THE DAY OF HIS POWER

THE DAY OF HIS POWER

A history of the International
Fellowship of Evangelical Students

Pete Lowman

INTER-VARSITY PRESS

INTER-VARSITY PRESS
38 De Montfort Street, Leicester LE1 7GP, England

© Pete Lowman 1983

First published 1983
Reprinted (with minor corrections) 1984

British Library Cataloguing in Publication Data
Lowman, Pete
  The day of His power: a history of the
  International Fellowship of Evangelical Students.
  1. International Fellowship of Evangelical Students
  —History
  I. Title
  269'.2'0601   BV2010

ISBN 0-85110-713-3

Typeset by Nuprint Services Limited, Harpenden, Herts.
Printed and bound in Great Britain by
Richard Clay (The Chaucer Press) Ltd,
Bungay, Suffolk

*Inter-Varsity Press is the publishing division of the Universities and
Colleges Christian Fellowship (formerly the Inter-Varsity
Fellowship), a student movement linking Christian Unions in
universities and colleges throughout the United Kingdom and the
Republic of Ireland, and a member movement of the International
Fellowship of Evangelical Students. For information about local and
national activities write to UCCF, 38 De Montfort Street,
Leicester LE1 7GP.*

Contents

Preface

'God wants His mighty acts in history to be remembered by future generations', wrote the general secretary of the Indian evangelical student movement recently. 'After the children of Israel had crossed the river Jordan to possess the promised land, God told Joshua to send twelve men to go back to the middle of the river and bring twelve big rocks. These rocks God told Joshua to heap up as a memorial. When in future their children would ask about the heap of stones, they were to be told of the mighty hand of God. This incident shows clearly that God expects us to look back, think of His wonderful leading in the past and give Him praise and thanksgiving from grateful hearts.'

And that is the purpose of this history: to be fuel for praise and to stimulate a vision of the greatness of God's power and purposes. It is not a complete, exhaustive chronicle of IFES. That would need a dozen volumes, and is perhaps unlikely to be written this side of the millennium! It is intended as a popular account of the main features of God's work through IFES (and similar closely related student movements) in recent years.

To say it is a popular history implies several things. First, we have not attempted to list every individual who has made an important contribution to the IFES movements. If we had, the result would have read more like a telephone directory! Secondly, we have adopted whatever narrative approach would lend continuity; for example, the history of the Latin American work has been told from a regional point of view rather more than that of Asia, where the individual countries developed more independently. Thirdly, we have quite consciously been very disproportionate in allocating space to different countries. We have sought to give space to incidents that demonstrate the power of God and the nature of what He has done through IFES. And where a particular development has occurred in a virtually identical manner in several countries, we have told the story in only one or two cases, and omitted the parallel events in other countries.

We have striven to avoid creating myths and legends. Sometimes we have found that the traditional account of a set of events is one that has been embellished considerably over the years, and we have attempted to give an accurate version. Equally, we have sometimes found the truth to be far more astonishing than the traditional version! But inevitably a brief history that covers nearly 100 countries in around 360 pages cannot avoid creating a somewhat distorted impression. Six points should be borne in mind as the reader proceeds.

First, to telescope the passage of several years, even a decade, into a couple of sentences implies an orderly, almost inevitable progress that is probably very far from the truth. It omits the long, empty years of sweat and tears when nothing happened – omits them precisely because nothing happened. It fails to tell of leaders who failed to lead, of opposition that was not colourful enough to be newsworthy, of the depressing accumulation of minor disappointments. As we stand back and look at a whole decade or more, it is easier to see the shape of God's working. While we are in the thick of the problems, we simply have to march on by faith.

Secondly, there is sometimes no way to measure progress except by statistics. Yet qualitative growth is as important as quantitative growth. In many countries, the expansion of higher education in recent years almost guaranteed *some* expansion in the Christian student groups.

Thirdly, the use of names distorts the reality. Comparatively few student leaders are named in this account; it is staff, rather than students, who are involved in a movement's life for several years running, and who write the reports that get quoted in a history like this. But the fundamental principle of IFES is that it is a fellowship of *students* witnessing to students, not of people coming in from outside to do the job. The names quoted in these accounts may often not be the key people who have witnessed on the front line.

Fourthly, an account such as this stresses the milestones in a movement's development. During the pioneering stages, those milestones come thick and fast. But as a movement grows larger – like Australia, Germany, Norway – the milestones grow fewer. The really important thing will still be happening – that is, the local student groups will be continuing the steady work of winning numerous converts and turning them into thorough-going disciples of Christ, month after month and year after year. It is that ministry that the national movement exists to strengthen, rather than to make a name for itself. But there may be fewer spectacular advances on a nationwide level. This causes problems sometimes for the older movements: it makes it harder to retain the vital sense of advance, of pressing on and extending the frontiers of the Kingdom. And it also causes difficulties for the historian who seeks to write about them!

Fifthly, a popular history describing so many countries in so few pages cannot avoid simplifying trends. But reality is always more complex than any summary. There are always contributory factors and important exceptions that had to be omitted for reasons of space. And most of what is recorded in these pages is far too recent for our assessments to be anything more than provisional.

Finally, this history is selective, because it leaves out all mention of many of the real heroes. When we get to the next world, we shall undoubtedly discover that many of our most significant pioneers were the people – some of them aged – who dedicated hour after hour daily to cry to God in prayer for the universities, colleges and high schools of the world. We cannot record the names of these people: we can only seek to imitate them.

But when all these qualifications are made, there remains a story that we find thrilling. 'The half has not been told'; we stand in the middle of a mighty work of God. He still desires to do more than we can ask or think. For example, most of this history focuses on the universities and colleges, where the IFES began;

but there are vast challenges to future evangelism in the high schools of many countries, and it may be that some future IFES history will redress this balance. We look forward with joyous expectation to the things God will do through the students of future years, and we dedicate this history in the words of an earlier history of IFES in Latin America: *A los que vendrán* – To those who will follow.

To God be the glory in this day of His power!

Prologue

The first recorded student fellowship in history was made up of four international students, on three-year government scholarships in the educational institutions of one of the world's great powers. As their course progressed, they found that the dominant cultural patterns conflicted with what they knew of the Word of God, necessitating a radical discipleship...

'Then the king ordered Ashpenaz, chief of his court officials, to bring in some of the Israelites from the royal family and the nobility – young men without any physical defect, handsome, showing aptitude for every kind of learning, well informed, quick to understand, and qualified to serve in the king's palace. He was to teach them the language and literature of the Babylonians. The king assigned them a daily amount of food and wine from the king's table. They were to be trained for three years, and after that they were to enter the king's service.

'Among these were some from Judah: Daniel, Hananiah, Mishael and Azariah. The chief official gave them new names: to Daniel, the name Belteshazzar; to Hananiah, Shadrach; to Mishael, Meshach; and to Azariah, Abednego.

'But Daniel resolved not to defile himself with the royal food and wine, and he asked the chief official for permission not to defile himself in this way. Now God had caused the official to show favour and sympathy to Daniel, but the official told Daniel, "I am afraid of my lord the king, who has assigned your food and drink. Why should he see you looking worse than the other young men of your age? The king would then have my head because of you."

'Daniel then said to the guard whom the chief official had appointed over Daniel, Hananiah, Mishael and Azariah, "Please test your servants for ten days. Give us nothing but vegetables to eat and water to drink. Then compare our appearance with that of the young men who eat the royal food, and treat your servants in accordance with what you see." So he agreed to this and tested them for ten days.

'At the end of the ten days they looked healthier and better nourished than any of the young men who ate the royal food. So the guard took away their choice food and the wine they were to drink and gave them vegetables instead.

'To these four young men God gave knowledge and understanding of all kinds of literature and learning.' (Daniel 1:3–17).

May such a spirit of biblical obedience be ours today!

1
Roots

'I have often speculated concerning the choice the apostle Paul would have made if he were alive today, in determining his sphere of service for the Lord Jesus Christ', a well-known professor of medicine told an Inter-Varsity Fellowship conference in Britain in 1932. 'I have a strong suspicion that he would make straight for some of our large universities... It is very noteworthy in the New Testament records how he selected the strategic centres. He sought those points where gathered men and women, whose influences were likely to be far-reaching. Such points are found in the universities today. At these are being trained the leaders of the future – the school teachers and the college professors; the doctors, the preachers, the writers, the administrators...'[1]

And certainly, a cursory glance at history reveals the important part played by university centres in the development of the church. John Wycliffe and his band of itinerant preachers were based in Oxford, England, in the fourteenth century. It was as a professor of biblical studies at the recently-founded university in Wittenberg that Martin Luther made his thrilling discovery of justification by faith, and promulgated his *95 Theses*.[2] On the eve of the English Reformation, Thomas Bilney brought together a group of men from Cambridge University – including Latimer, and very probably Coverdale – in the White Horse Inn, to read in secret from the Greek New Testament and the works of Luther. Some of this group were to become prominent Reformers; some

[1] W. M. Capper and Douglas Johnson, *The Faith of a Surgeon: belief and experience in the life of Arthur Rendle Short* (Paternoster Press, 1976), p.112.
[2] *The Lion History of Christianity*, ed. Tim Dowley (Lion, 1977), p.362.

were to be burnt at the stake. Two centuries later, the 'Holy Club' – which gave rise to the Methodist movement – was formed by Charles Wesley when he was a student at Oxford.[3]

A further example is provided by George Muller, the early nineteenth-century Brethren leader who built his orphanage work on complete dependence on answered prayer and in so doing became an inspiration to millions. He wrote, 'I am a graduate of the University of Halle. There were 1,200 students in the University when I was there. For the most part they were a wild, swearing, hard-drinking set. And I was ringleader among them in their mad pranks. At the time there were but eight Christian students in the whole 1,200. We who were not Christians made it hard for them, but they were brave, manly fellows and had a weekly prayer meeting.

'Along toward the close of my university course, something seemed to go wrong with me. I was not sick, and I had had no misfortune, but I was unhappy... "You aren't studying hard enough", I decided. I studied harder than ever, but still I was unhappy. "Go more into society." I went into society but my unhappiness continued... Then I remembered the eight Christian students who had a prayer meeting... I was promptly on hand at the hour. A chapter in the Bible was read, a few prayers were offered, some remarks were made, and the prayer meeting was over. But I detained the young men and told them my case. I said, "I don't know if it is what you have that I need, but tell me what it is." One and another told me of Christ. They prayed with me. I prayed for myself. At last I saw Christ as my Saviour... and a great love for Christ filled my soul... I loved Him more the year after, and more every year since.'[4]

He was a forerunner of scores of thousands of students who have come to Christ through student groups in subsequent years, and gone on to build up the church of God.

UNDER A HAYSTACK, UP A TREE

The earliest record of an organized, student-initiated Christian group concerns a Religious Society led by Henry Scougal in Aberdeen, Scotland, in the 1660s. Other student groups appeared sporadically in different countries. The influence of the German

[3] Much of this section is taken from Douglas Johnson, *A Brief History of the IFES*, published in 1964.
[4] Quoted in *His*, Spring 1942, p.7.

Pietist leader Francke (1663–1727) was responsible for the emergence of a remarkable Bible study and missionary movement in the University of Halle. And in the second decade of the eighteenth century, Count Zinzendorf (later a leader of the Moravian missionary movement) was a teenage student at the Paedagogium in Halle, and formed a secret praying and evangelistic society named the Order of the Grain of Mustard Seed.[5]

In America, Christian student societies existed in Harvard during the same century, with records dating back to 1706. These continued into the next century, changing their names and purposes but forming a recurrent chain of student fellowships.[6] The purposes of these societies varied, but included prayer, mutual edification and exhortation to a moral life, and philosophical and theological discussion. (It is interesting to see topics cropping up that have continued to appear in more recent times – 'Whether Heathens can be Sav'd according to the Terms of ye Gospel', 'Whether it be Fornication to lye with ones Sweetheart (after Contraction) before marriage?'[7])

Most of these groups were not evangelistically-oriented; and most of them were secret. Members of the Adelphoi Theologia, formed in Harvard in 1785, for example, had to make 'a most solemn promise' to keep whatever the president should disclose as 'an Eternal Secret'. In these days before the rise of widespread intellectual opposition to Christianity, hostility took the form of objections to 'enthusiasm': in 1789, for example, 'it was thought prudent to defer assembling...by reason of many suspicions unfavourable to the existence of this society prevailing among the Students'.[8] Across the Atlantic in Britain, university authorities were anxious to prevent 'Methodism'. In 1768 an Oxford tutor complained to the Principal of St Edmund Hall of 'several enthusiasts who talked of regeneration, inspiration and drawing near to God'. The end result was the expulsion of the

---

[5] Arthur J. Lewis, *Zinzendorf, the Ecumenical Pioneer*, quoted in David M. Howard, *Student Power in World Missions* (IVP-USA, 1970; revised ed. 1979), p.65.

[6] Clarence P. Shedd, *Two Centuries of Student Christian Movements* (Associated Press, N.Y., 1934), gives a thorough account of these groups. Shedd is so impressed by the continual reappearance of student initiative that he writes, 'The history of these societies indicates that, if we were to wipe out entirely the present local and national Christian Student Society organization, an organization of the same general characteristics would presently reappear, possibly under a different name' (p.xvii).

[7] *Ibid.*, p.13.   [8] *Ibid.*, p.20.

undergraduates concerned. The authorities' action was satirized
in a ballad: *opposition even then.*

> My thanks, and the nation's, to the Doctors be given,
> Those guardians of virtue, those Porters of heaven,
> For their timely wise care in suppressing the growth
> Of praying, expounding and hymn-singing youth.
>
> Should praying be suffer'd by our learnèd Sages
> (What has not been known in Ox...d for ages)
> Instead of gay parsons, with cassock and band,
> There would be none but Puritans all o'er the land.
>
> Expounding the Scriptures! This still is more wicked,
> Therefore from college be they instantly kickèd,
> For Scripture and priest-craft as distant do dwell
> As some parsons from virtue, or Heaven from hell.[9]

The beginning of the nineteenth century saw the emergence of
a missionary-oriented student group in America, which in turn
led to the development of strong inter-collegiate links. A small
group of students at Williams College had been meeting for
prayer in the home of a Christian lady in 1805–06, and saw a
religious revival come to their campus. One day five of them
were caught by a sudden storm while out walking. They sheltered
under a haystack, and began to use the time for prayer. One of
them was Samuel J. Mills, Jr. a student described by his room-
mate as having an 'awkward figure and ungainly manner and an
unelastic and croaking sort of voice; but he has a great heart and
great designs'. His mother, apparently, had 'consecrated him to
the work of missions' – a remarkable action in a time when
missionary interest was virtually unknown and no missionary
societies existed in North America.

As the students prayed under the haystack, their intercessions
turned to the sending out of foreign missionaries, and Mills
urged them to become the answer to their own prayers. 'We can
do this if we will', he affirmed. The result was the formation of a
student society – again secret, with records in cipher – aiming 'to
effect in the persons of its members a mission or missions to the

[9] Quoted in Douglas Johnson, *Contending for the Faith* (IVP-Britain, 1979), p.29.

heathen'. They were required to express 'a firm belief in those distinguishing doctrines commonly denominated evangelical'. The activities of this group led within six years to the formation of the first American denominational missionary society. Kenneth Scott Latourette goes so far as to say that 'It was from this haystack meeting that the foreign missionary movement of the churches of the United States had an initial main impulse'.[10]

Mills went on to play a part in the formation of the American Bible Society, to do Christian work in the New York slums and as a missionary among the American Indians, and finally to help form the American Colonization Society for the evangelism, liberation and repatriation of slaves, whom he saw as the best possible missionaries to Africa. (It was on the voyage back from an exploratory journey to what is now Liberia that he met his death, aged 35.) He and his friends were also the pioneers of an inter-collegiate vision. One member of the group at Williams transferred to another college to spread their concerns; and in 1809 Mills became a graduate resident at Yale, with the 'ostensible subject' of theological studies, as his 1820 biographer records, 'but his real object, the discovery, exciting and encouraging of some kindred spirits'. In 1810 he moved on to Andover Seminary, where a Society of Inquiry on the Subject of Missions was formed. Similar groups using the same constitution and model sprang up throughout the country. Altogether, more than ninety voluntary student Christian societies came into being between 1810 and 1850.[11]

In the 1850s, the Young Men's Christian Association spread from Britain to the USA, as a result of an enthusiastic letter from an American student in Scotland (an example of the significance of foreign students, as Ruth Rouse points out).[12] Within a few years it formed branches on college campuses, and a number of Societies of Inquiry chose to affiliate to it. One of these, an evangelistically effective group at Princeton, held a mission through which scores of students were saved during 1875–76. They were invited to send delegations to other colleges to tell 'what great things the Lord has done'; and they began to feel a concern for the formation of an inter-collegiate branch of the

---

[10] Quoted Howard, *op.cit.*, p.75. The material on Mills and the Haystack meeting is taken from Howard and from Shedd, *op.cit.*, pp.48ff.
[11] J. Edwin Orr, *Campus Aflame* (Regal, 1971), p.28.
[12] Ruth Rouse, *The World's Student Christian Federation* (SCM Press, 1948), p.25.

YMCA. Delegates from twenty-five colleges were brought together at Louisville in 1877, and as a result the world's first inter-collegiate evangelical student movement came into being.

'It was a real student decision made on student initiative,' writes Ruth Rouse, 'for the older YMCA leaders wisely stayed away from the meeting.' Diligent Bible study, prayer and personal evangelism were stressed as recommended activities; evangelical church membership was mandatory.[13] Princeton student president Luther Wishard soon became the first-ever travelling secretary. By 1885 there were 181 affiliated groups, with a membership around 10,000.[14]

Meanwhile, student witness was developing in Europe too. The early nineteenth century saw student groups appear in Tübingen and other German centres, and in Basel, Geneva and Lausanne in Switzerland. (The groups in the last two cities were, however, dissolved by order of the church authorities.) In 1843, a group called Sechor Dabar ('Remember the Word') was formed in Utrecht, Holland, where the churches had become thoroughly rationalistic. Its enemies in the student body referred to it scornfully as the 'Chocolate Club' or the 'Pious Circle'; one of the students who joined it, despite the warnings of his professors, was Andrew Murray, later to play a key role in the formation of what is now the IFES-affiliated Student Christian Association in South Africa.[15]

In Scotland, student prayer societies were recorded in St Andrews in 1733 and Edinburgh in the 1760s. The three original Edinburgh members could find nowhere to meet, and as a result their first meeting-place was up a tree. They continued to meet (in more conventional surroundings) until 1807.[16] In 1824 a Theological Missionary Association existed at Glasgow University that was in correspondence with the Americans at Andover.[17] A number of other theological and missionary societies existed in the country.

---

[13] Shedd, *op.cit.*, pp.134, 145.   [14] Rouse, *op.cit.*, pp.28–29.

[15] The material in this paragraph is mostly drawn from Douglas Johnson's *Brief History*, which in turn depends on Clarence P. Shedd's *The History of the World's Alliance of YMCAs* (SPCK, 1955) and the biography of Andrew Murray by J. du Plessis.

[16] M. G. Barker, 'Praying Societies in Scottish History', *Christian Graduate*, March 1963.

[17] Rouse, *op.cit.*, p.150.

BEGINNINGS AT CAMBRIDGE

But the most significant event for our purposes is the rise of a group that is still in existence today and linked with the IFES. That group was the Cambridge Inter-Collegiate Christian Union, or CICCU;[18] it was to play a unique part in the history of student witness, and today it is still the second largest IFES group, second only to that of the University of Singapore.

Cambridge was a university with a significant evangelical heritage from the time of Charles Simeon (1759–1836) onwards. CICCU's antecedents go back to 1827, when a group of evangelical undergraduates established a Sunday School in Jesus Lane, Barnwell, a poor area with an unsavoury reputation. Like their counterparts in Latin American IFES groups 150 years later, they became involved in a combination of literacy work and Scripture teaching. Children would be taught a few letters, then the teachers would dictate a text for them to write down, after which the meaning of the text would be explained. In 1848 – a year when revolution was sweeping Europe – a Union for Private Prayer was established; members covenanted to pray for each other every month. But they did not meet together. The first regular student gathering came into being after a visit to Cambridge by David Livingstone, just back from Africa. 'The sort of men who are wanted for missionaries are such as I see before me', he told a specially-convened meeting in the Senate House. 'I leave it with you.' The Cambridge University Church Missionary Union was formed in 1858 as a direct result of his visit.

The next step came four years later. Two new students came to Cambridge who had been converted in the 1859 Revival, had started to pray together and seen something of a spiritual awakening result among their schoolfellows. They now called on the two main evangelical leaders in Cambridge and proposed a daily prayer meeting. But student initiative – above all, the initiative of first years – was not a welcome commodity. Several objections were raised – the dangers of 'excitement', the

[18] CICCU's history is probably better documented than that of any other group in the world. The material on Cambridge in the next two chapters is taken almost *verbatim* from John Pollock, *A Cambridge Movement* (John Murray, 1953), which covers the period from the beginnings until 1952, and Oliver Barclay, *Whatever Happened to the Jesus Lane Lot?* (IVP, 1977), which besides covering this period takes the story up to 1977, and draws out many important lessons for student work.

suggestion that 'sufficient means of Grace and perfect Liturgies' already existed, and that 'assuming the propriety of the movement, *you* are not called upon to undertake it'.[19] They sought the advice of other friends, however; and as a result twenty students met together 'in fear and trembling'. They 'met with the disapproval of many of the most esteemed men' in the University. But they had begun a tradition which has continued unbroken to the present time, apart from a few months during World War One. Daily student prayer meetings for an evangelistic event in the city led to the establishment of a similar regular gathering in Oxford in 1867.

By 1875 226 of Cambridge's 2,000 undergraduates were involved in the Missionary Union. The growth of scientific agnosticism was now beginning to raise new, intellectually-based objections to faith. But as one student wrote in 1873, there was 'a large number of out and out Christian men...whose one aim and prayer was the desire to lead others to Christ'. In October five undergraduates and a recent graduate, Algernon Coote, were praying together one evening. 'As we rose from our knees', recalled Coote, 'someone quoted the words, "Launch out into the deep." We felt that it was a message from God.'

They determined to do something unprecedented: to take the largest hall in Cambridge for a major evangelistic meeting, and see that every undergraduate was invited personally, 'whatever the consequences might be, whatever the language used might be.' When the evening came, Coote sat by the door and with mingled delight and awe watched over half the undergraduate population 'literally pouring in'. There was intense interest; and it was an enormous encouragement to the Christians to venture out into bolder and more active evangelism.

Meanwhile, England was feeling the first effects of the 'holiness' or 'higher life' teaching that was soon expressed in the Keswick Convention. This movement was not without its excesses nor free from controversy, but it awoke many lukewarm Christians to a deeper consecration and a fresh sense of God's presence. Coote invited one of its leading figures, an American named

[19] Student initiative tended earlier to be seen as dangerously close to political radicalism. A student attempt to form a branch of the British and Foreign Bible Society in Cambridge in 1811 met with opposition because 'if they were suffered to proceed in this way about the Bible they would soon do the same about politics'.

Robert Pearsall Smith, to Cambridge. In 1874 a considerable number of Cambridge undergraduates attended a conference at Broadlands, which was the immediate precursor of the Keswick gatherings. They returned with deepened zeal, and further ambitious plans for evangelism were put into effect.

In November 1876 an evangelistic outreach took place, where the speaker was Sholto Douglas, one of the original founders of the Daily Prayer Meeting, and a man with 'a new, blazing method of evangelistic proclamation'. During his visit to Cambridge he urged the students to consider how better to co-ordinate their efforts. On his last day a breakfast was held at the Hoop Inn, where the guests discussed 'how best to carry on God's work among undergraduates by undergraduates'. Douglas had started something. Early the following term another meeting was held; one of the observers invited over from Oxford described the mood as 'rushing life and assured enthusiasm, young men buoyant and even rollicking, overflowing with animal spirits, but still more with the Spirit Divine... the shout of a King in the midst.' The decisive step was taken, and the CICCU was formed. Oxford's ICCU followed two years later.

The American Student YMCA had come into being as a direct result of a university mission involving D. L. Moody at Princeton; CICCU likewise was born as a direct result of an outreach, and one of its first moves was to invite Moody for a week's meetings, in 1882. The idea was that of the CICCU student president, Kynaston Studd, who was also university cricket captain (and later Lord Mayor of London). Senior friends feared it was a rash idea: Moody was neither British nor middle-class nor a university man. 'The older men were right', says Oliver Barclay; 'it was rash. But it was also of God.'

The first meeting drew an audience of 1,700. But many had come to 'have some fun', and had little goodwill for Moody. 'If uneducated men will come and teach the Varsity they deserve to be snubbed', said one (he was converted later in the week). The audience sang rowdy songs, built a pyramid of chairs, and responded to prayers with 'Hear! Hear!' Moody returned to his hotel, took off a collar that was dripping with sweat and remarked, 'I guess I've no hankering after that crowd again.'

But the meetings continued, with much prayer support. Students began to be converted. On the last night over half the university's undergraduates were present; Moody asked for those

21

who had received blessing during the week to rise to their feet, and 200 stood. A senior friend heard Moody whisper under his breath, 'My God, this is enough to live for.'

The mission had lasting results. The Daily Prayer Meeting increased in size. But the most striking effect was growing missionary commitment. This came to a head in 1884 when the 'Cambridge Seven' offered themselves to the China Inland Mission. The news caused a national sensation. One of the Seven was Kynaston Studd's brother C. T. Studd, 23 years old and at that time probably the most brilliant all-rounder in England's cricket team. Others of the group were also well known. Studd and another nationally famous sportsman, Stanley Smith, set off with 'a Bible and toothbrush' and addressed crowded meetings throughout the country. 2,000 students gathered at Edinburgh to hear them speak. After the last meeting there the room was still full at 10.30 p.m. with men asking 'What must I do to be saved?' When they were turned out of the hall at midnight, the work was still going on!

All seven were to carry out a long spell of missionary work, and C. T. Studd became founder of the Worldwide Evangelization Crusade. However, they went out at a time when many missionaries faced probable early death. (The cause – let alone the cure – of malaria was not discovered until 1895; the average life of Bishops of Sierra Leone was at one stage just two years!) Their inspiration shook the student world; in Cambridge, thirty-one CICCU members offered their services to the Church Missionary Society in 1886, and 140 in 1893. CICCU's senior friend Handley Moule, principal of Ridley Hall and later Bishop of Durham, had to plead with his students not to forget entirely the needs of the work in their own country!

The next years were years of tremendous blessing characterized, said a theological opponent of CICCU, by 'open, ardent courage' and 'passionate fervour' of devotion to Christ. Much open-air preaching and personal evangelism took place. A tradition developed of praying earnestly to get friends to services, and then talking with them personally afterwards. A Morning Watch Union was set up whose members determined to set aside at least 20 minutes each morning, and if possible an hour, for prayer and Bible study – the 'quiet time', as it is more generally known today. (The instigator took a personal responsibility for ejecting from bed any hapless member who failed to respond to his knock.) 'Interest in matters religious seemed unlimited in the University' is Pollock's summary of the situation at the beginning of the 1890s.

There were, however, difficulties resulting from the 'holiness' teaching that bore striking parallels to more recent disagreements. Both sides of the dispute shared the same longing for more of God, but differed over whether a single crisis experience could raise the believer on to a new plane. The 'holiness' movement had its extremists. One of them, John Smyth-Pigott, preached 'an almost passionate desire for entire deliverance from the power of sin', and was convinced that the Keswick Movement did not go far enough. His ministry on a visit in 1884 brought obvious blessing to many, in terms of greater depth and humility: but it came dangerously close to teaching that the believer could achieve sinless perfection.

Pigott returned to Cambridge in 1886, this time as a student for Anglican ordination. His presence challenged students to reach for the highest. The CU organized a convention in July and found men standing up to announce themselves entirely free from all internal sin. The president – a student of renowned devotion and holiness – decided that sin in a life committed to the Spirit was a contradiction of God's power; he and others believed themselves to have passed into a new state where the Spirit totally controlled them. Divine guidance was directly available, and had to be obeyed even when it conflicted with the moral commands of Scripture. Shipwreck followed. Senior friends worked hard to help those caught up in the excesses, but some CICCU members who had become convinced of their own sinlessness had nervous breakdowns, while others abandoned the faith. The president left to join the 'Abode of Love' community of the Agapemonites, a sexually deviant group. (Pigott joined him there a few years later, and proclaimed himself the Immortal Messiah in 1902.)

The casualties were few, however. By the end of the summer most extremists had seen their error; and Moule himself wrote later that the result of the stress on holiness and consecration was 'nobly good, and many a day since then I have almost prayed for the aberrations back again for the sake of the wonderful life'. More sober leadership took over. A series of meetings for the deepening of spiritual life was held in January 1887, with one of the main Keswick speakers, Evan Hopkins. 'A growing tone of humility and balance' was noted, and an increase in prayer; and

CICCU's evangelistic work went forward unhindered. In 1893 one member could write in the *English Churchman* that 'a vast majority of the most brilliant undergraduates are known to be decided and fervent Christians'!

THE BIRTH OF A MOVEMENT

Despite the brief crisis in the summer of 1886, CICCU was for most of the 1880s and early 1890s a model of what an evangelizing, biblically-based student group could be. But it was to be caught up in a bigger work of God.

It was a remarkable period. The CICCU was formed in March 1877, the American Intercollegiate YMCA in June. A Christian Association existed in Toronto University, Canada, from at least 1873, and the first Canadian Student Conference was held in 1879. There were developments in other continents too. Japan had had only ten baptized Protestants in 1872, but on 30 January 1876 thirty-five students from the Kumamoto Student Band climbed the hill of Hamaoka and solemnly took an oath of loyalty to Christ.[20] And ten days before the formation of CICCU, a group of students in Sapporo, Japan, drew up a 'Covenant of Believers in Jesus'.

An American graduate from Massachusetts had been invited to help found a college in Sapporo, and he refused to be involved unless an express prohibition against teaching the Bible was withdrawn. A good number of conversions occurred during his year there, and a student group came into existence, committed to Christ and to the Bible as the 'only perfect and infallible guide'. They wrote to the Christians in their founder's college in Massachusetts, 'We are one body in Christ and every one members one of another, and so we wish to work together with you for our Lord...We wish very much to hear how you are getting on with your good work of fighting against the kingdom of hell.'[21]

It happened that YMCA travelling secretary Luther Wishard was in Massachusetts, and heard the letter read. It had a powerful effect on him, giving him a new passion for work overseas. He wrote to Williams College to ask for a student to be sent to the

---

[20] Bobby Sng, 'Student Work and the Church', *IFES Review* 1982, 2, pp.32–33.

[21] *Cf.* Shedd, *Two Centuries...*, p.158; Rouse, *op.cit.*, p.30; Douglas Johnson, *A Brief History*, pp.137–139, which draws on an article by David Michell in IFES' East Asian magazine *The Way*, No.3, 1963.

next Intercollegiate YMCA conference to tell the story of Samuel Mills and his missionary-minded friends; and he filled the movement's magazine with accounts of D. L. Moody's missions in the British universities.

When Moody returned to the USA, he invited Kynaston Studd of CICCU to America, and Wishard arranged for Studd to tour twenty American colleges, telling the story of the Cambridge Seven and challenging them with the needs of the world. Wishard hoped that Studd's tour would result in the development of an intercollegiate YMCA in Britain. But Studd showed no great enthusiasm for the project, much to Wishard's disappointment. Wishard was not to know that God had used Studd's visit to Cornell University to set alight the man who would found a world-wide Christian student federation, John Mott.[22] As usual, God had a better plan than any human strategy!

But if Wishard had seen one dream die, he was ready with another. Moody proposed to Wishard that they gather all the YMCA staff for a conference at Mount Hermon, Massachusetts; Wishard responded with the suggestion of a month-long national Bible conference for *students*. Moody was nervous: he was still doubtful of his ability to speak to 'educated men'. Wishard was persistent: finally Moody said reluctantly, 'Well, I guess we better try it.'

Wishard went to work,[23] and finally brought together 251 students from 89 colleges. Among them were John Mott and Robert Wilder. Wilder was the son of a former member of the group formed by Mills and others in Andover; he was a student leader in the Princeton Foreign Missionary Society. He and his sister Grace had been praying for a year for a 'widespread missionary movement in the colleges and universities of North America'. He was to be the catalyst in the rise of the Student Volunteer Movement. Later, when that movement had ceased to be evangelical, he would play a key role in the events leading to the formation of the IFES.

The 1886 conference was God's answer to the Wilders' intercession. Wilder recalled afterwards, 'Before leaving, my sister said to me, "I believe our prayers will be answered at Mount Hermon"'; and she also predicted that 'there would be a hundred

[22] Rouse, *op.cit.*, p.34.
[23] Wishard was so nervous that Moody would change his mind that he got the circulars announcing the conference printed and posted within a couple of days!

volunteers enlisted there', willing to serve Christ abroad.[24] At the start, however, 'nobody had thought of it being a missionary conference', said Mott. Moody stated the object as being 'to stir you up and get you in love with the Bible'.[25] But Wilder and twenty-one other students met regularly to pray for the missionary aspect. Then there took place a meeting where representatives of ten nations – including an Armenian, a Japanese and a Thai – spoke of the needs of the mission field. 'Seldom have I seen an audience under the sway of God's Spirit as it was that night', said Wilder. Afterwards, the students withdrew quietly to pray.

From then on, recalls Mott, they 'talked missions everywhere – running, tramping, eating'.[26] The prayer meetings continued; students began to commit themselves definitely to the foreign field. Before the closing night, there were ninety-nine such volunteers; and as they gathered for a final session of prayer, the hundredth student slipped in to join them. Robert Wilder returned home with joy to tell his sister of their answered prayer.

But that was only the beginning. The students were anxious to spread the vision. Mindful of the massive impact made by the Cambridge Seven, they sent Wilder and another student, John Forman, to tour the universities of North America for a year. Forman was a man of prayer. More than once Wilder awoke in the middle of the night to hear him in the next room, 'pouring out his soul' to God. Together they visited 162 institutions, during 1886-87. Wilder's health broke down halfway through, but they continued. Time and again it seemed that they needed only 'to strike a match, and the whole college blazed up', wrote Wilder. Over 2,100 students signed a volunteer declaration; these included Samuel Zwemer, the great missionary to the Muslim world.[27]

In 1888, fifty volunteers met again at Northfield. They sensed that momentum was being lost now, and unity was evaporating. Some form of organization was necessary if the impetus was not

[24] Most of the material that follows on the SVM is drawn from Joe Cumming's detailed history of the movement in Cindy Smith and Joe Cumming, *Rebuilding the Mission Movement* (National Student Missions Coalition, 1982), pp.303–598.
[25] Pollock, *op.cit.*, p.126.   [26] Shedd, *op.cit.*, p.260.
[27] There was a price to be paid. Wilder returned home from Mount Hermon to find that his father might not live for more than six months. When his father heard of the planned year's journey, he was silent for two days; then told his son, 'Son, let the dead bury their dead; go thou and preach the kingdom.'

to disappear. And so the Student Volunteer Movement came into being. Mott was chosen as chairman, Wilder as travelling secretary. The watchword of the movement was 'The evangelization of the world in this generation'. It was united around a simple pledge, stating, 'It is my purpose, if God permit, to become a foreign missionary.' The Volunteers' intention was to overcome the inertia of the natural tendency to stay at home. It placed 'the burden of proof... on God', said Wilder. 'The pledge means *We are fully determined to become foreign missionaries unless God block the way.*'[28]

Inevitably, the American students wanted to share this vision with other students world-wide. But as Luther Wishard tried to export the idea of an Intercollegiate YMCA, he became frustrated. Kynaston Studd had been unenthusiastic; Edinburgh student leader Henry Drummond was brought across in 1887 for a similar tour, and 'highly surpassed' Wishard's expectations in the impression he made – but again seemed 'utterly disinclined to carry anything home in the way of organized methods'. In 1888 Wishard himself went to Britain, and ended up bringing ten British students across to the Northfield conference the following year. They must have been a somewhat gullible group; Wishard had raised their support from interested British laymen, and told the students (with questionable honesty) that by a 'special arrangement' with the steamship company they could make the return trip for £10 each!

It is interesting, however, that no Intercollegiate YMCA ever arose in Britain, although that was where the overall YMCA began. When an international Christian student movement arose a few years later, it was after John Mott's decision to adopt 'a different plan from that which had been followed hitherto... Instead of attempting to organize the Christian students under any one name and according to any one plan or organization, it would be better to encourage the Christian students in each country to develop national Christian movements of their own, adapted in name, organization and activity to their own particular genius and character, and then to link these together in some simple and yet effective Federation.'[29] Instead of imposing an organization and a methodology from abroad, such an approach would build on student initiative and the work of the Holy Spirit

[28] Quoted Cumming, *op. cit.*, p.450.   [29] Rouse, *op.cit.*, pp.36–37, 54.

in each place, with its distinctive flavour. (It is to this approach, of course, that the IFES has been committed since its foundation).

Wishard did not return to America from England, however. He had not forgotten the letter from Sapporo, Japan, and dreamed of turning 'the colleges of foreign mission lands into strongholds and distributing centres of Christianity'. Any young American professor teaching in these lands could start a Student YMCA, Wishard believed. He shared this dream, and as early as 1882 received a letter announcing the formation of a Student YMCA in Ceylon; others followed, in Turkey, Syria, India, Japan and China. In 1888, therefore, Wishard himself set off on a journey through these countries – and Germany, Malaya, Thailand, Burma, Egypt, Bulgaria, Greece, Russia and Bohemia too – sharing his vision.

In Japan, he held remarkably successful evangelistic meetings and by the time he left the country twelve Student YMCAs existed. The Japanese students decided to hold a national conference, under the theme 'Christian Students United for World-Conquest'. They cabled a greeting to the American student conference, 'Kyoto, July 5, 1889. Make Jesus King. (Signed) Five hundred students.' That cable was read out to some student leaders in Denmark, Sweden and Norway, where a large number of student groups had started meeting for Bible study, prayer and missionary concern as a result of the evangelical awakening of the 1880s. Their reaction was, 'If students can gather round Jesus Christ as their King over there in the Far East, why not also here in the north?' And so Scandinavian student conferences came into existence the following summer.[30]

Wishard had also been invited to South Africa, by the principal of a South African college whose imagination had been fired by attending the Northfield student conference. Before he arrived, however, a number of South African educationalists and clergymen became interested in this project. In 1896, a conference of 400 student delegates was held at Stellenbosch, under the chairmanship of the well-known Bible teacher Andrew Murray (who had been involved in the student work in the Netherlands while studying there, as we have noted.) A Student Christian Association was formed; and this movement – unlike the others formed

[30] Rouse, *op.cit.*, pp.41–46. Ruth Rouse explicitly states the evangelical origins of the movements in Scandinavia and Germany.

around this time – is the direct ancestor of an evangelical student movement affiliated to the IFES today.

Meanwhile, Robert Wilder had not been idle. In 1891, he set sail for India as a missionary, but decided to stop over in Britain to see if the SVM's vision would take root there. It did. A brief appearance at the Keswick Convention resulted in a deluge of invitations to university groups. Soon there were 300 volunteers, and in 1892 a British equivalent of the SVM was formed,[31] with one of the Cambridge Seven, home on furlough, as its first travelling secretary. Within four years it had sponsored an International Conference at Liverpool, with 927 delegates from twenty-one countries, and speakers including C. T. Studd and the evangelical bishop J. C. Ryle. The theme was 'Make Jesus King', which the British students had taken from the Japanese telegram seven years earlier. Out of SVM came a general intercollegiate Christian grouping, formed in 1893 at Keswick, and soon to be known as the Student Christian Movement. The SVM's travelling secretary was a key figure in the wider movement's formation; he was finding it hard to arouse missionary interest in colleges where no general Christian association existed.[32]

Wilder had gone on to Denmark in 1892 and seen an SVM formed there. Similar movements emerged in France and Switzerland in 1895, in India (as a result of a visit by John Mott) and in Germany and Scandinavia (as a result of the Liverpool Conference) in 1896. The German movement had as its mottos, 'We can only advance on our knees' and 'If Thy presence go not with us, carry us not up hence'.

Mott was SVM's chairman in America for thirty years. His main concern was not for specifically missionary groups, however, but for student Christian movements active in the whole range of Christian activity. In 1894 he walked into the rooms of the CICCU president at Cambridge, a student ten years his junior, and said he wanted to learn as much as he could about how CICCU operated. 'Note-book in hand', he cross-questioned

---

[31] An SVM-type Union had been formed in Britain after a visit by John Forman in 1889, on the initiative of Hudson Taylor's son Howard Taylor. But it had no travelling secretary and failed to make a permanent impact. Wilder, however, was anxious not to compete with it, and succeeded in arranging its merger with the new movement.

[32] Rouse, op.cit., p.57.

the president, then asked if he might come to the meetings and see for himself. For several nights, therefore, 'this unknown American would steal in and take up his position in the corner, saying nothing, but noticing everything, and slipping away as unceremoniously as he had come.'[33]

That spirit of learning and humility was the equipment needed by a man who would found a genuinely international movement. Mott travelled all over the world, despite being a bad sailor and, in the early days, almost invariably train-sick. In 1895, he met with representatives of the student movements of five other nations at Keswick, and the 'main lines' of a plan for a World's Student Christian Federation were sketched out. The WSCF finally came into being a fortnight later at the third Scandinavian Student Conference, in a mediaeval castle in Vadstena, Sweden. The Scandinavians (and the Germans too) were strongly prejudiced against anything 'Anglo-Saxon'; but Mott won them over with the assurance that 'the object would be to strengthen not to force the weak movements, to advise and never to control them'.

That was only the beginning, and rapid expansion followed. Between 1895 and 1897 Mott made a world tour that led to the formation of seventy local Student Christian Associations and four national movements, each with their own staffworkers. In Australia, for example, he stimulated the merger into a single witnessing Christian Union of two groups formed by Melbourne students in the previous four years; he also helped in the formation of Christian Unions in Adelaide, Brisbane and Sydney, plus a national movement to link them all together! (The new movement's convention was held before Mott left, and it drew 258 delegates from thirty-four institutions in Australia and New Zealand!) Mott raised the money to enable a former secretary of the Yale YMCA, a Canadian with a speciality in Bible study, to be their first staffworker.

Nor were Mott's dynamism and enthusiasm leaving behind his love for evangelism. In Australia and New Zealand, he held evangelistic meetings in every university city. In Japan, he spoke to audiences of up to 1,200 students, nearly all of them non-Christians. Over 200 accepted Christ, and to ensure 'intelligent and pronounced decisions' three after-meetings were held after each address. (With interpretation, his talks lasted two hours.)

[33] Pollock, *op.cit.*, p.131.

And in 1896, 1898, 1905 and 1908 he was back with the CICCU in Cambridge leading their university missions, and seeing many conversions.[34]

It may seem that the spirit of the early SVM and WSCF was more or less identical with that of the IFES today.[35] And it is indeed so. All the early leaders were convinced evangelicals. 'If we do not have absolute and complete authority for the great missionary designs in the writings which God has given, and in the word of Jesus Christ, we do not have it anywhere', said Mott in 1911; adding that 'absolute faith in the authority of the Christian Scriptures' was fundamental to what had happened at Mount Hermon. 'It is back, back to Christ and His redeeming blood', he affirmed, 'or it is on, onward to despair.' 'The Student Volunteer Movement has been largely a result of Bible study', said an 1891 SVM publication. At SVM's first convention A. T. Pierson criticized scholars who were 'denying the plenary inspiration of the Word of God, overthrowing this trust on miracles as well as prophecy, and shaking hands with rationalists'. Wherever the SVM took root, says Cumming, it was instrumental in spreading the notion of the Morning Watch or 'quiet time'.[36] Mott himself wrote pamphlets on *Bible Study for Personal Spiritual Growth, Secret Prayer, The Morning Watch*, and *Personal Work* (on personal evangelism). Thus the marks of an evangelical student movement were obviously present.

If we seek the work of God through biblically-based student initiative in the late nineteenth century, then, we find it manifested gloriously in the SVM and the WSCF. But the WSCF became irretrievably liberal; and the SVM died.

THE DEATH OF A MOVEMENT

Some of the problems that beset these movements were perhaps the consequences of the establishment of a large organization; some were part of the inevitable difficulties involved in passing on a pioneering vision to a succeeding generation. Joe

[34] The previous two paragraphs are based on Rouse, *op.cit.*
[35] It is very noticeable that when Douglas Johnson – one of the key figures in the early years of the IFES – wrote his history of the IFES, he depicted it very clearly as the successor of the earlier movement (*cf. A Brief History . . .* , pp.vii–viii, 17, 41, 46). WSCF staffworker Valdo Galland, writing in WSCF's Latin American publication *Testimonium*, IX–1, p.42, likewise recognizes the IFES as standing in the tradition of the WSCF's founders. (I owe this reference to Samuel Escobar.)
[36] Cumming, *op.cit.*, pp.323f., 378, 380, 399.

Cumming's summary of the American SVM's situation in the 1890s and 1900s describes them, and makes thought-provoking reading. Financial depression struck the American economy in the late 1890s; mission agencies did not have enough money to send SVM's recruits abroad, so SVM ended up spending more and more time fund-raising.

'In an overall view of these years, one finds that the SVM grew in numbers; but one finds, along with that numerical growth, the seeds of the movement's later spiritual decline. The Executive Committee in 1894 reported this danger, "to depend more upon the numbers than upon the Holy Spirit's power." In reading the correspondence of the movement's leadership through these years, one finds less and less often phrases like, "The Spirit fell upon us," or "God has done a wondrous work in our midst." More and more often, one reads phrases like, "Careful supervision," or "Cautious, balanced approach," or "Approved of by every leading denomination."

'Speaking subjectively, one may say that an attitude expressive of the movement's earliest years might be, "God is able to win the world in this generation. Our task is obedience to His Word." An attitude expressive of the Movement's leadership in its middle years might be, "This mighty assemblage of students joining together from all over the world has a potential and opportunity unparalleled in history for the evangelization of the world and the building of the Kingdom of God." In the Manual for the 1898 SVM Leadership Conference, John Mott wrote a revealing statement: "Without doubt, the greatest weakness of the Movement is its comparatively feeble prayer life."

'As the organization of the SVM grew, the correspondence, reports and minutes seemed to describe less and less a movement and more and more an organization. Fund-raising and financial debts became an increasing problem. In reading these documents, one senses at times a tendency to promote the "cause" of the SVM, more than the "cause" of foreign missions. During these years, the letters of individual volunteers continued to be quite spiritually-minded, but the correspondence of the movement's hierarchy became decreasingly so. Letters which had once been signed, "Yours for God's greater glory," or, "Yours for the cause," were signed, simply, "Sincerely yours."'[37]

---

[37] Cumming, *op.cit.*, pp.487f.

More deadly problems were manifesting themselves in Britain, where the SCM were at last having to face the challenge of theological liberalism. Rationalistic higher criticism of the Bible, with its brash confidence in its ability to assess the reliability of Scripture by the latest scholarly opinions, had hitherto not made much of a mark on the movement. During the 1890s, however, this influence grew. Particular problems were faced by students who had been committed evangelicals and went on to theological college. Little evangelical theological scholarship existed, and these students lacked support to stand against an overwhelming liberal consensus. No-one had prepared them for it, says Oliver Barclay, and 'in this decade and the next, very few theological students remained orthodox if they worked hard at theology, unless they were the kind of men who were set on learning only what would serve the interests of evangelistic service'. Some evangelicals reacted into a negative attitude to all theology and intellectual activity. Many of their best intellects were away building up the church on the mission field. 'Speakers tended to be either devotional *or* theological, and if theological to be commonly influenced by rationalistic liberalism.'[38]

The disastrous consequences of this dominance of liberalism did not become evident immediately. Many of those affected were from strongly orthodox backgrounds and continued to emphasize prayer, Bible study and missionary concern. The attitude to the Bible, and the *content* of the missionary message, might be changing, and the preaching of Christian truth tending to be prefaced by 'It seems to me...' or 'I suppose we would all agree...' rather than being presented as the proclamation of God's authoritative Word.[39] But the apparent spirituality of the men concerned made it seem that all was well. And so there came into the leadership of SCM a group of men who saw liberal criticism as 'a great movement of the Spirit'.[40]

Another important factor was SCM's deliberately inclusive policy. The emphasis on the 'evangelization of the world in this generation' was not matched by an equal concern to 'contend for the faith which was once for all delivered to the saints' (Jude 3). In their anxiety to draw all the churches, and the theological colleges too, into the missionary movement, they began to

[38] Barclay, *op.cit.*, pp.34, 55.   [39] *Ibid.*, p.53.
[40] Tissington Tatlow, *The Story of the Student Christian Movement* (SCM Press, 1933), p.272.

compromise with points of view that were alien to their own original vision. 'The *number* of missionaries seemed to be all-important', comments Oliver Barclay. 'Everyone began to care too much about the size and influence of the movement.' The price that had to be paid for ecclesiastical respectability was the growing influence of prominent but liberal church leaders (some of whom had never been in a student Christian union).[41]

It is important to note that it was people who were themselves evangelicals who were at the forefront of these developments. One of the powerful personalities in the formation of the British Student Volunteer Movement had been Douglas Thornton. He had a consuming passion to enlist every possible labourer for the missionary vision. As a student, he was a fervent evangelist, the kind of person who went missing from an open-air service and was later found kneeling in prayer with a barmaid in a local bar. (He was also the inventor of a device combining an alarm clock with a fishing-rod, which removed his bedclothes at 6 a.m. to ensure his waking for a 'quiet time'.)[42] A man of intense self-discipline, he left for Egypt as a missionary in 1898, and died there of typhoid seven years later. Yet Tissington Tatlow, the SCM general secretary of this period, wrote that it was Thornton, 'more than any other man', who led the SCM to draw into its membership 'Christian men of all types and points of view'.[43]

But the supreme example is John Mott himself, a God-gifted evangelist and a Bible-believing evangelical to the end of his life. Even in 1905 Mott was urging the CICCU to involve non-evangelicals in their university mission, and a few years later he was advocating to SCM that CICCU – by then the only major evangelical SCM member – be disaffiliated. Mott stayed on this ecumenical path; he was one of the key people in the formation of the World Council of Churches.

Accordingly, from the time of the British SVM's second quad-rennial conference in 1900, non-evangelical speakers were used. The chairman at that event already feared that the movement's message was being forfeited in the desire for unity with anglo-catholics and liberals. Two years later, Tatlow wrote that the SCM was 'making for true catholicity'. In 1903, several older leaders, including Temple Gairdner, Mrs Thornton, Ruth Rouse

---

[41] Barclay, *op.cit.*, pp.57, 60.   [42] Pollock, *op.cit.*, pp.118f.
[43] Tatlow, *op.cit.*, p.381.

and G. T. Manley, urged the executive to return to the original vision and 'recapture the spirit of the time when increase of Bible study, Prayer, Personal Work and full consecration were our sole objectives'.[44] But they were swimming against the stream. In 1906 the SCM decided 'to adopt frankly the modern position about the Bible' and to 'shake itself free' from the conservative approach.[45] It was thirteen years since the SCM's foundation, and twenty since Moody had led the conference at Mount Hermon 'to stir you up and get you in love with the Bible'.

But at Cambridge the CICCU, still evangelical, had suddenly found new verve and deeper prayer concern as a result of an effective and thoroughly biblically-oriented university mission in 1903. Their leaders were hardly likely to be enthusiastic, therefore, when two years later their Oxford University counterparts suggested that the SCM should be widened to include Unitarians![46] That same year, they had to face the question of whether to co-operate in a mission led by a well-known anglo-catholic. A talk by G. T. Manley (one of the SVM pioneers) on Luther's treatise concerning justification by faith helped the students focus their understanding of the issues involved, and they did not take part.

Between 1907 and 1909, however, CICCU had a series of presidents who were concerned to bring it into line with the rest of the SCM. (It was a time when the national SCM was receiving an increasing number of letters complaining of speakers 'forfeiting all that really matters in the Christian Faith', and requesting 'more speakers such as Robert P. Wilder', the original SVM firebrand.) John Mott's Cambridge mission of 1908 was a joint outreach with the other religious societies, but although 300 students 'decided for Christ' and the follow-up was thorough, very few converts stood firm. Lethargy set in; attendance at the Daily Prayer Meeting fell very low. The president, A. C. B. Bellerby, was convinced that the remedy was to broaden theologically, drop the open-air meetings, and perhaps replace the DPM with something more formal. But the more strongly evangelical students felt CICCU had moved from its heritage; could the new atmosphere foster the 'passionate and even reckless enthusiasm for the kingdom of God' that made a C. T. Studd or a Douglas Thornton?

[44] Pollock, *op.cit.*, p.161.   [45] Tatlow, *op.cit.*, pp.260, 213.
[46] Pollock, *op.cit.*, p.164.

By 1909 there were no undergraduates left who could remember the days before the 'reforming presidents'. Bellerby brought matters to a head: 'Either we enlarge our views and adequately represent the SCM, or we resign our affiliation.' Tatlow was invited to Cambridge to address the crucial meeting. Bellerby was convinced he would 'win the day' for 'a bigger Christian Union reaching a bigger circle of men'. A long discussion followed an able speech by Tatlow; the voting was close – but to Bellerby's horror it went against him. Soon afterwards, CICCU's general committee met, and there was a 'real fight' to reverse the decision. It failed by seventeen votes to five; CICCU informed the SCM of its withdrawal, so that both parties could work unhindered in Cambridge.[47]

It was a crucial moment. To Tatlow, the issue was CICCU's 'traditional evangelical theology', which was, he felt, of a kind that 'among thoughtful men was giving place to new theological formulations'. He saw its 'basic tenets' as 'the literal, verbal inspiration of the Bible, the penal view of the Atonement, and the near return in physical form to the earth of our Lord'.[48] As Douglas Johnson says, 'Compromise could not have papered over the gap for long. Two essentially different Christianities were confronting each other.'[49] The issues – is it true that what Scripture says, God says, or should Scripture be corrected by human opinion when the two conflict?[50] and did Christ really bear the penalty for our sins? – went to the heart of the faith.

That made it no easier for CICCU. In Britain, only the London medical schools were on their side. As far as they knew, they stood virtually alone against the shared assumptions of a WSCF of 148,000 members. Pressures were heavy; they were being forced to disagree sharply with personal friends, and were gaining themselves a reputation for being old-fashioned. 'At the time there was no glory...no certainty of success or influence on anyone else, only an awareness of being very much criticized by many whom they respected.'[51] But their loyalty to what they

---

[47] Cf. Pollock, *op.cit.*, ch.13, and Barclay, *op.cit.*, ch.4.

[48] Tatlow, *op.cit.*, pp.381, 383f.

[49] Douglas Johnson, *Contending for the Faith*, p.77.

[50] CICCU's phrasing of this issue was 'It is sufficiently reasonable to hold that view of the Old Testament which Christ Himself held' (Pollock, *op.cit.*, p.178).

[51] Barclay, *op.cit.*, p.70. The main reaction even of Manley and Wilder was 'keen

found written in the Bible was of crucial importance. At a time when liberalism had captured the theological colleges and even the once-conservative high-church leadership, CICCU was one of the few outposts of a biblical faith left in Britain.[52] And from Cambridge, plus the London medical schools, would come a national movement, the IVF; from the IVF, plus its Norwegian counterpart, would stem the IFES. Much was at stake when the students said goodbye to the SCM and their own reputations in Cambridge in 1909.

The immediate consequence was a decline in membership. But there was also 'a widespread sense of liberation, an eagerness to go forward in the work of evangelism, with the Sunday evening sermons once more the focus of the CICCU's life and the Daily Prayer Meeting its strength'.[53] Inevitably, there was controversy, in which intolerant attitudes came all too easily. Nor would every CICCU member necessarily be capable of articulating a complete defence of their stance. However, 'they were evangelists and knew what they and the new Christians needed and had found in the hurly-burly of student life'.[54] And that brought clarity of vision to their work, in contrast to the blurred outlook of previous years.

In 1911 the American evangelist R. A. Torrey was invited to Cambridge University to lead a mission. He had spent seven years at Yale, and been a thoroughgoing disciple of biblical criticism ('I was so wise that I believed so much of the Bible as was wise enough to agree with me'). But he had come to accept the 'absolute authority of the Scriptures' as a result of further studies under liberal teachers in Germany. There was a tremendous unity and intensity of prayer for the mission. There were problems too; a group of non-Christian students planned to kidnap Torrey and confine him for the mission week! The first night had a number of police present in readiness for disturbances. Two of C. T. Studd's daughters saw some men sitting near them who were carrying stink bombs – 'but before they

---

regret' that the one group to have remained faithful should have left the SCM (Pollock, *op.cit.*, pp.175f.).

[52] 'The whole Protestant world seemed to have been swept away. That some old-fashioned Church of England parishes, the Brethren, isolated Free Churches and a few students in Cambridge should hold fast was of little consequence' (Barclay, *op.cit.*, p.72).

[53] Pollock, *op.cit.*, p.176.   [54] Barclay, *op.cit.*, p.73.

could throw them they were converted!' There were large numbers of lasting conversions, and Torrey stayed on for a second week, primarily for follow-up.[55] He also emphasized the 'quiet time', and when he left there were reputed to be 200 students committed to spending an hour each morning in personal prayer and Bible study.

So much for the results in Cambridge. Also noteworthy are the long-term implications of this controversy for the SCM and for the world-wide WSCF. Tatlow wrote in 1910, 'The movement, as such, does not determine what is orthodox and what is unorthodox.' The same year, SCM's basis of membership came under question. After three years' debate it was amended from 'I desire in joining this Union to declare my faith in Jesus Christ as my Saviour, my Lord and my God' to a statement that avoided affirming the deity of Christ.[56]

This was not so much the result of anti-Trinitarian influences as of a concern to make students who had not yet reached a fully orthodox position feel that they belonged fully to the group.[57] Whether Christ and His apostles were not more concerned that someone who was lost should be aware of the fact was another question. Certainly, with both the deity of Christ and the meaning of the cross apparently open to debate, not much was left of the Pauline gospel of 'Christ crucified' (1 Corinthians 1:23). Inevitably, members unconvinced of the fundamentals came eventually to be influential in the SCM; there was no further doctrinal basis for SCM leaders, and within a few years a number of them would be people describing themselves as 'seekers'. A gradual paralysis of evangelism and of Bible-based devotion and thinking slowly followed. By 1926 the basis had changed to 'The SCM is a fellowship of students who desire to

[55] Each convert was assigned to a CU member who was to have Bible study and prayer with him until he was 'well grounded...in evidence of it taking part audibly in prayer meetings and speaking in the Open Air' (Pollock, *op.cit.*, pp.187f.).

[56] Mott had argued forcibly and successfully in 1899 that voting power in the SCM should be restricted to those who believed in the deity of Christ (Tatlow, *op.cit.*, p.199). And as late as 1908 he affirmed confidently that 'the battle will continue to be waged in our colleges on both sides of the Atlantic as to the Person of Jesus Christ; but the Student Christian Movement has sounded, and will continue to sound, no uncertain note with reference to the Deity of our Lord' (Cumming, *op.cit.*, p.377).

[57] *Cf.* Tatlow, *op.cit.*, chs.11 and 26.

understand the Christian Faith and to live the Christian life. This desire is the only condition of membership'.

The WSCF may perhaps be said to have reached a watershed with its Conference at Constantinople in 1911. This event was marked by a determination to welcome into full membership students holding the official positions of the traditional, sacramentalist Orthodox churches. The WSCF was clearly no longer a firmly evangelical movement basing itself on the Bible as its final and supreme authority.[58]

A number of WSCF-affiliated movements continued to be evangelical. In the 1930s the new evangelical student movements that eventually came together to form the IFES were in friendly contact with the WSCF-affiliated movements in Hungary, Germany, South Africa and Finland at least. But the full outworking of the world-wide movement's refusal to affirm the nature of its authority, or indeed of the way of salvation, may be seen if we move forward fifty years from Constantinople, to the 1960s.

In 1965 Wolfgang Löwe of the German SCM stated that its main concern could 'no longer be one of maintaining itself and multiplying its membership, nor can it any longer think it important to draw lines of distinction between its members and secular "outsiders", between "Christian" and "irreligious" students'.[59] In 1963, the secretary of the British SCM declared that 'I'm not kidding myself that we can go and convert these people in the old way, arrogantly saying "We've got something and we're going to give it you"... We're all of us feeling our way.'[60] Canadian SCM leaders at a meeting in 1965 stressed that though they were still using the term Christian 'We immediately apologize for being Christian by being open'.[61] *Federation News* of November 1964 suggests that words like 'witness' and 'mission' are 'too big and too definite. They suggest a certainty of faith and purpose, and an ability to conceptualize faith, in terms which create difficulty for many people...'. *The Student World*, no.3–1964, included the assertions that 'There cannot be found in, or

[58] *Ibid.*, pp.418–420. [59] *Andover Newton Quarterly*, November 1965, p.10.
[60] *Sunday Observer*, 7 April 1963. Even in the 1950s WSCF general secretary Phillip Maury asked, 'What about the good Biblical word "conversion" which has almost completely disappeared from our SCM vocabulary? Why is it that we have almost stopped thinking in terms of conversion?'
[61] *Canadian Churchman*, November 1965.

extracted from, the Bible a divinely revealed ethical system...
We are not bound by principles and prohibitions which have
been meaningful at other times or in other situations.'

In the absence of scriptural authority, national SCMs lacked an
anchor to enable them to assess the value of new emphases. This
became apparent in the politicization and ideological tempests
of the later 1960s, when some of these movements disappeared
altogether. Perhaps the saddest document of all is a paper
produced by WSCF general secretary Risto Lehtonen in 1972,
just after the high tide of the radicalism of the counter-culture.
He describes WSCF as facing attempts at takeover by two in-
compatible options, dogmatic Marxist and dogmatic anarchist.
For many members, he writes, the 'possibility of death' for the
'Christian dimension of the movement' is the most likely one.
He speaks plaintively of the demand for ideological conformity
leaving 'little place for compassion, forgiveness, joy and love –
even among the elite leadership'. And he notes 'outright reluctance to acknowledge membership in the Christian community
or to participate in its worship...almost total silence or even
disarray in the realm of personal ethics...the conspicuous lack of
any explicit or implicit reference to the Bible...If there is not in
all SCM activities even a fleeting hint of the life and liberation to
be found in Jesus Christ, it is not really surprising if many
students find it difficult to respond to such efforts in terms linked
with their Christian faith.'[62] It was, perhaps, an unusually
tempestuous phase. But these extremes were the logical
consequences of the refusal to affirm either the full authority of
Scripture, or the need for a closed membership, that marked
SCM's position at the time when the CICCU students disaffiliated.

Finally, what of the American Student Volunteer Movement,
that gave the initial impetus to this movement? After the First
World War, liberals in the SVM were asserting that all religions
were fundamentally the same, which made the exclusive
promotion of Christianity foolish or even offensive. Many
students at the 1920 Convention in Des Moines were not even
professing Christians. Some of them asked Sherwood Eddy,
'Why do you bring us this piffle, these old shibboleths, these old
worn-out phrases, why are you talking to us about the living

[62] Risto Lehtonen, *The Story of a Storm: An Ecumenical Case Study* (WSCF, 1972),
pp.8–12.

God and the divine Christ?'[63] For many liberals, the stress was primarily on the rebuilding of a just society. For a while there was perhaps a possibility of holding together a concern for personal salvation and world evangelism with the social implications of the gospel. But many of the students lacked the commitment to biblical authority on which such a totality would have to be based, and were simply 'determined to work for reforms – either with or without the help of God'.[64]

Des Moines was the movement's numerical peak. It was attended by 6,890, and the following year saw the largest-ever number of Volunteers enrolled (2,783).[65] But this was no guarantee of health; it merely reflected the postwar mood. The figure immediately began to plunge, falling below 1,000 in 1925 and below 700 from then on.

Robert Wilder returned as the SVM's general secretary in 1920. (He had served on the staff of SCM in Britain from 1905 till 1917.) He still hoped to hold liberals and evangelicals in a single movement. When he described his view of world mission in the SVM *Bulletin* in 1920, he described as its ultimate aim 'to bring into all parts of the world the Kingdom of God in all its fullness and with all its implications for individuals, for society, for nations, and for international relationships'. But the 'immediate aims' whereby this would be achieved were '1) To give every person in the world now living an intelligent opportunity to accept Jesus Christ as personal Saviour and Lord; 2) To win as many as possible... 3) To build up the converts in their faith... 4) To establish self-supporting and self-propagating indigenous churches... 5) To work for the Christianization of the social order.' This, however, was not the order of priorities of the movement as a whole. After the 1924 Convention he reported, 'Some fear... there may be an over-emphasis of what is called the "Social Gospel" and an under-emphasis of the gospel for the individual.'

By 1925, evangelical groups were beginning to disaffiliate from the SVM. Wilder reported to the executive that such groups could be retained 'if we continue to render the colleges a deeply spiritual contribution and if we avoid theological discussions' –

---

[63] Most of the following material on the SVM is again taken from the detailed account in Cumming, *op.cit.*

[64] Report in *The Missionary Review of the World*, quoted in Howard, *op.cit.*, p.101.

[65] William H. Beahm, *Factors in the Development of the Student Volunteer Movement for Foreign Missions*, quoted Howard, *op.cit.*, p.98.

obviously a disastrous and untenable position to have reached. One student leader wrote to Wilder complaining of speakers seeking 'to show that the old Gospel of the Cross of Christ was trite and powerless and altogether inadequate for our present needs'; he cited remarks like 'We used to speak of folk being saved and unsaved, now we are starting to wonder whether the state of the heathen is really as serious as we thought it was'; or again, 'We used to think that Christianity was right and every other religion was wrong until we are starting to wonder whether Christ was the fullest development or whether there isn't something beyond.' 'Brother Wilder', concluded this student, 'we desire to support the Student Volunteer Organization just so long as it seeks to maintain its original purpose.'

In 1927, Wilder resigned. In his 'farewell' report, he asked whether SVM was recruiting 'apostles with a passion for souls', and pointed to the plunge in numbers of new Volunteers. He singled out the problems of universalism and syncretism removing the note of urgency; of 'destructive criticism' which 'has led many students to doubt the trustworthiness of the sacred scriptures'; and of a lack of time being given to prayer and Bible study on the grounds that 'we cannot be mystics in the modern age'. He had tried to keep the SVM a powerful force for the biblical gospel; but it had not proved to be possible. Seven years later, he played a key role in the events leading to the formation of the IFES.

In 1932 SVM published a pamphlet entitled *A Philosophy of Life that Works*. The basic tenets were 'that all peoples are essentially alike, that we all stand or fall together, that the only solution of the problem lies in persons, and that it is the way of love that works'. Three years later, Wilder's chosen successor, Jesse Wilson, who had been trying to synthesize the liberal and evangelical approaches, resigned. He wrote to another leader, Raymond Currier, of his reluctance to accept that a real divergence existed: 'I have tried to think...that when allowance is made for differences of temperament, etc., we are, in the deep things of the spirit, essentially one. But the convictions deepen that you and I are really pulling the SVM in two opposite directions...The things that matter most to me – the things I live for and if need be must die for – are the things that do not count much with you...You do not deny them, you do not affirm them.'

By 1940, says Beahm, SVM had 'almost ceased to be a decisive

factor...in student religious life'. Twenty-five Volunteers enrolled in 1938, compared with the 2,783 of 1920; 465 attended the
1940 Convention, compared with the 6,890 of 1920. Even if its
ability to spread missionary vision had collapsed, however,
SVM's leaders were involved in a successful navigation of the
enormously tricky waters of ecumenical unification. In 1936, the
SVM co-ordinated its activities with those of the National Inter-
collegiate Christian Council (a union of the YMCA and YWCA)
and the University Christian Mission (a union of denominational
groups). In 1944, the YMCA, YWCA, SVM and denominational
groups joined together in the United Student Christian Council.
In 1956 the USCC and the Interseminary Committee merged to
form the National Student Christian Federation. In 1966 the
NSCF combined with the Roman Catholic National Newman
Student Federation and some other groups to form the University
Christian Movement (WSCF felt 'a tremendous sense of excitement' over this 'ecumenical breakthrough'[66]). In 1969, the UCM
voted itself out of existence.

To a Christian holding a robustly biblical faith, the story of the
WSCF and SVM offers no theme for triumphalism. Although
these movements shifted so far from their original beliefs and
purposes (and indeed WSCF has at times been virulently opposed
to the establishment of evangelical student work), yet they undoubtedly began as a glorious work of the Spirit of God. From
the beginning, many fine and dedicated people have poured
their efforts into them out of love for Christ. That the fruit of
these labours should so largely have been lost (as it must seem to
any evangelical) is a stark tragedy. We can only echo Jeremiah:
'How like a widow is she, who once was great among the nations!
...All the splendour has departed from the Daughter of Zion.'[67] In
the terms of Revelation's letters to the seven churches, the Lord
has removed His 'lampstand' from movements that have so
clearly moved away from and 'forsaken their first love'.[68]

Members of IFES-linked groups cannot afford to view these
developments with secure complacency. For this writer, the
most chilling part of compiling this narrative has been working
through Ruth Rouse's history of the WSCF up to 1924. It is a
chilling experience because of the uncanny resemblance the
early WSCF bore to the IFES. There is the same working philo-

---

[66] Lehtonen, *op.cit.*, p.5.   [67] Lamentations 1:1, 6.   [68] Revelation 2:4–5.

sophy, emphasizing student initiative and national, indigenous leadership, backed up by travelling secretaries and strategic conferences. Miss Rouse narrates the rapid growth of the first few years and asks what were its secrets; she immediately singles out the 'dominant passion... to lead students to become disciples of Jesus Christ. Each student was regarded as a man or woman needing, desperately needing, the power of God unto salvation'. All the Federation pioneers, she says, '"did the work of an evangelist" before all else'.

As a second cause, she highlights the 'steady and continuous emphasis on Bible study', including evangelistic Bible study. In Asia, and 'amongst masses of nominal but unbelieving "Christians" in European universities, the secretaries, after evangelistic meetings, invariably aimed at gathering those who had been touched into Bible circles, usually, especially in non-Christian countries, for the study of St. Mark... It was through such circles that tens of thousands of students won through to faith in Christ.' She also mentions the securing of prayer supporters as the first preparation for any new enterprise; and the certainty that 'the Federation movements grow in spiritual vigour just in proportion as they are gripped and held by the world-wide missionary idea'. There is the passion to reach for Christ students studying outside their own country, a vision that gripped Thornton, Manley, Wilder and Mott.[69] There is the awareness (from 1887 on) of the vast opportunities open to teachers of English in foreign campuses; and that Muslim lands will require a type of pioneer 'ready to spend years in one place in breaking up the ground before the seed could be sown'.[70]

In short, WSCF had virtually all the ingredients of an evangelical student movement of lasting effectiveness. What it lacked was a doctrinal concern that would have ensured its voting members – and above all its leaders – stayed loyal to a faith based unambiguously on the Word of God; a commitment like the apostle Paul's, that would have seen the maintenance of the divinely-revealed gospel as more crucial than unity with all who seemed religious. Only one weakness; but through that weakness the WSCF made shipwreck. IFES-linked groups have no cause to be

[69] Tatlow, *op.cit.*, p.550.
[70] These two paragraphs are taken from Rouse, *op.cit.*, pp.25, 87, 293, 81–83, 83–84, 89, 93, 142, 80, 78.

complacent. There, too, but for the grace of God, we might be drifting.

But the grace of God is never thwarted. As the twentieth century wore on, He brought new beginnings once again.

2
Fresh winds from God

In 1920-21, the years in which the American SVM began its final steep plunge towards oblivion, there came the first signs of a new movement of God among evangelical students in Norway.[1]

Here, again, the equivalent of the SCM had started out as an evangelical movement. But, as Ole Hallesby explained later, it 'went through an unhappy metamorphosis' in 1899. 'Before liberal theology became popular...we used to hear of sin and grace, sorrow for sin, and questions from the troubled conscience; *now* it is intellectual problems which are put in the centre. There is no further room for Christian repentance and conversion. Men have become satisfied with some vague religious experience...For us who were standing on a positive biblical basis, the door to the student world was tightly shut, and during these long years we were in the greatest distress.'

What had happened in 1899 was that an alliance had been formed linking together five different Christian student groups. The resulting body was the usual turn-of-the-century mixture of liberals and evangelicals. By about 1910 there were two tendencies in the movement, one very concerned for numerical strength and emphasizing a 'cultural Christianity', the other emphasizing an inner strength based on the fundamentals of the faith.

All this was taking place in the context of a similar conflict between evangelicals and liberals within the state church, which came to a climax in the early 1920s. Ole Hallesby was a young

---

[1] Much of what follows on Norway is taken from Aage Haavik's essay in the NKSS jubilee publication *Laget 50 Ar: 1924-1974*. The quotations from Ole Hallesby are from Douglas Johnson, *A Brief History of the IFES*, pp.178ff.

professor of systematic theology at the 'Menighetsfakultetet', the free evangelical seminary, and although he was a layman he became the standard-bearer of the evangelicals. (In the history of the Scandinavian churches, pietistic movements of laymen have often kept a biblical, personal faith alive during periods of coldness and formalism.) He was to be an influential evangelical leader for many years, known internationally as the author of such books as *Prayer* and *Why I am a Christian*, and as the first IFES president. During the war he became something of a national hero after being jailed by the Nazis for his courageous protest against the transportation of Jews and Norwegian youth to Germany.

Hallesby had been a popular speaker at the student alliance's summer conference. But from 1917 onwards he felt he could no longer take part. He became concerned about the need for a conference where the whole programme would be centralized on 'personal decision for Jesus Christ and life in Him'. In 1921, therefore, he arranged a gathering in Haugetun for students and graduates. Its success was by no means a foregone conclusion, and it came as a considerable relief to the anxious leaders when ninety participants came to hear preaching oriented towards spiritual revival. The event was repeated, and by 1923 there were over 200 present.

Meanwhile, a student named Gunnvald Kvarstein came up to the Menighetsfakultetet. At high school, he had seen two groups in operation, an evangelical group and a liberal group; so when he came on to higher education he knew that there existed more than one way of operating a Christian group. On arrival in Oslo, he went along to the gathering arranged by the student alliance for the new students, but was greatly disappointed. 'The most essential thing was missing,' he said, 'a message from God.' However, when he discussed the matter with fellow-students at the Menighetsfakultetet, the general feeling was to have one last attempt at reforming the alliance from within. Kvarstein accepted this, despite his doubts about the possibility of permanent reform. At the alliance's general assembly that year there were two candidates for the leadership, Hallesby and a liberal theologian named Kristian Schjelderup, the author of a book strongly influenced by eastern religions. The vote went against Hallesby, 99 to 60.

For Kvarstein and a number of other students, the issue was now clear. It was impossible for them to stand outside the struggle that was taking place in the church, when the very nature of the gospel was at stake. 'Let us have clear lines at any price', wrote one student in the alliance's paper in April 1923. A crowded meeting was held in the oratorium of the Menighetsfakultetet, including many of the seminary's professors. Kvarstein spoke of their responsibility in the student world; Hallesby shared his experiences in the Haugetun conferences. And the Norges Kristelige Studentlag came into being.

The new evangelical movement was thus the result of the initiative of students, most of them from small towns where there were Christians faithful to the Scriptures, and who found that the kind of Christian life cultivated within the alliance went against what they knew of Scripture. They started out with just fifty-three members, and from their faithfulness grew a strong evangelical movement. The high schools were swift to follow the inspiration of the universities; a high-schools group was formed in the autumn of 1924, and fifty such groups existed within ten years. In 1926, the Norwegian Student Volunteer Movement joined the new evangelical group.

News of what was happening in Norway spread to other parts of Scandinavia. Two Swedes, the Roden brothers, were present at the first Haugetun conference. They were tremendously impressed to see a conference so markedly different from the liberalism of their own theological faculty. The following year they brought fifty Swedish students with them! In 1923 they formed a Swedish committee, and the following two years united Scandinavian conferences took place in Sweden instead. Students formed Bible study and prayer groups in at least three Swedish cities by 1933. One of their senior friends – indeed, the chairman of their national movement – was the King of Sweden's brother, Prince Oscar Bernadotte! The Prince was a keen Christian and an active evangelist; he gave up his royal privileges to marry a commoner who was also a Christian. He became an adviser to the international conferences that preceded the formation of IFES.

The British took a little longer to form a national evangelical student movement. At the end of the First World War, the only evangelical student groups in existence were those in Cambridge and the London medical schools. In Cambridge, the SCM restarted 'like a rocket'; in contrast, CICCU's Daily Prayer Meeting could only muster some fifteen students in the first term of 1919. 'Move with the times', they were told, 'or CICCU will be dead within a year.' Most of their members, however, had a keen faith

48

that had come through the war. Two of the key student leaders, Godfrey Buxton (on crutches from a war wound) and Norman Grubb (later C. T. Studd's son-in-law) had both received military decorations for bravery. The CICCU soon moved back into personal evangelism and open-air preaching.

Their zeal and prayer life attracted attention. Charles Raven, a senior friend of the SCM, told CICCU, 'You have got the thing we want',[2] and he and others tried to persuade them to become a 'devotional branch' of the SCM. So Grubb and D. T. Dick, the president, met with the SCM leaders, and the Daily Prayer Meeting that day was continued until they returned. But 'after an hour's conversation which got us nowhere', they asked, 'Does the SCM consider the atoning blood of Jesus Christ as the central point of their message?' 'No, not as central', was the reply, 'although it is given a place in our teaching.' That was decisive. 'We explained to them at once that the atoning blood was so much the heart of our message that we could never join with a movement which gave it a lesser place.'[3] They could no more collaborate with 'another gospel' than could the apostle Paul;[4] the question was one of whether as a Union they continued to preach a gospel that really would lead to eternal salvation.

In July, several CICCU students were at a houseparty at Keswick. A couple of them began to feel that they were not 'hearing and responding to God's voice as we should', says Norman Grubb. They arranged to meet for half an hour's prayer. It seems that God stepped in. One of the youngest students present began to pray 'with no self-consciousness or inhibition. We began to do the same'. The meeting did not break up until around 2 a.m., and the students came out of it changed. Some went into the fields in the following days to pray. When they

[2] Raven felt that SCM was becoming a great debating society; he even found himself cold-shouldered for preaching the atonement 'emotionally'.

[3] From then on SCM's position hardened. When London evangelical students met with SCM general secretary Tatlow in 1926, Tatlow declared that 'the doctrine of the verbal inspiration of the Bible is as dead as Queen Anne' (who was very dead indeed), and that 'no theologian worth the name accepts the penal view of the Atonement'.

[4] Galatians 1:6–8. SCM's approach to evangelism was changing anyway. They still ran university missions, but Raven wrote of the 1920 Cambridge mission (in which CICCU joined, without overmuch success) that 'it was natural that the missioners should lay stress rather upon social duty and corporate righteousness than upon personal conversion and individual salvation' (Tissington Tatlow, *The Story of the Student Christian Movement*, p.645).

returned to Cambridge, there was a new mood; they might have become a 'hard barren defensive clique', but instead there was a 'terrific atmosphere of prayer'. 'With the decision against re-union' (with SCM) 'came *faithfulness*', wrote Norman Grubb later. 'At Keswick came *fire*.'

Flames spread. One of the students at Keswick, Noel Palmer, was from Oxford, where he had recently become SCM secretary. When he returned to Oxford, 'Things began to hum. Word went round that Tiny Palmer' (he was 6 feet 8 inches) 'had got religious mania.' If he had, it was certainly infectious. Within four weeks forty students were meeting in Bible study groups, and small, spontaneous prayer groups were meeting at all hours of the day in Palmer's rooms. They started street preaching too. 'The Varsity rugger fifteen were going to throw us in the river, but the local communists drew their fire instead because they were running a huge strike meeting.'

God's flames continued to spread. Grubb recalls that one day 'God gave me a vision of the IVF that was to be. I saw that not only must there be this witness in every university, but that God was going to do it.' And in December, students from Oxford, Cambridge and London met for an 'Inter-Varsity Conference' – so called because the date chosen was that of the 'Inter-Varsity' rugby game between Oxford and Cambridge, and therefore the time (it was thought) when the most Christian students would be in London. That conference soon grew. In the following years, students began evangelical groups in university after university.[5]

To begin with, a number of these were scarcely evangelistic; some of the students involved had such a minority complex that they did not think of going outside their own circle of mainly Christian friends. But that changed as they prayed and studied the Bible. Others were SCM members who had grown weary of having to debate with other members in front of non-Christians when they wished to proclaim the gospel. Such students were forfeiting the opportunity of influencing a large SCM, for a part in what then seemed a small 'hole-in-corner' group.

In Aberdeen, five students met for prayer and Bible study in 1921, and were arranging evangelistic meetings with eighty pre-

[5] In addition to the two histories of CICCU quoted extensively in the previous chapter, this section draws heavily on the two official histories of the British movement, *Contending for the Faith* by Douglas Johnson (IVP, 1979) and the briefer *For the Faith of the Gospel* (UCCF, 1978).

sent the following year. In St Andrews, five students met somewhat furtively in the ruins of a cathedral to try to form a group;
one of these resigned when they were joined by some women! At
Bristol, a medical professor, Arthur Rendle Short, had begun a
student meeting in his home before the war, and handed it over
to student leadership. He travelled extensively through the
country encouraging handfuls of evangelical students.[6]

In Edinburgh, a group was formed in 1922, and three years
later held a university mission led by one of their own number,
Eric Liddell (the hero of *Chariots of Fire*), who had won an
Olympic gold medal in the 400 metres the previous year. (That
was after refusing to run in the 100 metres – in which he was a
favourite – because the heats were on the Sabbath.) In Cardiff, a
student put up a notice asking 'all those who know that their sins
are forgiven and have thus accepted the Lord Jesus Christ as their
own personal Saviour' to contact him. The notices were mutilated,
but a lasting group was begun. One of the early leaders wrote,
'Thus far we had imagined our position isolated. Our surprise
and joy, then, were unbounded when... we discovered that our
experience was only similar to that of students in many other
universities... How we blessed God for His work!' Certainly this
spontaneous uprising of student initiative bore the marks of
divine rather than human organization.

By 1924 the Inter-Varsity Conference had acquired a doctrinal
basis which all its leaders and speakers would sign. The initiative
for this came from the women students in London and the theological students of the London College of Divinity. They were
keen to ensure that the young student groups now emerging
would – unlike their predecessors – stay faithful to the essence of
the gospel. They entered on an enthusiastic search for a statement
that – while obviously not summarizing the whole of Christian
doctrine! – would define the fundamentals of the gospel on
which all biblically-based Christians could join together. They
spent much effort in discussion with Christian leaders, and staff
and students of the London College of Divinity; they drew heavily
on older documents such as the Anglican Thirty-Nine Articles, the
Westminster Confession, and the doctrinal statement of the
Evangelical Alliance. Those students did their work well. The

[6] W. M. Capper and Douglas Johnson, *The Faith of a Surgeon: belief and experience in the life of Arthur Rendle Short*, pp.115–117.

resulting document is substantially the same as the doctrinal basis of the IFES today. It has enabled the student groups through sixty years to ensure they have the kind of leaders Paul insisted upon, who 'must hold firmly to the trustworthy message as it has been taught, so that (they) can encourage others by sound doctrine and refute those who oppose it' (Titus 1:9).

Doctrinal certainties have their price, and in 1925 the Conference had to face the loss of its Oxford representatives. The Oxford group had taken up the offer rejected by CICCU in 1919, becoming the 'Devotional Unit' of the local SCM. To the Inter-Varsity Conference committee, this meant returning to a situation where the biblical gospel was being presented merely as one of a number of equally valid options. So, while individual students were welcome to the conference, the Oxford CU's delegates were not present at its general committee.

The Oxford experiment was not a great success, however; the liberal outlook of the SCM was simply not conducive to evangelism. There was increasing unease, and in 1927 eighteen students restarted a new evangelical union with a strong doctrinal basis. (The key figure in this was a new student called Freddy Crittenden, who played a vital role in the expansion of evangelical student work in Africa in later years.) One of their first actions was to hire the Town Hall for evangelistic meetings led by three CICCU members. Much prayer took place, the Hall was packed out, a collection at the door covered the formidable expenses to the nearest penny, and there were many conversions. Doctrinal clarity and evangelistic zeal went together!

By this time the needs of the small groups that God had raised up across the country were obviously calling for the appointment of a full-time travelling secretary. CICCU president Hugh Gough (later Archbishop of Sydney) was appointed in 1927. In 1928, the Inter-Varsity Fellowship came together as a national movement. It was not until another four years had gone by that a part-time general secretary was appointed, 'at the rate of £150 per annum, subject to the money's being in hand'. He was Douglas Johnson, a London medical graduate who had been honorary secretary since 1924, and who now proceeded to divide his time between the IVF and a medical mission in Bermondsey, a poor area of London then severely short of doctors. He had intended going abroad as a medical missionary, and had doubts about accepting the IVF post. When he consulted Rendle Short – a renowned recruiter of medical missionaries – the latter urged him to stay at home and build up a movement that would send many more labourers. (On leaving, Douglas Johnson asked, 'Well, what shall I say at the Judgment Seat if I am asked why I did not go to the mission field?' 'Oh,' replied Rendle Short, 'you just leave that to me!')

Douglas Johnson was someone with a far-reaching vision. As a student, he managed to arrange to dissect the different parts of a human body each in a different medical school, and so help the group in each! He was to be IVF's general secretary until 1964, and (according to the first IFES general secretary, C. Stacey Woods) he did more than any other man to bring about the birth of the IFES. Throughout his life he has been characterized by complete loyalty to the biblical faith; his leadership combined the expenditure of extraordinary hours – many of them writing large numbers of warm and perceptive letters – with a self-effacing modesty (and a morbid hatred of cameras) that became legendary. He was utterly committed to the maintenance of student leadership, insisting that 'we graduates do *nothing* in local leadership which an average student can reasonably be expected to do'. In the student executive, he would sometimes refuse to express a view till a decision had been made.

John Laird, a former president of the Glasgow group who became Scripture Union's general secretary, describes 'DJ' as a 'voracious reader, and although he would probably deny it, a far-sighted strategist...His favourite quotation was from a nineteenth-century author of naval strategy, "When you are trying to accomplish something you should first decide what is the *final objective* you are seeking to attain, and then *never lose sight of it*."' Laird cites a typical letter from 'DJ' after a heart attack brought on by overwork at the time of the Battle of Britain: 'Result bed for twelve weeks and no work for six months. Result for me: have done more reading than ever!...Sorry you aren't here to be bombed with us so that we could spend time in shelters planning the next advance. Looking forward to meeting you again on earth if the Lord doesn't return; if not, then in heaven. N.B. I hope there's a library there!'[7]

Whether or not there is a library in heaven, there was no IVF office in London until later in the year, when 'DJ' and the editor of the student magazine – Donald Coggan, later Archbishop of

[7] John Laird, *No Mere Chance* (Hodder, 1981), pp.82–83.

Canterbury – came across a suitable room, put down £50 each, and then persuaded the rest of the student committee to accept that 'the Secretary's bed was no longer big enough to serve as an office desk'. This was perhaps a justifiable assessment. By then the movement was branching out into literature, with the publication of seven booklets, mostly on topics of science and faith. They had covers of 'dull brown paper, which was made more sombre by the black type', says 'DJ'. 'Art, advertisement and publicity were certainly not the strongest points in the early IVF days.' Several books followed, including *The Quiet Time* and *The Bible and Modern Research* in 1933, *Effective Witness*, the first volume of the Bible study guide *Search the Scriptures*, and an IVF history by Donald Coggan in 1934. The student committee had also broadened their field of interest geographically – to include Canada, Australia and New Zealand!

THE MISSIONARY JOURNEYS OF HOWARD GUINNESS

In 1927-28 Norman Grubb visited Canada on deputation for the Worldwide Evangelization Crusade. He was naturally on the lookout for evangelical students; but the Canadian SCM had become outspokenly rationalistic since the end of the war. All he found was a single evangelical student group in Vancouver, formed in 1926. In the USA, too, the picture was grim. During 1927 Robert Wilder had resigned as SVM general secretary, and shortly before doing so had lamented that 'all of the student movements of the world have gone over' to theological liberalism apart from the the SVM, 'and they have nearly captured the Student Volunteer Movement' – a prophecy that was fulfilled all too accurately within the next eight years.[8] There were reports of a League of Evangelical Students formed in 1925, but this still consisted mainly of theological students in the Philadelphia area.

Norman Grubb brought back to the IVF appeals from the retiring principal of McGill University, Montreal, and from the editor of *The Evangelical Christian,* for a student leader to be sent across to start something similar in Canada. He shared this challenge at the IVF conference, the first since IVF's formation as a movement. The students responded enthusiastically to this 'definite challenge from God'; and the student vice-chairman, Howard Guinness, was chosen.

[8] Quoted Joe Cumming, in Cindy Smith and Joe Cumming, *Rebuilding the Mission Movement*, p.514.

Howard Guinness was no ordinary Christian student. The grandson of Grattan Guinness, and son of the founder of the Regions Beyond Missionary Union, he was a fine rugby player and had a passion for evangelism.[9] He had made a habit of speaking to passengers on the bus each morning and evening about Christ; and when he changed his mode of transport to a motorbike, he duly purchased two notice-boards to hang on his rear wheel, and continued to do the work of an evangelist that way! He describes himself as 'impetuous, untidy, stubborn, dramatic, and over-optimistic', and without doubt some of his pioneering was done without much forethought. But God often uses people like that, and then uses other members of the Body of Christ to tidy up the pieces! Certainly there was no-one else at this stage of the movement whom God used to pioneer a wider area.

This, then, was the IVF's chosen ambassador to answer the 'Macedonian call' from Canada. Unfortunately, the students only remembered at the last minute that, if they were going to send out missionaries, they had financial responsibilities. IVF's assured annual income was only £25, which they kept in an Ovaltine tin! 'We hadn't a clue how the money would come in', recalls Douglas Johnson. He phoned Rendle Short – for years their sole benefactor – with the result that a one-way ticket to Canada was promised. Then the students organized a 'bring-and-buy' sale of their belongings – books, hockey-sticks, *etc.* – to raise a further £14. Norman Grubb bought Guinness an enormous overcoat for the Canadian winter; and off he went.

He arrived in Canada in early November 1928, having been seasick for much of the voyage but having nonetheless led his cabin-mate to Christ. His diary for 7 November records the text *'My Word shall not return unto ME void'*. He adds, *'My first duty to the students of Canada is to lead them out into the fullness of the Spirit's power... Unions of man-made energy – however true to God's word – would be a disaster to Canada. However, the Holy Spirit has been brooding over some of these Varsities and preparing certain hearts to receive this message and power through me and then to DO something! Allelujah!'*

McGill was his starting-point, with some useful contacts with

[9] One of his aunts was Hudson Taylor's daughter-in-law; another was the first woman travelling secretary of the American Student Volunteer Movement. It was quite a family!

55

members of the Student Volunteer Movement. He was not merely aiming to found student groups, however, but young people's camps as well, having been much involved with such work in England. Little of the kind was being done by evangelicals in Canada at this time, so he prepared an article on the subject, which was published by several Christian periodicals. But individual Christians were pessimistic about the idea. The British camps were frequently staffed by IVF students; in Canada students often had to use their summers to earn their college fees for the following year.[10]

The Montreal students decided to arrange a lunch-hour prayer meeting and a Saturday evening Bible reading, but did not yet take Guinness's advice to form an organized group. *'Praise God'* was his response in his diary, however, and he moved on to Toronto. Here he stayed in the house of former Oxford president Noel 'Tiny' Palmer. Here, again, the keenest Christians seemed to be SVM members. Guinness hoped to be able to make an impact with some big meetings. *'God will guide in this matter infallibly'*, he wrote in his diary. *'Oh for the faith and God abandonment of Abram who with but little knowledge of theology, yet knew His God and trusted Him!'*

The following day, *'The Holy Spirit seemed to say "Don't leave Toronto even if it means 6 weeks or more until the root has gone deep. It is the strategic position for the whole of Canada".'* That was Friday; he spent Saturday in prayer, and on Tuesday went to see the chaplain who was in charge of the local SCM affiliate at Hart House. *'This seemed to me like putting my head inside the lion's mouth, for he is a very advanced modernist'*, he wrote on the Monday. Not so. *'He said that he must use me whilst I was here and offered me the midday prayer meetings each day! Someone must have been praying.'*

The next Thursday he was at Knox College, where a prayer meeting already existed. After he spoke, there was an almost unanimous reaction: *'We have been hiding...We will come out of our hiding place and form a definite Evangelical witness for Christ so that the whole college shall know!'* Five days later, a Toronto Bible College student informed him they wanted *'a finger in the pie'*. A week later, he met two reporters from the *Varsity Daily* and one of

---

[10] Some of the material on Howard Guinness's pioneering is taken from his autobiography, *Journey Among Students.* (Anglican Information Office, Sydney, 1978). Sections in italics are from Guinness's diary.

them was converted. *'Praise the Lord!'*

That weekend, he and Noel Palmer left for the League of Evangelical Students conference in Chicago. They seemed to have formed their impressions of it rather more rapidly than an IFES staffworker in a new country might do today; but even allowing for exaggeration, the picture was still unpromising. Virtually all the twenty branches were in seminaries. *'The main University centres are not touched. There seemed to be nothing left of Borden's work at Yale...In the reports from each branch only one mentioned anything about soul-winning and that was not amongst students but in the town!'* Obviously they were hard at work combating liberal theology, but Guinness was yearning for a sign of *'aggressive evangelism'*.

Next Wednesday he was back in Toronto – meeting the SCM general secretary! *'I told them what I was doing,'* he recorded; he had no desire to appear underhand. The SCM leader invited Guinness to join their work. *'How I sweated!...In the end they said they would warn the rest of Canada of my coming as an Emissary of the Devil'* – but that was not quite as abusive as it might have seemed: *'I'm not sure that they believe in him!...We parted friends.'*

On Thursday evening, the university's evangelicals met and resolved to form an evangelical union. The doxology was sung, the meeting dispersed, and Guinness wrote in his diary, *'Bless the Lord O my Soul.'* The following day was volleyball in the afternoon, and an evening *'in conference with the Holy Spirit over a map'*. It was evidently going to be difficult to 'finish' (his word) Vancouver, Edmonton, Saskatoon and Winnipeg and get back to England to take up his appointment three months later! *'I found a great urge within me saying stay until the job is finished. What did a few months setback for my medical career count beside the evangelisation of the world in this generation to which the completion of my job here would give such an impetus!...There was no mistaking the call. It was stay right through until the job was done. Hallelujah! He leads, I follow.'*

That decision did not give him the money to cross Canada, however! Not until six days later did a cheque for $250 arrive from a wealthy Montreal Christian. Christmas Day dinner was a 'dubious affair alone in the dining car' of the westbound train – he decided he could not afford more than one course – but by 8 January 1929, he was with the three-year-old group in Vancouver. *'We discussed the reasons for no conversions since the Union was* started. *They confessed cowardice, powerlessness, lack of prayer, lack of consecration etc... The Lord began to break up the deeps. Then we had a time of prayer which was characterised by confession and repentance together with fresh consecration and utter dependence on His grace and Power. This is the beginning of Revival and it has started in the right place!'* And the next week saw conversions at last!

Now he turned east. He arrived in Edmonton with just over 30 cents left and no money to travel further. He could have asked for money from his sympathetic hosts, who would 'undoubtedly have come to my rescue', as he wrote later. 'But the Lord would not let me do this. I found that I wanted to prove that God could provide...in answer to prayer alone, so I simply told Him all about my need and left it at that.' The day before he was due to leave, a cheque arrived with enough money for a ticket back to Montreal. In Saskatoon, the evangelical students were keen to meet with him, and an evangelical union was formed; but he left them with some problems, as he wrote later. 'It would be difficult for a visitor from England, however tactful, doing my particular work not to arouse some antagonism in most Colleges. And tact was not my strongest suit.'

Then on to Winnipeg. Here he found – as many IFES pioneers since have done – that the Lord had begun the work before he arrived. On the train he met the senior student of the Anglican theological college, who had found God in a fresh way and had become the centre of a group of keen believers. Guinness stayed with him for several days; there were nearly a dozen conversions, he thought, and the Manitoba Varsity Christian Union was formed. The time in Winnipeg was an education for other reasons too. He met an SCM staffworker who had 'heard Norman Grubb the year before but had failed to grasp what he was talking about. None of the SCM students had understood him.' That forced Guinness to do some hard thinking about the way he was communicating.

Back in Toronto, the newly-formed group had survived critical articles in the university newspaper, and was putting Guinness's dream of youth camps into operation, with *'good backing from the Evangelical clergy...Hallelujah!'* He moved on to London, Ontario, where the SVM was still made up of strong evangelicals. It served as a nucleus for the formation, on 22 February, of an evangelistic Christian Students Fellowship.

The rest of his university visits did not yield any fruit until later. But living by faith continued to be an education. In Montreal he had enough money for a train ticket to Halifax, but nothing for food or any subsequent expenses. The morning he left, he was given $50. 'God always provided', he recalls. 'Whether the sum needed was great or small it always turned up, although often at the last moment.' At Halifax, a different kind of trial awaited him. The students were somewhat sceptical of their English visitor and challenged him to swim the 'Northwest Arm' – an inlet of the Atlantic which at that time of year was kept from freezing only by the movement of the ocean. He took the challenge – but on entering the water found it far colder than he had dreamed! He reached the far bank as fast as the college champion, but found he could not feel his towel when it touched his body. 'I was scared. Back to the college I ran full speed...'

From May his diary ceases. But that summer came the long-awaited camp. And one night 'God descended on the camp in a way I cannot possibly express'. The campers had been invited to share their own testimonies of what Christ meant to them, and suddenly one broke down and fell flat on the ground. Guinness was inclined to close the meeting and send the boys to bed. 'I am a very conservative person and I had a certain amount of medical knowledge and the last thing in the world that I wanted was anything emotional...Somehow I didn't stop the meeting. He seemed perfectly at ease and nobody else was disturbed at all by this extraordinary thing. Possibly the Holy Spirit was at work in an unusual way. So the evening was allowed to proceed with one or two others speaking while the boy on the ground quietened down. Then with a final song and a prayer we broke up for the night.

'But there was no bed. They were in little groups over the hillside singing hymns, talking again of what Christ meant to them; and indeed, the officers themselves had come into my tent and were kneeling in prayer...Now let me say again that I'm quite an ordinary man and it's very rarely that I've wept...As we prayed for our friends God had come upon us in a way that for me was a very, very, very rare experience...It's only once in a lifetime and I can never forget God so taking charge of a meeting and a whole group of people...leading them to heights of prayer, devotion, faith and love such as they had never experienced in their lives before and, I believe, doing very deep things as a result.' Out of that visitation – which took place on a camp where the participants were being encouraged to make decisions for Christ privately rather than publicly – grew the Pioneer Camp work. This is still a crucial part of Inter-Varsity's ministry in Canada today.

In the middle of the summer a cable came from a Sydney businessman inviting Guinness to visit Australia. He eventually accepted, and persuaded the British IVF to send out their latest student chairman, Kenneth Hooker, to succeed him as full-time staffworker in Canada. In the autumn, Canada's own Inter-Varsity Christian Fellowship was formed, with the presidents of the London (Ontario) and Toronto groups as student president and vice-president. Kenneth Hooker stayed six months, and was succeeded by Noel 'Tiny' Palmer (for three difficult years), then Arthur Hill (who had been the first student president), then, in 1934, an Australian, Stacey Woods; of whom we shall have more to say. Kenneth Hooker, incidentally, relates that during his time on staff he too found God providing for his financial needs in an exceptional manner – including a total stranger coming up to him on a railway platform and giving him money.

When Howard Guinness turned westwards, he had no money for his passage to Australia. But he booked it anyway, and set off to study Romans for a week in Seattle. Here he was used of God in the formation of an evangelical student group at the University of Washington. When he returned to Vancouver, there was £40 waiting from Douglas Johnson; enough for the passage.

On arrival in Sydney – having led two fellow-passengers to Christ – he found that the Lord was, again, already at work. A student Bible League had been formed in 1919, with a daily prayer meeting. Guinness encouraged them to get involved actively in evangelism, and to develop into a witnessing Evangelical Union, which they did. He spoke ('a little fearfully and not too well') at their first public meetings soon afterwards.

His thinking about pioneering student work had taken a new turn in Canada, however. He had become convinced that the strength of the British movement was due to the solid work being done by CSSM (which became part of Scripture Union) in the schools. This guaranteed a succession of evangelical university students. In March 1930 Guinness received an invitation to visit New Zealand, and replied in terms of his new strategy: 'What I want to aim at...is to get an entrance into the important schools of N.Z. and speak to them, stay one or two days at each and form definite CUs "run by the boys for the boys", thus starting a witness for Christ where it is 100% easier to get results. In this way the Varsities will find themselves being *fed* by *Christian boys* rather than heathen...Let the Evangelical Varsity men make their main field of evangelism *the schools* and they reflexly will more than double the effectiveness of their own witness at the university.'[11] (Presumably by 'main field' he meant 'main field after their immediate surroundings at the university'.)

In Sydney, therefore, he soon had the newly-formed Evangelical Union running a camp for schoolboys. He moved on to Melbourne, where a group of evangelical medical students were meeting with frustration in their attemps to initiate an effective outreach through the SCM. They had met for a half-day of prayer on several occasions, and now felt the time had come to start an Evangelical Union. About seventy people packed the lecture theatre when the EU was launched. Guinness also visited Brisbane and Adelaide (where the SCM invited him to conduct a mission). Apart from helping stimulate evangelical student work in two more universities, he was involved in setting up 'Crusader Unions' to continue the schools work.[12]

The choice of name was somewhat typical of his personality! He had been converted through a Crusader class in London; but the Crusader Unions he was enthusiastically setting up throughout Australia – and soon right across New Zealand too – were rather different from the Sunday afternoon Bible classes of the British Crusader movement. 'This did not trouble him', comments Peter Lineham. He 'had never asked permission to use the Crusaders' name and was carefree about organizational details. What appealed to him was the symbolism...The other thing he liked was the Crusader badge which was awarded to faithful members. He cheerfully modified the design of the hallowed badge by the addition of four stars to represent the Southern Cross, and he endowed the symbol and dozens of badges to the new organization.' By the time he returned to Canada he had decided that Inter-School Christian Fellowship might be an even better name. But he had exasperated the British Crusader Union,

[11] Peter Lineham, *No Ordinary Union* (the official history of Scripture Union in New Zealand; SU-New Zealand, 1980), p.42.
[12] John and Moyra Prince, *Tuned In To Change* (the official history of Scripture Union in Australia; Anzea, 1979), pp.97–99, and Guinness, *op.cit.*, pp.66–69.

who had no guarantee that the work set up in his high-speed tour would have any permanence. CSSM likewise were not over-enthusiastic about his having pirated the Scripture Union card for the Crusaders to use![13]

In New Zealand, again, evangelical groups were already developing. Here, as in Australia, the SCM had been founded through the evangelizing and encouraging labours of John Mott back in 1896. But like the other WSCF movements, it had broadened theologically. When in 1926 it appointed a full-time general secretary, the nominee was a man deeply influenced by theological liberalism. There were evangelicals within SCM, particularly W. H. Pettit, who were vocal opponents of the movement's new direction. By 1927 discontent had grown, till in Auckland a student group was formed with an evangelical doctrinal statement. It was called the Student Bible League by its members, and various other names – 'Bible Bangers', 'University Salvation Army' – by other students! Linked with it was an evangelical lecturer, E. M. Blaiklock, who was still conducting mini-missions with the evangelical students as late as 1982. The Auckland group was in contact with the British IVF by correspondence.

In Dunedin, R. S. Cree Brown – like Pettit, an SCM graduate who had subsequently done a few years as a missionary in India – had begun a student group in his home. It was he who in March 1930 invited Howard Guinness to tour New Zealand's universities. Guinness wrote back in April suggesting a June visit; he then postponed this date twice, to Cree Brown's frustration, on the grounds that it would have been irresponsible to leave the Australian work so early. New Zealand, he argued, had a group organized already in Auckland, and one in Dunedin that could organize itself 'at any time with or without me'. They compromised: he would arrive in September, speak in Auckland and hasten on to the southern colleges to try to make some impact before the exams.

Relations with SCM were complex. Guinness had seen that the Australian SCM still contained evangelicals; in New Zealand an evangelical had been the Otago SCM president in 1929. Cree Brown feared that SCM opposition to a specifically evangelical work might mean the doors became closed; and he wrote a scrupulously honest letter to SCM's secretary, informing her of

[13] Lineham, *op.cit.*, pp.43, 62. The material that follows on New Zealand is mostly drawn from pp.35–53 of this book, and Guinness, *op.cit.*, p.71.

the visit and making clear his desire to see SCM become evangelical again. Some SCM supporters were desperately anxious that at a time of financial crisis no rival organization should emerge. SCM responded that Guinness could speak at each university, providing discussion followed: 'The point is that Dr Guinness does not stand for an attitude which is that of the majority of SCM members... (but) we are very much aware of the fact that he is a fine man and has a message to give.' Privately, even though there were active SCM members among the students meeting at his home, Cree Brown was pessimistic. 'You can't do much in a mixed movement with unsaved and doubting leaders... Privately I rather dread the (SCM) being half-awakened, just enough to avoid the formation of an Evangelical Fellowship, and not enough to be a red-hot testimony...' He slowly began to believe that the Lord was preparing the way for a new group to be formed.

The issue did not arise except in Dunedin. Guinness spent much time in the schools; he would aim to speak at a school assembly at 9 a.m., address a voluntary meeting in the same school at lunchtime, and organize a Crusader group – or else speak at the university – at night! Each day he spoke two to four times, and seven nights out of two months in New Zealand he slept on trains. In Auckland, the Bible League's reputation kept the university SCM away; but a meeting at the Town Hall drew 1,600, and twenty responded to an appeal. The Bible League redesignated itself the Evangelical Students' Fellowship, and soon found that its new world-wide links opened doors among the university authorities.

In Dunedin, Otago SCM organized a meeting attended by 300 students, where some forty responded to an appeal for trust in Christ. An Evangelical Union was formed during the visit. Guinness and Cree Brown were so grateful for SCM's assistance that they were willing to see the EU form part of the local SCM group. However, EU membership was to be restricted to students confessing faith in Christ, and the EU's constitution would include the IVF doctrinal basis. The SCM president felt that co-operation along such lines was impossible; but the separation was fairly amicable. An impact was also made at Wellington (where the meeting was officially organized 'to question the fundamentalist from England'), and Christchurch, where a small Bible study group resulted.

In the schools there were many conversions, although in some cases, reported Guinness, 'the devil has been kicking up an awful fuss'. The New Zealand tour was the most strenuous task he had ever undertaken, however, and when he was addressing a farewell meeting in Auckland he had to stop halfway through from nervous exhaustion: 'If I had said another word I would have found myself in tears.' To say it was a whirlwind visit is something of an understatement. 'Do not copy me, please', he wrote to New Zealand friends later; and he commented in his autobiography that the Crusaders work he had begun 'would have collapsed entirely but for Dr John Laird', another IVF graduate 'whom God raised up at this very time'. Laird arrived in Auckland on the way to Asia, a month after Guinness's departure, and was persuaded to stay and set the Crusaders on a firm footing.

Peter Lineham's assessment is that though the wounds caused by haste and indiscretion in some places 'took many years to heal, he had dramatically shaken the liberal hold on New Zealand schools and universities. That success...was the product of Guinness' consecrated personality.' Other, different members of the Body of Christ would pioneer tertiary groups at Wellington, Lincoln and Massey; a 1935 visit from Stacey Woods, the future IFES general secretary, would give a new vision. It was to be on the combined initiative of the Auckland student leaders and the Crusader committee that a conference was held in 1936, where thirty-seven students met from thirteen colleges to form the New Zealand IVF. John Laird was its first chairman.

Howard Guinness returned to Canada with his head full of the possibilities of high-schools work. Noel Palmer, now IVCF's general secretary, was waiting for him in Vancouver – and they launched the Canadian ISCF with the formation of a group after an engagement in Victoria High School the following morning! They recrossed Canada together; after Christmas Guinness took a ship back to England. He arrived to find the IVF student executive had arranged a tour of the British universities in the immediate future. It was too much; his psychological reserves were exhausted and his voice was giving out. 'I couldn't bear the thought of meeting anyone...I wanted to retire into a corner and to be alone.' Fortunately IVF were willing to give him two months' leave of absence. He and his brother set off for a tour of southern England: 'Besides playing golf and being thoroughly lazy, we talked and prayed together about our vision of Christ's work and Kingdom.'

And he was not finished with Australia. In Sydney, the Evangelical Union was being split over the teachings and approach of the 'Moral Rearmament' movement. One of the student leaders, Paul White, knew that the rest of the Australian universities were weaker still, and bombarded the British IVF with requests for help. As a result, Guinness returned for a year in 1933-34. This time he had a team of several Australians to travel with him.

He needed them. 'Each State as we came to it was a whirl of meetings and interviews interspersed with occasional sight-seeing and games...School Assemblies, Hotel Receptions, University addresses and Missions, living in colleges, discussions until the early hours of the morning, camps, conferences and conventions, all were entered into with one objective – to make Christ known. And everywhere we went we saw people accepting Him and beginning to serve Him.' Twenty students from Sydney and Melbourne came to help in an outreach at Adelaide. In Melbourne, one Australian observer reported that 'for the first time (in our memory) the foundations of materialism and rationalism in the University were shaken'. Evangelical unions were formed in Perth (the SCM's vice-president being responsible) and Adelaide, after Guinness's departure. The network of groups now existed that would join together to form the Australian IVF in 1936.[14]

The six years since Guinness's first journey to Canada had been busy. He was as aware as anyone of the mistakes that had been made: 'My complete belief in God's guidance, which made the enterprise possible, also tended to preclude the possibility of seeing that some of my judgments might be wrong.' He felt he had been 'brash and self-opinionated...But God knew this and He chose me. He was evidently planning that all the glory should be ascribed to the only wise God and not to fallible man.'

He arrived back in England in August 1934. A main speaker at the IVF conference that year was another indefatigable world traveller: the founder of the Student Volunteer Movement, Robert Wilder.

'WE ARE CERTAINLY NOW IN THE HOUR OF GOD'

After his resignation as SVM general secretary, Robert Wilder had gone to Egypt, to work with the Near East Christian Council.

[14] Prince, *op.cit.*, pp.99–102, and Guinness, *op.cit.*, pp.84–88.

While there, he heard of the rise of the British IVF, and wrote to them urging them to adhere to the basic essentials of the evangelical faith, and the missionary obligations of the Christian.[15] IVF responded by inviting him to speak at their 1934 conference.

The atmosphere was not unlike that of the early SVM. The IVF students had just formed their own Missionary Fellowship for intending missionaries, under the impulse of David Adeney (later a pioneer in the student work in China, and now IFES president). (Within a year, Howard Guinness would have helped IVMF acquire a Watchword very much in the spirit of the SVM, 'Evangelise to a finish to bring back the King'.[16]) The zeal and missionary enthusiasm of the conference participants reminded Robert Wilder of his own undergraduate days, says his biographer; in turn, the British students were captivated by his sincerity and prayerfulness, and 'filled with a vision of what God might do through them'.[17]

But that was not all Robert Wilder did to point the way ahead. He brought with him two recent graduates from the Norwegian movement, his wife's niece and her future husband. The latter was Carl-Frederick Wislöff, later to become a theologian of very high reputation in the Norwegian church, and the IFES chairman 1959-67 and then president 1967-79. He saw that the British IVF was clearly caught up in the same task as the slightly older Norwegian movement. So, during lunch at the Cadena Restaurant in Oxford, he suggested to Douglas Johnson of IVF that some more formal contact should be arranged. He then returned to Norway and consulted with the NKSS leaders; and an invitation was sent to IVF to bring across a group of leaders in the autumn.

The British students took up the idea with enthusiasm. Something of this can be caught from the flavour of Donald Coggan's words in the IVF history *Christ and the Colleges*, written not long before the meeting. He speaks of news IVF had heard of evangelism in the universities of Holland, Germany and China, and then adds that 'incipient movements are springing up in almost all the Baltic countries... As this page goes to press (September, 1934) the programme is already prepared for the first International

---

[15] Douglas Johnson, *Contending for the Faith*, p.192.
[16] This was taken from Matthew 24:14 and 2 Samuel 19:10 (*ibid.*, p.196).
[17] Ruth Wilder Braisted, *In This Generation* (Friendship Press, N.Y., 1941), quoted in Douglas Johnson, *A Brief History...*, p.14. Much of what follows is from the latter source.

Conference of leaders of these various kindred Christian student circles. Those who have their future at heart will meet in order to discuss an informal basis of co-operation – particularly in order to reach those universities of the world where no distinctively evangelical witness is yet to be found. Their prayer is that the Conference may result in a new world-wide student missionary up-rising...May God grant that this present generation may strain every nerve to complete the task and – "EVANGELISE TO A FINISH TO BRING BACK THE KING."[18]

Besides the British delegation,[19] the Norwegians invited representatives of the Christian students in Finland, Denmark, Germany, Hungary, Latvia, Estonia and Sweden (including Swedish pioneer Nils Roden); plus Robert Wilder as interpreter. Ole Hallesby, Howard Guinness and Robert Wilder spent much time in prayer together. The conference discussions resulted in warm friendships and demonstrated a similarity of vision between the evangelical movements represented.

In particular, Ole Hallesby's address struck a prophetic note. He shared the history of the Norwegian movement, and the fears with which they began: 'These...made us realize, too, how helpless we were, and forced us into the fight of prayer. Our fears are now our greatest asset. Our work started as a praying work. God Himself had to bend our stiff knees.' Then looking at the wider scene, he declared, 'The Bible talks much of "the hour of God". In God's hour something always happens. We are certainly now in the hour of God. When movements so alike suddenly and spontaneously spring up in so many countries at the same time, then we must see that God wishes to do something. It is God's hour. It is an unspeakable privilege to move forward at God's time.

'It is as if I see the glow of morning, the dawn of a new day over the old unhappy world after a long, dark night. For many years a rationalistic theology has held most of our churches. On Christian work amongst students this theology has also laid its clammy hand. The Christian world movements have become liberal and at the same time have monopolized Christian work amongst

---

[18] *Christ and the Colleges,* ed. F. D. Coggan (IVF, 1934), p.28.
[19] The British delegation was made up of Howard Guinness, Arnold Aldis, Jean Strain (IVF's first women's travelling secretary, later Mrs Coggan), Dorothy James and Douglas Johnson. The last two of these became engaged on the journey back!

students. We have had no door into the great unhappy student world; everything has looked hopeless.

'This was the situation until just a few years ago. Today we are here, representatives of our many nations, and we can each tell of a Christian student work based on the Bible as the Word of God. We can tell of a door which God Himself, in grace, has opened unto us...'

WALKING THROUGH THE DOORS

The mood at Oslo in 1934 was not one of hasty and impetuous planning or of facile optimism, recalls Douglas Johnson. Rather, there was a sense of 'quiet assurance that God was with them and that He was clearly guiding them into some fruitful new acts of service for His kingdom. The prevailing mood was rather like that of a prudent landowner who puts acorns or plants seedlings in his ground, confident that in the providence of God they will one day develop into full-grown oaks, although he himself may not live to see them.'

No master-plan and no 'Federation', or even formal 'Fellowship', was envisaged; simply another International Conference. An executive was elected to plan this event, with Robert Wilder as chairman, plus Carl-Frederick Wislöff, Nils Roden and Douglas Johnson. It was agreed by a unanimous vote that details 'should be decided upon by the countries chiefly concerned, viz. – Norway, Sweden and England'.

The next gathering took place at Johannelund, Sweden, a year later, and a Conference Constitution was adopted. The meeting opened the way for increasing co-operation between the movements in the years following. This sometimes took the form of Christian academics associated with the student movements (*e.g.* Professor Hallesby or Professor Rendle Short) making speaking tours of other countries; but it also involved the exchange of student teams, most of whom travelled at their own expense. At the time of the Johannelund Conference, Howard Guinness led a team of seven IVF students on a tour of Sweden. The Swedish papers labelled them the 'English Seven' (after C. T. Studd's 'Cambridge Seven'). The team included three students at least who would play a key part in IFES: Tony Wilmot (later a widely-used evangelist in Africa), David Bentley-Taylor (later IFES regional secretary for the Islamic world), and Jim Broomhall (later a missionary with IVF-China). They were publicly welcomed by

Prince Oscar Bernadotte, who was on the advisory committee of the Stockholm Conference; and they attracted large gatherings of students throughout the country. The following year, former Cambridge president Godfrey Buxton led a team to Denmark, Sweden and Finland, and Professor Hallesby a Norwegian team of six students to Iceland.

The Iceland expedition was of considerable importance. It was undertaken in response to an invitation from a few students at the university in Rejkjavik. It was a time when Icelandic evangelicals were experiencing great difficulties. The Norwegians were asked to bring their evangelistic message, tell of their activities, and help to establish something similar. Hallesby found himself attacked as a 'hellfire' preacher; but something of a revival took place. A lasting student group was formed, and some of the Norwegian students stayed behind for some weeks to encourage and foster it.

An international camp in Beatenberg, Switzerland, in 1936, was another example of the potential of co-operation. René Pache (later IFES vice-chairman) had begun student camps in Switzerland in 1932; as a result, a Bible study group was formed in Lausanne, and another a little later in Geneva through a medical student named Rodolphe Bréchet. He attended the British IVF conference, and came back enthusiastic for contact with other countries. And it was obvious that holding an international camp in a more central European country might facilitate links with students from nations that had not been involved hitherto.

The results of the camp were indeed beneficial to all concerned. It strengthened the Swiss student work, which expanded into the high schools that same year and continued – albeit with 'frequent deaths and rebirths' – through the years of the Second World War. (The high-schools work was indeed the area of most rapid growth during this period, through the stimulus of a Scripture Union leader, Gabriel Mutzenberg.) And one of the new contacts – Ferencz Kiss, a leader of the WSCF-affiliated but largely evangelical Pro Christo student movement in Hungary – persuaded the gathering that the next International Conference should be held in Budapest. He then insisted that Douglas Johnson accompany him immediately back to Hungary to begin preparations! Hungarian students urged that this event should include large public meetings, and these were arranged jointly with the Hungarian Evangelical Alliance and Keswick Convention, in a vast hall normally used for horse-riding and exhibitions.[20]

The last pre-war International Conference was held in Cambridge on the eve of war in 1939. This was the biggest of all, and drew over 1,000 students from thirty-three nations. The Sunday morning address, by Harold Earnshaw Smith, was broadcast by the British Broadcasting Corporation. Amongst the participants was a staffworker with the DCSV, the German SCM, which had been largely evangelical up to its suppression by the Gestapo in 1938. He had written an article entitled 'Christ is our only King' in the movement's magazine; he was eventually arrested, and is believed to have died in a concentration camp. Another participant, and indeed a speaker, was the former general secretary of the Russian SCM, V.Ph. Martzinkovski. The Russian SCM had been through severe persecution after the First World War, before its suppression in 1927 and the exile of its leaders to Siberia. During that period an affirmative answer to the question 'Are you willing to die for Christ?' became a condition of membership. Vladimir Martzinkovski and another Moscow leader were imprisoned, and their fellow-members went short of food to send them something to supplement their 'rat soup'. Every night the police had come to the jail to take a batch of prisoners to be shot, and they had never known when their time would come. Nonetheless, they had gone on witnessing to their fellow-prisoners.[21]

The General Committee at the 1939 Conference had delegates or observers from Australia, Britain, Canada, Holland, New Zealand, Norway, Sweden, Denmark, Finland, Iceland, South Africa and the USA. (Hungary and Switzerland would have been

[20] Professor Ferencz Kiss was a close friend of Rendle Short, and a figure of some importance in the Hungarian churches. Throughout the war he held meetings for students and intellectuals, drawing around 100. He had the respect of the Hungarian governments both during and after the war. He was capable of delivering a prophetic rebuke to the wartime (pro-Nazi) premier, and after the war the Jewish community publicly thanked him for his services. Under the Communist government he became the free churches' representative to the State. In 1948 he wrote in *His* of weekly student gospel meetings drawing audiences of over 200, including many non-students, and of groups of students 'from the Christian Union' going out in the country for a day praying and studying a book of the Bible. On one occasion he was sentenced to exile in Siberia, and released through the intervention of a Russian officer he had cured of syphilis. When he died, his death was announced on Hungarian radio and television.

[21] The material on the Russian SCM is taken from Rouse, *op.cit.*, pp.163, 221.

represented too, but missed the committee meeting.) Evidently, there was a growing international family. And from Budapest onwards, there had been increasing awareness of the need to pioneer elsewhere, appointing staff for this purpose if necessary. The British delegates had suggested on that occasion that 'We now know and trust each other... We ought to think of taking the next step in advance.'

But all further progress was interrupted by the outbreak of war. The favourite hymn of the Cambridge conference had been appropriate to the hour:

'We rest on Thee,' our shield and our defender;
We go not forth alone against the foe;
Strong in Thy strength, safe in Thy keeping tender,
'We rest on Thee, and in Thy name we go.'

AWAKENING ANOTHER GIANT

Canada's general secretary during these later years of the 1930s was an Australian who was to be at the centre of much of IFES's later history. Stacey Woods had been co-leader of a boys' camp to which Howard Guinness came directly after his arrival in Australia in 1930. In 1934, Howard invited him to help with work among schoolboys in India. Stacey accepted immediately, and had booked his ticket when a letter arrived from IVCF-Canada inviting him to become their general secretary at $100 a month. 'My plans, however, were fixed', recalls Stacey. 'Without even praying over this invitation, I wrote my "thank you" but declined.

'The days following the despatch of this letter were filled with depression. God seemed to be saying to me, "You have made your decision without consulting me, yet you claim to be yielded to my will." In an agony of repentance I told the Lord I would go to Canada for one year, providing he would make this unequivocally clear. Within the next three days letters from my parents expressed their serious concern regarding the plan to spend two years in India. There was a cable from Howard Guinness stating that suddenly he had been recalled to England, and that the plan to work with him was cancelled. Then there came a second letter from Canada stating the continuous conviction that I should be that movement's next general secretary and asking me to reconsider and to come immediately. Incidentally, on this second invitation the salary offered was $50 a month. In the providence of God that one year in Canada was lengthened to eighteen.'[22]

On arrival in Canada, Stacey was faced by two immediate tests. One was a public debate with the SCM general secretary on the *raison d'être* of IVCF. 'With fear and trembling I entered the hall of debate, but God in His grace was with me.' Stacey affirmed IVCF's identity as a movement that based itself on the Bible as God's infallible word. 'This primary point was publicly and fairly conceded by the Student Christian Movement, and at that moment we stood justified as an independent biblical university student movement in Canada.' In McGill University, however, the IVCF group's vice-president, a brilliant man from a prominent Presbyterian family in the city who was a leader amongst McGill undergraduate society, had reached a point where he was no longer able to accept this very principle of the Bible's infallibility. There was no alternative, therefore, but to ask him to resign; which he graciously did.

Under Stacey's leadership the Canadian movement became firmly rooted. A team of staff developed including workers such as Cathie Nicoll and Joe Curry who would continue to be with the movement into the 1970s and even (in the case of Cathie) the 1980s! There began to be strong outreach among nurses and teachers too. The camp ministry, which had been so great a concern to Howard Guinness, contined in Ontario; Pioneer Camps were also held in Quebec during 1936-41, and in Alberta from 1940 and Manitoba from 1942. With the diversification of the movement's activities in this geographically huge country, and the accompanying increase in staff, the student leaders requested the formation of a supervisory board of senior friends.

South of the border, as has been indicated, there existed a League of Evangelical Students. The European movements were anxious to draw the LES into their International Conferences, and an LES leader, Clarence Bouma, was a speaker at Cambridge in 1939. However, LES's concern was primarily with theological students in seminaries, and graduates at that; and as time went on its programme and publications were growing more philo-sophically-oriented.

Stacey Woods was invited as an observer to the League's 1936 convention. Here, five American undergraduates, including Charles Troutman (later general secretary of the Australian and

[22] This section, and also much of what follows on Canada and the USA, is taken from C. Stacey Woods' history, *The Growth of a Work of God* (IVP-USA, 1978).

American IFES affiliates in succession), challenged the movement to a greater concern for the undergraduates on secular campuses, and a greater emphasis on personal devotional life and evangelism. But the convention did not respond. Stacey Woods, noting Charles Troutman's vision, invited him to join the staff of IVCF-Canada, and he spent the next three years in Ontario and Quebec.

Evidently an evangelistically-oriented movement was needed to reach the secular campuses of the USA. And during the next couple of years, students began independent evangelical groups on a number of campuses. One of the first was Badger Christian Fellowship at the University of Wisconsin, formed in 1937. Others followed between 1938 and 1940. Meanwhile, says Stacey, 'Another indication of God's leading was that Christians in the United States began sending to the Inter-Varsity Christian Fellowship of Canada financial gifts to help pioneer a similar work south of the border. Although we explained that we had no such present plan, gifts continued to be received and these were banked in a special account pending future developments.'

But eventually, in response to increasingly insistent requests, Stacey and his wife Yvonne crossed the frontier to visit some students in the University of Michigan. As a result an evangelical union came into being there. One of the first two groups of the previous evangelical student movement was formed in that same university, eighty years earlier! Three more groups soon followed elsewhere in Michigan. A group began to meet around the same time in Swarthmore College near Philadelphia, and later another at the University of Pennsylvania.

It was in April 1938 that after much heart-searching and prayer the Canadian Inter-Varsity board hesitantly gave approval to the commencement of work in the USA – feeling, adds Stacey, 'like a mouse trying to swallow an elephant! Too much cannot be said of the vision of the leaders in Canada then. They only partially realized what the cost to the Canadian movement would be and the degree that such an undertaking would lead to the weakening of the Canadian student work. Suffer it did! For the next 25 or 30 years.' During the war that soon followed, IVCF-Canada had no male staff. And the difficulty of finding a replacement for Stacey Woods in Canada meant that their general secretary was responsible for the USA too. (And IFES as well, from 1946 – but that is running ahead.) A successor to take over the Canadian work did not appear until 1952.

Once the initial decision was taken, Charles Troutman was authorized to spend two months working in the USA. In 1939 six IVCF groups (or 'chapters', as the American groups began to be called) were formed south of the border, including fellowships at New York, Columbia and John Hopkins Universities. The independent group at Wisconsin chose to affiliate with IVCF. And their example of student initiative in pioneering a group 'was to be repeated on scores of campuses during the following decade', says Stacey. 'It was a case of staff following or trying to catch up with Christian students of faith and daring.'

The rumour that 'Troutman's back!' was greeted with excitement, recalls Frank Cassel, who was a student around that time. His stories of what Canadian students were doing – Scripture distribution, ski-camps – inspired their American counterparts. Perhaps they could achieve more than simply preserving themselves from the pressures of a godless university!

In the autumn of 1939, IVCF-Canada appointed three staff for work in the USA: Charles Troutman was joined by Grace Koch and Herbert Butt. Substantial support was promised by a number of American Christians, including Margaret Haines, H. J. Taylor, and Howard Kelly (who had tried unsuccessfully to persuade Howard Guinness to launch student work in the States a decade earlier). Three Americans were invited on to the Canadian board in spring 1940; and in May 1941 IVCF-USA was officially formed. Had things been postponed a little later, the United States' entry into the Second World War would have made such development impossible. It was God's timing.

Obviously, the question arose of what relations should exist with the League of Evangelical Students. Stacey Woods was convinced that competition between Christian organizations was 'hateful to God...The Bible presents the Christian life as a brotherhood of love, fellowship, sharing, bearing one another's burdens and esteeming others better than ourselves. These virtues should be the hallmark of a relationship between organizations.' IVCF had originally come into the USA to do a job that LES was not doing. So, 'taking the initiative, we undertook to go on to no campus where the League' (or, indeed, any independent evangelical student group, such as existed at Princeton) 'was active. We notified one another about our intentions in pioneer work so that if the League planned to begin a work in a university that university was off-limits to Inter-Varsity.' As it happened, the LES began to disintegrate around this time. 'But our rule of thumb was that if a League chapter applied for membership in Inter-Varsity, this application was refused. The only course open at that time was for such a group to disaffiliate with the League and to continue as an independent society for a year. Only after that would the application be considered.'

The coming of the Second World War had a sobering effect on the campuses. 'Daily prayer meetings were crowded and prayer became urgent. The gospel seemed to become less of an option and more of a necessity. The meagre Bible study guides that we had were snapped up. Apart from our thinly spread staff, new groups of students were springing up spontaneously. There was no time for form or structure, let alone standard operational procedure... Our object as staff was to keep on running from campus to campus, doing our best.'

Stacey himself was spending one week a month in Toronto, one in Chicago and the rest on the road. 'The movement in a sense was characterized more by things left undone than by things done decently and in order, but many students were converted.' God was ensuring that IVCF kept a clear sense of their need of Him! And He was giving growth. In 1941, there had been 41 IVCF-USA chapters, with nine more universities being pioneered. By 1942 there were 46 chapters, but there was unofficial participation on 100 campuses. By 1943 there were 69 chapters; by the end of the war in 1945, about 200.

During these years IVCF encountered the Student Foreign Missions Fellowship, which was also student-led. SFMF had arisen at a conference of fifty-three students from fourteen colleges and Bible institutes, and ten high schools, held at Ben Lippen in 1936. Robert McQuilkin of Columbia Bible College played an important part in its development. He had been an adviser to an evangelical-led SVM group in South Carolina, who had found it 'increasingly difficult to have any fellowship with the leaders at national headquarters because of the increasing Modernism and even paganism evident in the programme... Naturally we began to pray for another missionary movement in colleges and Bible institutes'. The students at Ben Lippen formed a new committee to consider what could be done, and also appointed two delegates to share their concerns at a similar event in Keswick, New Jersey, soon afterwards. A constitution and doctrinal statement were adopted at another student conference in Keswick in 1938. Teams of students travelled across the country sharing the dream of a new student missionary movement, and by 1941 2,600 members were involved in forty-one groups. Inevitably, they met with IVCF, which was also concerned to spread missionary vision among students; there was increasing co-operation from around 1942, leading to a full merger in 1945.[23]

Another achievement of the wartime years was the launching of a magazine for IVCF groups in USA and (it was hoped) Canada too – although ensuring sufficient Canadian content was evidently something of a struggle. Birth-pangs were plenty – more than one early issue has a cover photo printed the wrong way round; and there are other aspects that read somewhat strangely today. 'Brunette Margaret Maddy is this month's *His* cover girl', announces one issue. The lady in question is photographed posting a letter, so the announcement adds jovially, 'Sorry fellows, the letter is addressed (firmly addressed, also) to Pfc. Richard Davis, US Army Air Corps, Madison, Wis.' Then there is the slang: 'The South has its conferences, too. Just ask the gang at Dallas... Meanwhile at McGill, Joe Curry tells of a walloping good conference where between 300 and 400 attended... Camp will be held July 4-13. For additional dope write Stan Cummings, Edmonton...'!

Such a style was not universally welcome. The first issue's invitation to readers to respond ('Let's have all you've got – pop bottles, brickbats or bouquets') produced a negative response from one Iowa student, which was printed in the following issue: 'What vain imagining prompted you to hope for bouquets after issuing a sloppy, pseudo-literary magazine called *His*. Your obvious and poor attempt at imitation of a conversational, racy magazine style...neither glorifies Christ nor impresses, attracts or stimulates the college student. What strange figment of the mind leads you to believe that your vulgar, slangy hodge-podge could in any wise be effective?' But the 'vulgar, slangy hodge-podge' was also getting reactions such as 'tops' or 'really swell', and already contained a fair number of solid and stimulating articles. Despite the scorn of Iowa, it was to become one of the most intelligent, edifying and well-presented Christian student magazines in the world, picking up regular awards from the

[23] The material in this paragraph is taken from David M. Howard, *Student Power in World Missions*, pp.106ff., and Cumming, *op.cit.*, pp.513ff., besides Stacey Woods' history of IVCF-USA.

Evangelical Press Association, and holding a circulation of at least 30,000.

Having seen IVCF-USA ushered safely into the world, the Canadians were not going to consider their missionary task completed. Instead, in 1943 Toronto students began giving money towards the extension of IVCF into Latin America. Obviously, the movement's leaders had to decide whether to encourage or discourage this student initiative. The Canadian board voted unanimously to send Stacey Woods on a month's survey of the possibilities of work in Central America and the Caribbean. The USA board was a little more hesitant: war was raging, their young movement was desperately short-staffed. 'It seemed madness even to consider another pioneering endeavour', says Stacey.

Yet – like the British students at their movement's first conference deciding to send Howard Guinness to Canada, and like the Canadians venturing to pioneer the USA when their own movement was still in its early stages – the IVCF-USA leaders were filled with the authentic missionary spirit. They had needs and problems of their own; but still they had a responsibility to the world's unreached campuses. Stacey Woods made his tour in the spring of 1944. When he returned, IVCF staffworker Ed Pentecost applied to serve abroad, and was sponsored by the two North American movements to pioneer student work in Mexico. The Mexican movement he founded still exists today.

FORWARD TOGETHER

It is hardly surprising, then, that when the war was over the North American movements were enthusiastic about joining hands with Christian students elsewhere to reach the unreached campuses of the world.

Several of the other movements had come out of the war in militant mood. The NKSS had survived the German occupation of Norway, although some of their students had been shot by the Nazis. Olav Egeland in particular, a 'born optimist', had cycled many hundreds of miles around southern Norway gathering students and young people for Christian camps, both legal and illegal.[24]

In Britain, student groups had found real openness to evangelism during the war. In Oxford Douglas Johnson overheard

[24] Cf. the interview with Olav Egeland in *Laget 50 Ar: 1924-1974.*

complaints that hardly anybody had come to a meeting organized by local clergy, plus the SCM, on postwar reconstruction, whereas 'those ranting fundamentalists, those schoolboys in the OICCU, have only to offer tea and some buns and a Bible-punching evangelist and they get crowded out!' As 'DJ' observes, graduates and students stationed in the Forces locally had pressing personal reasons to be inquisitive about what the gospel had to say regarding eternal life. Many IVF members looked forward to the postwar years with enthusiasm. Enough suggestions and draft plans for expansion were appearing to divert the Fellowship's energies into 'a hundred and one desirable channels'. The student executive and senior friends had to work hard to pursue relentlessly the movement's essential aims.[25]

As soon as the war ceased, letters flowed rapidly between the European movements. It became clear that they had all felt deeply 'the isolation from our international friends' – this sentiment was expressed with particular force by the Scandinavians – and wished to renew the pre-war links.[26] Those who had earlier been reluctant were now in favour of some form of international organization. Accordingly, the British student leaders invited the members of the executive committee of the International Conference to come to Oxford in the spring of 1946. Nils Dahlberg of Sweden took the chair on this occasion.

There was a sense of growing momentum. The Swiss, who had chosen only to have observer status in the pre-war conferences, came to Oxford wishing to be full members. Australia and New Zealand were keen to play an active role. A national student movement had emerged in France, and was seeking representation. Above all, there was news of remarkable growth among Christian students in China and the USA. (The story of IVF-China will be told later, in chapter 4). IVCF-USA was now almost certainly the world's largest evangelical student movement. It was less debilitated by the effects of war than its European counterparts, and had the resources for a new evangelistic advance.

These resources were being offered at precisely the right time. Britain and Scandinavia had borne the main brunt of the earlier international activities. They now found themselves with small

[25] Douglas Johnson, *Contending for the Faith*, pp.216–218.
[26] Most of the material that follows is from *ibid.*, pp.269–271, and the same author's *Brief History*, pp.69–76.

resources and some difficulties in strengthening their own personnel. But the North American delegates, Stacey Woods and John Bolten,[27] needed no persuasion to bring their energies into the international work; they had come to Oxford for this very purpose. 'The fresh forces, which were so urgently needed for a new period of activity, had arrived', summarizes Douglas Johnson.

The enthusiasm of the North Americans was infectious. There were also clear signs of numerous student groups in new lands that were awaiting fellowship and encouragement. There was a unanimous feeling that God was calling the gathering to further action. Even those who had been cautious about the danger of developing something top-heavy now felt that further hesitation would be disobedience to a divine summons.

It was resolved, therefore, to circulate to the movements a draft Constitution, whereby the International Conference could be changed into an International Fellowship; and to meet again in August 1947 in Boston, Massachusetts. As the last steps were being made to complete the provisional Constitution, a telegram arrived from the new Chinese evangelical student fellowship, suggesting the formation of a world movement. This was generally agreed to be 'a striking confirmation that the step taken was in accordance with God's will and the present needs', say the meeting's minutes.

In August 1947, therefore, the International Fellowship of Evangelical Students came into being, at Phillips Brooks House in Harvard University, outside Boston, Massachusetts, and very close to Plymouth Rock, where the Pilgrim Fathers landed in search of a place where they could freely worship God. The founder members of the new fellowship were Australia, Britain, Canada, China (the newcomer, welcomed with enthusiasm), France, Holland, New Zealand, Norway, Switzerland and the USA. The representatives of these countries included some notable figures. The Canadian delegation was headed by one of their senior friends, Justice John Reid, of the International Court of Justice at the Hague; the Americans included the president of Rotary International, Herbert Taylor, the chairman of their board; among the Australians was the Archbishop of Sydney, Howard Mowll, who had been president of CICCU the year after it broke with SCM.

[27] John Bolten was to be IFES treasurer from 1946 until 1963.

But there was a real need for humility and mutual forbearance. 'The cloying, humid heat was beyond imagination', recalls Stacey Woods, giving 'little palliation to soothe strained and ruffled spirits...'. When it came to planning, 'there was the careful precise British way of doing things – "It's always been done this way"; there was the brash American assurance that the American way was God's way; there was the intolerant Australian conviction that everyone was out of step but the Australians; there was the quiet immovable strength of the Orient – regardless of anyone or anything, without discussion or debate they would do it their way... Simplistic, activist Canada and USA were eager to get things going with a full fanfare of publicity; but conservative Europe wanted to move carefully, deliberately, and with little public notice. Somewhat insensitively two Americans present took the British delegation on a tour of some battlefields of the War of American Independence, showing them monuments celebrating British defeat and US victory. This also produced a minor crisis...'

Nonetheless, with effort, a shared determination to overcome the frustrations, and the incisive chairmanship of Martyn Lloyd-Jones, a basis of faith was hammered out, the complete autonomy of every national member movement was agreed upon, and a constitution was accepted. The faith that the Christians in each country could be trusted to know best the ways of working appropriate to their culture was in fact what made it possible for the Fellowship to come together. The Americans present felt that the British were trying to impose IVF's way of working on the USA, including a national student committee. The British, on the other hand, found it very hard to see how a genuine movement of students could exist without one. It was not exactly easy, but the underlying determination to put first the continuation of God's work ensured that discussions did not break down altogether.

Ole Hallesby was appointed president of the IFES; Martyn Lloyd-Jones was to be chairman, and Stacey Woods general secretary.[28] Martyn Lloyd-Jones' addresses had been a great inspiration to the Committee. In Stacey Woods' opinion he was

---

[28] Ole Hallesby remained as president till 1954; Martyn Lloyd-Jones was chairman till 1959, and also IFES president 1956-67; Stacey Woods was general secretary till 1972. The original 1946 proposal was for the general secretaryship to be held jointly by Stacey Woods and Douglas Johnson, but this was allowed to lapse at Boston.

'a prophet...the greatest living expository preacher of his day in the English language. Tolerance and compromise on essential matters were intolerable to him. Black was black and white was white. He did not suffer fools gladly...He loved keen debate, liked to be challenged, but woe betide the opponent who entered into the lists of debate with him unprepared but full of self-confidence.' To both the British IVF and the international fellowship his keen mind brought theological clarity. Douglas Johnson relates that when he first encountered Lloyd-Jones, in 1934, the latter evidently regarded him as a 'sentimental, empty-headed evangelical'! – but the two became close co-workers in the years that followed.[29]

A still greater part was to be played by Stacey Woods. As an Australian, he was to some degree able to mediate between the British, American and Scandinavian strands within IFES. He was to perform the astonishing feat of serving simultaneously as general secretary of IVCF-Canada, IVCF-USA and the world-wide IFES, until a successor was found in Canada in 1952. Despite repeated attempts, it was not until 1960 that his successor was found for the leadership of IVCF-USA.

By no means did his every action meet with universal approval, yet to read the tributes of those who were his co-workers is to see the evidence of his greatness. 'Stacey knew how to fight', says Douglas Johnson, 'and how at great personal cost to adhere resolutely to the gospel and to all that was most vital in the movement. He made a most judicious selection of personnel, and he had a good eye for evangelists. Owing to the generosity of the North American movements, and to his capacity for work, travel and successful combination of various duties, he was able to carry the burdens of general secretaryship at very little cost to the IFES.' Martyn Lloyd-Jones believed that IFES 'would never have come into being, and certainly would not have survived the inaugural General Committee in Boston in 1947, were it not for Stacey Woods' exceptional blend of qualities...With a cheerful, open, and friendly disposition, he could make contact easily with people of widely differing backgrounds and cultures', and 'get into the skin' of culture after culture. 'How he was able to endure the inconveniences and rigours of his much travelling I

[29] Quoted in Iain H. Murray, *D. Martyn Lloyd-Jones: The First Forty Years, 1899-1932* (Banner of Truth, 1982), p.296.

do not know... All who know him will agree that his enthusiasm is infectious and his optimism unbounded... I have often seen him exasperated, but never depressed. He often exploded – generally in private – but he always knew how to "consume his own smoke".' 'A correspondent *par excellence*, capable of dictating 70 letters a day', said his successor in IFES, Chua Wee Hian. 'Staffworkers enjoyed his letters of counsel and exhortation. He was always at home with students, and happiest when he had occasions to point them to Christ or help them grow in faith. He was chief pioneer and a strong campaigner for the autonomy of each national movement. Without doubt he was God's gift to the International Fellowship.'

Still, in 1947 no IFES master-plan existed for 'conquering the student world'. Indeed, no full-time staff were appointed until the 1948 executive committee meetings; and of the first five appointments, three were originally for a year, and a fourth for three months! The budget agreed at those meetings was only $16,730.[30] In the years that followed, the convictions of the IFES leadership that God was able to use ordinary students to accomplish His work on the campuses, combined with the inevitable financial constraints faced by a young movement, led to an approach where administrative superstructures were kept to an absolute minimum so that money was directed to the work on the campuses; and the field staff team remained small with staffworkers sometimes travelling across whole continents.

Douglas Johnson compared the situation to that of the period of the Acts of the Apostles: 'Journeys by men "full of the Holy Spirit" and devoted to an outspoken advocacy of the Christian gospel now, as then, are the chief means by which the kingdom of God progresses.' And in turn, 'the early leaders of the movement were deeply influenced by the Pastoral Epistles of St Paul, which were studied with all the enthusiasm of personal discovery. Here were documents, claiming the fullest apostolic authority and, at the same time, significantly addressed to a youthful Christian leader!' – someone inexperienced who had been left with massive responsibilities after the rapid passage of Paul through the Mediterranean region. 'Each student leader felt

[30] With the approval of the 1947 General Committee, IFES as an international body was incorporated locally in Massachusetts, USA. The purpose of this legal status was to make possible an official IFES bank account and the issuing of tax-exempt receipts for donors.

himself personally addressed. Here is to be found the key to the
policy and action of the IFES': the trust in the Spirit of God to
work through the gifts He has given to ordinary people in the
local situation; the determination to guard the vital 'deposit' or
'treasure' of truth provided in the Scriptures; and the concern to
transmit it adequately to 'faithful men, who shall be able to teach
others also'.[31]

The history of the student groups linked with IFES since 1946
has demonstrated the viability of the apostolic approach. Local
groups led by ordinary students, and national movements often
headed up by young and inexperienced leaders, have found
God's Word and God's Spirit to be the equipment they need,
now as in the days of the early church. In the following chapters
we shall see how this has worked out in six different regions of
the world.

[31] Douglas Johnson, *A Brief History...*, pp.89, 99–102. *Cf.* 1 Timothy 6:20;
2 Timothy 1:13–14; 2:2.

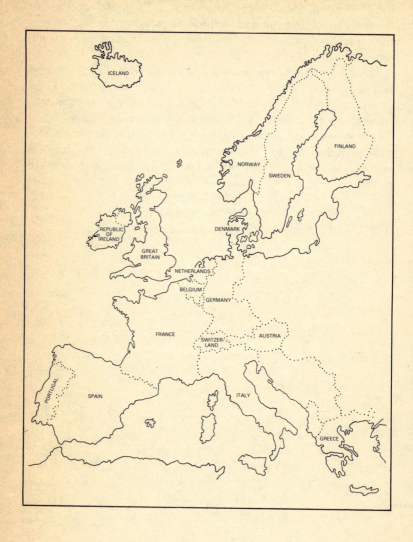

3
Europe

Europe had come out of the war shattered. In many parts of the continent there was considerable suffering. Christians who were not willing to trade on the black market or to steal were liable to come off worst.

Still, the British and Norwegian movements had come through the strife in fine spirit. In Switzerland, student camps had continued throughout the war years; the Dutch work reappeared soon after the conflict ended. And a national movement had been born in France during the Nazi occupation.[1] Half a dozen students in Aix and Marseilles had begun meeting for prayer and Bible study in 1942, and the following year they organized a student camp with René Pache (later IFES vice-chairman) at the foot of the Cévennes. Participants had to bring their ration cards if they wanted to eat! But the students were set on fire for the Lord, and went back to their universities as witnesses.

The following year's camp took place when the Allied forces were making their Mediterranean landings for the invasion of France, so there was no transport (participants came by foot or bicycle), and nothing but potatoes to eat. Through these annual camps, further university groups were formed in Montpellier, Grenoble, Lyons and Paris, and high-school groups in Nîmes and Arles. In 1947 a first national conference was held – at Vennes, across the border in Switzerland! – and Raymonde Brunel was invited to serve as staffworker.

---

[1] An evangelical union was begun in Paris in 1934 by some British students, but it had few French members and served mainly as a witness to international students.

It was not easy. 'I felt this impression of weariness, anxiety, sadness which is spread over France like a thick cloud,' she wrote. 'The people do not live, it seems; they just exist. Many Christians are tired by the hard life of these years of war; they are exhausted physically and spiritually.' In early 1948 she wrote again, 'Food is still scarce and very expensive. Many students do not eat enough to be able to work properly. Three of the leaders from Montpellier and Nîmes were obliged to stop work and rest because of lack of proper food.' Stacey Woods joined thirty students at Nîmes for an evangelistic meal made possible by a $10 packet of food (lard, flour, sugar and chocolate, *etc.*) from North America, which had turned into 'cookies, cakes and delicious pies as only the French can make them'.

Meanwhile, there were developments in Germany. John Bolten, treasurer of the newly-formed IFES, was a German-American, and he felt keenly the needs of the German students. News had come of foreigners in Germany being asked, 'Is there anyone who will ever speak to us in terms of friendship again?' At his urging, the 1946 General Committee in Oxford had spent several hours in prayer that God would raise up a free, biblical German student movement. Unknown to those founding fathers of IFES, several groups of students had started meeting for prayer and evangelism in the winter of 1945–46, in Marburg, Göttingen and Bethel.

Another delegate at Oxford had been Hans Bürki from Switzerland. Hans had learnt student work the hard way: during his studies he had prayed to be used as a witness, and had to wait three years before he saw any conversions and could start a group. And when one was begun, other students held open meetings to oppose it! But from then on God enabled him to pioneer an evangelical witness in the Swiss teacher training colleges, and in 1946 eleven were represented at Switzerland's first training colleges' conference. On Stacey Woods' advice, Hans went to North America for further studies, and saw how students there were being converted. Hans had believed he was called to China, but older friends advised him to think rather of Europe. So, while teaching at Wheaton College, he wrote to Erich Sauer, head of the Wiedenest Bible School in Germany, requesting names and addresses of believing students and teachers to whom letters and food parcels could be sent. Among the names he received were Bodo Volkmann, later IFES chairman;

Ernst Schrupp, a former army officer with a burden for student work; and Ulrich Wever, later general secretary of the German student movement.

In the summer of 1948, IFES planned a training conference for continental Western Europe at Vennes, and Stacey Woods and René Pache travelled from country to country to make it known. Hans Bürki visited Germany for the same purpose, and found the student work in a lively condition. Christian students had found Christ to be 'unshakeable in the midst of the complete collapse of Germany; the questions of the meaning of life and a sound basis for existence were of such great importance at that time that the message of Christ was willingly accepted', as one German writer said.

These efforts bore fruit. Nearly 400 undergraduates and graduates from twenty-eight countries and twenty-three denominations registered for Vennes, including eighty from Germany – but many more signified their desire to come. In faith, Hans rented six youth hostels in the hills near Basel, and – chiefly through generous giving by Swiss believers – an additional 180 German students attended evangelistic and training camps there under the leadership of Hans Bürki and Ernst Schrupp.

Before they arrived, Stacey and Hans met with thirty-five German leaders for a few days to wait upon God for His blessing. Their prayers were answered; and around seventy students professed faith in Christ at the camps. ('That made such an impact on me!' said Hans.) A further thirty conversions took place at the subsequent conference in Vennes, where the speakers included Martyn Lloyd-Jones, René Pache, Harold Ockenga and Erich Sauer. The IFES executive committee agreed to support Ernst Schrupp full-time in Germany (as well as financing Raymonde Brunel's ministry in France). A year later, Hans himself was appointed as a full-time staffworker – travelling in Belgium, France, Italy, Germany, Austria and Switzerland![2]

A number of German students at Vennes had made clear their

[2] Hans continued as general secretary of VBG-Switzerland until 1971; he also served as IFES literature secretary 1963-71, and continued as IFES associate general secretary until 1979, with a world-wide ministry. His counselling skills have been used by God to help student leaders and staff in numerous countries to a better understanding of themselves, their relationships with others and with God.

enthusiasm for the establishment of evangelical student witness in Germany. In the following months the developing movement gave clear proof of its zeal. Five hundred were present at the first German national student conference, in Wuppertal; three other such gatherings took place that autumn, and there were many conversions. Christian students transferred to other universities to witness, so commencing groups in Munich, Stuttgart, Tübingen and Hamburg. 'Spirit-led prayer groups are coming into existence in many universities,' wrote Ernst Schrupp.

In 1949 Stacey Woods visited Germany, in company with Hans and Ernst, to encourage attendance at that summer's Swiss training course. For three years he had been applying for a visa, only to be refused by the US Army on the recommendation of leading figures in the WSCF and World Council of Churches. Finally, however, a 'chance meeting' with a German YMCA leader provided the necessary invitation.

Germany was still in considerable economic difficulty. 'Food was poor, travel hard, but perhaps the greatest trial was on a number of nights to sleep in a student dormitory, three men in one bed,'wrote Stacey. 'I would pray fervently that I would not be in the middle, as occurred on several occasions! But this journey resulted in a substantial attendance later in the year.'

But before the Swiss training course came a pioneering evangelistic camp with the French movement at St Brevin. From an aesthetic point of view, the campsite left something to be desired: Swiss worker Elisabeth de Benoit went into one of the buildings and saw 'what looked like rain falling. In fact it was lice jumping all over the place'. 'We had rather rashly advertised the camp on bulletin boards in a number of universities,' recalls Stacey. 'We prayed and waited to see who would respond. Facilities were primitive and inadequate. Cooking was in the open air. Washing and toilet facilities were almost non-existent. Access to the one bathroom available for girls was by means of a ladder from the street to the first floor above the ground floor and through an open window. For the men we threw together a makeshift arrangement.

'The students arrived, about fifty unconverted men and women plus perhaps twelve Christians. The first crisis arose when they discovered there were separate quarters for men and women. Quite a few had cycled to St Brevin, sleeping together in the fields. They objected to what they called American and Anglo-Saxon morality being imposed on them. After much discussion and some humour, they agreed to this "strange segregation".'

After a few days, the cook became ill. Stacey volunteered to undertake the cooking: 'I can't speak French, I can't do anything else!' This helped build some bridges, since to the students it was incredible that the director of the camp should stoop to such a task! 'They were generous not only with advice and criticism but also with offers to help. And so we struggled through.

'The real crisis of that camp, however, was a virtual revolt against the Christian message – almost a refusal to listen. Meeting after meeting, speakers would face howls of derisive laughter at the mention of sin, God or salvation. Some students would shout, "There is no such thing as sin." Fortunately, the French speakers were much less perturbed by these demonstrations than I. God's man on this occasion was a French evangelist and Bible teacher named Gaston Racine. His unvarying love, sympathy and patience made some impression.

'But we were completely cast upon God. Unless the Holy Spirit worked, the camp would be a failure. We could do nothing. So three times a day the tiny minority of Christians almost literally cried to God that He would do what we could not possibly do. To have applied some of the new slick approaches to evangelism would have been worse than useless.

'God worked and performed His miracle. It began with a student from the Middle East, a nominal Muslim who really was an atheist. He had come to the camp because he wanted to be with his girl-friend, a Protestant whose evangelical commitment seemed limited to wearing a Protestant cross. One night he could not sleep. As he tossed on his pallet, he kept asking himself, "Does God exist?" Leaving his tent he went out into the starlit night alone and cried, "God, if you are there, make me know it." Evidently he had come under conviction during the messages given twice daily.

'In the middle of the night he was awakened and the message came to him, "Awake and read the Word of God." He was thoroughly upset by this and for several days was miserable in the realization that God had spoken to him. Finally, unable to sleep and in desperation, he confessed his sinfulness to God and accepted Christ as Saviour. In giving a voluntary testimony the following night, he said, "This Ahmed is not the one who came to camp...I am a new creature. And Christ possesses me."

'This announcement had an electrifying effect on the camp. A spirit of seriousness and conviction came upon a number of those French students. One I remember, a big, broad-shouldered fellow with red hair and freckled face from Marseilles. He had begun theological studies, but such was the effect of his theological lecturers that he became an atheist and abandoned theology to begin anew in medicine. During some of our meetings he had been particularly disruptive, loudly proclaiming his atheism and jeering at the biblical conception of sin. It was a startling, almost shocking sight to see him alone, sitting under a tree, sobbing under the conviction of sin. This clearly was God's work, not man's. He, too, became a Christian, as did quite a number of others.'[3]

Before the end of the camp, however, Stacey was almost at the point of exhaustion, and had to take a brief holiday before the four-week leadership training camp at Ballaigues. He continues the story:

'Altogether we were between 70 and 80 persons at this training course, the majority being Germans – some 40 students representing 17 German universities. The main theme of the conference was "The Bible as God's Word", its authentic, authoritative and infallible character.

'Right from the first we were faced with difficulties. August 1949 in the Jura was a period of drought and shortage of water, so washing facilities were extremely limited. The excitable Latin French and the more stolid organized Germans did not hit it off; but the heart of the problem was the doctrine of Scripture. Day after day one would see German theological students walking up and down the road arguing with one another regarding the Bible and its trustworthiness. A minor crisis arose when some students accused M. Racine of being possessed with a devil because of his view of Scripture, but the glorious anti-climax came one afternoon when a group of some 28 German students asked to see me.

'They had arranged the salon with one armchair at the end of the room and they stood around in a semi-circle. A student, Gunter Dulon, was the spokesman. He said, "We came to Ballaigues full of suspicion and doubt. We felt you were going to try to organize us and we determined that we would not be

---

[3] The above account is taken from C. Stacey Woods, *Some Ways of God* (IVP-USA, 1975), pp.61–64, and the same author's report in *His*, December 1948.

organized by any American association. You have not tried to organize us but you have taught us that the Bible is God's infallible Word and we have come to believe this. We want you to know that we return to Germany with a God-given conviction that there must be a German student movement. We have a mission to the students of Germany."'

It was a classic example of the strategic potential of student conferences. These men returned to their homeland; many of them gave up their studies for a year to travel the universities preaching the gospel. In those days it was not difficult to get a crowd of 400 or 500 students. Gunter Dulon succeeded Ernst Schrupp as leader of the German movement: and one month after the Ballaigues course German students met, drew up a constitution, and formed the Studentenmission in Deutschland. 'We cried to the Lord,' concluded Stacey Woods. 'He heard and answered.'

In France, however, there was a longer period of sowing before the harvest. Later in 1949 Hans Bürki came to Paris, and along with Raymonde Brunel and a few others set about pioneer evangelism. 'On Friday we went to the International House,' he wrote on one occasion. 'Each one of us sat at a different table at mealtime and began to talk to the student next to him. We had some difficulties at first from lack of practice, and I must confess that I had a hard time myself in prayer the day before. I feared to go again to the Cité, but the Lord gave me joy and victory to speak to others. At the end of our stay in Paris we had contacted fifteen new students in this way.'

But Hans had other responsibilities, including sharing in the German movement's university missions, which were seeing scores of conversions. Neither Paris nor the other French groups had yet the depth necessary to survive without considerable staff support, and after Raymonde Brunel left the work to get married in late 1949, it dwindled considerably. Suzanne Bernet, who served briefly as Raymonde's successor, wrote in *IFES Journal*, 'After two months' activity it seems to me that our crisis could be called a pre-death lethargy crisis, and not a growth crisis, as has previously been said.' Only the 'echoes of God's work in foreign universities' encouraged her that His love was 'the same towards all students in the world'.

Seeing this, René Pache urged Elisabeth de Benoit (Raymonde's sister-in-law, and the staffworker for French-speaking Switzerland) to move across to France. At that stage Geneva had only a couple of evangelical students; but the French-speaking Swiss work did have two or three small groups of graduates supporting it, so René felt the need was greater in France.

And with good reason. When Elisabeth moved to France in early 1951 she found 'two and a half' groups functioning. 'Try to do something,' she had been told. So she set off around France, visiting, not students, but any contacts whatsoever who might be sympathetic! The war and occupation had left the country in a mood of scepticism (unlike Germany); and she met with suspicion from pastors and churches, due to a recent major scandal in another parachurch organization, and the fact that pastors were backing the French SCM. (This organization, incidentally, became steadily more intellectual and politicized, until it was no longer at the level of the students and disappeared from the campuses.)

However, she was able to start several small student groups, although some of these were very unstable, with only two or three students. But the resources did not exist for the leadership training programme that was so badly needed in a country where no evangelical high-schools work existed to prepare students before university. In 1952, she was joined by IFES staff Frank Horton and his wife Anne, who was a former IVCF–USA worker. Their instructions were to concentrate on laying foundations by leadership training with a few hand-picked students. So their ministry was very much a personal one, and they did not see large groups emerging.

This kind of foundational ministry can be discouraging. In 1956, the Hortons were working with nineteen groups, many of them small, weak and on the verge of extinction; by 1959 the groups that remained were mostly healthy and much larger[4]– but only seven groups still existed. Looked at in terms of statistics rather than quality of leadership, it was depressing. 'I was very discouraged,' recalls Frank. 'There seemed nothing to show for nearly ten years', and the search for a male French staffworker continued to be fruitless. The 1959 IFES General Committee was held in Paris, tying up a good deal of energy in administration.

[4] But not all. 'Take Bordeaux, for example. One timid girl, a new convert at that, seeking to witness in the university. Ridiculous, isn't it – from a human point of view. Her parents think she's crazy. But she's found another Christian to help her, and together they welcomed 14 students to a recent Bible study.'

Over the next five years the work slowly expanded until by 1964 there were around 200 students involved in at least seventeen groups. That year Frank resigned, becoming a professor at the Institut Emmaus in Vevey, Switzerland. The Hortons were not to know that many of those who had been converted and trained in this time had caught a conviction about student work and would be key supporters in the boom years of the 1970s. It was only in retrospect that they saw the fulfilment of the biblical principle, 'One sows, another reaps.'

KEEPING MOMENTUM?

Netherlands
A similar period of sowing has marked the history of the Dutch student work. The Dutch ecclesiastical scene is marked by considerable denominational fragmentation. ('You can't find three Dutch people together that will hold the same theological attitude,' wrote one Dutch evangelical leader to the IFES office recently.) After the war, IFES had contact with two groups from large Reformed denominations, the Christelijke Gereformeerde Studentbond (CGS), and the Calvinistische Studenten Beweging (CSB) from the denomination of Abraham Kuyper and Hermann Bavinck.

These two groups formed a co-ordinating committee for international links in 1956; this developed into the Commissie Nederland IFES, or CNI, with the addition of two groups named Sermo in 1959. From 1963 onwards the CNI was joined by local groups of another Calvinistic movement, the Civitas Studiosorum in Fundamento Reformato (CSFR), followed from 1964 by local groups from Ichthus, a much more broadly-based movement that first arose from planning an evangelistic mission. In 1969, yet another Reformed group was added, the Civitas Studiosorum Reformatorum of Delft. The CSB was dissolved in 1968, the CGS in 1971. The final addition was a theological students' fellowship, the TSG, born in 1975. A complex situation, to say the least!

In the first ten or so years after the war, student evangelism tended to be left to the churches, and the student groups spent their time discussing problems of Christian apologetics and life in society. Around the end of the 1950s, a concern for Bible study and evangelism began to emerge, and some university missions were held. A part-time staffworker, Pieter Boomsma, was appointed in 1970; he was succeeded for four years by Edjan Westerman, who did a great deal for the groups in Bible study and leadership training. However, the Netherlands groups have never had more than one full-time worker.[5]

The joint appointment of such staffworkers was undoubtedly significant in turning the CNI from a merely formal link into something more coherent. By 1977 there were some eight Ichthus groups, and seven CSFR – though many CSFR groups were not very evangelistically oriented as groups, feeling that evangelism should be done within the church, rather than seeing themselves as 'the missionary arm of the church in the university'. Consequently a number were shrinking by the early 1980s.

Ichthus groups have shown more evangelistic vision, says current staffworker Niek Tramper, but 'the danger may arise of confusion of thought', since there is sometimes little concern with 'strong biblical and theological thinking. In most university cities Ichthus groups have held missions. But as far as we can see the outreach was not very successful. Often students put all their energies into one week and tended to be silent the rest of the time.' Still, Ichthus' evangelistic Bible studies and sailing camps have seen several conversions. In 1982–83 at least three new Ichthus groups were formed, and the national leaders of both Ichthus and CSFR are seeking to take further steps. IFES contacts are of importance, says Niek, in 'helping us develop a national vision and helping CSFR and Ichthus work together, because they need each other very much'.

Britain

Across the Channel, in Britain, there had been rather less of a problem in sustaining evangelistic momentum.[6] The student work after the end of the war was in a thoroughly positive mood: Christian students who had been through the war evidently intended to use their lives to some purpose, aggressive evangelism became normal and missionary enthusiasm ran high.

[5] Although in 1981 IVCF-USA staffworker Mike McDowell was seconded to CNI, to assist the ministry to international students pioneered part-time by IFES Graduate Team worker Janet Brown in 1978-80.

[6] Much of what follows is taken from two official histories of IVF/UCCF, Douglas Johnson's *Contending for the Faith* (IVP, 1979) and the briefer *For the Faith of the Gospel* (UCCF, 1978). (Inter-Varsity Fellowship's name was changed to Universities and Colleges Christian Fellowship in 1974, to recognize its non-university ministry.)

Sunday meetings of the Cambridge group, for example, would draw 600, of whom perhaps a third would not be Christians. Attendance at the IVF national conference rose to 500 – despite second-rate cooking at the 1947 event, which was greeted with, 'It is nectar compared with what we had for two days in the open boats after being torpedoed!' In Oxford and Cambridge, triennial university missions, major week-long outreaches which would reach a good half of a university's population, became an established tradition. Donald Barnhouse, John Stott,[7] Billy Graham and Martyn Lloyd-Jones were involved in such events, and large numbers of students were converted. In the following years, the practice spread to the other British groups.[8]

Inevitably, effective evangelism of this kind brought opposition with it. In 1955 an Anglican canon wrote to *The Times* attacking the proposed Billy Graham mission in Cambridge: 'Universities exist for the advancement of learning: on what basis, therefore, can fundamentalism claim a hearing at Cambridge?' A considerable debate followed, both in letters in the press and in books. IVF found its evangelicalism described as 'heretical' by the Bishop of Durham (later Archbishop Michael Ramsey of Canterbury)! Ironically, the book that perhaps lasted best from this controversy was not one of the volumes attacking evangelical Christianity, but J. I. Packer's thorough affirmation in *'Fundamentalism' and the Word of God* (IVP). At any rate, the debate made clear that the crucial divide within British religion was no longer between denominations but between those who were unambiguously committed to the Bible as final authority and those who were not. IVF and its associated Press were becoming a voice of major significance in the former group.

The same opposition appeared at local level. It was not uncommon for the year's first Religious Education lecture to college students to include a request for all 'fundamentalists' – or all who believed in Adam and Eve, *etc.* – to raise their hands; and this would be followed by a barrage of ridicule. College lecturers'

[7] John Stott was himself a CU member at Cambridge between 1940 and 1945, and exercised such an outstanding evangelistic and pastoral ministry that the committee deliberately refrained from appointing him as president, to avoid hindering it by time-consuming committee obligations (*cf.* Oliver Barclay, *Whatever Happened to the Jesus Lane Lot?* (IVP, 1977), p.111).

[8] See Roger Mitchell, 'Organizing a University or College Mission', *IFES Review* 1979, 2 for an in-depth study of mission evangelism.

hand-outs in such subjects were sometimes marked by dogmatic theological liberalism of a rigidity that astounded university staff into whose hands they fell – as did well-authenticated reports of evangelical students in women's colleges being invited to interviews with psychiatrists to help them 'adjust to the demands of modern and progressive education'! Evangelical groups might well be banned from meeting on college premises (although one group saw over twenty conversions in a year when the ban was in operation).

A less naïve form of hostility arose from the university Humanist Societies, which, for a brief period in the 1950s, became the largest university societies and were backed by a dazzling range of front-rank intellectuals. They were thoroughly opposed to the Christian Unions (IVF groups) – or 'God squads', as they were sometimes dubbed. In 1964, the Oxford Humanist Society, which had no less than 1,000 members, put up posters and distributed leaflets across the university attacking the CU's mission with John Stott: 'Join OICCU now. Membership fee: your intellectual integrity and your social conscience.' This particular attack raised challenges that deserved consideration and rebuttal. But it was the Humanist Society, rather than the CU, that was virtually defunct soon afterwards. Apathy, rather than intellectually credible opposition, has been the main obstacle to evangelism on British campuses in recent years.

The 1950s and early 1960s saw considerable expansion. By the end of the fifties some 6,000 students were involved in IVF groups, roughly triple the number in 1949. Higher education was expanding rapidly; IVF staffworkers were far too few to meet the needs, especially in such areas as the technical colleges, served by one worker only, where there were groups being visited only one afternoon a year – or less! In all this expansion the movement's leaders were anxious to preserve the emphasis on student leadership, where planning was done by a national student executive committee responsible to a representative student general committee. Roughly half of the university leaders would have been people converted there; a number of others came from high-school groups such as those linked with the Inter-School Christian Fellowship (which in Britain forms part of Scripture Union).

IVF's Graduates' Fellowship[9] has developed a steadily diversi-

[9] Now called UCCF Associates.

fying ministry under the leadership of Freddy Crittenden and his successors. Although his vision that the 'whole Graduates' Fellowship could be fully transformed into an evangelistic instrument' has not resulted in the massive mobilization of professionals for workplace evangelism that he might perhaps have wished,[10] nevertheless a number of effective professional groups have come into existence. The Christian Education Fellowship, for example, later merged with two parallel groups to form the Association of Christian Teachers, has helped to mobilize teachers in support of evangelical high-schools work while supplying a means for fellowship and professional help, as well as having an increasing voice in state educational policy-making.

Other groups of importance included the Christian Medical Fellowship, formed by a merger of the GF's medical section with an older Medical Prayer Band, and the Research Scientists' Christian Fellowship, which was in a position, as early as 1953, to give a series of five talks on BBC radio on the crucial apologetic issue of science and faith. In time these were to be joined by groups for agriculturalists, businessmen, dentists, college lecturers, historians, librarians, people in literary studies, social workers, university staff, and vets! More significant still, perhaps, was the establishment of the Tyndale Fellowship as a nucleus for evangelical biblical and theological scholarship, with the research centre at Tyndale House in Cambridge as its base. Scholars such as W. J. Martin, F. F. Bruce, A. M. Stibbs and D. J. Wiseman were actively involved in this project, from which such publications as the *New Bible Dictionary* and *New Bible Commentary* have emerged.

The movement's literature ministry, Inter-Varsity Press, under the capable leadership of former Birmingham CU president Ronald Inchley, became of considerable importance in the lives of student groups – and indeed the evangelical community in general – throughout the world. This reflected something of a change of policy from before the war. In 1938 IVF's publishing department was nearly closed down; and when in early 1939 the literature secretary took the bold step of getting engaged, it was agreed that he should seek other employment, since the ministry was unlikely to become sufficiently profitable to support a married man! Two years later, however, a new attitude was

---

[10] *Cf.* Douglas Johnson, *Contending for the Faith*, p.238.

becoming apparent, and the literature committee was urged to make plans for 'flooding the market with evangelical literature as soon as paper restrictions were removed'.

Sales in 1944 amounted to no more than £2,400; the 1945 figure was £3,375 (the literature secretary – now married – was invited back that year). But by 1951 the figure was up to nearly £14,000, reaching £32,000 in 1953, the year of the publication of IVP's first major work, the *New Bible Commentary*. This book was a great success, selling 30,000 in six months; a reprint had to be ordered almost immediately. Nearly 87,000 copies were sold before the 1970 revision, and sales of that edition reached the same total within half that time.

Other landmarks in IVP's history were the launching of the Tyndale Commentary series in 1956; the move into pocketbook editions in 1958, launched with a typical selection – *Authority* (Martyn Lloyd-Jones), *Basic Christianity* (John Stott), *'Fundamentalism' and the Word of God* (J. I. Packer), *The Story of the Church* (A. M. Renwick), *Towards Christian Marriage* (W. M. Capper and H. M. Williams), and a little later *Why Believe?* (Rendle Short); the *New Bible Dictionary* of 1962; and the expository series 'The Bible Speaks Today', launched in the early 1970s.[11] The number of titles expanded from 58 in 1945 to 250 in 1975 (dropping slightly in the late 1970s due to recession), and from around 1957 about 40% went overseas.

Still, this period was not without its problems, particularly in the area of unity. Many students were divided over issues of 'Calvinist' theology in the late 1950s and early 1960s, and over the charismatic movement from the mid-1960s onward. Student leaders and staff had to work hard at 'keeping the fundamentals fundamental', in Oliver Barclay's phrase: emphasizing that the groups were neither pro- nor anti-'Calvinist', neither pro- nor anti-charismatic, but existed for the specific purpose of a biblically-based witness on campus. Issues that divided equally biblically-minded evangelicals could be left to the teaching programmes of the churches.

---

[11] *Cf.* Michael Griffiths in *CU News*, Autumn 1979: 'When I was a student there was no *New Bible Commentary* or *Dictionary* and very little evangelistic material. I can still remember praying for *Basic Christianity* to hurry up and be published! What disappoints me is that today's Christian students simply haven't read the books which students in the past campaigned for...'

By 1977–78 God had given the movement some 14,000 members in over fifty university groups and 500 college groups. At the largest group, in Cambridge, over 1,000 students (not all of them Christians) met every week in Bible study groups: several hundred were involved at Oxford too, and the fact that such effective work existed in two of the world's most prestigious universities gave the lie to the suggestion that a biblical faith could not possibly be accepted by intellectuals. Up to 2,300 students came each night to Billy Graham's 1980 mission in Cambridge, and over 100 made professions of faith. Similar events took place throughout the country. By the end of the 1970s it was not uncommon for a third or even a half of a group's membership to have been converted at university. In 1981–82 Wales alone saw 100 conversions.

The Aberystwyth group, for example, adopted a year's strategy for 1980–81 which began with them going from door to door selling Gospels ('biographies'), and inviting fellow-students to a series of discussion groups on the life of Christ, based on these Gospels. They followed this by a mission where Leith Samuel gave seven talks from the book of John, and a good number were converted. (An unusually close relation existed here between the mission talks and Bible exposition.) These twin methods of evangelistic Bible study and unashamed preaching through university missions, backed by a great deal of prayer, are being used by God to bring many hundreds of students to Christ in Britain each year. A very large proportion will be students who have had long-term personal friendships with Christians. Certainly the most successful missions seem to be those preceded by plenty of friendship evangelism and evangelistic Bible study, and they leave many students ready for continued contact of the same kind in the months following a mission.

'This growth is wonderful, but it is extremely dangerous', was John Stott's warning to the British students at their 50th anniversary conference in Harrogate in 1978. 'We need extreme vigilance against Satan's counter-attack. We must never become part of the religious establishment; we must never sacrifice biblical truth . . . We are fooling ourselves if we imagine that the gospel or its proponents will ever become popular.'

Oliver Barclay[12] has spelt out some of the most significant

---

[12] Oliver Barclay served as UCCF student chairman 1942-45, then came on the

dangers. The apparent strength of the CUs, he says, can mean that 'the big meetings and the doings of the CU committee can seem remote to the ordinary member. The sense of belonging to the IVF/UCCF and of really going somewhere under God for the evangelization of this generation of students is not common.

'We used to pray specifically that we would become the main Christian student witness – because we weren't and spiritually hungry people went where they didn't hear the gospel. I think we've seen that prayer marvellously answered.' So, with the decline and widespread disappearance of SCM groups, students from a liberal background are more likely to join CUs. But that in turn means that 'People sometimes come into our groups with very little knowledge of the Bible. We've got to work enormously hard at this. Often the proportion of clued-up Christians is smaller than it used to be and the groups are peculiarly open to being swayed by diverse influences. We've lost some of the emphasis on the "quiet time" – personal prayer and devotion; on personal evangelism; on doctrinal clarity.

'But I think these are the problems of any work that's growing fast, with a lot of young converts. If the CUs can capture the Christian students of their generation for a truly biblical Christianity, the possibilities are enormous. If they become diluted in their Christianity by the weight of numbers and the carelessness of the leaders, they will produce a new liberal evangelicalism of the kind that dominated the scene between 1900 and 1930 and produced very little robust Christianity and a tragic inability to evangelize the following generation. We are going to have to "contend for the faith" again and perhaps the conflicts will be as sharp as ever. We must not repeat the 1890s, when apparently strong evangelical movements with no adequate doctrinal standards weakened into nondescript groups not even standing clearly for the deity of Christ.'

An enormous task still remains. Large sections of the student

staff – originally for two years – and was general secretary 1965-80. He was also a member of the IFES executive 1959-83 and IFES chairman 1971-79. His strategic perceptiveness and wise and unassuming counsel became something of a byword in IFES circles. Chua Wee Hian wrote of younger IFES leaders from other countries spending 'long hours at the IVF office, discussing specific problems and opportunities' with Dr Barclay and his predecessor, Douglas Johnson, both of whom were also 'great correspondents' whose 'painstaking comments on current theological and academic trends were greatly appreciated by their overseas recipients'.

body in the universities are unreached; in the colleges sector, there may be over 200 colleges without a group in any one year. UCCF's forty or more field staff usually work in teams of two, male and female, and in the colleges, such a team may be trying to cover 120 institutions, with established groups in two-thirds of them. Recession notwithstanding, even a movement with as healthy a tradition of student responsibility as UCCF is still in need of workers: not to mention the resources in prayer and finance to keep them going. And above all, the student leaders need prayer for the maintenance of a fervent, biblical, adventurously outgoing vision.

Norway

Not surprisingly, roughly the same story can be told of the Norwegian movement, that other IFES 'senior member' which hosted the first International Conference in 1934. Norway has always had the strongest movement of the five Scandinavian countries. Unlike Britain, it is a country where 95% of the population belong to a single denomination, the Lutheran church, which in Norway has remained generally evangelical. So an unusually close relationship exists between the student movement – which is active in high schools as well as tertiary institutions – and the churches.

The Norwegian movement, or NKSS, underwent considerable growth in the late 1970s. In 1977 there were about 10,000 members in 38 tertiary and 370 high-school groups; during the following years the Lord increased their numbers until by 1983 there were 82 tertiary and 484 school groups, totalling 14,000 members. 4,000 of these were tertiary students, out of a total tertiary enrolment of 40,000! NKSS's magazine *Credo* reflected these developments; around 1977 its editorial team became aware that it needed a thorough overhaul, so they gave some hard thought as to why they were producing it and the nature of their target audience. That in turn led them to make layout changes and to introduce more topical articles and thematic issues, with the result that their circulation, which had been decreasing, nearly tripled (from 2,500 to 7,200) in two years. Besides this, NKSS has an active graduate fellowship of 7,000 members.

But, like UCCF-Britain, the size of NKSS has brought its own problems. There was the question of how best to keep individual students involved in a large work, for example. The late 1970s saw a stronger emphasis on group Bible study; the university groups made use of NKSS staff in a 'Bible study pilot' system, where the staffworker trains six or seven students and each of these trains six or seven others. As in Singapore and Cambridge, the number of students in the Bible study groups resulting from this system is greater than the official membership of the groups.

At high-school level, on the other hand, the movement became aware that they had all too often simply imported methods of operation that were developed for university students. In this sector, therefore, they have built up a videotape ministry for use in the numerous high-school groups.

Secondly, increasing radical socialist influences on campus in the middle 1970s highlighted the need for thorough teaching on political, social and ethical issues. 'Unfortunately', said one NKSS document from this period, 'very few Norwegian theologians have been interested in apologetics, and it is almost impossible to find suitable literature on such subjects.' And like their sister movement in Britain, they were conscious that their very numerical strength could betray them into doctrinal slackness. 'It's very important to help people see what evangelical Christianity really is,' said Anfin Skaaheim. 'We have to emphasize the doctrinal basis in what is really a very unstable situation.'

But their evangelicalism was not intended to be a mere doctrinal stance. One missionary estimated that about 80% of Norwegian missionaries had been NKSS members, and by the late 1970s Anfin felt that 'a missionary revival had started', particularly among students with a profession that could be used abroad. He was anxious too that NKSS should produce graduates who would genuinely be of use to local churches. 'We want to give local congregations some people who have a vision for outreach,' he said. 'Our contribution to the church is to highlight just what evangelicalism is, to show what the people who want revival and renewal are talking about!'

REBIRTH IN SCANDINAVIA

The other Scandinavian movements have had the same aims as Norway, but have had to work in far less favourable circumstances. All four of them are confessionally Lutheran, although students from other denominations are welcome.

Iceland

In Iceland, at the beginning of the century, a number of Lutheran church leaders had turned to liberalism to strengthen what they thought to be a dying Christianity, and many pastors had become spiritists. Only a minority remained evangelical, and Professor Hallesby's visit, which led to the rise of the student movement, was of great importance to them. Iceland has only one university, with an enrolment of 4,000; and the movement's health has been significantly affected by contacts with other movements, particularly through the five-nation Nordic Student Conference for the whole of Scandinavia. This has been held in Iceland, for example in 1950 – when all the visiting students lived on a Norwegian liner, moored in the capital's harbour!

Soon after that event, the Nordic conferences stopped, and the student work in Iceland was often weak in the years that followed. Only in 1969–70 did the work recover momentum, after university students recommenced groups for prayer and Bible study. The Nordic conferences had restarted too; and in 1975 – one year after the appointment of their first-ever full-time staffworker – the Icelanders dared to host the event again. At that stage their university group had about fifty members, and the conference attendance from all five countries was to be over 1,300 students – which made it the largest conference of any kind held in Iceland! The capital's largest hall was hired, and some of the evening meetings were attended by 2,500 people – quite an event in a city of 85,000 inhabitants! The conference received coverage on national radio and television, and afterwards evangelistic teams travelled around the country with the gospel. The burden of organizing the conference left considerable exhaustion. Nonetheless, the movement has continued to develop, and is closely connected with a high-schools work of over 300 members.

Sweden

The Swedish work has gone through a similar dwindling and rebirth. Around 1950, the official WSCF-affiliated student movement of the Lutheran state church had become fairly middle-of-the-road in theological outlook and programme. Leaders of SESG (the Swedish IFES affiliate) felt there was no crucial difference between the two movements, and that they should integrate their work as much as possible; SESG ideas would thereby attain a wider influence. So the Lund and Uppsala SESG groups were disbanded, in 1950 and 1952 respectively, and the SESG students sought to form and lead Bible study groups within the other movement.

It seemed to be a success: Bible study groups flourished as never before. But within a few years the SESG students who had taken this lead had all graduated and the influence vanished; the organizational situation was not one that maintained the continuity of an evangelical vision. Meanwhile, SESG itself shrank for some years to a single group, in Stockholm. The dissolution of the movement was seriously considered.

'There is a general lesson to be learnt here,' comments Hans Lindholm, SESG general secretary. 'Two movements may appear very similar at one particular moment in time. Yet, if one has a clear doctrinal basis, but the other is broader theologically, the trends of a few years can drive the two movements very far from each other.'

Matters were worsened by a crisis in co-operation between the Scandinavian countries. The Swedish movement had always gained much from links with Norway, but the Nordic conferences never really regained their strength after the war. There were various difficulties – the Finnish movement in particular was hesitating between becoming a clearly evangelical, IFES-linked movement, or something more like the SCM elsewhere. In 1955, therefore, the Nordic conferences became Norwegian. The effect on Sweden was to underline the impression that evangelical work might be possible in Norway, but not in Sweden.

Sure enough, when the situation changed, international contacts played a crucial role. Students from Lund visited the Norwegian conference, and heard that evangelical student work had been restarted in Denmark, perhaps the most liberal of the five Scandinavian countries. So it *was* possible outside Norway! They made contacts with the Stockholm student group; the national movement was regenerated and a staffworker, Torsten Josephsson, was appointed in August 1959, with financial support from the EFS, an evangelical home and foreign missions society within the Lutheran church. (Nils Dahlberg, who had chaired the 1946 IFES General Committee, was still active in the leadership of EFS and the rebirth of SESG.)

Torsten was a formidable figure: a fearless street-preacher, a bearded giant of a man wearing a large wooden cross. Despite very strong opposition within the church and from other student movements, the work grew rapidly under his leadership, both in number of student groups and of staff (the budget increased by 50% every year from 1965 to 1972). By 1975 God had given SESG five groups in the universities and seventeen groups and about forty associated groups in the high schools, with a total membership of around 1,000. However, many high-school groups were negative towards anything organizational, or towards affiliation to a national movement, and hence, despite their eagerness for evangelism, they tended to lack continuity: 'they vanish as easily as they appear,' said Torsten sadly.

Once again, growth brought its own problems. 'You used to have to fight for the existence of the work, because it was attacked from many sides,' said Torsten in 1975. 'That was often hard: but it could be helpful, since it was necessary that the staff and student leaders knew where we stood and what our task was. Since the work has been recognized by many church leaders, much of this spirit has disappeared.'

SESG is still seeing a number of converts, many of whom are from a non-Christian background. This has necessitated a new emphasis on basic teaching – an area in which they have been learning from the methods of the Norwegian movement and also of the Navigators. 'We have to struggle continuously to keep the central themes of the gospel central to our work,' says Torsten's successor, Hans Lindholm. 'Nothing can be taken for granted, even in an evangelical student movement. Living in Sweden is like living on a mission field. The dominant ideology is agnosticism: and many Swedish Christians are so weak – and church-centred – that they are unable to become "dangerous" witnesses in everyday life. The future of Christianity in Sweden lies in a strong biblical faith that is reflected simply in everyday situations.'

Denmark

The Danish developments that triggered the rebirth of the Swedish movements took place in a similar 'mission field' context. As Flemming Kovod-Svendsen wrote, Denmark has had 'a great apostasy from biblical Christianity...In the wake of apostasy from the Word of God, godlessness became the hallmark of the nation.' Most of the Danish church became liberal around the turn of the century, and any evangelical work has faced an uphill struggle. In the student world, some evangelical students calling themselves the 'Credo Group' were in contact with Professor Hallesby in the 1920s, 1930s and 1940s, but at the beginning of the 1950s the group died out and there was no alternative to the more or less liberal SCM.

A group of medical students and nurses, mostly from the free churches, came into being in Copenhagen around 1953; three years later, a new 'Credo Group' was formed in the same city by students from evangelical movements within the Lutheran church. Unfortunately, the two groups proved unable to integrate their efforts, and the free church group ceased to function at the end of the decade. The new Credo grew in effectiveness, however, particularly with inspiration from the Norwegian movement, and encouraged students in Aarhus to begin a similar witness in 1958. The two city groups formed a national movement in 1959, to ensure the continuity of the work, and Niels Ove Rasmussen, who had been involved from the very beginning, became staffworker three years later. There was much opposition from different circles in the state church: even many of the more conservative Lutherans did not believe there was any future for an evangelical student work. (The Swedes had more faith in the matter, as we have noted.)

For the next few years the work grew very slowly and the fellowship of the evangelical movements elsewhere in Scandinavia was of great importance. In the early 1970s, however, new groups were founded throughout Denmark, and by 1977 twenty-six tertiary and fifty-eight high-school groups existed, with another thirty-three tertiary institutions and thirty-five high schools being pioneered. The largest university group had some 150 members. Fifty camps were being held each year. But the struggle continues. 'Liberal theology is completely dominant,' wrote general secretary Finn Kappelgaard in 1982. 'You meet it in the university classrooms, and also in the majority of the congregations. That means we are not accepted, because we want to be an evangelical, Bible-believing movement.'

Finland

The remaining Scandinavian country is Finland. Here the long-established Finnish Student Christian Federation, or SKY, had remained generally evangelical, largely because of its links with pietist 'revival' movements in the state church. Stacey Woods wrote of them after a visit in 1948: 'The calm, resolute fortitude and trust in God that these Finnish Christians have is something that all of us might learn from.' Nonetheless, SKY wished to retain its links with the WSCF, and although it affiliated to IFES in 1950, it was later decided that this action was against the IFES constitution, and it was discontinued – an 'awkward and unhappy decision', as Stacey called it.

In the later 1950s, however, the SKY came under the influence of leaders who were liberal, 'high church', or both, and its evangelistic zeal began to disappear. At the beginning of the following decade, a number of SKY students began to hold their own home meetings, besides attending the main SKY gatherings, because (as the first chairman Asko Jokiranta explained) they were 'thirsting for a closer relationship with the Saviour'. But as they studied the Bible together, 'the distinction between the regenerate and the unregenerate that SKY was all too often failing to recognize seemed clear... This difference between saved and lost could not be ignored by practical activity.' Their conviction was strengthened by the discovery of students with the same vision elsewhere in Scandinavia. 'We were not alone.'

In 1962, therefore, they began door-to-door work in the student residences, and this rapidly became a hallmark of their group life. There were many conversions, and the positive response forced them to begin evangelistic meetings, which were soon attended by over 100 students. Although SKY was still open to co-operation with this ministry, the students felt that such a unity 'would have implied our approval of new theological trends' within the SKY: co-operation in evangelism would have meant supporting the proclamation of an unbiblical gospel. From that decision, it was only a short step to the setting up of a new movement, the OPKO, to ensure that the work continued after the graduation of its first leaders.

Once again, the setting up of an independent movement brought opposition from various parts of the church; but this opposition lessened as SKY's concerns became manifestly political in the late 1960s. By the end of the following decade its work was much reduced. Meanwhile, OPKO's ministry spread to every part of Finland: and high-schools ministry began too. By 1973 groups existed in ten tertiary communities and nearly 200 high schools. Further pioneering was halted by the economic recession: OPKO's 1982 budget was four times that of 1973, but the number of staff was nearly the same!

However, they have been able to cover more ground with a literature ministry. Their high-schools newsletter, *Teinisanomat*, has a distribution of over 20,000 (though readership has gone as high as 60,000 some years); their correspondence courses have been popular, and a ministry has developed in cassettes for the 'day openings', or morning assemblies, in the Finnish high schools. These have met with an enthusiastic response. At the time of writing, however, the OPKO leaders are conscious that 'it seems to be more and more difficult to reach students with traditional evangelistic methods. Music seems almost the only way to reach the younger age-groups.' The rapid growth of the work should not make us forget the problems that are still appearing.

NEW DIRECTIONS

The Lord of history can use many different things as catalysts for new developments in His work. In Scandinavia, as we have seen, contacts with the strong Norwegian movement, especially through conferences, were a crucial stimulus in the development of work elsewhere. In countries farther south, the work moved into a new phase as a result of student unrest and the birth of the counter-culture in the late 1960s and early 1970s.

France

In France in particular, the events of 1968 – in which the student New Left nearly succeeded in bringing down the government – led eventually to a thrilling and long-awaited breakthrough in the GBU. There were two main aspects to this. Firstly, the demand for reforms in the French university system led to a much greater freedom for religious activities which had previously been forbidden on campus, including book-tables, posters, and the use of university premises for Christian meetings. Secondly, when the students occupied the universities, Operation Mobilisation teams encouraged the GBU members to set up book-tables, and helped stimulate a vision of what God could do through them. This contributed to a new evangelistic vision in the movement.

It was in the early 1970s that this vision really began to bear fruit. Ironically, one of the causes was probably the movement's lack of a general secretary after Roger van Dyk left the work in 1972. David Pollard, a former IVF-Britain staffworker who worked with the French movement from 1974 to 1977, comments that it was 'a blessing in disguise, because the impossible workload that was usually imposed on the general secretary was shared around among student leaders and graduates'. As a result, a number of students began to do some hard thinking about the work; one of them, Daniel Kuen, the son of a well-known French Bible teacher, had a particular gift for researching other movements and seeing what the French work could learn from elsewhere.

Partly as a result of the example of other European movements, the student committee began to make a real impact. The inclusion of regional representatives encouraged the development of the work at the grassroots, and the graduates set up a network of associates who were willing to help. More than half of these graduates had been active in the movement since the Hortons' time, and now they played a major part. Regional student activities 'helped groups who had felt "out on a limb" to feel that they belonged to a movement', says David, 'and also helped to engender the vision of a group in *every* university'. Prayer partnerships were set up across the whole country.

The atmosphere was right. The Vatican II Council had encouraged Catholic students to read the Bible, and a significant number of Catholics were being converted. There was widespread questioning and openness following the events of 1968. A major task was to encourage all the evangelical students to see their place in the GBU. There were many difficulties here. The 1973 annual general meeting was marked by a passionate debate on the place of Pentecostals in the movement, and they were finally accepted. With the fully interdenominational character of the GBUs established, a generation of students began to be mobilized who, in Frank Horton's words, 'took the Lord seriously and were ready to pay the price of being His servants and faithful witnesses in the faculties, in a way I have not seen before'.

Numbers at the movement's national Easter training camp, which brought together most of the groups' committed members, indicate what God was doing through the GBUs. The 1972 camp, held in a wing of a leprosy hospital at La Valbonne, drew about forty participants –roughly the attendance in the preceding years. The 1973 camp, however, drew eighty; in 1974 there were 120, in 1975 240, in 1976 and 1977 300, where the numbers stabilized. (This was more than were attending conferences of the much older British movement at this time.) University groups were springing up in areas where none had existed, and the number of high-schools groups likewise doubled from twenty to forty. 'The movement is growing at an almost unbelievable speed', said Frank Horton.

And it had no staff. Obviously, such growth was creating a need for a general secretary, and in 1974 Gerard Kuntz, who had been involved in pioneering a student movement in Madagascar, was appointed. Alongside Gerard, the student executive, led enthusiastically from 1974 to 1979 by Jacques Taurisson, stimulated the groups to continued outreach. Some groups were actively involved in developing the work in institutions 100 kilometres away. A massive distribution of Gospels was arranged for 1976–77; around 20,000 Bibles were sold between 1972 and 1977. Gerard also took the lead in regular programmes on Trans World Radio, and even a programme on French national television. (In later years, programmes were produced on TWR and then re-used by local groups on local radio.)

Between 1977 and 1979, Gerard, David and Jacques all left the movement, and there was a gap of a year before Yves Darrigrand assumed the general secretaryship. During the next few years, there were very few staff. (Britain and France both had about a million students, but the British movement had forty to fifty field staff, where the French had between one and three.) Even for a movement with such a successful emphasis on student initiative, there were problems in helping the groups feel their partnership in the national fellowship. 'Many things would be possible if we had four or five staff who would each ensure biblical training and pastoral care in one region', wrote Yves in 1982. 'Undoubtedly we could find such people: but we run up against the obstacle of finance. The future depends in part on our ability to promote more substantial support.' In the meantime, the movement aimed to establish a supportive group of associates in each town, and to remedy the inadequate training of leaders through training weekends, including an extended visit from IFES Bible study secretary Ada Lum.

The French academic year has now been changed, making the large Easter gathering an impossibility. Nonetheless, there is still an impressive camping programme: in 1982 the movement organized thirteen winter ski camps, and seventeen summer camps including events based on horse-riding, potato-planting, apple-picking, and ocean-going sailing from La Rochelle! Some

1,500 students (at the very least) are involved in the movement's fifty-five or more groups.

It continues to be a time of great potential. French universities are characterized by an 'ideological vacuum', wrote Yves in 1983. 'The students are deeply involved in securing their qualifications. You don't see many slogans or graffiti as you walk through a university. Successive ideologies have themselves demonstrated their own bankruptcy. We must seize this opportunity.' However, the work is still much stronger in the east (*e.g.* Strasbourg or Mulhouse) and south-east (*e.g.* Montpellier) than in the west, where most groups are still small. And one staggering fact puts the whole ministry in perspective: France is said to have seven Muslims for every born-again Christian!

Germany

The 1970s were to see expansion in the German movement too, although the decade began with a period of collective self-examination. During the 1960s much growth had taken place, till there was a group in almost all West German universities, a strong work among schools and graduates, and developing missionary concern fostered by the 'Arbeitskreis für Weltmission' section within SMD. There emerged a call for greater efforts in building up Christians. The student unrest of 1968–69, while it gave new evangelistic opportunities, also drove into the groups a number of students who were feeling great uncertainties in the prevailing ideological atmosphere and who were seeking support and security. Many of these proved unable or unwilling to play an active part in evangelism.

These developments forced the movement to do some hard thinking. General secretary Hartwig Lücke emphasized that the student groups existed not just to gather people but for mission: 'concentrating together so as to be sent forth!'[13] The problem was how to maintain the evangelistic emphasis when many students were coming for personal help rather than to participate in outreach. SMD's solution was to concentrate on its aims and doctrinal basis, so as to equip their members with new strength and vision for evangelism.

But at the high-schools level, the movement's commitment to

---

[13] *Cf.* his essay in the SMD graduate magazine *Porta* 25 (an issue devoted to SMD's history), p.33, and also Ernst Synofzik's article in the same issue.

'going forth' in mission was unmistakable. The first half of the 1970s saw a sudden expansion in this sector, until by 1975 there were 400 groups; and a further 600 groups were to be added by 1983! A crucial part in this development was played by SMD's two-week summer camps, led by graduates, mostly teachers. In 1975, for example, twenty-seven such camps were held, with about forty students in each; in 1979 forty-five camps were organized, totalling 2,000 participants, and fifty-five camps in 1982. A number of these were abroad, especially in Norway, since camps abroad are very attractive to German students.

As Wilfred Ahrens explains, 'Sometimes students from densely populated areas like the Ruhrgebiet who are used to lots of noise all the time have problems for the first few days! But the solitude provides a chance to rest from the bustle of everyday existence, and start thinking about one's life. Besides, solitude forces you to talk with the people who you are living with, which is particularly valuable in an evangelistic camp.' And during the late 1970s more and more non-Christians were coming – sometimes making up half a camp.

'The most impressive thing to most students is the fellowship,' says Wilfred. 'They are used to competition in everyday life at school. You hardly ever talk with each other openly and honestly: you hardly ever speak about personal problems. You have difficulties with older students, parents and teachers. But suddenly, here, at camp, the generation gap is no longer important. There will be up to eight leaders to a group of forty students, including university students who provide a useful link between campers and leaders: and these leaders try to establish good fellowship with the students, everybody seeks to be available for the others, and the planning is done together. For many students it is quite an experience to live together with forty other students without ending up competing and quarrelling.

'Small group Bible studies are at the centre of the programme, and the students' problems and questions from everyday life come in as they work through the text. Quite often the day will begin with half an hour's "quiet time", so each student has a chance to think through the passage prayerfully. Afternoons are usually free, while in the evenings there are social programmes as well as thematic evangelistic ones. Students return to their schools concerned to start groups for Bible study, prayer and evangelism: church youth groups will be affected too.'

In the tertiary sector, however, there was a lack of momentum. 'No new college or university groups have come into existence for some time,' wrote Wolfgang Heide in 1975. 'We experience many difficulties in getting into conversation with totally non-Christian students.' Another problem was that half the membership of many groups was made up of theological students, who were grappling with the problems and doubts raised by their own discipline in the main fellowship rather than in specific theological students' groups. But SMD were anxious to see the problem solved, praying that God would make their leadership training an 'empowering for moving *out*' and give 'a new enthusiasm for Jesus, fresh courage, opened eyes to see the needs and a love-motivated imagination to think up ways of seeking students'. By the early 1980s the number of SMD tertiary groups had risen from thirty-two to forty; all-out university missions were becoming a feature of more and more groups, drawing good numbers of outsiders; an effective camp ministry had developed in the universities; and conversions were resulting. Staff appointments were being extended to between three and five years to provide greater continuity.

And, as might be expected, the student work has wider repercussions. A growing graduate work exists: Friedhardt Gutsche, its co-ordinator in the early 1970s, would urge graduating students to consider prayerfully working in pairs. Two teachers could seek appointments in the same school, so finding fellowship and being doubly effective in outreach; two theological students could seek pastorates in neighbouring towns, and encourage one another in the German theological climate (which is not favourable to evangelicals). SMD were anxious also 'to be more aware of our responsibilities as Christian graduates in intellectual controversies and worldwide', and in the late 1970s and early 1980s specialist groups have been formed reaching out to doctors, teachers, psychologists, lawyers, scientists, engineers, economists and social workers.

There has been a growing vision for world mission. SMD's twenty-fifth anniversary conference in 1974 had world mission as its theme, and the movement commissioned four graduates for missionary service and prayed for twenty more by the end of 1975. 'One was tempted to ask, "Why so few?"' commented the report in *In Touch*: and sure enough, by 1978 SMD's conference was praying not for twenty but for seventy. Under Wolfgang

113

Heide's leadership, SMD came to play an important part in the worldwide work of IFES. At the level of finance, 10% of the SMD budget went to IFES, and in addition by 1979 students were collecting 30,000 DM each semester for IFES or another missionary project. (A number of German churches have also played a crucial role in providing finance to develop student work in country after country.)

In keeping with this there has been an increase in ministry to international students in Germany. Former IVCF-USA staff-worker Terrell Smith went to Germany with IFES in 1978 to help SMD develop this work. Terrell found himself identifying with the problems of the foreign student all too easily: 'There were endless forms to fill out for the university, the police and a visa, all written in a language I could barely read. High-school German hadn't prepared me for this! I was plunged into conferences where it became clear that I could never (so I thought) learn the language. (Everyone else would laugh, and I had no idea what was going on!) One of those first nights I wandered outside at 2 a.m., looked up at the stars, and in quiet frustration wept.

'The simplest things of life had become difficult. How does the telephone work? That looks like a washing-machine, but... Standing there with dirty laundry and a German-English dictionary I tried to decipher the instructions. Finally another international student came to my rescue. I was tempted to walk places because I didn't know how to buy a bus ticket and was tired of having to ask.'

Still, living in a dormitory gave many opportunities to meet international students. An evangelistic Bible study was begun, leading to a number of conversions; and a group was set up where international students – many of whom were very lonely – could 'make friends, get to know Germans, talk about their own countries, play games together, sing, cook national dishes, and learn about Jesus through Bible study'. Friendships were deepened through 'weekends together, picnics, volleyball, going to concerts together – and most important, simply dropping in for visits'. After the first semester, Terrell began to travel round Germany stimulating similar work in other centres, and by 1982 half the SMD tertiary groups were reaching out to foreign students.

Switzerland

A third country where the work moved into a new phase during the late 1960s and early 1970s was Switzerland. Here the work had been divided along linguistic lines in 1953, with the Groupes Bibliques des Ecoles et Universités working in French-speaking Switzerland and the Vereinigte Bibelgruppen in German-speaking Switzerland. Hans Bürki remained general secretary of the latter. The French-speaking work was the weaker of the two, being limited to three very fragile groups, until in 1956 Paul Decorvet was appointed as part-time staffworker – the first staff since Elisabeth de Benoit left Switzerland for France – and it began to increase in effectiveness. When Paul left to become a missionary in Haiti (where he founded the Haitian student work), he was succeeded by Louis Perret. Louis extended the work to Neuchatel and the Jura, before likewise leaving to become a missionary (he was IFES's first staffworker in French-speaking Africa).

By the end of the decade, the two Swiss movements had nine tertiary groups, thirty-five groups among teachers and graduates, and twenty among nurses. The student magazine had a circulation of 4,300 – rather higher than that of many IFES member movements' magazines at the present time! – and circulated widely among intellectuals outside the movement.

Throughout the 1960s, and indeed until 1975, the general secretary of the French-speaking work was Raymond Gallay. At this stage evangelism was taking place mostly through camps. In 1968, a camp held at Florence gave a new direction to the movement's life. The speaker was Maurice Ray, and his expositions of Acts impressed the student leaders very forcibly with the importance of Christian community life. As a result, the emphasis of the work was switched from large-group meetings to small cell groups, meeting together in larger units as little as two or three times a year. The immediate results were remarkable and the movement doubled in size within a year: undoubtedly the small group emphasis, free from any sense of an organization imposed 'from the top', was well-suited to the mood of that era. At that size, however, the growth halted and numbers slowly decreased again until they stabilized at fifty regular participants in the two main universities.

Five years later, rapid growth came to German-speaking Switzerland, where between 1973 and 1975 the Zürich group grew from fifty to 100 participants, Bern from thirty to seventy, Basel from thirty to 110, and St Gallen from five to twenty. 'Deeper repentance and more fulfilment in the Holy Spirit were major factors in this development', says Ewald Rieser. But at this stage, again, the massive growth ceased, with some of the groups growing a little but others shrinking. VBG's successful outreach to student teachers ensured a well-grounded work in the high-schools sector, that was reaching nearly every German-speaking school (except the strictly Catholic institutions) by 1976. Further penetration proved hard to achieve at either level, even though VBG as a whole had the second largest staff team in continental Europe (14 in 1976, 18 in 1983). Ewald commented in 1982 that the movement was seeing only about twenty conversions in a year. The affluence and financial well-being of Swiss students made them hard-hearted, he wrote: 'Most students just want a good job, a fine house and to live in peace and quiet.'

VBG's strategy has been to seek to develop communities where discipleship would be shown to be more than words, through the centres at Casa Moscia and Rasa (a remote mountain village without roads and with twenty inhabitants), and through Christian houses. Half the committed VBG members in Zürich, Bern and Basel live in such houses. But no great impact on non-Christian students has been made, and the VBG feel the need to be 'stronger in prayers' for 'the opening of heaven...for God to break the barriers around our hearts'.

The movement in French-speaking Switzerland adopted a similar strategy for the difficult situation in their region. The failure represented to many by the student unrest of 1968 had left a sense of pessimism about all ideals; in the established church there was widespread deadness, while free evangelical groups were still very much in the position of outcasts. To make matters worse, students seldom left home to study; time spent in university was usually limited to study, and after lectures 'the student's mind turns to his town where his work is waiting for him (many earn their living), as well as his leisure activities', wrote Christian van den Heuvel, the general secretary from 1975 to 1982.

GBU's response, like that of VBG, was above all to attempt to use their small groups as 'real Christian communities', Bible study groups that had taken the time to get to know each other and deepened their relationships by sharing experiences, witnessing together and spending time together outside the group meetings. These groups were to be linked together by the leadership team: in Geneva, for example, the fifteen or more leaders would spend five hours together at weekends. Their feeling that the image of the church was 'so negative among students as to have vaccinated them against Christianity' led to a heavy emphasis on '*living* the gospel' where proclamatory activities such as widespread tracting or large evangelistic gatherings were rare. The groups staked their evangelism on 'the desire for personal contact, the attraction of a week's skiing or a visit to Florence', activities in which it was hoped that non-Christians would be drawn into the warmth and love of the Christian group and confronted with the Christian message.

In 1977–78 the GBUs created a 300-square-metre exhibition entitled 'Barrières', presenting the gospel through a focus on 'the barriers which prejudice, masks and materialism create between individuals', linked to discussion groups on areas such as violence, the establishment, sexuality, culture, or urbanization. Considered from an artistic point of view, it was one of the most impressive productions ever produced by an IFES movement. But, as Christian wrote, while it 'united the leaders in a very close communion' (which in Lausanne's case may have paved the way for later growth), it added very few people to the groups in the following weeks. It was the last major evangelistic effort for some years.

Christian's assessment of the situation in 1982 is of interest. 'There has been good pastoral work in the groups,' he said, 'good leadership training and good group Bible studies. The movement has become much more church-oriented: many people active in the GBU in the early 1970s had failed to get involved in the church. But in evangelism a certain lack of enthusiasm will be noted, yet with some original experiments: a puppet theatre in a university residence, an audio-visual, an artistic evening where Christians and non-Christians were invited to display their gifts in music, mime, drama, photographs, *etc.*, and the Christian message was very well received. Our evangelistic camps take equally seriously the individual's creative capacity to express by such means what challenged them in expositions and Bible studies. But although our camps are more and more successful, the proportion of non-Christians is becoming smaller and smaller.'

In 1982 a new general secretary took over, Shafique Keshavjee. He was a graduate of the Lausanne group, which had seen very considerable growth in its groups in the previous four years. 'He is more oriented towards evangelism', said Christian. The first evangelistic training camp for eight years was organized, with a component of actual door-to-door evangelism besides the theoretical training. 'I want our students to be *proud of God*!' says Shafique. 'So often there are people for whom Christ *is* important, and yet they are ashamed. And we need a vision for world mission. Paris has 150 GBU members out of 200,000 students. In Lausanne we Swiss now have nearly 150 out of 8,000-9,000. We have a responsibility!'

Shafique, it is worth noting, is an Indian, born into a Muslim family in Kenya. At one stage in recent years the only travelling secretary in the thriving French movement was Gabriel Moussanang, from an animistic, ancestor-worshipping background in Chad in Africa. And Brazilian workers Tacito and Glacy Pinto brought new energy to the Italian work around the same time. As the European church has grown cold and stale, God has called Christians from different cultural heritages to be His messengers to students in Europe. World mission must be seen as 'from all nations to all nations' in this generation.

NEW OPENINGS

Evangelical student work was pioneered in three countries during the early and mid-1970s: Austria, Spain and the Republic of Ireland.

Austria

In Austria the roots go back to around 1966, when an American TEAM missionary, Richard Baarendse, met some Norwegian students while doing language-study in Vienna, and a meeting of international students began in his home. Numbers soon rose to forty, mostly Norwegians but with Indonesians and Chinese too; there was not enough floorspace, and some students were having to stand! In 1967, therefore, separate meetings began – a Norwegian gathering that was soon drawing eighty, an Indonesian group and a Chinese group, both numbering around thirty. The Norwegians in particular began witnessing to Austrian students, and at least three were converted; and in 1969 these three were among a group of Austrian students who attended a conference of SMD, the IFES affiliate in Germany, with a view to finding out how they could begin something similar. On the way back from the SMD conference of autumn 1969, a serious car accident took place which resulted in several weeks of hospitalization for a number of the Austrians. It was a time of deep fellowship and prayer that was later seen as a turning-point.

By 1970, four student groups existed in Vienna – Austrian, Norwegian, Indonesian and Chinese; personal evangelism was taking place in restaurants and lecture theatres, besides prayer and Bible study groups. Some Austrian students urged IFES to take an interest in the situation, and so in 1971 Noor van Haaften and Janice Wheeler were asked to make fact-finding visits to Vienna and Graz and see if any help was needed. Noor was from Holland and had been converted through being dragged by her sister to an IFES Bible study conference at Schloss Mittersill in Austria – albeit with such unwillingness that at first she had been determined not to attend any meetings – and Janice was secretary at the Schloss.

In Graz, they found that Norwegian students had started a fellowship group, as in Vienna, but only a very few had a vision for reaching Austrians. Noor began a daily prayer meeting with those who did: through this – and a bookstall they manned for four to six hours a day! – a witnessing group was born. Noor went to Bible college in June; Janice joined IFES staff in October and settled in Graz. Unlike virtually all other IFES workers, Janice had never been a student. 'I was scared,' she recalls.

And not without reason! She soon discovered that the some-what authoritarian Austrian educational system meant that at Bible studies the Austrian students expected a monologue from their staffworker! 'It seemed to me that the group was becoming a model of all the wrong ways of doing things,' says Janice, 'but I was powerless to change it.' After six weeks they decided to hold an open meeting, publicized by a book-table. When the time came, no-one was willing to take responsibility, and Janice herself was ill. Five days before the meeting, 'I gave in and committed the whole mess to the Lord.' The next day Janice's illness had cleared up, and she met a student who was not a group member but was willing to come with her to get permission for a bookstall. The problems continued – the person who was supposed to bring the film fell sick, the heating at the venue was inadequate – but now Janice knew that 'the Lord was in control'. Only four outsiders came, however, three of whom spent the film making mocking noises, and the luckless student who had volunteered to speak afterwards hardly had the courage to do so. The next night, they held a frank post-mortem: everyone spoke freely, and in a time of prayer afterwards 'it became clear that something quite new had begun'.

One week later, after listening to a tape on the 'New Life For All' evangelistic movement in Nigeria, one of the students suggested restarting a daily prayer meeting. This became a regular occurrence at 6 a.m. each day, and from then on the group began to grow. By April 1972 thirty students were coming to the Bible study; in the following months they became involved in a mission to the city, a series of open-air services, and a prison outreach.

In their prayers for each other, they had 'learnt much of the value of being specific, of asking for the seemingly impossible under God's guidance, and asking others to pray about our individual difficulties,' said Janice. 'Impossible examinations were passed; work, accommodation and transport all materialized overnight in a crisis situation; a boy was released from hospital after only three days, instead of as many weeks or months, to the amazement of the doctors covering his case. The new Christians' faith was built up as they experienced the power of prayer, and several non-Christians changed their attitude when they saw the unmistakable intervention of God. How good of the Lord to take the work out of my hands.'

In Vienna, however, the Austrians' group had fallen on hard times. Most of the members had left simultaneously, leaving only three members; the group's leader had been converted only six months earlier. They asked the Lord to send them help; and a letter came from IFES offering to send four graduates to Vienna for a year! The result was that Noor returned to Austria in 1973, with Anne-Johanne Karlsen of Norway and Andrew Cranston and Paul Pearman from England. They had some problems to begin with – the team had no first language in common, and one of the Englishmen grew so frustrated with his language problems that he almost left – but through book-tables, evangelistic Bible studies and an open home, new contacts were made and the group grew to forty.

In Innsbruck, meanwhile, three students began a group,

encouraged by two free church ministers along with Ewald Rieser and another leader from VBG-Switzerland (then at a stage of rapid growth, as has been mentioned). Here again, evangelistic Bible studies and open meetings in a student restaurant led to a conversion every two weeks, and the group grew to thirty within a year. In 1974, a group was begun in Salzburg through four church leaders, and another in Linz. Viennese students went to Linz with Noor every Wednesday to do book-tables, door-to-door work and evangelistic Bible studies in the student restaurant, with the Viennese group paying for most of the travel expenses and free literature.

In 1975 Innsbruck and Graz officially joined Vienna in the Österreichische Studentenmission. A national student committee was formed, with the backing of a 'theological advisory committee' made up of local Christian leaders and pastors. Noor herself – now spending time with an average of fifteen students a day, from as early as 7 a.m. to as late as 1 a.m. – was appointed national staffworker, and soon left the Vienna group for the more pioneering situation in Salzburg. Noor commented on the way in which the student leaders were maturing: 'The necessity to grapple with the practical application of scriptural principles in the face of false teaching of various kinds has brought leading students to a spiritual maturity they would not have attained so quickly, if at all, had they been able to rely on a long-established organization.' Participation in IFES conferences at Mittersill and the conferences of the German, British and Dutch movements brought them added enrichment, as did the experience gained by one Vienna student from a month spent in England with a British staffworker. Also, added Noor, these contacts nurtured 'an even wider vision and a feeling of identification with evangelical Christians worldwide – most important in a country that is over 90% Catholic'.

In 1976–77, the OSM joined with the Gospel in Every Home Crusade for 'Aktion-KEFAS'. This project aimed to send every Austrian student a tract containing a gospel message, an introduction to the OSM with students' testimonies, details of the evangelistic programmes of Trans World Radio, and an offer of a Bible correspondence course. Student teams visited the churches to ask for support, and congregations all over the country got involved in prayer. 90,000 tracts were sent out, and 300 students asked for a correspondence course. There were some conversions, although not many students actually joined the group as a result.

The KEFAS project strengthened the movement's already healthy links with the evangelical churches. OSM was described at a national conference for evangelical leaders as 'one of the three main currents in the growth of evangelical work in Austria'. But opposition also increased with OSM's more public stand; families of converts threatened to stop supporting their studies. The Vienna group had already found themselves featured alongside Operation Mobilisation in a Catholic article warning against 'sects' – a marked contrast to some earlier Catholic reactions. 'Yet', said Noor, 'this opposition so often resulted in radical commitment to Christ and His cause!' Christians whose conversion had cost them something were becoming effective student leaders.

Above all, it remained true that 'OSM = evangelism!', with street preaching, bookstalls, evangelistic meals, Bible studies and weekly evangelistic meetings. A first evangelistic ski camp was held in 1977: the idea was that Christians could come only if they brought a non-Christian friend. This was not enforced rigidly, but a third of the ninety participants were non-Christians. The same year brought a four-week spell in hospital for Noor (including one night when the chief surgeon paid an unexpected visit and found her bed empty, since she was leading an evangelistic Bible study in another ward; when he returned next day all he said was 'a rather sour "I gather you were at mass last night"'!). Her enforced absence was a factor in the increase of student initiative around this time, as more and more active responsibility was taken over by the national student committee, particularly its dedicated president, Hubert Opitz. It was 'a breakthrough when the students realized more strongly that the work wasn't "Noor" but "us"!' Noor recalls. OSM was becoming indigenous, a process completed by the appointment of the first Austrian staffworker, Arthur Domig, the following year.

Also in 1977 was held the first week-long OSM in-depth Bible study conference with mathematics lecturer John Lennox, when forty students and graduates met in Graz to spend six hours a day on 1 Peter and Leviticus. The experience of grappling with Scripture with such thoroughness, treating Bible books as whole books rather than as bits and pieces, was radically new to most participants, and met with great enthusiasm. The conference was repeated in subsequent years, covering Romans (as a whole), much of Kings, Genesis, Luke and Judges, and considerable sections of Exodus and Hebrews, during the next five events. Numbers grew steadily from year to year, reaching 120 by 1982: and some conversions were occurring too.

The Austrian movement has been as evangelistically effective as any movement in Europe in the 1970s, despite being in a strongly Catholic context of a kind which has sometimes baffled evangelical student groups. Converts from a Catholic background have formed the greater part of OSM's membership. And it is worth noting that this has been achieved, not through the razzmatazz of vast spectaculars, but by the grace of God working through a few students and staff in book-tables, Bible studies, and similar mundane activities!

OSM has faced some difficulties in the early 1980s, for instance in the creation of appropriate structures for the movement. When Arthur Domig left the work in 1982, it proved difficult to find a successor, particularly as IFES Graduate Team worker Anna Johnston, who had worked alongside Arthur from 1980 onwards, was moving on at the same time.

Spain

In Spain, the development of the work owed a certain amount to IFES staff who were involved in pioneering Spanish-speaking Latin America. There had been sporadic contacts with evangelical students in Spain since the 1950s, but few such students existed – in part because as late as 1958 all students other than foreigners had to pass an examination in religion before a Jesuit priest.[14] Nonetheless, from 1959 onwards an annual student conference for evangelism training was organized by Rodolfo Gonzalez, in El Escorial. Many of the participants were foreigners – some Puerto Ricans in particular were being used by God in sharing the gospel with their fellow-students – and some small groups came into being, particularly in Madrid, Salamanca and Barcelona. Unfortunately, meetings for ecumenical dialogue with 'progressive' Catholics came in time to replace evangelism; and the work had to be recommenced. Similarly, groups begun by Latin Americans or other foreign students all too easily collapsed

---

[14] David Burt estimated later that there were perhaps a dozen evangelical students in Spain in 1966.

when their originators graduated. No cohesive movement emerged: and in 1964 an *IFES Journal* article declared that 'Unless it is viewed from the perspective of God's purpose, the idea of an evangelistic student movement in Spain is groundless optimism'.

Unless...In 1966–67, one of the key pioneers of the Latin American work, Samuel Escobar, came to Madrid University on a year's sabbatical. He too started a weekly Bible study, and when he left he recommended that Ruth Siemens, an American IFES staffworker who had pioneered the Peruvian work, be sent to Spain. In the summer of 1967, however, Operation Mobilisation sent a team of graduates to begin a student witness in Madrid. One, Stuart Park, had been on the executive of the IVF group in Cambridge: another, David Burt, had been missionary secretary of the Oxford group. They were able to continue where Samuel had left off with the four or five students in Madrid: and they were determined that the group should have a strong evangelistic orientation (some of the earlier groups had been more for mutual edification). This vision left its mark on the Spanish movement. By the summer of 1968 a permanent group had been established.

Ruth arrived in Spain, and seeing what had transpired in Madrid, she settled in Barcelona, where some medical students had been in contact with the British Christian Medical Fellowship and finally formed a group two weeks before her arrival. (A good example of the Spirit's power to orchestrate apparently unrelated developments!) It was not an easy time from the political point of view. One of the early members, Pablo Martinez, recalls 'the secret police keeping their eye on us, and coming to the student centre one day and asking many questions in a very polite way. We were not allowed to have more than fifteen students at a meeting – so if there were more than fifteen there was always the risk of being surprised by the police.' In 1969 the Madrid and Barcelona students held a 'national camp', along with two Valencia students who returned to their campus and began a group. (One of them, Arturo Ortega, was converted at the camp.) It was at that camp that the students conceived a vision for a national witness, which bore fruit two years later in the formation of the Federacion de Grupos Biblicos Universitarios with its own national student executive.[15]

---

[15] Not that the formation of an organization was a goal for its own sake. 'Our aim had never been to mount an impressive national structure,' wrote David. 'We

Ruth and David travelled around Spain making contact with isolated students and stimulating the formation of groups. Some groups started and died out again immediately; but there was a steady growth in the number of groups, determined, as David Burt says, 'in the last analysis by the Lord's raising up student leaders with the vision and initiative to keep a group together and stimulate them in evangelism'. In 1973 the team was strengthened by the arrival of IFES Graduate Team worker Alan Pallister; and in 1975 the first Spanish staff were appointed. Arturo Ortega, one of the Valencia pioneers, was one, and the other, Marisa Gimenez, started pioneering high-schools work.

Evangelistic methods posed problems. Films, singing groups, even evangelistic speakers had nearly always to be imported from abroad. This – and the fact that the groups were not legalized until 1975 – threw them back on personal evangelism and evangelistic Bible study, an area in which Ruth Siemens was a skilful and enthusiastic trainer[16] and which, says David Burt, became the 'most characteristic feature of our movement. Two or three Christian students will meet with their friends, usually in the faculty bar with all its noise and tobacco smoke, to study passages from the Gospels week by week. This has on the whole been our most successful form of outreach.' Beatriz, who was alone as a Christian in Pamplona University for two years, organized evangelistic Bible studies, at the price of being unjustly discriminated against, until eventually she was joined by four more believers. Three Malagan students handled as many as five Bible study groups, each with a different group of friends, for a whole year! In many situations, of course, the groups had far less vision.

By 1976 there were groups of twenty to forty in Madrid, Barcelona and Valencia, with four or five evangelistic Bible studies in each and a monthly 'open' evangelistic meeting,

---

have always believed that organization and structures must be at the service of spiritual vision, never an aim in themselves. Little by little however, as the GBU expanded, we found it necessary, or at least convenient, to give a more structured expression to this development, always with the proviso that the structure could and should be changed if ever it came to hinder spiritual initiative.'

[16] For a hilarious account of how under Ruth's influence one foreign student in Barcelona, Becky Manley Pippert, found her way into effective evangelistic Bible study, see Becky's superb book on evangelism, *Out of the Saltshaker* (IVP, 1979), pp. 15–31, 148–151.

besides a weekly prayer meeting and a weekly teaching meeting; groups of up to a dozen were meeting fairly regularly in four more cities, and contacts existed with one to four students in twelve cities, including two in the Canary Islands. Altogether, the movement had about 150 members. And at the end of that year, David took a five-month furlough, leaving a rather startled Arturo Ortega to take over as general secretary. ('It never crossed my mind that I would one day replace David Burt,' he wrote.) David returned later to Barcelona to become pastor of one of the largest Protestant churches in Spain.

There were still problems ahead. The movement acquired a deserved reputation for treating biblically such issues as corruption or divorce which Spanish evangelicals had generally not handled. But, as Pablo Martinez wrote in 1981, 'There came a decline in evangelistic zeal. We became more inward-looking, preoccupied with social ethics more from an intellectual standpoint than anything else. Slowly we realized this was wrong. At a general assembly, Arturo Ortega challenged us that either we became more active, more aggressive, in our evangelism, or we cease to be an evangelistic movement. This gave us new courage, and we are now at a stage that is again very encouraging in terms of evangelism.' The movement has been dogged by severe financial problems, however, and when Arturo left the work in 1982 it proved very difficult to find a replacement. All these things served to hinder the continuance of the movement's growth.

Republic of Ireland

Like Spain, the Republic of Ireland opened up in an unprecedented manner in the 1970s. Whereas Northern Ireland is politically part of Britain and has a Protestant majority, the Republic is an independent state, vehemently nationalistic and 96% Roman Catholic. (In 1976, about half its students attended church once a week.) Nonetheless, evangelical students from both north and south have been involved in the Universities and Colleges Christian Fellowship, transcending national boundaries.

At one of the Republic's universities, Trinity College in Dublin, an evangelical group had existed since 1920 – but this university was a Protestant foundation. At least one short-lived Bible study group existed in Cork in the 1960s; but it was only in the early seventies that a lasting and widespread work developed, when students began to meet regularly for Bible study in Cork, two colleges in Limerick, and two more in Dublin. In all these situations Christian lecturers played an important part.

As the decade continued, it became obvious that this country, which had appeared almost closed to evangelicals, was changing rapidly. In 1976 Margaret McVeigh described the key factors as 'encouragement to read the Bible from within the Roman Catholic church; disillusionment with the institutional church; the ecumenical movement, which has helped to remove some of the suspicion of Protestantism; and the Roman Catholic charismatic renewal'. A few years later, UCCF staffworker Sandra McMaster (who had worked with IFES in Belgium and the Lebanon) spoke of 'amazing openness, which makes it exciting to be in student work...The existence of God is not something that is questioned too much – He is very much a part of Irish culture and everyday life – but how we get to know Him in a real way certainly is. And so it is not difficult to set up a book-table and enter into very honest discussion, and invite students to study the Bible. In University College, Cork, over twenty-five students meet to study the life of Christ; a series of four or five studies is followed by a challenging talk. In some places there are many folk interested in Bible study and not enough people to lead the studies and do follow-up – a good problem to have!'

In short, there was the usual need for labourers! Group members had for years been praying that experienced students from elsewhere would come to the Republic for postgraduate studies; and it was noticeable that three Belfast postgraduates made a major contribution in Cork, including pioneering an entirely new group, while studying there from 1977. Likewise several postgraduates were involved in a period of growth in the University College, Dublin, group a year or two later.

Other groups have been springing up too: eighteen existed by 1983 (though some had only two or three members). 'It has been exciting to see God opening up opportunities to establish Bible studies in places we never expected,' wrote Sandra McMaster, 'and also to see a real sense of caring in the Irish family as prayer links and friendships are forged, and those involved in stronger groups look for practical ways to support isolated "troops" in other colleges.' The formation of a lecturers' fellowship meeting once a term to pray and discuss how they can support and pioneer the work should prove of strategic importance. More such lecturers are needed to give continuity to the work. The well-established northern groups continue to be eager to support the expanding work in the south – and to be challenged by the energy and courage of the small groups in the Republic. 'There is much still to be done,' summarizes Joan Strange, 'with 60–70 universities and colleges in the Republic. But it is a time of real growth and opportunity, and we praise God for all He is doing.'

FOUR PIONEERING COUNTRIES

In some parts of the world, the myth sometimes circulates that Europe is a 'Christian continent'. Indeed, there are parts of the continent where God has raised up very large numbers of active evangelical students. 1978–79 gave proof of this when 1,100 students met at SMD-Germany's world mission conference in Marburg; 1,100 more gathered at Harrogate, in England, for a conference on vocation, exploring the implications of the Lordship of Christ in areas ranging from medical ethics, management, education and the arts to political action, the family, the use of leisure and the use of the environment, besides the traditional emphases of Bible exposition, worship and world vision; and the Norwegians were welcoming around 2,000 Scandinavian students to the Nordic conference at Trondheim. But at the same time the work in several other European countries had gathered momentum only in the previous five years or so, as has been indicated. There remained four European countries where all the evangelical student groups together would have totalled less than fifty students in each country: Italy, Greece, Portugal and Belgium.

Italy

In Italy the work has had a long but difficult history. Many Italian students study and work at the same time; attendance at lectures is optional, and some students obtain bibliographies at the beginning of the year and then study at home. There have been very few evangelical students, and even fewer lecturers. As in other parts of Latin Europe, there is a widespread distrust of anything interdenominational among evangelicals. This has been a major hindrance to the development of a student movement, and in particular to the emergence of Italian staff. (One worker wrote in 1977 that there would be no strong movement in Italy 'until the churches encourage their students to take an active part and do not consider them as traitors if they do'.) There are slight signs that this situation is improving, as more graduates from the student groups become leaders in the churches. But staff-worker Marcella Fanelli wrote in 1981 that she feared there might still be 'a long work to be done which may take many more years' before the ecclesiastical climate permits 'developing the groups along the lines which are fruitful in other countries'.

As early as 1948 there were Christian students meeting in Genoa and Milan, and in *His* magazine Stacey Woods was asking for prayer for an Italian national staffworker to be found. A first camp was held in Florence in 1950, with twenty to thirty students from eight cities; Hans Bürki reported in *IFES News* that there had been several conversions and, indeed, that a national student movement with an elected committee and a national graduates' fellowship had been formed. This proved to be a false dawn; but some small Bible study groups did come into being, led by Italians such as staffworker Maria Teresa de Giustina and Marcella Fanelli. A magazine, *Certezze*, was begun in 1952.

At that time groups existed in Florence, Naples, Genoa and Pisa, according to *IFES News*, and there was one known evangelical among the 60,000 students in Rome. In 1954 it was Florence, Pisa and Pavia, with high-school groups in Alessandria and Florence; in 1955 the two high-school groups from the previous year had ceased functioning, but one had started in Siena. In 1957 Maria Teresa left to get married, and Marcella became full-time staffworker and was joined by Jean Elliott from England. That year a national movement was organized, the Gruppi Biblici Universitari, with groups in Florence, Pisa, Milan, Turin, Naples (the largest group, with up to eight dependable members), and shortly afterwards Rome (two members). In 1959 there were seven groups with membership from two to six, although Bible studies might attract ten and special meetings fifteen or even more.

In 1962 a Reading Room in Rome was opened to attract students, and there was a steady trickle of conversions. 1969 saw a new staff couple, Paul and Elaine Finch, from Britain and the USA. But in 1971, the estimated membership was still only twenty-five nationally. Four years later the movement's largest-ever group existed in Genoa (ten students), but that and groups in Rome, Pavia and Milan were virtually the whole movement.

Two years later, in 1977, there were six groups again; and then a new lease of life came briefly to the work with the arrival of two workers from the strong Brazilian movement, Tacito and Glacy Pinto. They rapidly raised up three groups around Genoa – but by 1980 the old problems were recurring. 'The novelty of our being new workers has worn off,' wrote Tacito. 'Less students are coming to our meetings. It is hard to share the gospel in a tired culture. The Italians have experienced everything, even religion...After two years we have no prayer support from any Italian church.'

They kept on trying, experimenting with imaginative out-reaches – concerts, lectures on guruism, besides the regular Bible study. In Rome and Florence too the groups had 'bent over backwards' to further the witness, wrote Paul Finch, but to no effect: and the Turin and Pavia groups 'have not moved forward into student witness as such'. Not long after Tacito and Glacy Pinto departed at the end of their two-year term, the Genoa work came to a halt.

The Finches have now left the staff, and the movement consists of groups in Rome, where Marcella and Jean are based, and Florence, where former IVCF-USA staff Tom and Nancy Balma are working with international students; plus an effective pub-lishing house built up by Marcella over the years, and camps at the movement's site, 'La Salsicaia'. Tribute must be paid to the staff who have given their lives so faithfully for so little fruit – for well over twenty-five years in the case of Marcella and Jean. The movement's committee are convinced that progress depends on finding an experienced male Italian worker to give leadership; for many years this search has been unsuccessful, and it must be a major prayer target. Clearly, a miracle is needed. But God is sovereign: and it is not long since the Spanish situation too seemed hopeless.

Greece

Greece is a country without a developed national student movement affiliated to IFES, although a Greek Evangelical Students' Fellowship existed around 1964–65. Greece and Italy make it clear that strong local unions, rather than the formation of a national movement, are the one thing indispensable in student work. However, where no national movement exists, a local group may not survive the graduation and departure of key leaders; and unfortunately Greece also illustrates this principle.

In the late 1970s a number of fine Greek student leaders emerged; a group sprang up in Athens, and grew from ten to fifty during 1979–80. Ten people were converted at a single conference. 'We continuously receive letters from people asking for Bibles and material about God,' wrote one of the leaders.

But sadly this interdenominational work did not meet with universal encouragement from the evangelical churches, although they were receiving new members from it; and – as in many other countries – the demands of church schedules left little time for the students to function effectively as a missionary arm of the church inside the university. The pioneering leaders graduated, campus activities dwindled and the group tended to become a more general youth fellowship. At the present time, there is encouraging news again from Athens. But it may well be that in this country, with so ancient a Christian tradition, Greek workers will be needed to ensure continuity of the students' efforts in a lasting witness.

Portugal

In Portugal, this process has already taken place: a national movement was born, affiliated to IFES, died, was born again (!) and now appears to be growing. Curiously, back in 1943 David Adeney (who later co-ordinated IFES's pioneering work in East Asia) visited Portugal and met a group of evangelical students and an IVF-Britain graduate anxious to pioneer an evangelical witness!

It was in 1967 that TEAM missionaries, who had been holding youth camps in Portugal for the previous ten years, decided the time was ripe for a camp intended specifically for students. One of the speakers was Latin American IFES leader Samuel Escobar, then on study leave in Madrid. Meanwhile, some pastors requested that an evangelical student movement be formed, in view of theologically liberal initiatives taking place in the university. As a result the Movimento de Estudantes Evangélicos de Portugal came into being, and requested affiliation to IFES. This was approved by the IFES executive committee in 1968 and confirmed by the full General Committee of 1971.

But whatever existed on paper, the MEEP was not firmly rooted on the campuses. In 1970 IFES sent a staffworker to Portugal, a Brazilian named Alex Araújo who had been president of an IVCF group in California. When he arrived only one group was still operating, in Coimbra. Before the end of 1971 it was recognized that the MEEP no longer really existed as a national movement. However, Alex's hard work led to the formation of groups in Porto and Lisbon; and a national student committee came into being.

The 1974 *coup d'état* led to a considerable change in the legal situation of evangelicals, who gained more freedom of speech and freedom to distribute literature. But a large number of the evangelical students, who had received little orientation on Christian involvement in society from their churches, proved unable to involve themselves as Christians in the new situation, joined political movements and abandoned their faith.

In 1976 the Grupo Bíblico Universitário de Portugal was registered as a national movement, and appointed its first staffworker, Celeste Jorge, who had been president of the Coimbra group in the days of the MEEP. The following year, Celeste married former IFES Graduate Team worker Alan Pallister; he came back on IFES staff, and since then they have been working together in Portugal.[17]

The new movement faced hindrances in its growth because of widespread denominationalism among evangelical churches, based on a refusal to distinguish between vital Christian truths fundamental to the gospel and the more minor secondary issues that divided biblically-based Christians. In particular, a number of GBU members left the movement to become involved in a separatist 'renewal movement' which claimed to make all decisions on the basis of direct revelations.

Expansion, therefore, was slow: an attendance of seventeen at the 1980 national meeting was greeted with great joy, since it was the largest for many years. As late as 1981 there were rarely more than eight students at any of the three groups. The staff team went through difficult personal and family problems that year, and grappled with real discouragement, when some of the students who had taken on leadership responsibilities in the enthusiasm of the national gathering found the task too difficult for them. But it may well have been the darkest hour before the

[17] Since that time the team has been augmented by the addition of national staffworkers Helena Pais Martins from 1978 and Rui Franco from 1983, plus Norwegian IFES staff Hakon and Sissel Bech-Sorensen from 1978 till 1982, when Sissel's terminal cancer forced them to return to Norway. Their place was taken by another Norwegian graduate couple, Oivind and Tone Benestad.

dawn. The following year the Coimbra group doubled in size, the Easter houseparty was attended by over thirty, and the student leaders were regaining their enthusiasm. At the time of writing some sixty students are involved with the GBU groups, a number of Portuguese student leaders have emerged, and there seem grounds for hope that the work has gathered momentum.

Belgium

Similar hopes seem to be justified in Belgium, a country where GBUs have been starting and disappearing again for over thirty years. A group was formed in Belgium as early as 1948–49, and Hans Bürki organized a national student camp in 1950 by writing to all known Christian students and contacts of the evangelical student work, so bringing nearly thirty people together. But Belgium presented special problems for student evangelism. On the one hand, Belgian Catholicism was very conservative for some time after the war; on the other, this had provoked a strong rationalist reaction. To join the student association at the Free University of Brussels, for example, it was necessary to sign a 'principle of free examination' discounting 'all possibility of revelation'. (Membership of the association was required for entry to student facilities such as restaurants, student bookshops, *etc*.) Frank Horton, IFES staffworker in France, visited Belgium occasionally and comments that in the more rationalistic situations there was 'something diabolical about the place, a deliberately anti-Christian atmosphere'. It was difficult to find anyone who would commit themselves to the student work.

A group was formed in the Free University, but died out again and had to be revived several years later, in 1957. Around the end of that decade moderately strong groups existed in several centres; but their numbers dwindled again around 1963. There was no full-time staffworker. Finally all the groups died out except Brussels, where an OM team were supporting the work.

In 1970, therefore, Claude Vilain was appointed as an IFES staffworker and was able to pioneer work in Charleroi (another institution with a 'free examination' statute designed to exclude religious faith) and Liège. 'Pioneer' is the right word: in 1974, for example, he lamented that the Brussels students lacked evangelistic vision, and when he went to help them with a book-table it was 'three hours behind a table and wait and wait...someone comes along: "What's this? Oh, Christian, ugh...goodbye!"' In

1973 they sold just one Bible and one or two other books. 'I do many things – and nothing' was Claude's summary of how he often felt. Nonetheless, like the Hortons in France, his four years' persistence had sown seeds from which something could grow.

In 1975–76, Elizabeth Grey from Oxford and Terry Snodgrass from California went to Louvain-la-Neuve as an IFES Graduate Team, and pioneered a group there; while fellow-GT Sandra McMaster was hard at work in Brussels, with a team of Irish students linked to a local Baptist church. An OM team had begun a group in Leuven, with the help of some Dutch students; other more temporary gatherings took place in Woluwe and Mons. In Ghent, three students found Christ during the summer vacation and met each other in a local church the next term: and so a witness came into being there. Probably an important factor in these developments was the new openness among Catholic students as a result of the Catholic charismatic movement. (Belgian Cardinal Suenens was a charismatic leader with a world-wide reputation.) But above all, the Spirit was placing His hand on different people in the various universities, and small, fragile cells were commencing as a result.

Elizabeth, Terry and Sandra moved on; new GTs, Mark Hopkins and Kees and Kathinka Streefkerk, took their place. Mark, an Oxford graduate, went to work with the Louvain-la-Neuve group in 1978; Kees and Kathinka, from Holland, settled in Ghent. In both towns they were working with a team from Operation Mobilisation. Mark's goal was to give a good deal of input to one group so that it became strong and self-supporting, then to move on elsewhere as capable student leaders emerged and took over responsibility. This took a couple of years, but in late 1980 evangelistic Bible studies led to some ten conversions, and by early 1981 Mark and the OM team moved to Liège, where the group had died out. Restarting it was a chilling experience: when Mark approached the university authorities about recognition and the conversation turned to the group that had been pioneered in the early 1970s, the administrator reached for a file and pulled out the constitution of the group before that, formed in 1960!

Meanwhile, Kees and Kathinka Streefkerk had shown the *Joni* film in Ghent and Antwerp to impressively large audiences, of 650 and 100 respectively. No-one from the huge attendance at Ghent had turned up at the Bible study afterwards, but in

Antwerp four or five students were found to start a group. In early 1981, therefore, groups of at least fifteen students were established in Louvain-la-Neuve, Leuven and Ghent, and a nucleus existed in Liège, French-speaking Brussels, Antwerp and Kortrijk. Again, scarcely a mass movement: but the purpose was that 'each generation may get further than the previous one', said Mark.

In 1981 came a milestone, with the replacement of Mark and the Streefkerks by two Belgian staff, Dirk Lemmens (for the Flemish-speaking half of the country) and Jacques Lemaire (for the French-speaking half). OM's contingent increased to three teams and another couple, and they were working hard in helping the group's evangelism through questionnaires, book-tables, door-to-door work and evangelistic newspapers. The Antwerp group grew from five to fifteen in 1981–82; new groups began in Woluwe, in Mons and among Flemish students in Brussels. The Kortrijk work still consisted of a single evangelistic Bible study.

Altogether, nine groups were functioning – although even the largest of these would not have twenty students, and each year meant a fresh struggle as key members graduated and no influx of Christian first-year students could be depended upon. Nonetheless, fifty-five students met at a national conference in September 1982; a group of graduates came into being to support the work, and a national consciousness has slowly been developing. It appears that the Belgian work has started putting down roots at last.

Such, then, is the situation in western Europe. In eastern Europe, matters are obviously different, and evangelical campus groups are not permitted. Even so, it is impossible to tell what God will do in the years to come. The 1979 IFES General Committee in Norway was addressed by an East German pastor in contact with Christian students and other young people, and in 1981 IFES general secretary Chua Wee Hian and two other leaders were officially invited to visit the evangelical youth fellowship of the Lutheran church in the German Democratic Republic. This included a visit to a prayer meeting where 100 students had gathered. For many years IFES and national member movements have been keen to make places available at conferences and training events to anyone who was permitted to come; and at times it has been possible to respond to requests for assistance with Bible exposition or similar programmes. God is sovereign, and still has His plans for the students of eastern Europe.

Europe remains a continent where many campuses are virtually unevangelized. Less than one tertiary student in 500 is involved in the IFES-affiliated groups in Portugal, Spain or Italy; or the closely associated student groups of Austria, Greece or Belgium. The evangelical student work in several Catholic countries of Europe has been considerably less effective than in Catholic countries elsewhere such as Brazil or the Philippines. At the 1979 General Committee, IFES's European regional secretary, Brede Kristensen of Holland[18], declared most of the continent to be a pioneer area. 'At the moment there are very few gifted student evangelists in Europe,' he said, adding that most Christian students were 'flabby, with a typical middle-class mentality'.

There is a need for prayer that God will equip *every* group and *every* member to be an effective witness in fact as well as in theory. In Europe, the harvest is white and waiting for the labourers to get to work.

[18] Brede was succeeded by Lindsay Brown from Wales in 1982.

4
Asia and the Pacific

By the time IFES was formed in 1946, Asia contained an evangelical student movement, IVF-China, whose growth soon outstripped most of IFES's founder-members. IVF-China no longer exists, but the Asian movements still include some of the world's most remarkable instances of the power of God on campus.

FIRST FRUITS
China

In the later part of the Second World War, God used evangelistic conferences among students in the universities of the Chungking area of west China, and something like a revival broke out. Liberal Christian groups already existed in the area, but these were little more than social groups; so the new converts, who felt a strong desire for prayer and Bible study, began to hold their own meetings, against bitter opposition. Such groups sprang up with amazing speed, and in July 1945 169 delegates from forty of China's sixty universities met for an epoch-making conference at Chungking. There were signs of a deep work of the Holy Spirit: some students were converted, many yielded their lives for consecration, and several answered the call to Christian ministry. Towards the close of the conference, they began to feel the need of a national fellowship to unite them in the gospel. So the China Inter-Varsity Evangelical Christian Students Fellowship was born, with Calvin Chao, a gifted Chinese evangelist much used of God at this time, becoming general secretary.

IVF-Britain graduate David Adeney arrived in Chungking in January 1946 in the middle of the new movement's winter con-

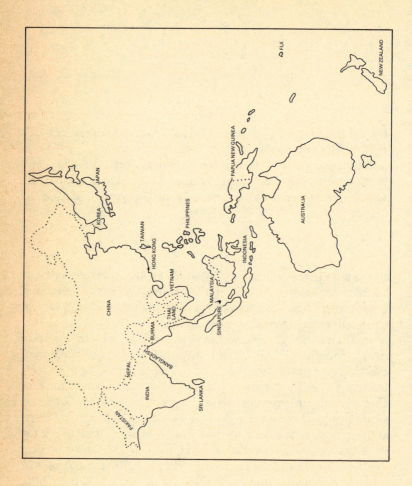

ference.[1] 'I shall never forget the tremendous enthusiasm among the several hundred students who gathered,' he recalls. 'The Holy Spirit was working in a very wonderful way, and constantly between the meetings students would come and say, "Pray with us for some of our friends who have not yet received the Lord." There were people coming to know Christ every day.'

The spirit of revival spread from college to college. Calvin Chao wrote in *His* in March 1946 that there were a thousand members among the fellowships of Chungking, Fu Tan and Central Universities. From Kulupa in Shensi, CIM missionary Paul Contento reported how two students had begun a daily prayer meeting on a hilltop early in the morning. Two weeks later, thirty students were meeting; curious non-Christians came and were converted. Some went to the authorities and confessed stealing books or cheating in exams. David Adeney met the same signs of revival in a western university where 'even the boatmen knew that something had happened because students came and gave them money to make up for the times when they had used forged tickets'.

At the end of the war, the universities which had been evacuated moved back east, and groups were established all over the country. Students from the west returned to Peking, for example, and held a prayer conference, followed by an evangelistic campaign led by the famous preacher Wang Ming-tao. There were many conversions. A united fellowship was set up for students from Peking's fifteen colleges, with some outstanding student leaders, and rapidly grew to 150.[2] (Student prayer conferences

[1] David Adeney was student missionary secretary for the IVF group in Cambridge, then for the national IVF, and led the way in the formation of the Inter-Varsity Missionary Fellowship in 1933. The following year he went to China with the China Inland Mission (which later became the Overseas Missionary Fellowship). He and his wife Ruth remained in China after the Revolution, finally leaving in 1950. Afterwards he worked with IVCF-USA among foreign students, and was IVCF's missionary secretary from 1953 till 1956. From then until 1968 he was IFES associate general secretary in East Asia, and played a crucial role in the development of the work throughout the continent, as will become plain from the rest of this chapter! At the time of writing he is IFES president. Some of the material in this section is taken from his book *China: Christian Students Face the Revolution* (IVP, 1973).

[2] For a fuller account of the Peking group and the important part played by Wang Ming-tao, see Leslie Lyall, *Three of China's Mighty Men* (OMF/Hodder, 1980), pp.123ff. (CIM missionary Leslie Lyall was another IVF-Britain graduate and a former student leader at Cambridge.)

were to continue in Peking each year till 1955.) David Adeney, who was now working full-time with students, moved to Nanking and found the same happening there. 'We have unbounded opportunities,' he wrote, 'but a great shortage of workers.' By early 1947 he was speaking an average of eleven times a week!

In July 1947, despite economic crisis and runaway inflation, 350 delegates from sixty fellowships right across China attended the IVF national conference on the slopes of the Purple Mountain outside Nanking. Speakers included David Yang, Andrew Gih and Calvin Chao. (Nanking's students had prepared the conference; they divided up into two groups, and one would sweep floors and set up beds while the other group prayed for the event. Later they would change over.) IVF-China was soon thought to have become the largest movement affiliated to IFES. There were some thirty staff, including missionary helpers. Conferences continued to be packed by students hungry for Bible study.

God's blessing continued. In the summer of 1948, 800 students attended the national conferences; 400 students made a profession of faith in a single outreach in Wuchang. The advance of the People's Liberation Army of Mao Tse-Tung was causing 'unprecedented confusion and near panic', but a report in *IFES News* insisted that 'There is no thought of retrenchment or abandonment of the present work', and asked for prayer for south China and Canton, where little IVF work yet existed. But political developments caused inevitable problems. Communist cell groups were set up in each university, seeking to infiltrate every organization,[3] and the Christians were accused of being 'reactionary'; on the other hand, the Nationalist government suspected them of providing cover for Communists, finding it incomprehensible that so many students should gather at conferences just for prayer and Bible study! Just before the fall of Shanghai several Christian students, found with a duplicator and a copy of a banned newspaper, were arrested and narrowly escaped being executed.

It was a difficult situation. Students could not be indifferent to the great needs of society, and knew they were 'bound to proclaim the Word of the Lord against injustice and oppression', as David Adeney says, 'for the servants of God in every generation are

[3] One IVF group with a large membership including a number of nominal Christians arranged a three-hour prayer meeting before electing their officers, feeling that only the true Christians would remain right through!

called to "love righteousness and hate iniquity".' Individual members became active in the relief of suffering. At the same time, political action in such a climate could hinder them seizing the brief opportunity for evangelism, and involve them in methods of protest contrary to Christian principles. 'Their message was bound to bring change in the lives of those who accepted the Lordship of Christ, but, following in the steps of their Master, they chose the way of suffering and death rather than seeking to change society by the sword', making their priority 'the preaching of the gospel and the building up of a fellowship that would manifest the real love that exists between Christians'.

They kept to this task throughout the thickest of the fighting. 'A student conference in a besieged city hardly seems a practical proposition,' wrote David Adeney in *IFES News* in April 1949, 'and yet while the armies were hammering at the gates of a city, 150 students were gathered for the winter conference.' In Shanghai, thirty student leaders from a dozen universities met for two weeks' intensive training; and 'even when Nanking was being struck by wave after wave of panic', IVF staff carried through a month's Bible school there. IVF groups were now active in nearly eighty colleges.

Four months later Robert Finley visited the groups and reported, 'Only one out of every 400 Chinese is a professing Christian, but of the university students, Calvin Chao estimates that at least one in fifteen is connected with the IVF. The Lord is daily adding to this number. The mid-winter evangelistic meetings in Shanghai revealed the intensity of the Chinese students' hunger for God. Some 500 students overflowed a church for seven consecutive nights. They came in the bitter cold, riding in an open truck; when the truck arrived at a campus, before it was hardly stopped the students would climb aboard and occupy every inch of standing room. Many were left behind because there was no room for them.

'The meetings were a sight to behold. The students hung on every word. Many were hearing the gospel for the first time and anxious to know if it might be true... Afterwards, all over the building little groups of students gathered, a key Christian in the centre of each... Each night the converts were instructed to come an hour earlier for Bible study. By the end of the week there were more than 150. Truly this is the Lord's doing... All over China today in conferences, evangelistic meetings, Bible studies and individual conversations, the students are being brought to Christ in numbers unparalleled in history. Conditions are difficult and often chaotic, but God is using these very conditions.'

David Adeney sounded a note of caution. 'Evangelistic missions have been held in many centres and hundreds have indicated their desire to follow Christ; but spiritual results can never be measured in terms of numbers of decisions made at meetings. It is during a time of testing that the real value of the work appears... There must be the steady "building-up" work in the college prayer meetings and Bible study groups...' Hence the leaders' concern to seize every opportunity for teaching and training in the light of the 'time of testing' that might be approaching.

The triumph of the People's Liberation Army in 1949 did not disrupt the work. 'We hardly hoped for the liberty we now enjoy,' wrote David Adeney in January 1950. 'On Christmas afternoon about a hundred representing a number of fellowships gathered for a time of praise, and as we listened to the various testimonies we were conscious that the Holy Spirit has been working in our midst. The fellowships are absolutely autonomous, and it was grand to hear of the way in which the students on their own initiative had been actively witnessing. There were also stories of failure...'

But the pressures were increasing. Sundays were often chosen for political meetings. Students faced intense indoctrination and the complete organization of their time, making it hard for them to have fellowship. They would be required to join in extravagant hymns of praise to Mao; some told how, when they came to the words 'Our eternal liberator, we want no other saviour', many of them refused to sing. Testimonies were given in meetings and printed in newspapers of students claiming to have been delivered from the burden of religious superstition. In one university, students were given six months of indoctrination; the Christians were divided up, and after the first two months were not allowed off campus to go to church. Eventually it was almost impossible for them to speak to each other openly, and in the group meetings they were constantly attacked.

In March David Adeney wrote, 'It would be hard to exaggerate some of the difficulties many young Christians are facing.' And yet, 'Wherever the Christians have possessed abundant spiritual life and have witnessed boldly, victories have been won in the name of Christ. Where believers have been gripped by a spirit of

142

fear, non-Christians have pressed the attack, the witness has been severely restricted, and a blanket of depression has settled over the believers. "I never knew what depression was until I visited the pastors of that area," said a friend of mine. Possibly one reason was that some of them had been trusting too much in the organization of the church and on help from abroad, but not enough in the living God....

'A Christian professor writes, "The anti-Christian atmosphere is so tense that it is hard for the Christians here to stand. But we are bearing our testimony whenever and wherever we have the opportunity." There are many who take their Bibles to their political discussion groups and include the story of their conversion in the "thought reports" that they have to write. Although not agreeing with the ideas expressed, it is often said of the Christians that their reports are the most sincere and truthful of all. We have been encouraged by the very real hunger for the Word of God and eagerness to pray that has been manifested in recent short-term Bible schools. In one place 60 or 70 met for three weeks of intensive Bible study. On several occasions they ran out of food, and more than once were able to eat only thin rice gruel all day long. Waiting upon the Lord for their daily bread, and seeing meals provided in answer to prayer, resulted in a real strengthening of their faith, and was an excellent preparation for weeks of study of the principles of Marxism with which the new term began.'

And then in April: 'Each evening during the indoctrination course the Christians met to pray and discuss together the questions that they had met in their small groups during the day. Non-Christians were impressed by the clear witness given. One of the non-Christian leaders told students not to argue about the existence of God, for he said it is hopeless to make a direct attack on the Christians. "They are like a glass of water: normally calm and contained within certain limits, but if you attack it, the water gets stirred and spills all over the place."'

Whenever a Christian was under pressure, group members would do their utmost to surround them with love and prayer, and to establish them through teaching and testimony to the presence and reality of the living Christ. In Shanghai, seventy or eighty students would come every Sunday to the IVF house. The membership came to know each other intimately, and anyone ill or unable to attend knew they would be missed. A record book was kept with answers to prayer. This bond of fellowship kept many from falling.

Christian students were forced to spend hours in ideological discussions where they were not allowed to remain silent, so it was important to give help on such problems as suffering, the Christian's hope for the future or his attitude to injustice. Wu Yung-chuen, the IVF editorial secretary, produced a book in 1950 entitled *Questions Concerning the Faith*. It was immensely effective. One Communist leader found Christ through reading the book and observing the Christians' care for each other and for refugees in the area. 60,000 copies were issued in the first six months, besides pirated editions! One political officer told his students he could give no answer to the book – which made them all want to read it. Yet, as one student said, 'Although we might answer a hundred of the non-Christians' questions, there still would be a hundred and one waiting for a solution.' 'Being able to answer questions is not really the most important thing', said David Adeney afterwards. 'Walking in close fellowship with God is what really counts. If communion with Christ is maintained and there is honest searching for the truth in fellowship with Christian friends, the temptation to unbelief will be overcome.'

Interestingly, an ecumenical Christian leader, Charles C. West of the Ecumenical Institute, Bossey, Switzerland, wrote at this time that 'Christian Liberalism turned itself easily, too easily, into Christian-Communist Liberalism in China. Christian Liberalism failed to recognize the depth of sin, and hence the need of personal salvation...The most vigorous Christian life in Peking today lies not in the churches but in Inter-Varsity organized student groups and sects.'[4]

But matters worsened. From 1951 on, students were forbidden to take part in religious activity outside registered churches. In the August 1951 *IFES News* David Adeney – now outside China – wrote that 'it is now impossible to meet on the campus', although 'in one centre about 100 students attended three days of special meetings'. But 'Most news tells of increased difficulties. Some have already followed in the footsteps of Stephen, while others are seeking to glorify their Lord in circumstances similar to those experienced by Paul and Silas at Philippi. In one place, because

---

[4] 'Barnabas', *Christian Witness in Communist China*, p.63 (SCM Press, 1951), quoted in Eric S. Fife and Arthur F. Glasser, *Missions in Crisis* (IVP, 1962), p.77. I owe this reference to Samuel Escobar.

of constant opposition and questioning, a girl who was very bright spiritually and a leader in the Fellowship has had a mental breakdown, but others have taken her place and the witness continues. These young Christians are surrounded by those who watch for some unguarded word.

'Their attitude is perhaps best illustrated by an article written recently by a Fellowship leader in a large government university: "Recently we have had an immense burden to preach the gospel ...because after all the preaching of the gospel is the duty of every Christian. Even if we can't preach we must preach, and if we are not willing to preach we still must do it...And for this we will gladly die..." "They overcame...by the blood of the Lamb ...and they loved not their lives unto the death" (Rev. 12:11).'

Even that was not the end of the story. After the organizational IVF was dissolved, Christian students continued to meet for prayer and Bible study, and in January 1953 *IFES Journal* reported that about 300 Christian students had gathered together on campus for a meeting that had not been openly advertised! Reports of several Bible study and prayer conferences in different universities appeared in the September issue. In Peking, the annual student prayer conferences continued and students flocked to Wang Ming-tao's church until his arrest (along with a number of student leaders) in 1955. His example of courageous faithfulness to the gospel inspired many of them to stand firm.

Two years later came a period of lessened restrictions. In 1957, *IFES Journal* reported that a 5 a.m. prayer meeting took place each morning on one campus. Leslie Lyall tells how, although the Peking group had been forcibly disbanded in 1955, 'their successors obtained permission to meet again in 1957 – a large group which, like its predecessors, spent much time in prayer, even half-nights of prayer, as well as maintaining a clear witness...In 1957 a student conference in Swatow was attended by representatives from universities in Peking, Tientsin, Shanghai, Wuhan, Nanking, Kweilin, Nanning and Canton... Over a thousand attended a student rally in Wenchow.' But these examples of revived witness were soon disbanded again.[5]

Many former IVF students and staff suffered greatly during the Cultural Revolution. After the downfall of the Gang of Four, David Adeney was able to revisit China and meet some of them. The choir leader of the Nanking conference spent years in prison, and

[5] Leslie Lyall, *New Spring in China* (Hodder, 1979), pp.172–173.

then during the Cultural Revolution was 'sent to a labour camp where there was not enough food, and life was very bitter. Some of his friends committed suicide. He and his wife kept the faith all through these times of testing. His experience is perhaps typical of many former IVF students. But for some, the pressure was too much. There were those who openly denied Christ, while others internalised their faith and have only recently associated themselves with Christians once again.' One former IVF member suffered for twenty years in prisons and labour camps.

A prominent scientist told David of the sufferings through which he had passed because of his connection with IVF, but added that 'in spite of all that had happened, he was still very thankful for the IVF work and believes that its fruit still remains'. IVF no longer exists: but after its final dissolution, small groups of Christian students continued to meet in homes near the campuses, and doubtless this has recurred. Even in 1979 a report came of Christian students starting a daily prayer meeting in one such home. This, however, is exceptional, and the vast majority of Chinese students today have little opportunity to hear the gospel. 'It is not impossible for God to raise up a witness once again in the student world of China,' concludes David; but it will come primarily through 'humble service and the manifestation of the love of Christ in the lives of young Chinese Christians. We are called to join in fervent prayer.'

Japan

Across in Japan the work likewise made remarkable strides in the years following the Second World War. As in the case of Germany, it was a story of partnership between believers from countries recently at war with each other. Early in 1947 there was a single student in Waseda University, Tokyo, praying for a Christian friend; God answered his prayers, and a daily prayer meeting began amid dust-covered piles of desks in the ruins of a bomb-damaged storeroom. In March, Roy Hasegawa, a Japanese who had studied in the USA, returned to Tokyo under the auspices of the Far Eastern Gospel Crusade, and began weekly meetings in the Nippon Medical College. In April he was followed by Irene Webster-Smith, a British missionary with the Japan Evangelistic Band, who had served as IVCF staff in California during the war.

In May, Roy arranged for a young American serviceman named

Charles Hummel to speak to the medical college students. Charles had been involved with IVCF at Yale, and his brief was to speak on the new sulfa drugs and penicillin, and also to present Christianity. On May 13 he addressed 100 students by interpretation for thirty minutes; during the following weeks he learnt as much as possible about penicillin, then proceeded to give a series on this new 'miracle drug', staying behind afterwards to talk to interested students about Jesus Christ.

He remained in Japan until November, using that time to develop Bible classes at several universities, and to encourage the commencement of a weekly inter-collegiate gathering at Kanda, which included the Waseda group. It was student-led and had fifty or sixty attending by the end of the year. (One of the early leaders, Hisashi Ariga, was to become the first Japanese general secretary, and the mainspring behind the development of the literature programme. His wife was one of the first lady staffworkers.) Daily prayer meetings now existed on three campuses.

The following year saw the commencement of a magazine, *Kirisutosha*, and the first summer conference, attended by forty-five students from seven campuses. These annual conferences were to play a key part in the movement's growth; students who committed themselves to Christ at the conference returned to their campuses and set up fellowships there. It was a time of real spiritual openness. 'The way they are buying New Testaments is amazing, and there are many enquirers,' wrote Irene Webster-Smith. At one meeting in Tokyo, 100 students confessed Christ as Saviour for the first time: many attended daily follow-up meetings afterwards. At Meji University, almost 500 students indicated a desire to become Christians. 'The greatest need is for trained leadership,' said a report in *IFES News*. 'The multitudes who are turning to Christ are as sheep having no shepherd.'

Roy Hasegawa began regular training sessions at the student centre for key leaders who could themselves train others; meanwhile, more conversions occurred at almost every meeting of the Tokyo inter-collegiate group. The 1951 conference was attended by students from outside Tokyo – Osaka, Kobe, Hokkaido; one of the Kobe students who received assurance of salvation at the conference, Takashi Baino, went back and pioneered the work in the Kansai region. (Today he is a professor, and an associate staffworker to the Japanese movement.) Another student at that same conference was turned out of her home for a year because a gift of cakes had been brought for Japanese New Year and she refused to offer them at the family god-shelf.

But appearances could be deceptive. David Adeney told of a Tokyo street meeting in 1952 where 'large numbers were kneeling in the street signifying their desire to be Christians', but 'it would be a mistake to describe them as converts'. A Christian student wrote that 'those who raised their hands in response to the message are not seeking God nor salvation. Usually we are asked about God's existence, miracles, Satan, problems of peace, the Christian's attitude towards war.'

On the campus, many Bible classes were still led by missionaries. 'It is vitally important that this witness should become truly indigenous,' insisted David Adeney. Two years later, New Zealander Ken Roundhill wrote to the same effect: 'In a land of strong national consciousness, the leadership of a Japanese student movement should not even appear to lie in foreign hands.' It was a cry God answered: the first Japanese staffworkers, Reiko Ishikawa and Hisayuki Takahashi, were appointed before the end of that year.

Nonetheless, there were still difficulties ahead. Several of the key leaders in the late 1950s were close friends who had known each other from the earliest days of the movement, and, as David Adeney wrote, 'It became very easy for the initiative to pass from the students on the campus to the graduates and staffworkers off the campus.' Students felt that their responsibility was being stifled, and also that the development of literature work, particularly the ambitious translation of the *New Bible Commentary*, limited the time which staff were able to spend on campus. Around 1960 there were organizational and financial crises, and after much heart-searching the magazine had to be abandoned. The encouraging outcome was a new wave of student initiative, with the establishment of a national student committee in 1962. Still, the *Commentary* itself became a bestseller (it was the only complete commentary on the whole Bible in Japanese); it went through several editions, while other publications from the movement could be found in secular bookstores.

The sixties saw numerous opportunities for expansion. The movement was invited to sponsor a 1.45 a.m. radio programme, which was very popular with students working late, and was drawing eighty new letters and requests for correspondence courses a week. Michael Griffiths[6] verbalized their dilemma: 'Can we afford to do this? Rather, can we afford *not* to take this opportunity?' They accepted the challenge: and by 1967 400 students were doing the correspondence courses. And although one contributor to *IFES Journal* expressed a fear that the 'early zeal for personal work among the first members is not now always so apparent', the movement continued to expand.

Perhaps the most encouraging sign of all was the survey taken at the 1979 national conference, which revealed that 74.5% of the 345 participants attending did not have Christian parents, and hence were by no means predisposed towards the faith. 29.6% had been converted while at university. By 1982 the national conference attendance had doubled, to 700 students. Significant, too, is the growing number of missionaries coming from the movement: and Koichi Ohtawa, former general secretary of the Japanese movement, is now IFES associate general secretary, responsible for co-ordinating the IFES ministry throughout East Asia. The work has come a long way since that first prayer meeting among the debris of the wartime bombing. Yet, although there are now over 250 groups involved with the movement, Japan has 700 campuses still unreached.

THE SECOND GENERATION

Japan was the sole Asian IFES affiliate until 1959, when the Fellowship was enriched by the addition of India, the Philippines, Korea, Singapore and Malaya.

India
The story of the Indian work matches that of Japan. As early as 1949 *IFES News* spoke of 'an active group of staunchly evangelical students' in Calcutta holding a regular 6 a.m. prayer meeting: and when the IFES executive had appointed its first group of staff, Norton Sterrett, formerly missionary secretary for IVCF-USA and Canada, had been appointed to work in India. Norton Sterrett and his wife Eloise were a remarkable couple: they laboured among Indian students until 1975, during which time they were said to have moved house forty times!

But when the Sterretts arrived in India, the only Christian

---

[6] Formerly national student chairman for IVF-Britain, and at this time seconded to the Japanese movement by the Overseas Missionary Fellowship, of which he later became general director.

organization among more than a million Indian students was the SCM. 'It is difficult to characterize the movement as a whole and be fair,' Norton wrote of it. 'One is glad to recognize that certain local groups have evangelical leadership and are endeavouring to do a spiritual work.' Its literature, however, seemed to 'bypass the most important question of the new birth as a necessity for everyone', and 'reflects attitudes at variance with the evangelical faith, particularly on the trustworthiness of the Bible'.

Still, he was not in a hurry to set up a new organization. 'Indian Christian students must themselves determine the course they believe God would have them take. Unnecessary un-Christian strife is to be avoided. If a fresh start is to be made, the primary question is not one of a new organization, but a new vision of Christ crucified, a new conviction that the gospel of God's grace is God's only message to fallen man and that the Scriptures are the inerrant, authoritative revelation of God.'

In the meantime, Norton had brought the Moody film *The God of Creation,* and travelled 6,000 miles throughout north and central India, showing the film eighty times, mostly in schools and colleges. Apart from proclaiming the gospel, he hoped to 'disabuse educated Indians of the all-too-common idea that Christianity belongs to the outcasts and the ignorant'. Uncounted numbers of the intelligentsia were hearing the gospel for the first time: he even managed to show the film in a strict 'purdah' Muslim girls' school. ('We went out while the girls filed in. We were permitted to show the film then from the rear of the room where we men could not see the faces of the girls assembled.')

And soon God's time came for 'Indian Christians themselves' to take a decisive step. In Madras, a group of students were meeting for prayer at the home of Professor H. Enoch. Professor Enoch had been president of an evangelical SCM group at Visakapatnam, but had been troubled to find at provincial SCM level that conversion was generally felt to be 'an emotional experience which was not necessary, and belief in the Bible as the Word of God was thought to be unscholarly'. He continued as president at Vizag hoping to 'revive the movement'; but when he moved to Madras in 1949, and was invited to join SCM there, 'I had to politely decline as I found no lasting influence among students with whom I had worked at Vizag.'

Something else was needed. But nothing was known of the evangelical student movements that had developed elsewhere in the world. However, 'I discovered the Lord had been working in the hearts of some students and senior friends. I shared my burden and dissatisfaction and we began to pray regularly.'

Then one afternoon Professor Enoch was introduced to an IVF graduate from England, David C. C. Watson. A warm friendship sprang up between the two. At the same time, Bakht Singh, the famous Indian evangelist, told Professor Enoch of Norton Sterrett. As a result Dr Sterrett was invited to show his film in Madras, 'to collect those who were really interested in the Bible'. Within a few months, the Madras Inter Collegiate Christian Union came into being, in July 1951.

Meanwhile, in Vellore, a group of six medical students had been meeting on Sunday afternoons for prayer and Bible study since 1948: and in November 1951 an Australian dental surgeon, John Moody, encouraged them to set up a fully-fledged, witnessing Evangelical Union, which met in the home of Dr S. C. Devadatta. A little later, an engineering student from Madras, H. S. Ponnuraj, transferred to Coimbatore, and established a student witness in company with D. Jeyapaul. The foundations of a wider movement were laid; but still, insisted Norton Sterrett, 'they are not yet a national IVF, and will become so only if they wish, since we do not believe we should make any such decisions for them'. The common bonds were, however, irresistible: and at a retreat on a farm near Katpadi in 1954, the Union of Evangelical Students of India was formed.

Thereupon, says Professor Enoch, 'An avalanche of criticism descended on us from Christian groups and friends in the academic world.' One Christian organization passed a resolution demanding that Christian colleges permit no-one but themselves to work among the students, and David Watson wrote sadly, 'Most Principals seem to have acceded to that request.' The All-India president of SCM expressed a fear that 'a lot of American money was being brought into India to start new movements', recalls Professor Enoch, and that 'I was being used as a cat's paw. I only answered that he would know the truth by and by... This criticism challenged us to eschew dependence on foreign financial aid lest the glory of the Lord should be tarnished and His testimony dimmed.' Finally a meeting took place between the leaders of UESI and SCM, very similar to that in Cambridge after the First World War. 'It was pointed out that we believe that the Bible is the Word of God... and so new birth is essential for salvation.

They were not able to agree with us on this and so we parted.'

Indian evangelical students had other difficulties to face too. Converts in 1952 faced expulsion from home and threats of dismissal from college. In Madras, a convert from Hinduism was deprived of his scholarship. As late as 1961, Bruce Nicholls, writing that 'the work of the Evangelical Unions is one of the most strategic in India', could also say that for these students commitment 'could mean being thrown out of their homes, being cut off from any family inheritance, a knife between the shoulder blades, or death from poisoned food. Discipleship costs in the East.'

But there were those who were willing to pay the cost. Early in 1956, P. T. Chandapilla became the movement's first Indian staffworker. Chandapilla was a gifted and single-minded figure: he was reputed to have gone to study at Columbia Bible College before coming on staff, leaving with one suitcase of personal belongings, and returning with one much smaller suitcase – plus boxes full of books, as might perhaps be expected from the staffworker of an IFES affiliate! Chandapilla was to serve with UESI until 1976, when he moved on to become the general secretary of the Federation of Evangelical Churches of India.

1957 saw the first All-India camp, with participants from areas as far apart as Nagaland and Tuticorin near Madras. 'Financing this camp appeared an impossible question,' recalls P. T. Chandapilla, 'because we were paying for the travel and boarding of all our campers.' And this on their first attempt! But 'this gave us a major lesson in the effectiveness of prayer and faith. To our surprise there were a few hundred rupees left over. Most surprising was that contacts for EU work began to explode on a national level with that camp.'

'Explode' is not too strong a verb to use. 1958 saw a group started in Andhra Pradesh, 1959 in Calcutta, 1960 in Shillong and in Assam, 1961 in Uttar Pradesh, Gujarat, Maharashtra and Karnataka. Thirteen of India's twenty-one states had at least one group by 1964. In other respects too the work was expanding. 1961 saw the first city-wide UESI Mission, in Madras. 1962 saw a national graduates conference, from which emerged the Evangelical Graduates Fellowship, as well as the appointment of the first staffworker among women students, Mary Beaton, a former IVCF-USA worker who had pioneered with IFES in the Philippines. This was a significant appointment, since men staffworkers were not normally able to work among women students, due to the prevailing cultural pattern. By 1967, two Indian lady staffworkers were appointed. P. T. Chandapilla was delighted: 'We could hardly think of lady staffworkers from India coming to this insecure and strenuous work,' he wrote.

A literature ministry was likewise developing, including the *Jyoti Pocketbook* series published in collaboration with Gospel Literature Service of Bombay. In 1972 came the first national missionary conference, which resulted from the Indian contingent at the North American Urbana Convention in 1970 asking, 'Why can't Christian students in India have a Missionary Conference like this?'

The event faced financial difficulties similar to the first All-India camp. UESI conferences had never been attended by more than eighty, but this time at least 150 might be expected – except that very few students could afford to travel to Madras, nor could UESI's tight budget subsidize them. The organizing committee were exhorted, 'We must pray and then believe that God will send the extra money.' They accepted the challenge: and an unexpected cheque from Indian friends in the USA was God's answer as the conference attendance rose to an unprecedented 365! 'For the last 250 years God has sent men and women from other countries to be watchmen here,' general secretary Chandapilla told the gathering. 'But now God in His mercy, and maybe in His judgment, will remove those watchmen, and your house and mine will lie desolate if there are not men and women here to be watchmen...Get involved!' State missionary conferences have followed in Maharashtra, Orissa, Gujarat and Karnataka.

The twentieth anniversary conference in Nagpur in 1974 was attended by 500 and gave further impetus to the work. Simultaneous programmes were held for those involved with theological studies, teaching, medicine, the civil service and business. Papers focused on practical problems posed by widespread corruption: the government service and businessmen's group passed a resolution to 'establish a clear witness for the Lord Jesus Christ in our professions by scrupulously upright conduct regardless of consequences'. In each of these professional areas a nationwide fellowship was formed.

Later in the decade an awareness of the need to work in the state languages as well as in English led to a deliberate decentralization of the geographically gigantic work on to the state level, drawing extensively on the Evangelical Graduates Fellowships. Such a move could be problematic: 'We must pray that the national integrity and unity should not be lost, and the national vision should be passed on,' wrote the staffworker from Tamil Nadu, the state that led the way. The change seems to have borne some fruit. Within five years of decentralization the Tamil Nadu budget had increased fivefold to support an enlarged staff team (including a worker for north India); publications had been issued in Tamil, the number of student groups had increased from sixteen to twenty-four and the graduate groups from ten to forty. Some hundreds of Hindu students turned to Christ in that state, and also in Andhra Pradesh, during the early 1980s.

Still, it was estimated at the end of the 1970s that 98% of India's six million students remained unevangelized. Only forty of Delhi's 70,000 students were involved with UESI, and there were no groups in the states of Rajasthan, Haryana, Himachal Pradesh, Sikkim, Goa, Tripura or Arunachal Pradesh. 2,500 colleges remained unreached in 1982. As with Japan, the sturdy Indian movement has still a huge task ahead.

The Philippines

The first recorded student Bible studies in the Philippines were taking place around 1950, particularly among students in the University of Manila and Silliman University. Far Eastern Gospel Crusade missionary Ray Larsen, a former IVCF-USA staffworker, arrived in the Philippines in 1952, and met with half a dozen students at the University of the Philippines, plus about twenty-five medical students in downtown Manila. 'The liberals, Seventh Day Adventists, Jehovah's Witnesses, etc. are very active here,' he wrote, 'and the students will listen to anything that is presented to them...I am convinced that today is the day of salvation as far as the student world in the East is concerned.' More labourers followed: Peter Kemery and his wife, graduates of IVF-Britain, and IFES staffworker Gwen Wong, who was born in San Francisco's Chinatown and was a professional baseball player for a short period, before joining IVCF-USA staff and pioneering the work in Hawaii.

There were problems. Deep denominational divisions existed among the evangelicals, and real tensions between Christian Chinese and Christian Filipino students. Besides this, the IFES

154

concept of student work – 'students witnessing to students, students responsible to develop their own programme, to lead their Bible studies, conduct their prayer meetings' – was somewhat novel to the Filipinos. It 'did not initially appeal', Ephraim Orteza wrote afterwards. 'Ordinary students were ready to join a group if no responsibility was expected and if a programme was provided.'

Nevertheless, daily prayer meetings, Saturday afternoon discussions, and evangelistic meetings took place, and by 1954 student-led groups began on campus. 1956 saw a week-long evangelistic conference attended by 100 students from at least ten campuses: shortly afterwards the first two Filipino staff joined the movement, along with a second IFES worker, Mary Beaton. The increased staff numbers made possible more training in leadership for the students, especially in inductive Bible study.

By 1958 the young national movement was no longer dependent on outside Bible teachers, and graduates were returning to their homes in places like Cebu and Davao and encouraging the undergraduates there in campus witness. This created a still greater need for training. Graduates and Christian friends inside and outside the Philippines gave sacrificially to equip a site generously donated by the Orteza family in a mountainous area of Negros Occidental, and IVCF-Philippines' first month-long Kawayan Camp was held. ('Kawayan', incidentally, is the versatile bamboo plant.) Here students were encouraged to lead Bible studies – with evaluation and constructive criticism – and teaching was given on the life of Christ, discipleship, the 'quiet time', and so on.

Gwen Wong and Mary Beaton had told the Filipinos that they would be leaving the country within a very few years of their arrival. True to their word, they wrote to IFES general secretary Stacey Woods in 1959, 'Our task in the Philippines is finished. We leave behind a National Committee, a corps of national staff workers, a supportive Christian constituency, and so we are sailing for India.' Stacey saw it as a classic example of 'the New Testament pattern of those who could found a work and then move on, instead of following the disastrous pattern of so much missionary paternalism'.[7]

But to the first Filipino general secretary, Ephraim Orteza, and his fellow-workers the situation was slightly more problematic!

[7] C. Stacey Woods, *The Growth of a Work of God* p.35.

All of them were in their early twenties, and, as Ephraim says, 'Many shook their heads believing it was quite impossible for such young, inexperienced men and women to carry on a national student work; and, humanly speaking, they were right. Nevertheless they were convinced that God had called them, and this was a binding force in spite of much testing and discouragement.'

And God continued to bless the work. By 1960 IVCF was working in twenty-four campuses, and soon a strong work began to develop in the high schools too. Four years later some 200 students came to the first National Missionary Conference in Baguio City.

In 1966 Isabelo Magalit became general secretary, and his emphasis on staff training, combined with a strong commitment to evangelism and missionary concern, helped produce a movement able to communicate to a changing university situation. For the student unrest of the second half of the decade made it necessary for IVCF to discover and affirm a holistic discipleship. A number of student radicals turned to Christ: one such activist was Melba Maggay, who quickly produced an evangelistic newspaper which, appearing after a week of violent clashes between students and police, sold 5,000 copies in seven days at the University of the Philippines. Melba expressed her new-found vision in an article entitled 'Revolutionary Truth':

We have been conditioned to think of Christ as an effeminate symbol of oppression emanating from the gilded thrones of the papacy: a tool for the continuing exploitation of the masses by the collusive tie-up between the ruling class and the clerical-fascist order... While it is true that to a large extent the so-called semi-colonial, semi-feudal structure of our society has crippled the Filipino for so long, it is also true that the root cause of our corruption and exploitation is NOT the system but WE who are in the system...

It is man who corrupts his environment. Any blueprint for change must take into account the ugly side of man... Anyone who seeks change must realize that change in the power structure is simply *not enough*. It must be accompanied by a change in man. A total restructuring of the whole man. And the Christian experience has shown that Christ does not simply politicalize man. He changes man and everything that he is.

It it not perhaps too much to say that such a holistic vision was expressed in the activities of IVCF-Philippines during this period. On the one hand, there was the concern to expose students to Christ who alone could empower real change in man; in partnership with the Bible Society they printed and distributed 50,000 copies of a selection of Bible passages under the title *Jesus, Who Are You?* Meanwhile IVCF graduates sought to become involved in their country's needs in areas such as legal aid to the illiterate (and so defenceless) tribes people, or in medical relief. Through the Lubang Medical Mission, for example, a team of volunteer doctors, dentists, nurses, medical and paramedical students would visit the Mindoro tribes each summer in collaboration with OMF, bringing medical aid along with the gospel.

The seventies saw continued evangelistic vision. On 21 September 1972, university classes were suspended as martial law was declared. Two IVCF members at the University of the Philippines returned to their hometown, Naga City in Bicol, and began small group Bible studies among the students. One of them eventually stayed to study there, while working in his family's business. This approach to pioneering was adopted as a deliberate strategy when the first 'Graduate Team' was appointed in 1975. There were many opportunities to pioneer student work that the small staff team were simply unable to take up: so the challenge was presented to the graduates, and a group of five (an engineer, a nutritionist, a high-school teacher, a commerce graduate and a premedical graduate) sailed for Davao City to help the growing work there. They had no security, no home and no jobs: it took almost three months before they all found employment.

The following year three graduates went to Bicol, where there was again no student witness, and a group of graduates in Cebu City formed a team to assist the local staffworker. Meanwhile the original Davao team had visited neighbouring cities to challenge other graduates to share the vision: God answered their prayers, and three more teams were formed!

By 1980 there were twenty-eight graduates forming twelve teams, financed through their secular jobs, and involved in evangelism, training, counselling and praying with key students, providing literature, *etc*. Each Graduate Team member is considered an assistant staffworker of IVCF, and attends a ten-day training conference before being assigned, including workshops on training Bible study leaders, expository preaching, counselling and running conferences. Most GT members work outside their home region: all agree to serve for at least a year, and to postpone marriage or courtship during the first year. Some are faced with learning a new dialect and being alone and jobless for months.

Today, there are more Christian students involved with the tertiary-level groups in the Philippines than there are in any European country except Norway, Britain or Germany. And yet the Philippines is not a rarity in Asia. Singapore likewise has seen tremendous blessing on campus during the past three decades.

Singapore

Here, as in Tokyo, Madras, Vellore and Manila, the story begins with a small group of students praying together. The SCM group in the University had adopted a liberal position. Bible study after Bible study saw disagreements between the evangelicals and the more liberal element, who felt that all religions led to God and that salvation through Christ's blood was a pagan notion. It was scarcely a 'unified witness'. One of the evangelicals addressed the SCM on 'Faith and Prayer' and found himself confronted by the SCM chaplain asserting that the Genesis creation account was a myth, and probably less accurate than the Hindu equivalent!

Some of the evangelicals felt a concern to stay within SCM and work for its renewal: their efforts were unsuccessful, however, despite an evangelical majority on the SCM committee, since 'several not-so-evangelical church leaders' were *ex officio* committee members. The result was the beginning, in September 1950, of a prayer meeting among the medical students, who felt that 'a clear-cut stand had to be made for the sake of a pure witness for the Lord'. In mid-1951 Ewan Lumsden and his wife, graduates of IVF-Australia, arrived in Singapore, and two regular Bible studies were held under the leadership of Ewan, Phoon Wai On and Tow Siang Hwa, two of the original four students. On two occasions, the possibility of forming an IVF-style group was raised, but did not meet with widespread support: minor doctrinal differences on the subject of church government being a major hindrance. In the middle of 1952 the Lumsdens left Singapore.

'The fortunes of our group were at the lowest tide,' recalls Dr Phoon. 'Even the most stalwart among us were daunted. My low spirits, however, were freshened by God's grace. In a farewell meeting with the Lumsdens I told them soberly, humbly, yet with a strange confidence that when they returned in five months time they would see an organized evangelical body in existence. It was not a prophecy at all. Somehow I felt it deeply in my heart that the time had come. I was sounding the note of triumph on what seemed the eve of calamity.'

His faith was not misplaced. An inaugural meeting was held for a 'Christian Students' Union' in August, and the Varsity Christian Fellowship began with twenty members in October. Soon afterwards, IVF-Britain graduate Leon Dale arrived in Singapore as a geography lecturer, and became a tower of strength to the fledgling group as he opened his home on Sunday afternoons.

Little by little the work expanded. 1956 saw the formation of a second group, at Nanyang University, 1957 a third at Kuala Lumpur, and two years later a Fellowship of Evangelical Students was formed for Singapore and Malaya, which duly affiliated to IFES.

In 1963 FES acquired its first staffworker, Chua Wee Hian (later IFES associate general secretary for East Asia from 1968 to 1971, and now general secretary internationally). He was supported entirely from Singapore, a fact of some significance since at that time there were few self-supporting ministries in the country. Wee Hian's wife, King Ling, was offered an associate professorship at the Chinese-speaking Nanyang University, then heavily Marxist. As a result, strong links were created between the Chinese-speaking Nanyang students and the believers at the more English-speaking Singapore University. (Such links were by no means common in Singapore life.) The next staffworker, Choong Chee Pang, was from Nanyang and supported primarily by Nanyang graduates.

By 1971 some 450 students were involved in FES. The next decade was to be one of remarkable growth in the Fellowship. This may be illustrated from the developments in the VCF at Singapore University, which had 127 members in 1971. VCF main meetings were drawing satisfactory numbers, but the fellowship seemed impersonal, and many members were becoming inactive 'passengers'. The executive committee, headed up by William Wan, were anxious to solve this problem.

They turned to a medical student, Chua Choon Lan, who,

though only twenty years old, was already a leader in a local church and had been involved in setting up small groups for following up young converts. He was invited to adapt the system for the VCF, emphasizing the existing cell groups – which functioned mainly for Bible study and did not involve the whole fellowship – and turning them into a 'contact group' system.

The groups were so named because of their stress on developing relationships with God, with their fellow-believers, and with non-Christians: Bible study, prayer, sharing, outreach. It was perhaps the emphasis on evangelism which was distinctive: many student cell groups in different parts of the world have an introverted preoccupation with 'fellowship'.[8] The Singapore groups were intending to 'divide and multiply', splitting into two groups once their membership rose above six. Evangelistic Bible studies, coffee evenings and gospel camps became built in as the system developed. From 1972 a Contact Group co-ordinator was appointed: and in each faculty or hostel a sub-committee developed to co-ordinate the integration and outreach of the groups in that area.[9]

The VCF members were organized into thirty contact groups, led, writes Serene Wee, by 'dizzy-headed student leaders (some of whom had never sat in a Bible study before), and co-ordinated by a few determined student bulldozers'. But the employment of VCF's first staffworker, Thomas John, and the rapid – if sometimes haphazard – arrangement of training camps for group leaders helped the idea catch on. (Early in his appointment, Thomas had six camps in two weeks.) The Lord blessed: VCF members began to share their vision and faith. By 1977, VCF's membership had more than doubled, to 300 – but an astonishing 700 students out of the university enrolment of 6,000 were involved in the contact groups! Nor was that the end of the story. By 1979 that figure had risen to 900: at the time of writing, 1,500 of the university's 9,000 students are said to be in the groups. Obviously much prayer is needed for the VCF leaders, that this numerical strength should be channelled and not permitted to stagnate into spiritual fat!

---

[8] As one Australian staffworker wrote, 'Some cell groups seem to have misunderstood the word "cell". The sooner they roll away the stone and come out of prison, the better!'

[9] Further details are contained in *Guidelines on Contact Groups* by Soon Guat Eng, published by FES-Singapore (later revised by Pamela Lau).

It need not have been so, of course. Soon Guat Eng, a VCF graduate who joined FES staff in 1974, regards the contact group system as 'fraught with dangers...If CG leaders in particular do not understand the importance of a corporate witness for Christ, the results may be disastrous', both for the contact group and the larger fellowship. A 1977 FES document emphasized that '(1) The leaders must be well-trained, *e.g.* in programme planning, leading Bible discussions; (2) there must be suitable study materials; (3) there must be good co-ordination with the Fellowship's executive committee.' There were of course other factors in the spectacular growth of the VCF during this period. Their 1977 magazine stressed the significance of 'the work of Scripture Union and Youth for Christ in schools; and the staffworkers, who provided counselling and teaching', besides a vital sense of history. Nonetheless, the contact groups were of fundamental importance both in VCF and the other FES fellowships.

In such a growth situation there are inevitably problems in preserving momentum. 'There is a danger in only maintaining things,' says Guat Eng. 'The question always has to be, How can this be improved? We would teach the groups: Improvise! Improve! Revise!' But on a wider strategic level, the question arose as to what lasting impact was being made. Here the Graduate Christian Fellowship, formed in 1955, had a crucial role. One of GCF's leaders, Bobby Sng Ewe Kong, expressed it when he wrote: 'To graduate is more than just to acquire a privileged passport into working life. It is to realize that the Lord Jesus is now sending us out into the world to help Him in establishing His Kingdom...some of us to industries and others to offices, and yet others to distant lands...This sense of mission is fundamental to our graduate life...How can we now make our life count for Him?'

The Singapore graduates found various answers.[10] A number have used the training they acquired in evangelistic Bible studies while at university to pioneer lunchtime witness and fellowship groups in offices and hospitals, among lawyers, bus workers and employees of government departments. A group of Christian lawyers and doctors got together when a major alteration to the divorce law was in view and made representations to parliament that resulted in the legislation being withdrawn. Others have gone into leadership in various parts of Singapore society,

[10] *Cf.* Bobby Sng, 'Make Your Life Count', *In Touch* 1981, 1.

including the higher echelons of politics and the academic world. (By 1973 over 10% of the national university's teaching staff were committed Christians.) It was made a deliberate policy to encourage graduates towards full-time and pastoral ministry, and more than forty responded between 1970 and 1978. Still others have used their qualifications in missionary service; at one stage a number of doctors – including Bobby Sng himself – deliberately chose postings in rural areas of Malaysia, and as a result were in every instance able to establish new churches or to encourage fledgling work.

And, at the most basic level, the organization of graduates from the same year into groups – Group 81, Group 82, Group 83, and so on – meeting two or three times a year for perhaps the first five years after college, has not only created communities able to give badly-needed financial backing for FES staff, but also mutual support in facing the difficult changes in lifestyle after university. The scheme was in fact the result of student initiative, when some prominent casualties induced the 1971 leadership to place graduate dropout at the top of their list of problems needing tackling.[11]

Malaysia

Across the Causeway in Malaysia a slightly different situation exists. Malaysia is an Islamic country, and although freedom of worship is allowed, the Malay majority are Muslims by law and non-Muslims are forbidden to take the initiative in propagating their faith. Indeed, when a Malay Muslim was converted in Singapore, her parents removed her from university, permitting her to return only when she promised not to attend Christian meetings. Privately she continued in fellowship with Christians, and read her Bible daily: but on returning home after graduation she was placed under the protection of Muslim families, and escorted back and forth to work by Muslim men who would also censor all her letters.

It is to be expected, then, that the Malaysian groups will be made up of students from the Chinese and Indian sections of the population. The group in Kuala Lumpur received much impetus from a number of Christian students and staff moving to their campus in 1959; by 1963 they were able to hold their first major university mission, with John Stott as speaker. (This was part of

[11] *Cf.* Soon Guat Eng, 'Year Grads in Singapore', *IFES Review* 1977, 2.

a tour that also included missions in Vellore, Singapore and Manila.)

The political separation of Singapore from Malaysia necessitated the organization of FES in Malaysia as a separate movement, which affiliated with IFES in 1967; it formed an administrative joint committee with Scripture Union in 1975 to avoid duplication in a common constituency of supporters. There were obvious advantages in terms of co-ordination with SU's high-schools ministry, and the mobilization of trainee teachers for that task. Malaysia now has an active Teachers' Christian Fellowship; in East Malaysia in particular it is not unknown for teachers in their early twenties to be responsible for a high-schools fellowship of up to a hundred, and it is common to be the only Christian teacher in a school of several hundred. FES graduates have a fine record of involvement with struggling rural churches – something that is by no means a universal phenomenon among Christian graduates worldwide.

FES Malaysia sponsors a three-week training camp in the Cameron Highlands, similar to the Kawayan Camp in the Philippines, which has helped to cultivate student leadership. One year, early on, the leaders received word just as they were departing for the camp that the conference venue could not be used. 'We went forward in faith,' says David Adeney, 'and it was amazing to see the way in which God provided an old British military hospital, with beds and furniture. So we had our conference, even though when we started up the mountain we did not know where we were going to sleep that night!'

One of the most successful evangelistic approaches early in the '70s was the musical evenings, when a choir from the student group would perform a cantata, or perhaps excerpts from Handel's *Messiah*, followed by a message. To the amazement of the Christian students, many Malays would come along to such an evening, particularly when the theme was the resurrection.

The latter half of the '70s saw much blessing and rapid growth in the movement. In 1971 about 300 tertiary students were involved; by the middle of the decade this had risen to about 330. But by 1982 one of the training colleges contained a fellowship of 300 members, while there were 400 in a Christian fellowship at one of the universities.

Korea

The work in South Korea has a different story again. Not long before the Korean war, some Korean leaders were in touch with IFES enquiring about a link with the Fellowship: and after the war attempts were made to start a student witness through mass evangelistic meetings. However, as David Adeney wrote, the work 'made a false start in some respects, as it became involved in church politics and began from above rather than from among the students themselves'. In 1959 a new general secretary, Samuel Yoon, took over, and the Inter Varsity Christian Fellowship work was more or less restarted. (They affiliated to IFES that year.)

Samuel was a remarkable man. During the Korean war he had been captured by the North Koreans and condemned to death on false evidence, but was unexpectedly freed after the intervention of a Communist friend. On the previous night this friend had urged him to save his life by becoming a Communist, and had been challenged with the gospel in reply! When United Nations forces recaptured the area, most of the young men in the People's Court which had tried Samuel were themselves facing death at the hands of the South Korean police, and Samuel pleaded for their lives at the police station for three days and nights, 'fasting and weeping'. Finally they were released – and as a result Samuel's family were converted. However, when he took over the leadership of KIVCF, 'I found so many difficulties and problems that I was tempted to be discouraged...I did not pray enough,' he wrote in *The Way*. 'This coming year I will pray more in secret and with others, so that I may see the hand of God move in the hearts of many students.'

The problem at this time was not that it was difficult to get students to make a 'decision for Christ', but rather was in the area of effective follow-up. 'Many will volunteer to serve on a committee,' reported David Adeney, 'but few are prepared to persevere with Bible study, prayer and personal evangelism.' Those 'few' were the work's foundation, however, and by the 1970s the work was growing steadily, from fourteen groups with 200 members in 1971 to thirty-four campus fellowships and twelve graduate groups by the end of the decade. There is a flourishing literature ministry in the area of Bible study guides, which are much appreciated by the churches: and 1980 saw a first-ever camp for Christian medical students, with an attendance of seventy.

A number of evangelical student organizations are operating in the complex ecclesiastical situation of Korea. Their inter-relationships have been complicated by denominational and regional tensions, and the role of IFES has not been an easy one. For some time during this period IFES had contact with the University Bible Fellowship, formed in Kwangju in 1961 through the efforts of a graduate, Lee Chang Woo, and an American missionary, Sarah Barry. As they began to reach out to students they encountered IFES staffworker Gwen Wong, who introduced them to the notion of evangelistic Bible studies. Many such studies were set up: many students were converted and taught to be missionary-minded. One of the movement's slogans was 'Every Christian must be a fisherman'. The movement spread rapidly northwards into all the main university centres, and in its heyday had several thousand members. More than ninety of 100 UBF students surveyed in 1972 had been converted at university, and most of these were not from Christian backgrounds. All staff were UBF converts.

It is interesting that this evangelistic momentum resulted from a stress on systematic study and continuous exposure to God's Word (though conscious and thoroughgoing Koreanization was of significance too), rather than through evangelistic meetings or through training in particular evangelistic methods or formulae. UBF meetings would be almost exclusively Bible expositions or inductive Bible studies. Students met daily to study the Bible: new converts would do 'quiet times' with older believers for at least thirty days.

A merger was attempted between IVCF and UBF, but it broke up within weeks leaving many wounds. During the later 1970s UBF grew somewhat more authoritarian and heavily centralized. At the present time the Student Bible Fellowship, an offshoot of UBF, has a sturdy witness on a number of campuses. SBF has currently sent three of its senior staff abroad for theological training to ensure a thorough grounding for the work in the late 1980s, but nonetheless the movement has continued to thrive.

FIVE POST-1959 MOVEMENTS

Taiwan

Another independent evangelical student movement, working in close association with IFES, is the Campus Evangelical Fellowship of Taiwan. God used various missionaries, particularly from OMF, to lay its foundations in the 1950s. Pauline Hamilton began student work in Taichung in central Taiwan in 1952, Dick Webster in Tainan in the south in 1953, Wesley Milne, Margaret Aldis and Frank Wuest in Kao-hsiung in 1954, and four more missionaries along with two Chinese lay Christians developed a similar ministry in Ping-Tung in 1956.

Dick Webster had been an honorary staffworker with IVCF-USA: he and his wife began their work when, after 'praying all the way across the Pacific for student contacts', they arrived in Taiwan and were immediately asked by a fellow missionary to take over her position as English teacher at the Engineering College. 'Before long we were so busy with interviews and Bible classes among these students and teachers that we had to drop teaching English!' So the Tainan Christian Fellowship was born; and high-schools work developed rapidly too. The meeting-place became crammed to capacity, which meant that the students were unable to advertise their gatherings as widely as they wished. So they built an inexpensive student centre; and by the end of 1955 they numbered two hundred. Prayer meetings were held six days a week from 7.30 till 8.30 a.m.; the groups were also involved in witness to the unevangelized peasant people of the neighbouring district.

Around that same time there occurred a fateful 'chance meeting'. David Cha, who had been converted in an IVF meeting in Shanghai on the Chinese mainland, was on a train journey from Taipei to Tainan and found himself travelling with David Adeney, whom he had known some years previously and who was then on his first trip to Taiwan. David Cha had served briefly as a student worker for a large Baptist church, but now he was preparing to move on. That evening they talked in the home of the Websters, and wondered if God's time had not come for the establishment of an IVF-type ministry in Taiwan.

So David and his family rented a small room, and he began to go on campus and ask students, 'Are you a Christian?' As a result a group came into being in Taiwan National University. He also began a bi-monthly magazine, *Campus Fellowship,* which became widely appreciated. The next step was to invite his readers to attend a summer conference: and as a result more interdenominational, student-led groups were gradually formed in the universities.

For six years David was the sole staffworker; but God led a

Christian professor, Chang Ming-Che, to take an active part in the work. Almost a hundred students attended a class in his church, and he was much in demand at student conferences. He set about leading two long Bible studies each week, believing that the top priority was to provide student leaders with spiritual depth and solid foundations for their faith: 'One student fully saved is better than a hundred half saved!' Gwen Wong spent two months in Taiwan, teaching group Bible study to the graduates and OMF missionaries who were getting involved. Finally in 1962 a national movement was formed.

Since then it has grown steadily, with a succession of unusually gifted leaders, such as Morley Lee, Nathaniel Chow, Daniel Rao and Andrew Lin. In the late seventies there were forty-five staff, serving 2,200 university and college members in seventy-six groups, plus 135 high-school groups with an average attendance of 2,600. In 1965 they started a literature work, which had an annual budget of $10,000 for some while, publishing a book every two or three years. In 1973, however, contacts through IFES led to Edwin Su spending some time with Inter-Varsity Press in Britain and the USA; ten years later their budget had risen to $1 million annually, and they were publishing two books each month! God has given CEF a headquarters right opposite the Taiwan National University, and the ground floor is now a bookshop that is very strategic for evangelism.

A major factor in the movement's growth has been God's blessing on CEF's extensive summer programme of evangelistic camps. In 1973, for example, half of the 1,150 university students at the camps were non-Christians and 235 professed conversion; likewise, half of the 2,240 students at the high-schools camps were non-Christians, and 900 professed conversion. In 1980, 2,000 students and graduates attended the camps; 700 were non-Christians, and 400 professed conversion.

Such instances of God's power must be expected to bear widespread fruit. Graduate groups have grown up in fifteen cities, with up to 100 members, and are reaching non-Christian graduates who are unwilling to attend church. Some of these groups have set up gospel teams, to work with small churches.

Worldwide concern is increasing too. CEF's first Missionary Convention in July 1979 drew some 1,400 participants, including sixty pastors (a cause for rejoicing, since CEF's relationships with the churches were at the outset plagued with misunderstanding); and 100 of these participants already felt sure God was calling them abroad. $4,000 was given for student work abroad, plus a further $1,500 raised by students fasting and praying in 'Watchmen' sessions. (These took place three times daily, with about 150 participating: IFES-East Asia's newspaper *New Way* suggested that they were 'the real secret of the abundant blessing on the conference'.) The second such conference took place in 1982, and drew an attendance of 1,800.

Hong Kong

God's grace has been visible in a different but equally remarkable way in the work in Hong Kong, where around 1951 something of a steady spiritual revival began among young people. Monthly rallies were held to reach secondary-school students; and on various campuses, students began spontaneously to meet for prayer and Bible study. This continued until 1957, when David Adeney came to Hong Kong with his wife Ruth to work with the nucleus of evangelicals actively witnessing in the university.

Once again, he was to play a crucial role as a catalyst. The next year or so saw several significant events: the first joint conference of evangelicals from Hong Kong's tertiary institutions, which led to the formation of the Inter College Christian Fellowship; the establishment of a Graduates Christian Fellowship by graduates from both local and overseas universities, particularly to support the evangelistic work among high-school students, which in turn led to the formation of the Inter Schools Christian Fellowship; and the opening of the Evangelical Reading Room in Kowloon, funded by the graduates, with books the students could borrow or buy. (By 1961 it was having 600 visitors a month.)

By 1958 the graduates were able to support the first local staffworker, Chan Pak Fai, followed two years later by Chan Hay Him. In 1959, a Teachers Christian Fellowship was formed. All these streams came together with the formation of Hong Kong Fellowship of Evangelical Students in 1961. By then Hong Kong University's Christian Association, which dated back to 1911, had become a strongly evangelical fellowship with a conservative basis of faith and an evangelistic approach.

In the 1970s, HKFES gave birth to some rather remarkable offspring. 'Unless we can produce attractive and contemporary literature to the Asian masses,' Chua Wee Hian had declared in *IFES Journal* in 1970, 'we shall lose the battle for men's minds . . .

Let us plan creatively and boldly. We can then expect the Spirit of God to guide us for a breakthrough in Christian literature.' It was doubtful whether he would then have imagined just how that dream would be brought to pass through FES.

Breakthrough was the name of a magazine launched in 1974 by a group of graduates, headed up by Philemon Choi and Josephine So (who was herself living under the shadow of a cancer that would kill her eight years later). It was a bi-monthly, in Chinese, aimed at a mass readership in the 15 – 25 age-range. Of the initial printing of 20,000, no less than 5,000 sold at the news-stands, and the reaction was positive and enthusiastic. 'Do not hesitate to take $2 from your pockets, friends, and buy one,' wrote a well-known local newspaper columnist.

From there on, the ministry began to snowball. In September 1975, extra-large posters all over the city proclaimed that the magazine had become a monthly; which, as Josephine said, 'meant more than doubling the amount of work...Many times staff members were bogged down by tension, anxiety and depression, but God helped them to meet impossible deadlines.' Circulation climbed to one target after another, and soon *Breakthrough* was selling over 30,000 copies a month, more than half of which went to non-Christians.

Such an impact was being made that the commercial radio – who had never accepted anything religious – offered *Breakthrough* the chance to do a regular programme. (In recent years, this has been broadcast six days a week.) '*Breakthrough* on Air' treated issues from a Christian perspective, directing its listeners to a way of life beyond the carnal, the superficial and the temporary, rather than presenting the gospel directly: but letters seeking guidance and counselling poured in – to the amazement of the radio authorities. The establishment of a 'hot-line' telephone service was decided upon: training courses were organized, Christian experts were recruited, the government – with an eye to juvenile delinquency problems – provided facilities in a new housing estate, and the *Breakthrough* Counselling Centre was opened before the end of 1975.[12]

By 1982, *Breakthrough* had an estimated readership of 120,000; *Breakthrough Junior*, launched in 1979 and aimed at the younger adolescent age-range, stood at 68,000. 100,000 people were listen-

[12] See Philemon Choi, 'The *Breakthrough* Counselling Centre', *Evangelical Review of Theology*, April 1981, pp.102–110.

ing to 'Breakthrough on Air'; 4,700 people had been helped through the Counselling Service in 1981. The multi-media youth rally 'Breakthrough Nite', which started in 1975 featuring a combination of popular and classical music, modern dance, poetry and drama, was by 1981 reaching 10,000 people, plus 1,300 in regional presentations.

The 1981 show was built around the book of Lamentations (which, it was said, 'communicates fittingly the rhythm of Hong Kong in the '80s'), and included an audio-visual using nine screens and twenty-four projectors, with live dance and choral groups. A massive follow-up scheme entitled 'Operation Andrew' trained follow-up workers for the project: and a cassette based on the presentation sold 5,000 within seven months. Inevitably, the magazine has had to match words with action, and its social concern has been expressed in an anti-pornography campaign, a fund-raising campaign for Cambodian refugees, and a Simple Life Camp which drew 400. Many *Breakthrough* readers have come to Christ at evangelistic camps.

In 1981 *Breakthrough* became administratively separate from HKFES, though remaining a 'sister organization', since its scope was now reaching well beyond the student world. The FES ministry has continued to expand both among students and graduates. Graduates have been involved extensively in counselling at FES's evangelistic high-school camps; at one stage nearly all the student participants would be non-Christians. No less than 4,000 students are involved in the high-schools groups at the present time, besides the 600 tertiary group members. FES has a vision to train and mobilize Christian graduates who will be salt and light in the world: the expansion of this ministry has included seminars on areas such as vocation, counselling, and family life, that have frequently been over-subscribed.

Vietnam

In Vietnam, the work began to crystallize at the same time as Hong Kong. At the end of the 1950s half a dozen students were meeting together, and in response to a request from them, an official invitation from the National Evangelical Church and the urging of Christian and Missionary Alliance workers in the country, OMF missionaries Paul and Maida Contento arrived in Saigon in 1960, as IFES associate staffworkers. The Contentos had already contributed a great deal to student work in both

China and Singapore. 'The gospel is the most exciting thing in the world,' Paul once told *The Way*. 'I'm 100% enthusiastic about that!' When they arrived in Vietnam, they spent four months travelling in the country to get a first-hand picture of the needs. 'What really hit us hard was the exploding student population and literally no-one with the time or knowhow to tackle this great challenge!'

To read their reports is to watch strategists at work. There was no Christian student literature available, and the education system was just shifting from French to English, so translators were in short supply. Yet such literature was 'an absolute must', and Maida Contento made it her personal challenge. There were no daily Bible reading notes, and 'how could Christians become strong in the faith if they did not read the Word of God daily and systematically? So obviously SU was a must at the earliest moment!' In the first year, they organized a student conference attended by thirty: and over the next two years a high-school work developed also.

Here student initiative and missionary initiative meshed together: a group of evangelical high-schoolers who had watched their older friends backslide at university banded together before going up themselves, resolving to pray and help one another to stand firm – not knowing that anyone else had ever done such a thing! So their enthusiasm knew no bounds when they heard that God had raised up similar groups elsewhere. The National Evangelical Church warmly welcomed the developing work and invited the student movement to affiliate to it.

For the first few years, membership stayed at thirty to forty: but this grew once the high-school group members began to enter university. Meanwhile, the Contentos had other dreams. 'Since students, once converted, must be brought into the church and the church is in need of revival, and revival blessing can only be the fruit of reading and obeying the Word of God, the need of knowing the doctrines and teaching of God's Word was obviously of tremendous importance.' So Bible correspondence courses were needed for the students – 'Another must!' (As it turned out, 'the mailman seems to be able to go where no Christian worker dare go!')

Finally, their anxiety to provide fresh blood for the Vietnamese church as a whole made them decide 'not only that we must focus our prayers and efforts on getting students saved, but that some of them with vision and dedication must go to some of the best evangelical theological seminaries abroad and come back with good theological degrees and burning fire in their hearts to evangelize their own country'. From 1961, for example, through the generous gift of a British Christian, Le Vinh Thach spent three years studying at London Bible College, after which he returned to student work in Vietnam. By 1970 ten such graduates were in training.

Right from the outset, the Contentos had stated their objective to be the establishment of an independent, indigenous student movement as soon as possible: and when these graduates began to return, and the church appointed one of them as staff, the Contentos stopped attending any IVF meeting and gently turned the high-school work over as well. 'Their philosophy of training the national leaders to take over the work has been strictly followed,' wrote the Vietnamese staffworker. And in April 1975 the Contentos left Saigon for Manila. By then, the national movement, or Tong Doan Sinh-Vien Hoc-Sinh Tin-Lanh, had 300 members active in five universities and seventeen high-school groups. The work had expanded so much that two more associate staff were needed: and still the conversions continued, especially among the high-school students.

Then came the fall of Saigon, and the gradual dissolution of the movement. What were the Vietnamese students to do? One of the leaders wrote to Chua Wee Hian, 'I have decided to stay and I do not encourage any of the Christian students to leave the country. Their faith needs to be proved under trial. And I believe that God will not let them down if they really believe in Him. I doubt the kind of faith that is easy-going. Moreover they need to be here to witness to those who need Christ the most. My ministry will be restricted but they will have more opportunity to witness and uphold one another than I do. If all desert Vietnam, who is going to be here to witness to the other side?...This is probably my last communication with IFES. Pray for us that we might have the courage, strength and wisdom to face the coming fiery trial. Our Lord has risen. We are going to suffer, to die and to be raised up with Him in reality. Please extend our warm greetings to all IFES member movements.'

So, despite its freedom from foreign domination and its treasured autonomy, the Vietnamese movement's history came to an end. Some of its leaders were sent to re-education camps.

172

Although the training the students had received in evangelistic Bible study is one that will stand them in good stead under any regime, the door has now closed to campus ministry. IFES East Asia missionary secretary Ellie Lau, who was in Saigon the year before it fell, recalls the students' last request just before she boarded her plane: 'You may not be able to return to visit us again. That's all right. We don't want mere visitors; what we really need is your support in prayer. Just tell our brothers and sisters that we are still alive!' That request summarizes the means God has provided for continued ministry to the universities of Vietnam.

Thailand

Soon after the fall of Saigon, Laos and Cambodia came under Communist influence: and IFES has no work in these countries.[13] The next country, according to the 'domino theory' current in some Western political circles in those days, was to be Thailand. Here, however, a real work of God had taken place. There had been earlier examples of campus witness in Thailand: *IFES Journal* reported an informal prayer meeting in 1954 in the house of Helen Smith, a geography professor from Wheaton (who came back to Thailand again during the crucial years of the late sixties). But perhaps the student work's history really began when an OMF missionary pharmacist in Thailand, Mike Richards, felt a burden to reach the university students. He returned to London to secure a PhD, and armed with that obtained a teaching post in Chulalongkorn University. A pharmacy student, Suttida, had started a Bible study there in 1965, and this group worked with Mike to start Bible studies in other faculties. By 1967 there were two such groups, four in 1968, and eight in 1969. In that year IFES associate staffworker Andrew Way, of OMF, started working with the students.

In 1970 Chua Wee Hian and Ada Lum were invited to Thailand to assist in a training camp. Wee Hian was IFES associate general secretary: Ada Lum, too, was a worker of considerable experience. A Hawaiian Chinese, she started work with IVCF in Hawaii in 1955, and at first sidestepped David Adeney's repeated promptings to work with IFES in Asia. ('I felt the Lord needed me in Hawaii and couldn't get along without me there!') In 1962, however, she had been persuaded to join the young work in

---

[13] Although IFES associate staffworker Andrew Way spent eighteen months working in Cambodia in the mid-1970s.

Hong Kong. It was a traumatic experience; she had a devastating sense of uselessness. 'I had to fall flat on my face time and time again. I was not in demand. Nor were hundreds being brought to the Lord. I found I had much more to learn from brothers and sisters than I could ever teach them. And for that, I will be eternally grateful to God.'

Ada helped to build up the movements in Hong Kong, Vietnam and Korea, and slowly found herself moving into an itinerant ministry. Her colleagues would say, 'The new student movement in Vietnam is getting off the ground with Paul and Maida Contento. But they must take their regular furlough. (That's once in a decade.) The students want to invite you to train them for a year in Bible study and evangelism. Will you accept?'

Or: 'At last we've found a few Christian students in Bangkok meeting for prayer and Bible study. They were amazed to hear that in other Asian universities Christians are doing the same thing and reaching out to non-Christians. These Thai students could be the nucleus we've been looking for for so many years. I've suggested that they have a training conference next summer, and they're interested. It would be good if both of us could go.'

Or: 'The student movement in country X is the fastest growing in Asia, but they have been very cautious about IFES or any overseas link, even though I've assured them that we are not a Western organization. Now they're willing to try you out for three months. They especially want to learn how to prepare and publish their own Bible study materials. They want you to concentrate on the women staff, but leave the men alone. This is the opportunity we've been praying for. How about it?'[14]

Requests such as these led Ada to spend the years between 1968 and 1977 with no home of her own and with what she called an 'uncluttered lifestyle', travelling around Asia with 'a baby typewriter and my entire home and office all in one suitcase'. She would generally spend between one and three months in a country, conducting Bible study workshops and training national staff to produce study guides adapted to their particular context. (By 1974 Chua Wee Hian described her as 'a continual headache...Over twenty fields and movements are asking for her services at the same time!'[15])

[14] John W. Alexander (ed.), *Believing and Obeying Jesus Christ* (IVP-USA, 1980), pp.253f.
[15] David M. Howard (ed.), *Jesus Christ: Lord of the Universe, Hope of the World*

This was Ada's role in Thailand for six months in 1970. The Huahin conference in June of that year was a turning-point for the Thai movement. Chua Wee Hian spoke on the principles of evangelism, Ada Lum trained the students in its practice and in evangelistic Bible study. On three afternoons the students went out in twos to witness in a nearby village 'with their knees trembling', as Wee Hian recalls, 'but after they began to open their lips to testify to their countrymen, they became courageous. When they returned to Bangkok, they were on fire with love for the Lord. Some of the leaders met daily at 5.30 a.m. for prayer.' At least six of the group won members of their family to Christ; many Buddhists came to faith. (At this stage Thailand had more Buddhist temples than individual Protestants!) The work spread into the high schools too. So the Thai Christian Students came together as a movement; and in June 1972 they appointed Prasarn Charoensuk as their first national staffworker.

Other leaders emerged too from among the students. Ada said of two of them in 1972, 'Krassanai and Tonglaw are young men who have God's hand on them. I am genuinely awed to observe how they are guided by Him and obey Him without hesitation... What they both have in common are discipline in their personal Bible study and prayer habits, faith, vision and hard work.' Both were to be key leaders in the movement, and Tonglaw Wongkamchai was to spend a number of years as the movement's general secretary.

Indonesia

Meanwhile, another pioneering field was opening up: the vast country of Indonesia, the world's fifth most populous nation. Christian students played an important role during the early years of independence, but as time went on a lack of truly biblical witness became apparent. In the late 1960s a number of Indonesians had been blessed through evangelical student groups while studying overseas, and felt a burden to share this vision on their return home. In 1970, Chua Wee Hian spoke at an Australian student convention where at least twenty Indonesians were present, and asked them, 'Has the Lord got someone here from these Indonesian brethren who might well be God's man for his own people?'

(IVP–USA, 1974), p.177. Ada spent the years between 1978 and 1983 as IFES Bible study secretary, exercising a similar ministry internationally.

The answer turned out to be Jimmy Kuswadi, a leader in the Overseas Christian Fellowship at Hobart, Tasmania. He returned to Djakarta later that year with the backing in prayer and finance of IFES student groups in Australia and throughout East Asia too. In June 1971, a movement named *Perkantas* was founded in the Indonesian capital.

The outlook was not entirely encouraging. John Chambers, an IVF-Britain graduate teaching in Bogor, wrote in *IFES Journal,* 'Several Christian groups working among students have already found it an uphill, disappointing mission... *Perkantas* faces the same problems. The students are willing to please, willing to say "Yes", but unwilling to commit themselves to anything... Unless we pray for this new movement, it will be stillborn. It cannot be imposed from outside; it must grow as the students themselves demand teaching, literature and fellowship. Let us take up the challenge and move the students of Indonesia through God by prayer!'

There was indeed a long journey ahead. Iman and Lea Santoso joined the staff to pioneer student work in the second largest city, Surabaya, in 1974; a third worker was added to pioneer Manado, Sulawesi, the following year, but there is no work there now. *Perkantas'* structure and strategy had to be different from that of other comparable movements, since a government directive forbade any off-campus organization being involved in campus activities. Consequently, *Perkantas* existed as a service organization, based on its student centre, having neither individual nor group affiliation. This could cause problems: some groups experienced God's blessing, grew rapidly, and no longer felt any need for the national movement. In 1980, therefore, *Perkantas* encouraged those who came to its student centres to form a federation of student leaders, meeting monthly for teaching and mutual support.

But recent years have seen rapid growth in the work. Fellowships in the *Perkantas* mould have been started in dozens of campuses spread across at least ten cities, even though staff have been located in only three. In a number of other cities groups have begun through students attending the national *Perkantas* camps. In Djakarta itself, the movement faced the embarrassing problem by 1980 of having eighty or more students coming each week to a meeting in a room that would hold only forty sitting on the floor. ('It's really like canned fish,' said a *Perkantas* report.)

And the high-schools ministry was growing steadily. But up to twenty cities were still unreached, and there was very little work outside Java; finances were very tight, and the handful of staff were overstretched.

In July 1981, therefore, *Perkantas* staff and council had a time of reflection and evaluation, in company with the IFES associate general secretary Isabelo Magalit and fellow IFES worker Ellie Lau (although *Perkantas* is not actually affiliated to IFES). The consequence was a move away from the somewhat decentralized structure that had existed hitherto, with the formation of a national office and the publication of a bulletin. A Potential Staff Camp was held for student leaders and graduates from nine cities, where each participant was encouraged to consider involvement as a full-time staffworker, a supporter in prayer and finances, or as a member of a graduate team similar to those in the Philippines. New staff have been recruited, and it seems that *Perkantas* is poised for very significant ministry in the late 1980s.

Certainly the doors have become wide open. John Chambers wrote in *Christian Graduate* in December 1981 of the vast opportunities presented by the compulsory religious education classes of Indonesian universities. In September 1980, 150 students came to the 'Protestant class' he was teaching: most were nominal Christians, and 'pretty turned off'. However, a number of senior students were 'totally involved and committed to the evangelism of the first year class'; and when the class finished in January 1981, 'more than half had made a commitment to the Lord and were dedicating themselves to His service in one way or another.' John adds, 'This is by far the largest proportion of conversions that we've seen in any religious education class since we've been here.'

NEW OPPORTUNITIES

Two other areas opened up in the second half of the 1970s, Central Asia and the Pacific.

Central Asia
Central Asia includes a number of extremely difficult countries. Bangladesh is 85% Islamic, Burma 75% Buddhist, Sri Lanka 65% Buddhist, while a fusion of Buddhism and Hinduism holds the adherence of 97% of the population of Nepal. In 1975, former UESI-India staffworker Viju Abraham was appointed as IFES

staffworker for the region.

Viju's dream was to see evangelical student movements from at least three of these countries affiliating with IFES by 1979. This did not come to pass, but nonetheless there has been steady growth. In **Nepal**, an Evangelical Students' Fellowship had come into being back in 1970. They faced difficulties in their outreach, since for much of the seventies the authorities frowned on Nepalis changing religions, and anyone found baptizing was liable to imprisonment or a heavy fine. (Indeed, even at the time of writing religious freedom cannot be taken for granted in Nepal.) One of the students in Kathmandu had just completed a two-year prison sentence for distributing Gospels and preaching.

This group died out by the mid-seventies; but there were a number of graduates who had a vision for student work. A Bible study group restarted in 1976. A little later a keen Indian graduate, formerly president of an Evangelical Union in Kerala, went to Nepal, and the work developed a more solid basis. This brother gave himself unstintingly to the development of the work, sometimes walking hours on foot to visit a lone Christian student in a rural area; he also succeeded in launching a literature work without finance from abroad.

In 1979, a completely independent national evangelical student movement, the Nepal Biswabidyalaya Christia Bidyarti Sangati, came into existence. Personal evangelism and student camps brought many to know the Lord. One letter in 1980 spoke of 'a wonderful camp arranged with three days' notice', which attracted twice the number expected: 'Many seekers came to a commitment and a few have joined the church.' Still there was a real sense of supernatural conflict: 'the power of darkness is unleashed... Local unrest and extremist movements' had made life very difficult for the few believers in some parts of western Nepal. Nonetheless, they were trusting the Lord 'to establish many group Bible studies, prayer cells and contact groups in strategic centres'. The following years saw at least two major steps forward, with the appointment of a Nepali part-time staffworker, and the quarterly, serialized publication of an adapted translation of *Search the Scriptures,* which was warmly received and widely used. NBCBS's emphasis on Bible study, and the materials it is producing in this area, may well prove to be of considerable importance to the life of the growing young church in Nepal.

In **Bangladesh** likewise there were thought to be no more than twenty Protestant Christian students in full-time tertiary education in 1973. Visits by UESI staffworker Narayan Mitra and a group of evangelical graduates from Calcutta had led to the formation of a group in Mymensingh in 1974; and here too the work spread to other campuses, with the encouragement of IFES associate staffworker Bob Cutler (an ex-IVF-Britain staffworker seconded from BMMF) and Australian Baptist missionary Ros Gooden (an AFES graduate), among others. Five towns were represented at the 1979 camp. Early in the eighties, the Bangladeshis were able to form a national Bible Students' Fellowship, and to appoint the first Bangladeshi staffworker. But at the time of writing the work is still at an early stage, although national camps have been attended by up to 150 students.

Sri Lanka is a predominantly Buddhist country with a small Christian minority. An SCM has existed for years, but its influence on students steadily declined in the latter part of the seventies. Small evangelical Bible study groups arose spontaneously in the island's universities, and a fledgling graduates fellowship also emerged. Vinoth Ramachandra, a Sri Lankan who had been an undergraduate and a doctoral student in nuclear engineering in the University of London, returned home as an IFES staffworker in 1980. Annual training camps for students on a national level were introduced that year. In December 1982 a national evangelical student movement (the Fellowship of Christian University Students) was formed. In **Burma**, too, there are groups of Christian students, and a crying need exists for Bible study materials and training in small group Bible studies. A student centre will soon be functioning, with a national worker.

John Ray, the current IFES regional secretary for Central Asia, was one of the founder-members of the Pakistani movement. In 1981 John defined the task for IFES in Central Asia as being 'preparation for evangelism by example and precept, writing of relevant small group Bible study materials, "formation" of national staff and student leaders, mobilizing graduates into fellowships which help them integrate all aspects of life (family, professional, recreational) under the Lordship of Christ, and seeing students, staff, graduates, all of us built up as part of the church'. It is a huge task, and it has only just begun.

The Pacific

The Pacific region also opened up in the late seventies and early eighties – somewhat more spectacularly. The old-established movements in **Australia** and **New Zealand** had continued to flourish since the war, although both have changed their names from Inter-Varsity Fellowship as their membership began to include many students from non-university institutions.[16] By 1959 2,000 students were involved with the Australian movement: the Graduates Fellowship could claim 1,500 members, and the Teachers Christian Fellowship 1,400. Under the leadership of general secretary Ian Burnard, the movement made considerable efforts to assist the development of student work abroad, for example by giving scholarships for Asian and Papuan New Guinean student leaders to attend Australian conferences, and also by giving warm encouragement to the development of groups of Asian students in the various Australian state capitals.

Yet this perceptive determination was accompanied in some leaders by a belief that Western missionary work was essentially paternalistic, and that the day of Western missionaries had passed, except perhaps as 'tentmakers' in secular jobs. It is interesting that the resulting decline in missionary involvement in the student groups was accompanied by a simultaneous decline in evangelism. The energies of the movement turned more to intellectual and social issues, producing some valuable work, but, as a whole, becoming somewhat cerebral and anti-pietistic.

These trends continued until the mid-1970s. Graduates Fellowship groups declined. On the campuses, protest, alienation and restlessness were widespread among students generally (as in many other countries during the late sixties and early seventies), and a small-group atmosphere prevailed. Still, even in the midst of this gloomy period, AFES groups were the largest voluntary student groups on most campuses.

In the mid-seventies, the Australian movement decentralized its administration, setting up area committees in each region. Although in retrospect the Australians felt the change was poorly prepared, it has led to a broadening of support and involvement. But it took place when many groups were introverted and not very concerned for an outward, biblically based ministry to the campus and the wider community.

[16] Becoming, respectively, the Australian Fellowship of Evangelical Students and, in New Zealand, the Tertiary Students' Christian Fellowship.

'A number of features came together to change the gloom of this situation,' says Tony McCarthy, who became general secretary in 1977. 'Student leaders increasingly recognized that the malaise was fundamentally a spiritual issue, and that the remedy demanded a change in theological conviction.' Campus missions, which had disappeared from the scene for some years, reappeared. In mid-1977, one of the oldest and largest student groups challenged the conventional wisdom that the university was too large and the climate inappropriate for such an outreach. This mission sparked off a chain reaction, where a mission on one campus stimulated a willingness to risk such an enterprise elsewhere. The resulting wave of missions has gone round Australia once since 1977 and still continues.

'One mission highlights some of these trends,' says Tony. 'After a succession of student committees most of whose leaders had backslidden within two or three years of graduation, the University of Western Australia group mounted a mission with John Stott and John Smith as principal speakers. Not only did ten per cent of the campus population turn out to the peak meeting, but a 120-strong fellowship among the university staff was formed as an ongoing result of the mission.

'The wave of missions is evidence of the changed convictions of student leaders, a change reinforced by significant staff appointments and the growing influence of the national conference to encourage student leaders. Cross cultural missionary interest is also growing, a sign that missionary vision is again a significant part of fellowship life.'

In New Zealand the student groups have continued a steady and effective witness. During the 1950s university missions were a key factor in securing the growth and character of a movement which had till then been viewed by many as fledgling and suspect. By the end of that decade the groups were becoming the strongest religious organizations on campus, if not indeed the strongest non-sporting clubs.

For some years the movement's general secretaries were from abroad – Warner Hutchinson, for example, a former IVCF staff-worker from the USA, and Robert Withycombe from Australia – but these were well-accepted. Warner Hutchinson in particular was remembered for his 'imaginative and creative leadership that introduced a whole generation of students to a new way of thinking about evangelical religion... Warner realized that the new generation had to face a different world and must hold to and communicate the evangelical message in a way relevant to the realities of the sixties and seventies.' He left his mark on a large number of New Zealand students who moved on into the pastoral ministry. All in all, the sixties and seventies saw what the New Zealanders described as 'boom growth' in numerical terms, enabling them to branch out in such areas as a social work scheme sponsored jointly with Christchurch City Mission. By the late seventies some 2,000 students were involved nationally. Numbers have diminished slightly since then, in part because many students now live at home and commute to university, with inevitable results in terms of lessening involvement in campus life. But a healthy witness is maintained on campuses throughout the country.

One significant aspect of the student scene in these countries has been the strong groups of Christian students from abroad known as Overseas Christian Fellowships. These groups are made up largely of Chinese from south-east Asia, with a small number of Africans and Pacific Islanders. The first Australian group, OCF Sydney, was officially formed by six students in 1957; similar groups sprang up independently in the main centres of Australia, and appeared likewise in New Zealand. Over the years the Australian groups have grown to be very large indeed: in 1982, the average weekly attendance in Sydney OCF's Bible study groups was over 300, while there were OCFs in Melbourne with 120 and 160 members. Tony McCarthy, general secretary of the Australian Fellowship of Evangelical Students, has commented that in some cases the OCFs have been a great deal clearer about their goals and objectives than the 'native' student groups. In New Zealand, the OCFs are much smaller at the present time due to marked decreases in overseas student numbers. Even so, at one New Zealand campus 25% of the Asian students were attending the OCF in 1982, while a further 15% were involved in an Asian students' group attached to a local Pentecostal church. Down the years, very many students from abroad have come to faith in these groups.

Still more remarkable, perhaps, is the work of God through student initiative in another Pacific country, **Papua-New Guinea.** The work in PNG dates back to 1966, when two students from the University of PNG were invited to the Australian movement's conference. These two returned home filled with enthusiasm and started a group of six at their own university the following year. It was only a small group: yet many young people were being influenced by the work of Scripture Union in the high schools, and the work expanded rapidly, with much encouragement from graduates of the Australian movement who were working in the country. By 1975 there were twelve groups: by mid-1977 there were sixteen, with 500 members. That year was the first time that applicants had to be turned away from a national camp because of lack of space: 230 attended, including many non-Christians, and about 85 made professions of faith.

The years since then have seen tremendous blessing: by 1982 there were approximately 3,500 students involved in the groups! Perhaps the most striking thing is that the movement has no staffworker. It is difficult to think of another place in the world where such growth has occurred without staff involvement. A key role has been played by graduates of the movement, who have continued to be involved with the care of the work: and the connection with the high schools, whereby tertiary groups will be connected with specific high schools and visit them once a year, is also undoubtedly of significance. So too is the attraction of a movement that is genuinely indigenous. Papua-New Guinea is a young country, having attained independence in 1975, and there is a great demand for trained people: some of the movement's graduates are already in positions of considerable responsibility, and need much prayer.

Many of the other Pacific nations send their students to the University of the South Pacific in Fiji; indeed, its students represent the future leadership of eleven countries, scattered across 11 million square miles of ocean. The Christian Fellowship is one of the few groups in the University where different islanders associate together voluntarily – itself a demonstration of the reality of oneness in Christ – and their vision is, in the words of staffworker Rig Reddy, to become a 'training ground for the Christian leaders in the Pacific'. The CF was formed in 1973, when a Tongan student, Meleana Puloka, and a British lecturer, Gordon Wynne, felt a desire for Bible study, prayer, worship and witness that was not being met by the existing SCM group. After discussion and prayer with other like-minded students, they formed the USPCF.

There was much intercession: the students met for prayer each morning at 6.30 a.m. The group grew in spirit and in number, and by 1977 about eighty of USP's 1,700 students were involved. It was an independent, student-led group, which meant that besides the backing of several keen evangelical lecturers from Australia, New Zealand and the USA, the group was able to draw on the assistance of a number of different parachurch organizations. Indeed, it was precisely because the student leaders understood that IFES stood for a policy of student initiative that they affiliated with it in 1978.

There was, however, another reason. They had been involved with assisting high-schools work in Fiji, in fellowship with Scripture Union, and now the students began to see the potential for reaching all the tertiary institutions – schools of medicine, teachers' colleges, technical institutes *etc.* – in the region that USP served. They approached IFES for staff assistance in this task, with the result that Roger Mitchell, an evangelist with considerable experience in university missions in Britain, went out to Fiji with his wife Sue in 1980.

It was, said Roger, a 'more or less ideal situation': a sturdy group already existed as a reliable foundation for the wider outreach, and 'the student leaders and their supporters knew what they wanted done, and had themselves initiated and approved the fact that I had come to help them do it'. However, there was also 'a more overtly supernatural element. From the moment I arrived, I sensed it was just the right time for the development of the work. That it was God's time. I've lost count of the occasions when we were confronted by the verses "I set before you an open door", and "Not by might, nor by power, but by my Spirit, says the Lord".'

It did indeed seem that God Himself was stirring up the Pacific students, and that He had led Roger and Sue there to play a part within the wider movement of the Spirit. During Roger's first week in Fiji, he and Rig went to visit Fiji School of Medicine, looking for an ex-USP student called Margaret. It turned out she had been praying about how best to set up an effective Christian witness: and she became the founder of the CF there, which soon grew to thirty in number. A Christian student at Fiji Institute of Technology was approached by two Samoans: 'We've seen you carrying a Bible: are you a Christian? We're thinking of starting a Christian Fellowship: what do you think?' It 'just so happened' he was going to meet Roger that evening to discuss the topic! And at the agricultural college, the students had started a group

184

the previous term and approached the university group for help.

Thus, within two years, and in part through the many students who knew or had belonged to USPCF or a high-schools group, seven new groups were started and several more discovered or strengthened. In 1981 a national movement, Pacific Students for Christ, was born. Nor was it to be expatriate-led for very long. Before arriving in Fiji, Roger had described his concept of Christian leadership as being 'like 2 Timothy 2: sharing the things you've been taught with other people, who will pass them on to others again: training someone, making yourself redundant, and moving on'. Soon after Roger arrived, Rig left for theological training in Regent College, Vancouver, on an IFES scholarship: and a few months after Rig returned, Roger handed over his responsibilities and went back to England.

To tell the story in this way, compressing a great deal of labour into so few sentences, gives the illusion that the work was very easy. Indeed, the Spirit had brought a national movement into being in Fiji in an unusual way: but the element of spiritual conflict was not removed. 'Now that the work is established,' wrote Roger at the end of 1981, 'the devil is making a determined effort to undermine it': there began to be murmurs of opposition, and 'at the very moment we committed ourselves in faith to find Rig's salary, we knew we had no money even for stamps for the latest newsletter!' Nor will PSFC's need for prayer support be any the less during these first few years of its history. It is, after all, far easier to maintain enthusiasm during times of spectacular growth, when milestone after milestone rapidly passes by, than in the times of consolidation, when the rewards are not so immediately visible.

One more story, however, may serve to emphasize the potential of this work. Not long before they left Fiji, Roger and Sue met one of their former students, Nemia. 'What are you doing these days, Nemia?' they asked. 'I'm working as an engineer up on the new road...I stay in camp with the other men.' 'You'll have to try and get a Christian Fellowship going for them.' 'Oh, I have already, last Wednesday night. I asked permission and they all came. About forty of them. Afterwards three men prayed prayers of commitment.' 'When did you become a Christian, Nemia?' 'Last year at FIT, through the Christian Fellowship...'

THE MISSIONARY FUTURE

Such, then, is the work of the movements linked with IFES in Asia and the Pacific. By the grace of God a great deal has happened since the apparently calamitous years at the beginning of the 1950s when all foreign workers were expelled from China, the China IVF was clearly on the way to dissolution by the government, and scarcely any group of any size existed elsewhere in Asia, apart from Japan.

The changes in the conference ministry in Asia demonstrate how the movements have developed. In 1957, a small group of about a dozen staff – Chinese, Indian, Japanese, Filipino, American and English – met in Hong Kong to plan for the expansion of the work in the new universities that were opening across Asia: and such gatherings, attended mostly by staff, continued through the sixties as the movements became established. In the seventies, however, the conferences began to be marked by large delegations of students and graduates: and, as the movements were now a little more established, the conferences came to have a strong missionary emphasis.

The epochal first Asian Student Missionary Convention took place in Baguio in the Philippines in December 1973, and was attended by 800 students and young professionals from twenty-five countries (150 more had to be turned away). Unexpectedly high numbers posed problems to begin with – over 300 beds had to be found, and the caterer, who had planned in terms of 400, had to be appeased. But the event was an eye-opener to many. 'Most wonderful for me was to pray for the first time with other nationalities for God's work,' said one Hong Kong student: and Philippines general secretary Harvey Co Chien told the gathering, 'Missions are no longer the monopoly of Western Christians. Asians have not sold their birthright.' As a direct consequence of the convention, Leni Sison, an IVCF-Philippines worker, went to Mexico in 1976 on IFES staff to pioneer a high-schools ministry in Mexico City – the first Asian to work with IFES in another continent, apart from general secretary Chua Wee Hian. The theme of the East Asia conference in Singapore in 1977 was 'Into All the World'; and later that year, in response to a recommendation from the regional consultation, Ellie Lau was appointed to travel throughout East Asia as regional missionary secretary.

Various national movements have held missionary conventions

during the seventies. India held its first in 1972, Singapore in 1974, Japan in 1976. To that tally may be added Taiwan, with its first such conference in 1979 attended by 1,400 people; the Philippines, where over 500 participants have attended the last two student missionary conventions; and, obviously, the long-standing missionary concern of the movements in Australia and New Zealand. Since the 1973 ASMC, Chinese, Filipino, Indian, Japanese and Korean graduates have gone out as missionaries: while the student groups in Hong Kong, Malaysia and Singapore have sent student missionary teams abroad for learning experiences in their vacations.

It must be so. Healthy growth in the IFES student movements must inevitably lead to a Christlike concern for the needs of the world: and in Asia those needs remain titanic, even at the level of student evangelism. In so many places the campuses remain unreached: vast areas of north India, Mongolia, North Korea, Vietnam, Laos and Kampuchea. IFES is still exploring the best ways in which to respond to the spiritual needs of the students in China. Less than one tertiary student in 1,000 is involved, so far as we can tell, with the movements in Japan, India or Bangladesh.

The call to the Asian movements, then, is to unceasing missionary involvement. Isabelo Magalit, whose passionate commitment to evangelism and missionary vision as IFES associate general secretary between 1972 and 1982 has left its imprint on the continent, summarized the needs: 'We are not going into all the world if we evangelize only in the cities and not the tribes; if we reach the professionals and students but not the labourers and factory workers; if we go only to the responsive and back away from the resistant; if we enter only the wide open doors and make no concerted attempt to penetrate the curtains of iron or bamboo or teak.' The task continues.

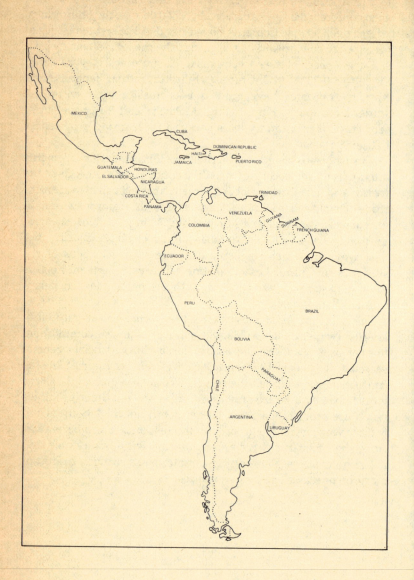

5
Latin America

The story of IFES in Latin America begins at the two geographical extremities of the region, in Argentina and Mexico.

In **Argentina**, an evangelical student group had been formed in La Plata through the efforts of a young British accountant as early as 1936.[1] One member of that group was a medical student named Gwendolyn Shepherd. While doing postgraduate studies in the USA she encountered IVCF; she attended the 1947 IFES General Committee at Harvard, and returned to Argentina with an enthusiastic vision for student work.

After months of prayer, the Pena Biblica Universitaria of Buenos Aires came into being. By 1951 it had had among its members a number who were to become leaders in various different denominations. Three prayer meetings were taking place each week, plus a Friday Bible study and an evangelistic meeting every fifteen days.

But **Mexico** was to be the first Latin American country to affiliate to the IFES. Stacey Woods toured Mexico, Central America, Colombia, Jamaica and Cuba in 1944, and wrote in *His* on his return that the 'need for a clear-cut fundamental witness...is far greater than I could have imagined possible'. Pioneering such a witness would 'probably be very slow and difficult and perhaps disappointing', he suspected, but there were openings for English teachers in the continent's universities, and much could be achieved through student hostels close

[1] The first third of this chapter draws very heavily on chapters 3 and 4 of *La Chispa y la Llama,* by Samuel Escobar (Ediciones Certeza, 1978), where more detailed information can be obtained. Samuel is currently IFES associate general secretary.

to the campuses. 'Because of the prevailing attitude of suspicion in Latin America toward North America, and also for the sake of the students and the work itself, this work must become a national movement just as quickly as possible and have a strictly autonomous set-up.' After his visit, an evangelical group was established in the University of Mexico; and, as has been indicated, Ed Pentecost enrolled as a postgraduate student there in February 1945, backed by the American and Canadian student movements.

It took some time for the work to gather momentum. The government was legally non-religious, but there was virulent anti-Protestant feeling in some parts of the country. 'Probably not six months have gone by in the last fifteen years when some have not been killed for being Protestants and many more burnt out of their homes,' Ed wrote in *His*. However, he had begun making friends. 'Yesterday I made contact with two believing students. They both tell me they know other Christian students, and are going to make a list of them so we can arrange for a get-together soon. This last week we have also gone further with contacts in the Polytechnic School, and are planning a social time with them in our home this Saturday. These are just the barest of beginnings; we know that only earnest prayer can make them become profitable.'

By 1949 many students without church connections would visit the Pentecosts on Sunday evenings for a time of conversation and singing. Ed was also able to take several students with him on preaching tours outside Mexico City, doing a combination of evangelism and health education. 'Almost every approach to student work as we know it is closed,' he wrote. 'There are no campuses...no dormitories or residences...Hence the importance of a home open at all times to students for personal interviews, Bible studies and prayer is evident.'

By mid-1950 Ed was working with some thirty students, most of them from Catholic backgrounds. There was still much opposition, but by the following year four groups existed in different parts of Mexico. There were also signs of student initiative, which had been a missing ingredient hitherto. Some students had attended IVCF-USA camps at 'Campus-in-the-Woods' – a 'veritable breeding-ground of North American leaders', as Samuel Escobar termed it. Mexico's own first student camp took place in 1952.

In Mexico City, a new house became necessary. Ed found what he believed was the right place – at a time when he had precisely $4! But 'the day we signed the contract the money was on hand, and the first month's rent of $110 was paid. Telephones are almost an impossibility, but four days after moving into the new house the contract for the telephone was signed... For three months we have been praying with the students, asking God for the furniture necessary. Last Saturday our prayer was answered definitely' – and the answer included a dining table and enough chairs to seat twenty, all a free gift. 'When some of the students learnt of this, all they could say was "Let's pray", and together they got down to thank the Lord.'

By mid-1953 the Puebla group had seventy-six attending its meetings, although a liberal theological organization had sent a worker to the university there with the avowed intention of destroying the evangelical group! The Mexican student movement affiliated to IFES in that year.

Ed had a concern for the rest of **Central America** too. As early as 1948 Ruth Petty of Latin America Mission had been working among students in Costa Rica, supported entirely by IVCF in Canada and the USA, along with former IVCF-Canada staff-worker Fred Denton. The January 1948 issue of *His* announced the formation of a Union Evangelico de Estudiantes Costarricenses by a group of seventy high-school students. Honduras likewise had five high-school groups at this time, and Ruth formed another group during a visit to Panama a few months later.

Most of these groups turned out to be short-lived (a problem that has dogged the area ever since). Still, when Ed toured the region late in 1954 he found that Christian students had been meeting in Costa Rica since June of that year, while a student group was gathering at the home of Presbyterian missionary Robert Thorp in Guatemala, and an enthusiastic fellowship existed in the university at Leon, Nicaragua. In January 1955 the first IFES-sponsored Central American Student Congress was held, in El Salvador, and a keen university group began in Honduras soon afterwards. A magazine, *Avance*, began in 1955, and was being sent to at least nine South American countries before the end of the year.

Meanwhile Ruth Siemens, an American schoolteacher, had gone to Lima, **Peru**, where several attempts to organize an evangelical student group had failed. Ruth was gifted with 'more

191

than average persistence and prayerfulness', wrote her fellow-worker, John White, later. 'Wide-eyed femininity gives no hint of her iron determination and teuton thoroughness! Most important of all, she has vision and a blithe optimistic faith.' She began Bible studies with seven or eight Christian students, who at times invited non-Christian friends. But the lack of students willing to take initiative forced a change of policy, and by mid-1955 there were two Bible studies in her home, primarily for the unconverted. Non-Christians were struck by the friendly atmosphere at these studies and by the discovery that the Bible was a comprehensible book! Thus the Circulo Biblico Universitario came into being. One of its student leaders was to be Samuel Escobar, someone who, in John White's words, grew 'increasingly obsessed with university evangelism'.

In 1957, Samuel pushed the young Circulo into showing the film *Martin Luther*. The film was sponsored jointly with the Student Federation, and, as Samuel recalls, the CBU 'utilized publicity techniques common to other groups active in the university and contradicted the exaggerated prudence of the complex-ridden evangelical minority'. Advertisements on blackboards announced '*Martin Lutero*, the prohibited film. Come and see why it is prohibited!'. The first night, hundreds of students crammed the hall. The Student Federation ended up arranging two additional showings, admission by ticket only. At the second showing of the film, Communist students were present in force. Audience restlessness seemed to call for a prompt start!

But there were other reasons for starting early. The Apristas – a political group with a reputation for strong-arm tactics – wanted the hall. Violence seemed possible, and nervous CBU members suggested the doors be closed. Sure enough, during a pause in the film Aprista officials came to the front and demanded the room. Samuel coolly suggested the matter be put to a vote, and won an overwhelming response for continuing the film. The Apristas retired, muttering threats.

Sitting beside Samuel was a young CBU member, himself an Aprista sympathizer. He 'marvelled at Samuel's grace and tact', says John White, but he 'still seethed with indignation at the Apristas' intervention. Sweating with anger, he clenched his fists in anticipation of swinging them when the meeting came to an end. He knew the Apristas were waiting outside the door.'

That student was Pedro Arana, later to be IFES associate general secretary for Latin America. Samuel, however, counselled non-violence.

So did some other CBU members, though not for the same reasons. 'Some of them (among them one student famous for his "Mr Universe" physique) slipped quietly out of the back door,' says John White, 'while Samuel and Pedro went to face the music. Mercifully, they were to suffer little more than hot words and ruffled clothes.' It was a price worth paying. An estimated 1,700 students saw the film; open discussion followed, and 500 duplicated copies of *Faith and Reason* by Swiss IFES leader René Pache were distributed. It was the first time since the University's foundation in 1551 that the evangelicals had been seen and heard!

The same year saw forty students at a national camp, with participants from Cuzco and Arequipa as well as Lima. When Ruth and Samuel left Peru for work elsewhere, Pedro, still a student, became the main Peruvian leader, travelling up and down the country encouraging the establishment of new groups, pushing the Lima students into inviting students from elsewhere to their conferences, printing tracts and Bible study materials. It was quite a task. To travel from Cuzco, where the students came from poor Andean villages and thought in Marxist concepts, to Arequipa, where the group faced bitter Catholic opposition, would involve him in a three-day journey in trucks and rattletrap buses over the wild Andes mountains, with two nights in chilly inns. But by 1962 a national movement was formed, with Pedro as its first general secretary, and members in five university centres.

'A wave of student initiative – a sign that this was God's time for the work – was not limited to one place or country,' recalls Samuel. 'Students moved from one country to another sharing their resources.' In 1958, for example, Lima CBU member Enrique Giraldo went to Chile to study and establish contacts for student witness. International links through camps were also of importance; Bolivian and Ecuadorian students were present at the CBU's 1955 camp to catch the vision for university witness, while Chilean, Peruvian and Bolivian students were at a conference sponsored by the Pena in Buenos Aires, Argentina, the following year.

Gibran Isaias wrote in *Los Viejos Leones* of these early years that the groups 'began in the midst of poverty...But what counted was the decisiveness and conviction of their action and faith. The sacrifice of a handful of students who know what they want and have a living faith and fellowship is a greater guarantee of success...than all the noisy apparatus, installations and abundance of resources. For true student work is accomplished with fervour, nerve, sacrifice, heart, tears and joy.'

The concern of the early IFES pioneers was to promote such a spirit, and it was rooted, writes Samuel Escobar, in their 'great respect for the missionary principles found in the New Testament...The respect for local initiative, the search for local leadership, the decision not to impose prefabricated patterns of action and witness – all these principles developed from the very beginning a strong team spirit between foreigners and nationals which has lasted down through the years.'

COCHABAMBA AND BEYOND

By the late 1950s the IFES family as a whole were being mobilized to pray for Latin America. René Pache, vice-chairman of the IFES executive, toured the continent in 1956 on the way to the IFES General Committee, in company with Robert Young. The latter was a very suitable guide: a former IVCF-USA staffworker, he had learnt Spanish, then enrolled in an Argentinian university to help the work there. With the backing of IFES, he travelled throughout the continent to share the vision for student work. ('We on the staff in Latin America cannot forget his example,' said René Padilla later. 'When I travelled through South America, everywhere I went I met people who had known Bob Young. I don't know how he covered so much territory, but the Lord had surely used him.'[2])

Together the two men visited six countries, speaking to up to 1,000 people at a time. René Pache was impressed by the tremendous openness he saw. 'This is the hour of God for South America, the continent of the future,' he wrote in *IFES Journal*. Roman Catholicism was visibly losing the universities, in part because of its all-too-evident alliance with totalitarian regimes. René cited one Jesuit writer's comparison of the 'dynamic passion' of the rapidly-growing evangelical churches in Chile

[2] David M. Howard (ed.), *Jesus Christ: Lord of the Universe, Hope of the World*, pp.167–168.

with Catholic indifference: 'For evangelicals Christianity is above all total adherence to a living Person, whereas the only religion that most Catholics know is a series of meaningless rites, wholly unconnected with daily living. People who have been victims of vice, and turn evangelical, experience a radical change. The evangelicals present to them a Christ who can change human beings.'[3]

Yet there were many places where a 'powerful evangelical work' existed, but nothing was being done in the universities and schools. Immediate action was needed, in mobilizing prayer, in supplying the necessary finance and workers: 'the doors are wide open, and we should be very careful not to let this unique opportunity go by.'

These two streams – the growing initiative of the fledgling student groups across the continent, and the prayerful concern of the wider IFES family – came together in a Latin American conference at Cochabamba in 1958. This event marked a growing awareness that, valuable though contacts through correspondence and camp exchanges had been, they only partially filled the need for fellowship and co-operation. At the same time, declared co-ordinator Robert Young, 'the purpose of these meetings is not of an organizational nature'. The Lima group, for example, had expressed the feeling that they were 'all tired of the many university and even ecclesiastical organizations which had no existence other than the letterheads of their stationery'. So any decisions taken regarding future partnership were not to be 'final nor will they imply any obligation on the part of the groups. In virtue of its autonomy, each group will take its final decision'.

The conference delegates represented seventeen groups from nine countries, and included pioneering workers such as Robert Young, Ed Pentecost, Wayne Bragg and Ruth Siemens, active graduates such as Samuel Escobar and René and Washington Padilla, and student leaders such as Pedro Arana and Nelly Garcia who were to play a big part in the years to come. The main speakers were Samuel Escobar, John White and David Phillips. John White had been student chairman of the British IVF, was a medical doctor at a Bolivian leprosarium, and was to become IFES regional secretary for Latin America (and later the author of

[3] Ignacio Vergara, *The Gospel Message*, December 1956.

popular student books such as *The Fight*). David Phillips had been an active IVCF student leader in British Columbia and was now director of Cochabamba Baptist Seminary.

The main address of the opening evening was given by Jose Maria Rico, a converted priest and former director of the Catholic university student movement in Bolivia. That meeting also included a letter of welcome from the President of Bolivia, and all its proceedings were broadcast by a leading Cochabamba radio station! Of more long-term significance was the fact that, as Robert Young knew, 'Christians were praying for the conference from Hong Kong to Germany, from California to France'. John White expounded from Nehemiah the principles underlying student leadership and responsibility, leaving 'a profound impression on all of us', as Samuel Escobar recalls. Samuel himself spoke on the characteristics of the Latin American student, and David Phillips on 'The Servant of Christ'. This too was 'of immense value. Latin American "caudillismo"[4] and the "political committee" kind of leadership were a temptation against which many of us would have to struggle.... Through these two men God gave us from His Word that portion which would be necessary for us on the road that we were starting to travel.'

In evening sessions, delegates shared what God had done in their countries. 'The hymn we perhaps sang the most was "Cuán Grande Es El!" ("How Great Thou Art!"),' says Samuel. 'It aptly expressed our feelings at the time.' In business sessions, delegates hammered out with oratorical fire and painstaking parliamentary procedure the doctrinal basis upon which the work would develop. Sometimes two lines of minutes would summarize two hours of heated discussion. 'For example, what was the best way to express our unanimous conviction that justification by faith is essential to our message? IFES was presenting to us their Basis of Faith as a proposal: it was through that discussion that it became *ours*.... The deliberations over the name of the Congress, the formulation of objectives and the doctrinal basis were in reality an exercise in expressing the reality of what the groups represented already were.'

The conference adopted a unified strategy. The continent was divided into four regions with their own workers and training camps; firstly, Mexico, Central America, the Spanish-speaking Caribbean and Venezuela, where Ed Pentecost and Wayne Bragg

---

[4] *I.e.* a strong, quasi-dictatorial style of leadership.

were recognized as the staff responsible, but with 'the prayer that God would raise up and prepare more national workers'; Colombia, Ecuador and Peru, with Samuel Escobar as staff-worker; Brazil, where Robert Young would continue pioneering until a Brazilian was available; and Argentina and the remainder of the continent, with Luis Perfetti as staff. IFES offered to support these workers during the initial period. Samuel Escobar insisted that the nominations and assistance be approved by the Latin Americans at the conference, and a vote of confidence was given. Francisco Gutiérrez and Enrique Giraldo were appointed as national workers in Bolivia and Chile respectively.

Literature ministry was given special consideration. Professor Alejandro Clifford and TEAM missionary Paul Sheetz of Cordoba, Argentina, shared plans for a first-class magazine in Spanish for students and professionals. Alejandro 'patiently listened to suggestions', recalls Samuel, 'tried to unify opposing linguistic criteria and immerse himself in the overall mood of the Congress. At that time he and Paul Sheetz represented the best team in Latin American evangelical journalism, and Stacey Woods' vision attracted them to the task of IFES. Clifford's vast literary and political knowledge as well as his encyclopaedic understanding of the history of protestantism in Latin America were the delight of many delegates who stayed up until midnight in conversation with him. This stirred up the expectation and enthusiasm for what would later be *Certeza*, "The magazine for thinking people"' – a publication whose influence in student work and the Latin American churches would be significant in the years to come.

A literature committee was also set up to plan evangelistic booklets and pocketbooks, especially in apologetics. This was a vital field in view of what Samuel called the 'ever-increasing Marxist ideological deluge, which forced Christians to think more seriously of a biblical world-view'. In the event, the first books published by 'Ediciones Certeza' were *Authority* by Martyn Lloyd-Jones, *Basic Christianity* by John Stott and the book of the same name by Margaret Erb. 'To a certain extent', says Samuel, 'they defined the nature of the movement which was emerging. In many places the magazine and books opened up the way for the formation of groups and an organized witness. In the absence of manuals, a stereotyped style of work or an elaborate programme of public relations, these publications were the calling card of the movement.'

The magazine in particular was designed for non-evangelicals, and very effective; it had a circulation of 10,000 – mostly sold by students – and an estimated readership of over 50,000 by 1962. A typical issue might include articles on science, literature and philosophy, showing that reason does not rule out faith; a testimony from a university professor; a conversion story of an ex-Communist; news, a Bible study, a direct evangelistic article, and so on.

An Argentinian student borrowed a copy and was converted; in the same country, a man from a prominent family, but with a severe alcoholism problem, was given a copy by a missionary. He was converted and cured, later going on to become a provincial vice-governor. In another city, a librarian, the president of the local Catholic Action, found a copy and wrote to the editor to commend it; and after prolonged contact, he announced that he had found Christ as his Saviour. In one Venezuelan university, the magazine was the topic of conversation among both students and lecturers for days after each issue's arrival, providing unprecedented opportunities for witness. All this took place despite colossal distribution problems. In some countries custom officials would hold up consignments for three months, and in one it was suspected that whole shipments were confiscated. Mail delays alone meant that magazines took three months from the south to the interior of Brazil.

These years saw new groups appearing. In **Puerto Rico** in 1957, IFES staffworker Wayne Bragg had a providential meeting with a Paraguayan student, Cesar Acevedo, who had gained enthusiasm and experience as president of the Paraguayan group. They began to pray daily for the emergence of an evangelical student movement. Less than a year later a group had come into existence and held its first camp. By 1959 some forty-five students were involved, and they were seeking to plant high-schools work, besides reaching out to the many foreign students in the country. In the **Dominican Republic**, likewise, eight students began meeting in 1957, without knowledge of any similar work elsewhere. Their first conference, in 1959, drew thirty-five students. It was illegal for them to meet openly, so regular gatherings for prayer and Bible study were held in restaurants!

The IFES General Committee in Paris that same year brought changes. Ed Pentecost, Robert Young and Luis Perfetti left the staff and René Padilla joined. The remainder of the team consisted of Wayne Bragg, Samuel Escobar and Ruth Siemens, plus John White who was trying to have a pastoral and administrative ministry to the team and also travelling throughout the continent. The team covered large distances by bus, train and (occasionally) air, labouring at pastoral work, intensive teaching and person-to-person discipling.

Their mobility, says Samuel, was made possible 'by their dedication and enthusiasm; but also by their age, by families who were willing to have the husband and father absent during prolonged periods, and by the generous hospitality offered by friends of the student work throughout the continent. The validity of this kind of travelling ministry has been the subject of discussion...but in those early years there was really no alternative. Open doors in many places, contacts made in regional camps, interested pastors and missionaries – all these demanded the continual mobility of the staffworkers.' There were disadvantages: the fact that regional secretary John White had to travel so much did not allow for strong co-ordination. But the team's itinerant style certainly allowed room for student initiative, and allowed the work to develop an indigenous character.

The goal of the staff was long-term disciple-making rather than setting up 'a mammoth para-ecclesiastical continental structure'. Nonetheless, national movements soon began to emerge. These were autonomous, but a certain basic unity arose from the literature, from some of the methods used, and from the emphases recognized as general goals at Cochabamba. The small student groups appealed for help in planning their activities, and as a result John White and Samuel Escobar prepared a manual. Every three months they would send each group a duplicated chapter, plus six or eight evangelistic Bible studies with suggestions on how to use them, materials and detailed instructions for an evangelistic project they could carry out, and other suggestions.

But this was only giving the national believers the tools they could use – or not, as they chose. The team's desire was that responsibility should pass from IFES to the students and graduates of the countries concerned, so that the work was genuinely self-governing, self-propagating and self-supporting. 'This can only take place as the Holy Spirit raises up people in each country who understand the work and are willing to sacrifice for it,' wrote John White to his prayer supporters. 'The shift of responsibility will usually be gradual. *But we want it to take place.*'

THE EARLY 1960s

The 1963 IFES General Committee at Nyack, New York, saw the Mexican movement joined as an IFES affiliate by several others: AGEUP Peru, ABU Brazil, AUC Costa Rica and ABU Puerto Rico. It also saw active participation by the Latin American delegates, characterized by an insistence that evangelicals take the social and political dimensions of the gospel seriously and that the gospel be related to the broader cultural context of the different countries.

Mexico

The old-established Mexican movement had been through a difficult phase. Ed Pentecost's departure from student work in 1959 left a major gap, and the movement virtually ceased functioning, except for Mexico City where the work was restarted by Fred Denton from the American Bible Society. Mexico City had 100,000 university students by 1962, and there was obviously an urgent need for a full-time staffworker! Miriam Lemcke (later Mrs Luster), a former IVCF-USA staffworker and a Brethren missionary, was seconded to IFES for this task.

It was not an easy one. In early 1963 she held some 'very poorly attended' training classes. 'Gradually, some students began to learn to lead Bible studies which were not boring: specific and honest praying emerged little by little. One girl was even willing, after much persuasion, to ask her friends to an evangelistic Bible study on the campus.' But when the time came, the group were willing to meet only deep in the safety of a group of trees!

However, they had made a start. 'As the students began to see that the studies were interesting, we moved out of the trees. One morning we sat on the angle of a low wall. As we studied, two fellows joined us from one side and later another from the other side. They participated in the discussion taking Bibles into their hands. The leader was thrilled at their response, and declared afterwards that we were not going to hide ourselves in the trees any more but study right out in the open, where others could see us and join us if they cared to!'

In 1964 the arrival of Cochabamba participant Nelly Garcia from Costa Rica helped to give a Latin touch to the leadership.

That academic year twelve evangelistic Bible studies began, some led by students, some by Miriam or Nelly. In almost every case the Christian students had to be persuaded to invite their friends; but the avid participation on the unbelievers' part began to speak for itself. 'It is quite refreshing to see a carload of eight or nine students, perhaps six of whom are not believers, with Bible in hand, honestly searching to find what God has to say to them today,' wrote Miriam. A number were solidly converted; attendance at the main weekly meeting rose from eight in 1964 to thirty-five by mid-1965, and the group was divided into two to avoid losing the personal touch. The students also began to feel a concern to restart the work in other parts of Mexico, and journeys to Guadalajara led to the establishment of a Bible study there.

In March 1967, Miriam returned to the USA to get married. 'Many who had witnessed the growth of the Mexican movement through her ministry began to question the wisdom of her decision,' wrote René Padilla. 'Who was now to take over? What would happen when she left? Would everything fall apart? Should she not postpone, or even forgo, her marriage for the sake of the work? The answer came from a handful of students and young graduates whose lives, in one way or another, had been affected through Miriam during her stay there – they were ready to carry on without her!'

Students had already taken over the arrangements for the first national conference, and at that gathering (which included people from four or five university centres) the movement was reorganized and a constitution was approved. Jorge Chao – Miriam's 'right hand man', just about to complete his studies – was appointed as staffworker. It was 'the culmination of Miriam's work', wrote René. Within a year, half the movement's budget was being raised within Mexico. A solid foundation of leadership training meant that the movement was not tied to foreign help.

A visit by IFES staffworker Hans Bürki in 1965 was also of importance. Hans spent two months in Latin America, visiting five countries, and made a considerable impact. 'His style of Bible exposition, his vast awareness of literature and philosophy, as well as his pastoral ability to draw each person he spoke with into a dialogue on a personal level, were something unprecedented in the university classrooms,' wrote Samuel Escobar. In Argentina, for example, Hans spoke on 'Biblical faith and existentialism', 'Christian ethics and contemporary psychology', 'Christ and the new humanism', and 'Pestalozzi: humanism and Christianity in conflict', as well as sexual ethics, creativity in education, and the thought of Nietzsche! In every country his audiences listened and interacted enthusiastically, and some came to surrender to Christ. For the Christian students, it was both an answer to prayer and a lesson in the communication of Christian truth. Hans fitted in much personal evangelism as well, including a dialogue in one Brazilian cafe that lasted till 2 a.m.

Inevitably there was opposition too. 400 students came to hear Hans speak on Nietzsche at 6.30 p.m. one evening in the University of Mexico. 'Suddenly disturbance', says his diary: 'my translator wipes his eyes, and seconds later my eyes are burning as from cut onions. We stop for a moment, some students get up and leave the room. An atmosphere of alarm fills the auditorium. Thank God we realize in time it is tear gas. I speak into the microphone, "I will continue to speak to you of Nietzsche even with tears." There is a burst of laughter and applause, and the situation is under control and we settle down once more ... Ten minutes later ... a second load of tear gas in the pipe of the ventilators, but it has been neutralized by one of the Christian students of chemistry....

'The evening continues until 11 p.m. The tear gas episode was probably organized by one of the leftist groups and it has been most excellent propaganda, for everyone is talking about it...' Not only that: one of the students who helped plant the tear-gas bomb, Carmen Perez, was a staffworker in the evangelical student movement thirteen years later!

However, successful evangelism of this kind revealed glaring weaknesses in the Christian student groups, and an urgent need for training. Pedro Arana, René Padilla and Samuel Escobar were among the Latin Americans present at an IFES staff training conference run by Hans Bürki at Casa Moscia in September 1965, and they felt a burden for something similar in their own continent. Hans was brought back to Latin America in 1966 for four leadership training courses, in particular a course in Lima, which combined teaching on discipleship, Bible study, and the social and ecclesiastical situation of the continent, with practical experience in evangelism and a strong emphasis on prayer and meditation.

The course, Samuel wrote later, was a landmark in the history of the Latin American work. 'We had begun to articulate something which was very evangelical but also very much ours, something which gave form to all that we had learnt.' The presence of older pioneers together with younger staff and professionals created a strong sense of community, and this, combined with the in-depth training in discipleship, proved to be a vital foundation for the years that followed. 'The difference Peru made in work here is like a miracle,' wrote Tom Hanks soon afterwards from Costa Rica, 'and if the students carry through with even half the momentum in vision they are showing at present, they will be fantastic.' 'Those who went to Lima have been very active in starting Bible study groups, and since they began they have already seen some coming to the Lord,' Miriam Lemcke reported from Mexico. 'The excellent work of organization and the initiative in evangelism that our staffworker is taking are no doubt the result of what he learnt in Lima,' commented a senior leader in Argentina.

GAINS, LOSSES, REASSESSMENTS

Three more Latin American movements affiliated to IFES at the General Committee held in Wuppertal, Germany, the following year: ABUA Argentina, MUEVE Venezuela and ADUCEP Paraguay. ADEE of the Dominican Republic followed in 1971. The history of some of these movements gives food for thought.

Venezuela
The Venezuelan groups began in 1958, through the initiatives of TEAM missionaries Dale Schanely and his wife in Merida, and were much helped in the early stages by the repeated visits of René Padilla. Groups of students went out from Merida and planted work in Maracaibo, Caracas and Cumana; church leaders José Liscano and Ramon Rojas began student fellowships in Valencia and Maracay. Training camps played an important role in the development of a national vision: MUEVE held its first National Congress in 1966. By 1978 God had raised up fourteen member groups.

However, in the early 1970s René Padilla noted that 'a tendency in some leaders towards giving more attention to politics than to the gospel' had 'endangered the witness' in two cities, while the fact that many groups included university and high-school students and graduates and teachers too had hindered them from making an impact on any single front. Samuel Escobar wrote a little later that the 'organizing genius and distinctively Latin American style of leadership' of general secretary Ramon Rojas gave the movement 'a dynamism and an admirable ability to penetrate the universities with the message of the gospel'. But at times the very ability of MUEVE to evangelize effectively among students from non-evangelical backgrounds resulted in a certain alienation from some more traditionally-minded leaders in the evangelical community, whose conservatism 'was more concerned with outward forms than with essentials...This area represents a difficulty for the movement'.

Argentina

Argentina, of course, was the IFES group with the longest history. Several IFES workers had their base in Argentina: Robert Young, Samuel Escobar, John White, René Padilla, José Young. Yet in 1962 there were still only three groups. However, Doug Stewart's strong pastoral ministry in the early sixties helped many who were to take significant leadership roles in their churches. This pastoral ministry was continued by Anibal and Ines Moreira working in La Plata, with David Evans – a former president of the Oxford CU, and later Bishop of Peru – collaborating voluntarily as general secretary. By 1977 there were five affiliated and two associated groups, totalling about 100 members.

Various difficulties existed in the Argentinian situation. Most students had to work their way through university, and work plus university classes could consume 72 hours per week. In Buenos Aires students might also spend up to four hours a day travelling! The majority lived at home, and therefore remained in their home churches. Some pastors were very loath to 'lose' their students for the duration of a university career that might last seven years or more. Hence the student movement faced considerable ecclesiastical opposition at times.

Political instability created other problems for many years: public meetings and book-tables on university premises were impossible, and the sale of literature was very difficult. Geographic distances between groups and strong denominationalist attitudes in some churches hindered national co-operation. By the end of the 1970s there were still fifteen Argentinian universities without any evangelical witness whatsoever, and the movement had come close to complete collapse.

However, the picture was not entirely dark. ABUA had begun to collaborate in a literature ministry in the *Peña* bookshop in La Plata. This ministry has continued, and has since been extended with the recent addition of the *Certeza* bookshop on one of the main streets of Buenos Aires, thanks to considerable financial aid from IFES and IVCF-USA. This centre is now becoming a focal point for Christian students.

There were other factors too that have given grounds for hope. In 1979 the present general secretary, John Harrower, and his family arrived from Australia, at the invitation of the ABUA. John and fellow-worker Sheila Dale from Scotland have found considerable scope for ministry in the early 1980s. Sheila was in Argentina during most of the South Atlantic conflict, and was overwhelmed by the caring love with which she was surrounded by ABUA members. It was one more proof of how God's Kingdom transcends national barriers! The number of groups has now grown to eight, plus two associate groups. In Salta in the north, a group that began 1982 with just three members organized a weekend camp later in the year with over fifty participants! In view of the distances, the worsening economic situation, and the lack of full-time staffworkers, the significance of such local student initiative is obvious. And as Sheila says, 'God delights to do what seems impossible to man!'

Paraguay

The Paraguayan movement also had a long history, having been formed in 1951 largely through the efforts of Professor Reynaldo Decoud Larroso. He was an expert in mathematics and psycho-analysis, and fluent in Guarani, Hebrew, Greek and Portuguese; and through the movement and his professorship he became the mentor of a whole generation of Paraguayan Protestant leaders. But from its formation the movement faced a situation where the Jesuits were attempting to restrict evangelicalism by both legal and coercive means. In 1953 the evangelical students numbered twenty-six. The problems of long working hours, widely-scattered faculties, and the small evangelical churches' desperate needs for the involvement of their student members led to general discouragement and from June 1954 until September 1955 they did not meet at all.

Then the group gathered again, and re-established their

leadership and a daily 6.30 a.m. prayer meeting. They were accepted as an affiliate of IFES in 1967. However, the small IFES staff team was unable to make regular visits to the country. Towards the end of the decade there was a failure to pass on the vision to new generations of students; and, with a Campus Crusade worker based full-time in Paraguay and working among the same constituency, ADUCEP went out of existence by 1971. Only in recent years has the situation been right for IFES work to recommence in Paraguay, as will be indicated below.

Bolivia

A similar story can be told of Bolivia. As late as 1955 it seemed impossible to penetrate the universities in a country that was fanatically Catholic, but the law was changed and in 1956 a student group 'caught fire' in Cochabamba. Further groups were formed in La Paz and Oruro, and a national conference was held in 1957, where plans were made to reach the remaining universities. Two hundred students came to one meeting in La Paz, and Sucre ('Little Rome') and Potosi had been pioneered by 1959. In 1964, the Asociacion de Grupos Universitarios Evangelicos de Bolivia came into being; by 1967 it had some seven member groups, and was participating actively in the Evangelism-in-Depth programme in that country. Around the end of the 1960s, however, the AGUEB dwindled in membership, and here too the work has only recently recommenced.

Ecuador

In Ecuador, again, student groups were formed as early as 1957, by students who had attended a camp organized by the Lima group. Since that time, various attempts have been made to establish a student witness in Quito and Guayaquil. Overall, however, there has been little lasting success, and no national movement has emerged as yet. The student members have sometimes tended to be over-dependent on the various missionaries involved. At the time of writing, fresh efforts have been made by a Norwegian missionary couple, Arne and Kari Aarstad, to establish work in Cuenca; in Quito, Everett Bruckner and his wife, who are closely linked with IVCF-USA, have an effective ministry. There continues to be a need for dedicated student leaders, and for prayer that, this time, a permanent student witness will develop.

As we consider these last four countries, and add Mexico (where the work nearly died out around 1962) and Costa Rica (which affiliated in 1963 but now has no IFES-linked witness), it is plain that IFES has faced greater problems in some parts of Latin America than in most other continents, barring Latin Europe (and the strongholds of the Muslim and Communist lands).

Jack Voelkel, writing in 1973 as a student worker not directly linked with IFES, has offered two suggestions as to why this may be so.[5] Firstly, he suggests, 'Although evangelism lies at the very centre of its concern and philosophy, IFES in many places has yet to break out of the small-group, quality-over-quantity psychology.' He links this to the fact that IFES 'is seeking valiantly to tackle the difficult problem of aiding and mobilizing second-generation evangelicals, who are all too often trapped in their own sub-culture without the friendships with non-Christians that would serve as a basis for successful evangelism. In some cases, the discipling they have received in their churches has consisted of little more than a list of "do's and dont's".'[6]

He is enthusiastic about IFES's concern for a total world-view in which 'students are forced to think and fit all of life's challenges into the spectrum of their faith'; but he fears that 'at times an emphasis on the academic has caused a tendency to talk about theological problems rather than to be personally involved in aggressive (not offensive) evangelism. IFES, in a desire not to be superficial, has shied away from teaching the students a simple outline of the Gospel for presentation... Training for witness has often been theoretical rather than practical.'

Secondly, he proposes tentatively that the 'effectiveness of student initiative and leadership has yet to prove itself fully in Latin America. Some observers wonder if the Latin psychology lends itself' to such an approach. Rather, he suggests that in this particular cultural context students may be 'strongest and most aggressive when closely supported and guided by resident full- and part-time staff'.

These comments deserve serious consideration, coming as they do from someone simultaneously expressing a high regard

[5] Jack Voelkel, *Student Evangelism in a World of Revolution* (Zondervan, 1974), pp. 109–110. He played a major part in the pioneering of UCU-Colombia, which chose not to affiliate to IFES until 1979, some years after its formation (see below).

[6] He discusses these problems in greater depth in pp. 69–89.

207

for the IFES-linked ministry. The point about student leadership has to be seen in the light of the part it has played in the history of the continent as a whole. But Jack's suggestions are worth setting alongside some remarks made the same year by René Padilla (a doughty defender of student leadership!) on the need for sufficient staff input if well-grounded students were to be mobilized. At this time, the IFES-linked work in the entire continent had only fourteen full-time staff, and René was convinced this was simply not enough. Quite apart from the unreached countries, he said, 'The existing work can hardly be expected to have a healthy growth without more staff help.' Staff had to travel over large areas, which reduced the amount of time they could spend with student leaders in any one place. But, he wrote, 'The emphasis on itinerant workers requires a "minimum condition" (including especially a strong church ministry)' that was not always available in Latin America. 'On the other hand, wherever a staffworker has limited himself to a group (*e.g.* Felicity Houghton in Santiago and Doug Stewart in Buenos Aires) the result in terms of mature disciples has been rewarding.'

Staff today have somewhat smaller 'parishes' to cover than those of 1973, of course. But the earlier problems in several countries and the examples of Doug and Felicity – both of whom have been keen to ensure that the work was genuinely student-led as soon as possible[7] – demonstrate the importance of student initiative in these countries being backed by close support, guidance and stimulus from co-workers near at hand.[8] It is such people that the IFES family must provide, until sufficient national staff and graduates emerge and assume this supportive role.

In the light of this we turn to two more countries, in both of which the work saw striking growth in the 1970s: Brazil and Colombia.

GROWTH IN THE 1970s

Brazil

The history of the Brazilian work can perhaps be said to date

---

[7] The growth of student leadership in the group in Santiago, Chile, is described later in this chapter.

[8] *Cf.* Samuel Escobar's comment that often students 'grew, organized the work and came to have a permanent impact' when the itinerant staffworker's visit was 'supplemented by the presence of an older person deeply interested in student work' (*La Chispa y la Llama*, p.72).

back to a prayer meeting in 1956, when Robert Young and Brazilian student Dirk van Eyken prayed that God would establish a student witness in this largest country of Latin America. One result was that Robert visited Brazil, making many contacts. These were followed up by Ruth Siemens, who had pioneered work in Peru and now covered thousands of miles by bus seeking out evangelical students in every state of Brazil; Ross Douglas, a Canadian professor of nuclear physics teaching in Sao Paulo; and Curitiba minister Walter Kaschel. The first student camp was held in January 1958, with just fifteen students; the first university group came into existence in Curitiba later that year, and five more groups were formed by early 1959. EUSA missionary Dennis Pape was invited to help with a summer course; he caught a vision for the possibilities and started a work in Fortaleza in the north. Years of prayer and sacrificial effort culminated in the first national congress of the Aliança Biblica Universitaria in 1962, attended by eighteen delegates from eleven cities.

Brazil had an SCM for some thirty years, with a large full-time staff and virtual control of the youth department of the Brazilian Evangelical Federation. But this movement lacked a clear doctrinal stance; and although it had carried out some worth-while social projects, it was moving away from an evangelical position. In the early 1960s it became infiltrated by radical political elements, and it did not survive the political upheavals of 1964–68.

1966 saw two major steps forward for ABU: the commencement of two periodicals linking the far-flung groups, and the appointment of the first national staffworker, Japanese-Brazilian Neuza Itioka. But it was not an easy time. Brazil is a huge country, and apart from Neuza the staff team consisted of three missionaries, plus Ruth Siemens and fellow-IFES staffworker Wayne Bragg. (Wayne had moved down from the Caribbean to become ABU general secretary.) The team was hopelessly overstretched. Ross Douglas wrote to the IFES executive of students catching the vision for the work at the camp and then losing it again: 'Many times the effort has been unsuccessful because the worker could not visit the group within six months or a year, or even two years. Needless to say, it is more difficult to start another group at a later date... The establishment of a student movement seems to require a certain "critical mass" or necessary minimum in terms of human, administrative and financial capacity for the consolidation of the work initiated in camps and missions. This necessary minimum would seem to be a wise investment...'

But the process of creating this 'necessary minimum' by bringing nationals into leadership was slowly gathering pace. Two more Brazilians joined the staff in 1968. Two years later, Wayne Bragg turned over the general secretaryship to Brazilian Manfred Loitzenbauer, while Dennis Pape brought Elizabeth Coutinho de Barros on to the staff before leaving for Canada. Just names, it might seem – but they amounted to the emergence of ABU as a genuinely Brazilian entity, rather than something controlled by outsiders.

IFES involvement continued. Hans Bürki and Samuel Escobar visited many campuses during 1967–68 on speaking tours. The political climate was very tense, and the Lord rewarded this courageous evangelism; interest ran high and large groups attended the meetings. Unfortunately, many ABU groups were so small and weak that they could not adequately follow up the many contacts. It was an important lesson. From that time, ABU has had an increasing emphasis on training student leaders.

The years that followed saw rapid expansion. In 1972 ABU had twenty university Bible study groups; three years later God had raised up 120 groups in forty-five cities. Neuza Itioka became acting general secretary, and showed herself to be a worker whose commitment to prayer and fasting matched her strategic vision. But she took over at a moment of crisis: she was handling the southern half of this immense country on her own, and both the staff in the north had plans to leave!

So, seeing the impossibility of ministering adequately to the rapidly-growing movement, she appealed to the student leaders' congress to appoint more workers. The appeal was answered. Werner Haeuser was invited to interrupt his theological studies in the USA, and he returned as staffworker; former IVCF-USA staff Bill McConnell was seconded to ABU by IFES, while the Evangelical Union of South America provided five workers. 'Campus Interns' were introduced – recent graduates, or students interrupting their studies for a year, some of them from seminaries. Former Curitiba student president Dieter Brepohl, now ABU's general secretary, was one of the first recruits.

For Dieter, however, that year's internship was only the

beginning. Halfway through the 1974 student training conference, which he was leading, he became ill. Day after day passed without improvement, despite prayers and medical attention. Finally the conference speaker suggested that God might have something to say to Dieter through the illness. It was then that Dieter understood what was going on. 'As a high-school student,' he explained, 'I committed myself to serve God on a full-time basis. I wanted to go into the family business, yet I felt constantly that I was compromising my commitment to God. That's why I became an ABU intern – I was hoping that this year would fulfil my obligation.'

Soon afterwards Dieter was back on his feet, and returned to his family to announce that he was joining ABU staff and would remain there until God showed him the next step. (At the time of writing Dieter is still serving ABU, as general secretary.) A few ABU leaders had been praying for a staff core who would commit themselves to building up the movement for at least five years. They had realized that that meant praying for a spiritual crisis to occur in some students' lives. God was answering those prayers.

1975 saw several major milestones. High-school work began, not by ABU's decision, but through the interest and initiative of younger brothers and sisters of ABU students. ABU recognized this ministry in 1975 and backed it with a full-time staffworker the following year; university students and graduates also became actively involved, and within four years high-schools work was going on in twenty-five cities, with a beginning in a further eighteen. Graduate work was recognized at the same time, and a staffworker was appointed.

Thirdly, the ABU Press was officially organized. ABU had produced books in co-operation with mission publishers from very early on (Brazil, unlike the rest of Latin America, is Portuguese-speaking, so imported books did not altogether meet the need). But now a fully-fledged programme of translations and original work was begun, under the leadership of Milton Andrade and Bill McConnell. Progress was not always smooth; the recession of the late 1970s brought the Press to the edge of extinction, with a $15,000 deficit. But, as Bill said, God was leading them 'into and through the crisis. He couldn't get us to change some things as long as we thought we were doing just fine.' The following year saw income rise by 120% (the inflation rate was 60%), and two ABU books appeared in a 'Best of the

Year' list in a Rio de Janeiro newspaper. By 1982 inflation had risen to 110% per annum, but the press was surviving, albeit in very inadequate premises. (Shortage of space was so acute that the kitchen area was used for storage and filing, and the entrance was a space nine inches wide between a filing cabinet and the wall. 'Thin staff are called for!' commented Dennis Pape – not to mention a new headquarters, which would involve expenditure of $100,000.)

Two other highly significant events occurred in 1975–76. Firstly, ABU requested that IFES terminate its direct subsidy, apart from supporting IFES staffworker Bill McConnell. 'The first year was a real crisis,' wrote Dennis Pape, 'but the staff, sometimes with salaries three months in arrears, pulled in their belt, and trusted the Lord. The ABU became self-supporting. Graduates rallied to the cause, and some churches helped. The movement grew muscle.' By the end of the decade, the Brazilians were raising an annual budget of over $100,000. 'The costly experiment produced a truly national movement dependent on the Lord,' concluded Dennis.

Such growth was naturally reflected in outward-looking vision. Neuza had attended the first IFES Asian Student Missionary Convention in the Philippines, and had come back dreaming of a similar event in Brazil. She shared the vision with her fellow-workers; and just over two years later, in January 1976, ABU sponsored the first Latin American student missionary convention, back in Curitiba, with the theme 'Jesus Christ: Lordship, Purpose, Mission'. Five hundred delegates came from throughout Brazil and beyond, selected from no less than 3,000 who applied. (A high percentage of applicants were from the northern borders, 1,000 miles away.) All participants had to be recommended by their pastor and staffworker, and had to complete a preliminary correspondence course.

At Curitiba, concern for mission was presented as no optional extra. Rather, declared Valdir Steuernagel, all Christians are called to service in this world by the whole of our lives, most especially our professions. 'The concept of mission must not be the exclusive concern of missionary agencies,' he declared; 'it must be the concern of the whole church. Either the church is a missionary church or it is no church at all.' 'Holy Spirit, Your divine inspiration has throughout history stimulated different movements and peoples to an active missionary life,' prayed

Neuza Itioka on the first evening. 'Now is our time!'

This missionary concern was being expressed in action. A group of medical students in Belo Horizonte had been moved by the needs of Brazil's poverty-stricken interior, and resolved to forgo the lucrative city practices and go to the interior to start a hospital. Amid immense hardships, they founded Hospital Maranata, and later another hospital too in a nearby town. Many more graduate missionary projects sprang up in the slums and tribal areas after the Convention, involving doctors, dentists, dieticians, social scientists and engineers.

An example of the results that could follow was provided when staffworker Tonica van der Meer and a team from Brasilia stayed in the Maranata Hospital for a week of practical evangelism. They visited almost every house in the town, besides working with the children and preaching in the public square. 'The first night', wrote Neuza, 'over 100 people came to the meeting. Those who wanted to follow Christ came forward right there in the square. They were all visited personally by the students, who opened the Word and prayed with them to confirm and establish their faith. Practically a whole new church came into being in a week! The field was ready for harvest because the ground had been well prepared by the ABU graduates who founded the hospital.'

Curitiba also stimulated the formation of a creative writing work-shop, and a Christian Psychologists and Psychiatrists Fellowship. The latter met a real need. Brazil's fastest growing religion is not Christianity but spiritism; Brazilians of all classes have been pursuing the African cultural heritage through such sects as 'umbanda' and 'macumba'. In 1977 a Sao Paulo newspaper reported that all but one of the president's top aides attended spiritist meetings regularly. In the universities, spiritism was taught as folklore; while Jorge Amado, Brazil's most widely read novelist, was arguing that Marxism must build on a spiritist base to win the masses. There has been a desperate need for teaching on the subject in the student groups, since some spiritist sects make use of the Bible, and sometimes second or third generation Christians dabble with spiritism out of curiosity, impressed by its claims to spiritual power. One student explained: 'God is good. We don't need to be afraid of Him. But demons have power to harm: that's why we must placate them with sacrifices and offerings.'

ABU weekend conferences have been particularly effective in reaching such students, because they demonstrate visibly the fruit of the Christian faith in conjunction with biblical teaching. 'A life of open fellowship and confidence in the good God who has overcome the power of the evil one is often more powerful than argument,' reports Bill. 'Students often hold prayer vigils while an experienced counsellor spends days helping someone seeking freedom from the power of demons.'

But in the fields of psychology and medicine, spiritist healers are particularly influential. They also support a large number of psychiatric hospitals. This, said one ABU staffworker, 'is just one result of their belief. Their minds become twisted and they all go for psychiatric help.' The fellowship for Christian psychologists and psychiatrists was designed to help students studying under spiritist professors, to promote a Christian response to the spiritist medical philosophy, and to bring those answers to serve clinical psychology.

The main area of development in the early 1980s was perhaps in high-schools work. In 1980 the IFES Latin American movements launched a 'Year of Evangelism': the Brazilian leaders announced the emphasis with a fear that it would be 'just another slogan'. But, as Bill McConnell reported, 'God has written "O ye of little faith" across the calendar. We saw more conversions this year than all the years we've been in Brazil.'

Dieter Brepohl told of a Christian teacher named Arlete, in a Curitiba high school, who was encouraged by an ABU staffworker to organize a Christian meeting. She found to her surprise that 'by means of Bible study, prayer and sharing, God began to touch hearts. Students themselves invited their classmates, and the group grew in interest every day. Fear took hold of Arlete and the staffworker each time they met for evaluation; the work was assuming proportions they had never imagined.' They organized an evangelistic camp, expecting sixty participants at the most. To their horror, over 150 turned up, and thirty had to be sent back. 'What were they to do with all these people? But the most incredible thing was not the influx of people, but the way in which the Spirit manifested Himself in their midst as the Bible studies were given. One by one, dozens of participants began to yield to this supernatural presence.'

Back in school, the witness of the new converts was contagious. Arlete and the staffworker felt they should plan another camp.

'To the surprise of all, dozens more came to Christ. At the same time, groups of pupils started meeting to guide newly converted friends. These leaders organized Bible study groups, and by this time the new converts themselves were using materials published by ABU Press to witness to their colleagues. Multiplication occurred. Dozens of young people began to join the local churches. Over seven denominations received new blood, new brothers.'

'Dozens of similar stories are found in Brazil, fruit of the action of God,' concluded Dieter. 'Staff have been very busy preparing Bible study guides, doing follow-up, and integrating converts into local churches.' Bill told of the Sao Paulo high-schools staffworker, a full-time seminary student named Nelson Bomilcar, who was supposed to be visiting ten schools. He happened to share the vision with a teacher in another school, who then began a group; the superintendent heard of it, and asked for an explanation. As a result, Nelson was invited to speak to a group of sixty school principals, and they approved ABU's beginning work in the whole district!

Developments like these have meant that the Brazilian high-schools work is coming to need more staff than the universities work. 'Please pray with us,' says Bill. 'The issue is acute, because other groups, like the spiritists, want the same privilege.' In the meantime ABU are doing their best to train more helpers, and to produce more literature for the high schools.

In the early 1950s, it used to be said that 80% of young believers entering Brazilian universities lost their faith. God has changed that! The careful discipling of a few students in the early days has borne fruit, and today there are 2,000 ABU tertiary members in sixty cities, besides the high-schools work in twenty cities. There are sixteen full-time and four part-time campus staff. Yet even now the movement is just a drop in the ocean of Brazil's million university students, and 75 million people under 25. And pioneering Portuguese-speaking countries elsewhere, like Angola and Mozambique, await ABU's outreach. Already ABU have sent their first IFES missionaries to Europe, Tacito and Glacy Pinto, who went to the tough country of Italy in 1978. It seems only reasonable to expect that more will follow.

Colombia

The Colombian movement has been marked by an equally fervent zeal in evangelism in recent years. After the Second World War, Protestants faced persecution. The Evangelical Confederation of Colombia announced in 1953 that fifty-one Protestants had been killed, forty-two church buildings destroyed by dynamite, thirty-one damaged and ten confiscated, in the previous five years. Nonetheless, student groups were meeting for prayer and Bible study in Cartagena and Medellin as early as 1948–49. René Pache found no groups when he passed through the country in 1956, and reported that 'terrible persecutions are constantly going on; chapels are closed or destroyed, houses burnt with people inside, believers arrested and fined on the false charge of being Communists'. Bob Young met a student who had just spent several weeks in prison because he had given tracts to his friends. Yet around the same time large crowds of believers had gathered for big celebrations of the centenary of evangelical work in the country, and there were many conversions!

But the history of the evangelical student movement in Colombia really begins in 1968–69, when Jack and Mary Anne Voelkel of the Latin America Mission arrived in Bogotá as members of the Evangelism-in-Depth advisory team which had been invited to Colombia by the evangelical churches. Their responsibility was to be a liaison between the Evangelism-in-Depth programme and Christian university students. They had already spent a year in Peru with the same programme, in close contact with IFES, and saw student work as a key part of mobilizing the Colombian church in evangelism. But when they organized student retreats for training, there was little interest: some students were not true believers, others were too timid to witness. And among the pastors, the Voelkels found much fear of the campuses. Church leaders did not feel able to answer the students' questions, and indeed the vast majority did not have higher education themselves.

So when the Evangelism-in-Depth team left Colombia, Jack and Mary Anne felt they had to stay on, join a local church where many students attended, and build up a student witness. They met two couples willing to share this task, Santiago and Margarette Botero (who had been involved with IFES in Venezuela and Germany) and Antonio and Ruth Cortes. In early 1969 they held their first meeting with fifteen students in the

Boteros' garden. RBMU missionary David James-Morse (a former graduate of an IVF group in Wales) spoke on the importance of the devotional life; he introduced inductive Bible study, and the students practised it in small groups. It seemed fresh and interesting. The students agreed to form weekly cell groups.

And so two weekly meetings came into being, Sunday for night-school and Friday evenings for day students. Bible study and prayer were emphasized. But there was just one problem. 'We were concerned about evangelism,' says Jack; 'we talked about it, studied it, prayed about it, planned meetings for non-Christians, *etc.*, but *no-one* ever brought anyone who was not in some way already part of the evangelical subculture. I was deeply burdened. We had succeeded in organizing a "nice little student group", but across the street was a massive university with 15,000 students, and we weren't reaching any of them. How could God break this impasse?'[9]

An evangelistic film was arranged. The Christian students were invited to a preview, so that having seen it they could invite their friends on the following Friday. The first showing was a sell-out: but on the following Friday nobody came. One or two students confessed the reason: 'We don't really have many non-Christian friends!'

More and more the Voelkels began to feel that if they were ever going to reach the students at the notoriously anti-American National University, 'we had to somehow become a part of the university scene; we had to *belong*'. Jack applied for a lectureship; the Lord provided personal contacts with the authorities – but there were no openings. Classes began, but they continued praying that God would open the door, encouraged by many promises from Scripture. A few weeks went by. 'Had I misunderstood the Lord? I had almost ceased to hope, when the phone rang...''Mr Voelkel? Are you still available to teach?'' (*Was* I!)

'During the months that followed, I learned a hundred lessons. Mary Anne became a part-time student in Social Work.... Gradually the walls began to come down. Friendships were established. We decided to invite one of my classes to a party in our house and show a Moody science film. (I thought my veterinarian students would like *City of the Bees*.) The party was

[9] This section and most of the material that follows are taken from Jack Voelkel, *Student Evangelism in a World of Revolution*, pp.156–159, 163–165.

great, but the spiritual emphasis of the film (even though it had been carefully announced ahead of time) was too much of a shock. It fell flat. Fortunately, this difficult experience didn't end the good relationships that were being established with individuals.

'The next time, though, we tried a new idea. We involved our Christian students in the party. They helped us plan it and put it on. It was a wholly social evening and loads of fun. Our Christian friends were surprised that the non-Christians had such a good time without drinking! At the end of the evening, the leader of the group said, "Many of us here have come to discover that Jesus Christ can meet the deepest needs in our lives. We would like to tell you more about our experience. We meet every Friday evening and we'd like to invite you. Next week we'll be having a...."

'From that day on we *never* had a meeting without non-Christians, and this new experience did something for the evangelical young people. There was a new boldness to put up posters, give out announcements, and even invite classmates. When there was an evangelistic meeting planned, we all knew that it would be attended by a goodly number of those who needed to find the Saviour. The Christian students felt a growing need for more prayer and study, so we organized a luncheon Bible study and prayer time and this proved to be one of our most effective means of building them up spiritually.

'The next time we had a party, the students said to us, "Don't invite *your* friends, we'll invite *ours* – otherwise there won't be room." (Eighty arrived to pack out our living-room!)

'As individuals began to accept Christ, this added the dimension we lacked – a dimension of excitement and joy, and the sense of the Lord's close presence. What is more, the new Christians began to bring *their* friends in goodly numbers. We had broken out of the mould.'

Out of the mould and on to the campus, indeed. The breakthrough occurred in September 1969; in October the National University students started their lunchtime Bible study group, and two lectures took place, at one of which Samuel Escobar spoke on the topic 'Dialogue between Christ and Marx'. In December, the Unidad Cristiana Universitaria was formed. The following month Victor and Elena Rodriguez joined the work. In May 1970, the Voelkels left the country for a year of study. This necessitated the development of student leadership.

Jorge Atiencia was one of the first students who came to spiritual maturity through the life and witness of UCU. An Ecuadorian, his conversion had come about through Jack's inviting him to share their apartment for a month while his wife was away, and then studying the epistle of James with him every morning. During the next few months, Jack discipled Jorge carefully. After his graduation Jorge came on the staff, leading a team of students who organized Bible study workshops in local churches, and beginning programmes in two universities where no groups existed. As a student president, staffworker, and (at the time of writing) executive secretary, Jorge's vision, dynamic leadership and love of the Scriptures have been decisive in shaping the movement, especially in recent years.

1975 saw the establishment of a group in Armenia, and further groups were formed in Cali, Pereira, Medellin, Cartagena and Barranquilla, particularly as a result of concerned students making visits to universities where no groups existed, and UCU graduates fanning out into the provinces. The first national congress was held, in Medellin in 1977; the following year the movement added several more staff and grew in financial self-support. In 1979 they affiliated to IFES. During that year, eight staffworkers produced the 400-page UCU Manual, an attractively presented combination of working philosophy and practical suggestions.

At the time of writing, God has brought some 700 students into the movement's nine groups. Graduate groups exist in four cities. There are twelve nationally supported part-time staff, and fifteen of UCU's graduates are involved in social programmes sponsored by organizations such as World Vision.

An important factor in UCU's growth has been the staff-workers' concern to be living models of active evangelism and discipleship. 'Evangelism is really caught when one observes another sharing the gospel,' says Jack Voelkel. 'The danger is that we leaders get absorbed in planning and administration, meetings, counselling, and editing materials – and thus end up spending most of our time in our offices. While these ministries are all essential, we must have front line leaders who are actively evangelizing and taking students with them. At the same time we must use all the opportunities the Lord gives to us and speak of them often in the hearing of our group members.'

FURTHER GROWTH

The 1975 IFES General Committee added two national movements to the family: GBU Chile, COMCEDE in Central America.

Chile

Bob Young had been involved in an attempt to start a work in Chile in 1958 – something he called 'crashing the devil-barrier' – and so had Enrique Giraldo. But the first student camp took place during a visit by John White in 1963. Only two students turned up, and they were outnumbered by the speakers! But two results came out of this unpromising beginning. A group began to meet in Temuco in the home of Alliance missionary Bob Newman; and Felicity Houghton, working with the South American Missionary Society, approached John White and said, 'If you think I can be useful, I am willing to give myself to helping form a student movement.' That had taken courage. 'My sense of inadequacy and inexperience moved me to tears,' says Felicity as she recalls that time. 'All I can say is that God in His mercy took me on: no-one else would have dared to.'

In Santiago, the capital, God provided Felicity with a prayer partner. She was Irma Iskuche, a research worker in the university, and she helped Felicity with student contacts. At first they encountered questions as to whether they were not attempting to duplicate the work of SCM, but meeting with the SCM leaders made it clear to the students that 'their priorities were not the same as ours'. During 1964 Felicity and Irma met with a small handful of students for Bible study: but none of the students was yet willing to accept responsibility for leadership, and when eventually Felicity left for her first furlough in 1965, the group stopped meeting.

On her return to Latin America, however, she attended the Lima training course mentioned earlier, and went back to Chile with renewed vision. 'A few weeks later, our dormant group awoke to rebirth, and slowly began to grow.' (One of the leaders at that time, an engineer named Alberto Bull, was to be a pillar of strength to the GBU for many years to come.) Visits from itinerant IFES staff played 'a vital part in forming disciples, and in giving us a vision of what the Lord wanted us to do and become'.

In June 1967 Stacey Woods wrote to Felicity, 'Are you seeing the emergence of any potential student leaders? If so, these are the people upon whom you should concentrate. I am sure that this kind of responsible leadership is something to be developed. It just doesn't spring like a phoenix from the fire.'[10] The answer was yes. A conference was held in February 1967; attendance was low, and exams and other responsibilities compelled a number who did attend to arrive late or leave early. René Padilla noted, 'Humanly speaking, there was nothing to lead anyone to believe that this gathering would come to anything.'

But the talks and expositions by René, Felicity, and Doug Stewart were to be the final impetus needed to mobilize the Chilean students' gifts and initiative. Soon after the conference the students took over leadership of the Santiago group, and two of the leaders travelled with Felicity to Valparaiso to establish a group there. Another SAMS missionary, Margaret Lutley, was on hand in Valparaiso to support the new group. Key student leaders attended the IFES leadership training courses in Lima, which were 'of fundamental help to the movement', according to Felicity. 1971 saw evangelistic missions with Samuel Escobar in Santiago and Concepcion.

Felicity went on furlough again, but this time there was a group of graduates available to take responsibility and organize the first national congress, at which the movement was officially constituted and a national student executive was formed. Three years later the first national staffworker was appointed, and the movement managed to pay the whole of his salary at a time when Chile's inflation rate was the world's highest. The development of student leadership had turned the students into missionaries where God had placed them, and had also ensured a process of indigenization of the work.

Just one step was needed to complete the process. By 1977 Felicity wrote, 'We are waiting for God's time to appoint our first general secretary', a Chilean who would 'co-ordinate, inspire and nurture God's work'. This stage was reached in March 1980 with the appointment of Josué Fonseca to take over as general secretary for a movement now made up of some 200 students and ten groups meeting regularly. It was a classic example of a key component of the IFES concept of leadership – sharing vision and knowhow with someone else until they could take over the job and the original leader could move on somewhere else. In January 1982, Felicity arrived in La Paz, Bolivia, to pioneer

[10] See René Padilla's comments above, p.208.

student work there, with the backing of the Chilean movement. For a century, Chile had been a 'receiving country': now they too could be involved in missionary vision.

Central America

The Chilean movement has had to grow in a troubled political situation. But still greater problems have surrounded the other Latin American movement to affiliate to IFES in 1975, COMCEDE of Central America. Work had been going on in this region since the mid-1950s, as has been indicated, but somewhat inconsistently. Groups were restarted in Costa Rica (by Wayne Bragg) and in Panama (by a local doctor and a businessman) in 1958; and annual regional camps recommenced in 1959, drawing participants from Guatemala, Honduras and El Salvador. An attempt was made to begin a Central American student movement, but this was a 'complete failure'. Some of the groups represented had links with the WSCF, and disagreements resulted over the doctrinal basis and, indeed, the basic purposes of a university group. As a result, only Costa Rica affiliated to IFES the following year, with Nelly Garcia (later Mrs de Mendoza) as a staffworker.

In 1966 Rodolfo Saborio joined the staff, and three or four students and a couple of graduates began a more active group in Guatemala, partly as a consequence of the Lima training course. At the 1974 regional camp, a single movement was formed for the six Central American countries. The camp gave a new evangelistic impetus to the El Salvador group in particular, which bore fruit in the distribution of 5,000 copies of the joint IFES/Bible Societies publication entitled *Jesus: Model for the New Man*. As late as 1976, however, the work was still at a very early stage in Honduras, Nicaragua and Panama; and it was hoped that the development of regional collaboration would supply the help they needed. Even in El Salvador, where there were thought to be some 400 Christian students in 1977, scarcely thirty were involved with COMCEDE, because of the heavy demands that church programmes made of student members. Mardoqueo Carranza took over as COMCEDE general secretary in 1979 and was based in El Salvador.

Some years later, however, it seems that the work has developed most effectively at a national rather than a regional level. The **Guatemala** group – which had a membership of fifteen to twenty out of the 24,000 students at the University of San

Carlos – held a remarkable mission in 1978, in collaboration with local graduates, other Christian agencies, and students from the Central American Theological Seminary, which went so far as to suspend its classes for the occasion! Training sessions were held before the mission, attended by some 200 students, and the vision was shared with some seventeen churches, all of whom responded enthusiastically with every kind of support. During the mission, 18,000 books and leaflets were distributed through six book-tables, and over 1,500 students attended the ten lectures. These were again based on the theme 'Jesus, Model for the New Man'. 'The evangelistic work was intensive', wrote Mardoqueo. 'Forty students were converted and we witnessed dramatic scenes as weeping students surrendered their lives to the Lord. They were kneeling in the streets and the corridors!'

There were immediate benefits. To begin with, the Christian students realized that their unbelieving friends were neither 'super-intellectual' nor 'super-hostile'! Mardoqueo felt the collaboration with the theological students, and with those who did not belong to campus groups, was a source of particular blessing. 300 students had asked to take part in a Bible study as a result of the mission, and over 500 needed some form of follow-up. The student leaders got to work on a programme of visitation.

It was, however, an enormous task for so small a group; and, as Mardoqueo reflected afterwards, 'We did not have the necessary structure to receive all the wheat.' The 1979 appointment of Israel Ortiz as staffworker for Guatemala may prove to have been the turning-point for the work in this country. Israel has worked hard to deepen the group's spiritual life and commitment to prayer. A number of evangelistically-gifted students have emerged, and at the time of writing there are some ten to fifteen Bible study groups meeting in three universities, with eight to ten students in each group.

A similar situation has existed in **Honduras.** Honduras was the last country to join COMCEDE; but by 1980 some fifty university students were involved in the group there. The university group was being 'fed' with students by an effective high-schools ministry, in which a medical student, Guillermo Jimenez, had been powerfully used by God in evangelism. More than once, Mardoqueo used the IFES *Praise and Prayer Bulletin* to ask for prayer for a similar vision and concerted effort in the university.

In April 1982, Pentecostal evangelist Pablo Finkenbinder came to Honduras for a campaign in the national stadium, under the auspices of the Alianza Ministerial Evangelica Nacional, and the university group were able to arrange a meeting on campus. The time – 3 p.m. – did not seem ideal, but the secular television and newspapers turned up, and the auditorium was packed out by a crowd variously estimated as being from 1,500 to 4,000 in size! After the message, the evangelist invited the audience to give their lives to Christ, and to Mardoqueo's astonishment nearly 400 students responded. Several new Bible study groups came into being soon afterwards; personal evangelism received a new impetus, and many evangelical students joined the group who had not known of its existence. But, as Mardoqueo says, the huge task of follow-up posed the same problem as in Guatemala. The recent appointment of Guillermo Jimenez as staffworker is of major significance to the work in Honduras.

In **Panama** a group of a dozen students emerged in 1979, and grew rapidly in enthusiasm and evangelistic concern. Immigration restrictions and other factors have made it difficult for Mardoqueo to visit them. In **Costa Rica**, in contrast, there was a failure to pass on the vision to successive generations of student leaders: by 1980 the group was down to eight members, with little local support to guide them, and soon afterwards it died altogether.

In Nicaragua and El Salvador the student groups have had to learn to exist in the midst of carnage. In **Nicaragua,** the final fifteen days of the 1979 revolution saw 47,000 deaths as the government started to bomb its own citizens. When the new government took over, the COMCEDE group chose to merge with an interdenominational youth movement that had adopted a large part of the IFES working philosophy. The results of this remain to be seen.

In **El Salvador**, the university group continued holding five weekly meetings as violence climbed to unprecedented proportions in late 1979 and 1980 (a year in which 10,000 people were killed). From June onwards the university was closed. The student group kept in contact through a weekly meeting, despite the suspicions that a gathering of students might incur from the authorities. Private universities emerged, but these were open only to people with a certain economic status; the members of the student group objected to them in principle, and hence, despite Mardoqueo's strong encouragement, did not become involved in their evangelization. Instead, the students' anxiety not to be mere spectators in their country's tragedy was expressed in seeing to the food, medical and pastoral needs of nearly thirty-five families – over 200 people.

El Salvador had nearly 200,000 refugees at this time, including thousands of widows and orphans. 'Every story makes one want to weep,' wrote Mardoqueo. 'There are women of hardly 24 years left alone with five children seeking work.' The students would give each family the minimum provisions for a month – rice, sugar, kidney beans, and in the most urgent cases tinned milk. Two young doctors and two final-year students provided medical attention – especially for children – that the overworked hospitals were unable to supply: first-aid, minor surgery, vaccines, medicines for intestinal infections. Besides this, Scriptures and Christian literature were distributed.

Mardoqueo and his family stayed in El Salvador to co-ordinate this work. 'Jesus Christ has not given up guiding our country's history,' he wrote. 'Whatever happens, we are His! Of course, three or four bombs explode daily. The capital is a fortress. Many medicines do not exist. Relatives or people you know die every little while. But...even though I walk through the valley of the shadow of death, I will fear no evil, because *Thou art with me. Hallelujah!*'

At the time of writing, the death toll continues to rise. The aid programme is assisting 2,000 people. 'Catholics, evangelicals, left, right – if they need help it is enough for us,' says Mardoqueo. 'We need relief funds, but we also need prayer, and news that people are praying.'

DISCIPLESHIP AND THE 'NEW MAN'

The pressures on the El Salvadorean students to join the guerrilla forces, and the urgent need that any aid they provided should be entirely free of political taint, symbolize the constraints under which many Latin American Christian students are working. In many countries, structures that visibly work for the continuation of poverty and institutionalized injustice are all too evident. In such a situation, the Marxist analysis clearly has had much to offer.

As early as 1963 the IFES team spoke of Marxism making 'unbelievable gains'. Doug Stewart wrote from Mexico in 1975 that 'Marxism is about the only ideology at Chapingo, because it's an agricultural school and they're dealing with the basic problems of the country'. More recently, Bill Asbury wrote that 'the dominant ideology on university campuses in Brazil today is Marxism and its revised forms'. A Brazilian student doing a Master's thesis found that her professor, a Marxist, was unwilling to accept the results of her research, for ideological reasons. In another case, a professor postponed the approval of a graduate thesis, asking for a change of the basic premises and an adoption of a Marxist viewpoint.

'It is a matter for prayer,' says Samuel Escobar. But it also means that 'our staff in this area must be conversant with Marxist ideology and with those aspects of Christian faith which answer it directly'.

There has not been overmuch written material available, although Samuel himself has written a study entitled *Dialogo entre Cristo y Marx*. Samuel recalls a visit to one evangelical seminary, where every one of ten theses presented during the previous four or five years had begun with a Marxist description of reality, imposed by the professors as 'scientific'. Outside the evangelical church, the synthesis of Christianity and Marxism propounded by articulate theologians such as Jose Luis Segundo and Gustavo Gutierrez is influential. These writers begin by asking about the meaning of faith in a context of oppression. Theology, they argue, must be committed practically to an ideology of struggle; not to take such a stand is to support the *status quo*. Christ is to be encountered, writes Gutierrez, 'in the commitment to the historical process of mankind'. Salvation is fundamentally seen as political liberation.

The response to this in IFES circles is not in the first instance to attack liberation theologians' leftist ideology. 'Many theologians write from an equally ideological perspective,' says René Padilla. 'They adopt a capitalistic attitude, it gets into their theology and they are not aware of it.' The problem is rather that in presupposing the 'scientific' accuracy of the Marxist analysis, liberation theologians have failed to be critical of its materialistic assumptions: 'if you begin with a system already made up there is no way Scripture can exercise its function of clarifying things.' However, says René, 'We can learn from liberation theology that salvation affects life in history. Theology has to have relevance to life. Often we have not seen the social implications of sin and the gospel: we reduce everything to the individual.' But 'faith is never mere assent to doctrine. It involves obedience...And the church is a community of those who have believed and live a life of obedience.'[11]

Accordingly, the evangelical response to liberation theology is 'not simply to criticise it, but to make an effort, by God's grace, to produce something better, more biblical and more relevant', says René. This goes for the evangelical response to materialistic Marxism as well. 'Before being a convincing intellectual challenge,' says Samuel Escobar, 'Marxism is a challenge to action and commitment. The challenge of Marxism lies in the call to *do something* about social evils, to *fight for justice,* to *align with the poor and the oppressed:* especially in the Third World where social evils can be so blatant.'

Yet it is at this very point of 'praxis' that the Marxist solution faces problems. Samuel himself had learnt from Peruvian Marxists a concern to meet the needs of his people that his church had never given him. But he became disillusioned through watching the effect power had on erstwhile idealists, and realizing that Marxism could not cure the basic selfishness of the individual. This question of how the new man is to be created is basic to the evangelical response to Marxism in Latin America. Hence, of course, the widespread distribution of the Scripture selection entitled *Jesus: Model for the New Man.*

But what kind of action should result from the Christian's 'new birth' and 'new life'? One day in 1952 Samuel invited a Communist leader called Hector – later a guerrilla leader – to his church's youth meeting. 'Songs, a Bible reading, prayer, and then some social games. After that, cocoa and cookies. All provided by the church. As we walked back to the street car stop I asked Hector what he thought of our church. He told me bluntly: "It is very nice and easy to be a Christian. You see, they give you a room, they provide you a nice place for your games and then they feed you. In my own case I have to give to the Communist Party several hours a day of hard work with no payment. I am risking my life every time I attend a meeting. I put my own money into publishing the youth paper of the Party that I edit.... Yeah, it is easy indeed to be a Christian."'

[11] René Padilla, 'The Roads To Freedom', *In Touch* 1978, 3. See also *Liberation Theology: An Evangelical View from the Third World* (Marshall, 1979) by Andrew Kirk, one of René's co-workers in the Latin America Theological Fraternity.

To Samuel the lesson was clear. 'Only a real committed Christian discipleship can match the attraction of Marxist commitment. Part of this discipleship is intellectual seriousness, but also necessary are the disciplined life, the attitude of service, the evangelistic zeal and the joy of a clear relationship with the Lord. A half-hearted, easy-going kind of Christianity is no answer to the challenge of Marxism... We have to work out a clear biblical answer to the problems of injustice, suffering and social evils in our societies. The spiritualizing phrases from well-fed, well-dressed and well-paid preachers, who speak from the distance of the stadium platform and the anonymity of a TV studio, do not work here. It is the presence of committed, serving churches that live and witness in the midst of the suffering that will be more convincing... What a challenge for Christian students and graduates!'[12]

A strength of the Latin American movements has been their commitment to thoroughly biblical social action that goes beyond mere theorizing. One example is the Huaylas Project. Huaylas is a community in the Peruvian highlands, where thousands of homes and villages were devastated by an earthquake in 1970. The student movement got involved in physical and spiritual rehabilitation in the area, first through summer work camps, then through a much more far-reaching, long-term community redevelopment project designed to take into account the whole man. They set about building a small centre as a base for research in agriculture (with technical aid to improve crop-growing and agricultural methods), and for home industries (*e.g.* beekeeping), handicrafts and schooling, with the aim of training community members to tackle their own problems. A programme was planned, including areas of health and hygiene, education and family life, to stimulate economic, moral and cultural development. The permanent staff – some of whom were postgraduates combining their involvement with research for higher degrees – sought to play a part in the community's spiritual growth too.

Caleb Meza recalls one morning when an old Indian chief visited the students. It was breakfast time, and the team were deep in animated discussion of the meaning of the word 'church'. 'During the student chit chat and the passing to and fro of bread and butter dishes an old man enters. He wears a faded brown poncho. There is so much tiredness in his eyes. He sits down

[12] Samuel Escobar, 'Marxist Ideology and Christian Mission', *In Touch* 1981, 3.

politely at one end of the table and listens to us...Across the table names, concepts, themes are bandied...Ecclesia, Barth, Marcuse – will the old man know who or what we're talking about?'

After breakfast three students approached the old man – and found out who he was. It turned out that his community had owned the land in the area since the time of the Incas and had papers dating back to 1700. 'But then those rich landowners came and took advantage of us because we didn't know how to read...If we complained they called us Communists and took us to prison, handcuffed us, made us go on foot for hours, days. They kicked us, tortured us...We were few, but we were going to give our lives for the lands they took from us.' To the old chief it seemed incredible that a group of students should decide to give their time to his people, 'huddled away like a sack of potatoes at the far end of the frozen Andes, and shut themselves up here instead of enjoying the round of books, girls and cafes in the distant city'. To Caleb and his co-workers, however, no alternative existed. 'In this matter of need there is no middle way,' he wrote afterwards. 'Either we stand out or – by our silence – we comply with injustice. We must decide today how strongly we are motivated to help the dispossessed and to what extent we will get involved.'

In many parts of the continent such involvement has taken the form of literacy work, particularly in association with ALFALIT. This is a programme developed by Justo Gonzáles, an exiled Cuban evangelical writer, which teaches illiterates to read in 30 hours, introduces basic biblical teaching and culminates in the reading of Mark's Gospel in a simplified translation. (A combination similar to that of the Jesus Lane Sunday School project, which grew into the IVF group in Cambridge, England!) Such a programme achieves something of considerable significance without a huge outlay in time or money. By giving a few hours a month, a student can not only teach illiterates to read, but also train teachers to continue the work. In a pioneer venture in Lima in 1967, eighteen students taught twenty-three illiterates in one of the most crowded and deprived slum areas, without electricity or sewage disposal, while six other students worked with twenty-one prospective teachers. The whole venture was carried out in partnership with four local churches, two Presbyterian and two Pentecostal.

A visit by Justo Gonzáles brought to the student group in La Plata, Argentina, the challenge of the problem of illiteracy and the 'disgraceful quietism of those (like us) who by the grace of God have access to the university'. The students decided to get involved alongside an evangelical church in a slum area. They began with literacy classes for children; but as they learnt more about the situation they discovered that a crucial problem was the high number of children dropping out of school. Many parents were unconvinced of the value of education (which was alien in cultural forms and even in language); there was no money for clothes and school supplies; and the poorer children, who were dirty or ill-kempt, might well be segregated or even sent home. So the students turned their efforts to a tutoring programme. Involvement with health care, Christian education, dentistry and physical education followed. 'Our protest against the situation of the poor is not now, nor ever can be again, simply another topic of discussion,' concluded one student.

In many parts of the continent such stories could be duplicated. In Chile and the Dominican Republic, the movements have set up hostels for poor students. The desperate poverty of many Latin American students causes many problems for IFES's ministry; such hostels not only strike at the problem but become centres of evangelism and discipling. The Venezuelan movement formed a social agency which was conducting more than thirty social projects by 1976, including a vocational school, literacy, education, Bible teaching, and distribution of food and medicine in Tacagua, a slum area in Caracas; and community development combining Bible teaching, medicine, dentistry, farming, education, handicrafts and nutrition among the Guaraos, a native group. The Brazilians created a team of graduates to co-ordinate several similar projects.

In 1977 IFES appointed a Peruvian staffworker, Victor Arroyo, supported financially by TEAR Fund, to give co-ordination and pastoring to the projects. For this kind of work has its own attendant problems, as the La Plata group found. 'When the students fully realized the situation in which the people were living, they wanted to throw themselves into many projects that went far beyond their material and human resources. They learnt that they had to set realistic goals for what they could do. At the beginning many people were very enthused about the work and offered their services, but it soon became evident that not all could be counted on. The students realized that in the end what really counts is not enthusiasm, but rather a profound conviction accompanied by constancy in putting it into practice. They comment: "Many projects which are started in poor neighbourhoods, whether by political groups or religious institutions, are characterized by a lack of continuity. They often betray the very hopes which they have raised, leaving the people with the sense of having been 'used'. We decided that a distinguishing characteristic of our work as Christians had to be its consistency. Great nebulous projects are less important than small but consistent actions."'

A major ingredient of effective social action is the mobilization of graduates and professionals, and this too has been a concern of IFES movements in Latin America. René Padilla insists on the importance of seeing university studies as a time when Christian students 'prepare themselves to serve others, especially the underprivileged', rather than seeking a degree as a 'status symbol, or a charter authorizing you to exploit others, or a means to satisfy your "small ambitions"'. Groups of Christian professionals concerned to use their gifts and knowledge for the sake of others have sprung up in connection with the IFES work across the continent. An important factor in this development was the stimulus of Peter Savage as graduates' secretary for the Latin American movements. The first continent-wide graduate conference was held at Itaici, near Sao Paulo, Brazil, in 1979. This brought together eighty-eight graduates, from ten national movements.

A ministry aiming to build up a faith that is thoroughly biblical and marked by a relevance to every area of life must also be supported by intelligent evangelical literature. Here Ediciones Certeza has continued to play a vital part, having recovered from a severe setback when a stroke forced Paul Sheetz to leave the work without a successor being immediately available. For some years Samuel Escobar and René Padilla served in turn as director of the operation. In the early 1970s the work began to expand rapidly, despite an inflation rate in Argentina that stood at around 300% per annum in the mid-1970s and was still 180% at the end of the decade. In the mid-1970s the books were printed in Spain and distributed from the United States, since that was the cheapest way of doing it!

Ediciones Certeza now handles some eighty titles, including

general interest books, such as David Adeney's *China: Christian Students Face the Revolution* or Walter Trobisch's *Love is a Feeling to be Learned*; evangelical theological works such as the symposia *Christian Faith and Latin America Today* and *The Gospel Today*; the *Tyndale* commentaries; and a series of Bible study guides for groups or individual study. Translations have been published of books by such authors as John Stott, Ada Lum, F. F. Bruce, Michael Green and Howard Guinness; besides the long-term project of translating the *New Bible Dictionary*. The more difficult problem has been finding Latin American authors – for the non-Christian public in particular. 'We still have no C. S. Lewis!' says René. Graduates who have written articles for *Certeza* magazine are encouraged to expand them into books, and writing competitions and 30-hour writing workshops have been held.

The financial problems have been less easy to handle. Continued inflation meant that administrative expenses continued to soar, while sales fell as students and professionals were less able to buy books. Finally the situation became desperate, and in 1982 the operation was taken over by IVP-USA (although editorial control remained with a Latin American committee). This expensive rescue was an act of considerable generosity in a time of severe recession. But it made possible the continued production of intelligent, biblical books for Latin American students.

EVANGELISTIC VISION

Although the Latin American IFES movements have spent a good deal of effort on the development of biblical and practical social action programmes, evangelism has remained their priority, as they reaffirmed clearly at their continental Congress in Armenia, Colombia, in 1981. This has by no means been restricted solely to the personal and small-group level. For example, one of Samuel Escobar's contributions has been the conducting of university missions throughout the continent – in over twenty Brazilian universities in 1968, in Brazil, Bolivia and Peru in 1970, Argentina and Chile in 1971, and many more since. These were followed up by Bible study courses and camps for those contacted.

Periodical ventures in the mass distribution of Christian literature have also been undertaken. In the late sixties and early seventies, several countries joined in the distribution of the tract *I Don't Agree With God*, offering a free Bible study course. In

Brazil, the movement printed 400,000 copies – one for each student in the country at that time – then obtained addresses from the university administration and mailed them out. In Argentina, 50,000 were distributed, and 300 requests were received for the course. In Chile, the response was even greater.

The Mexican students distributed this tract too; a little later, in 1973, they organized a similar effort to pass out copies of the *Good News for Modern Man* New Testament, in connection with an evangelistic mission. 20,000 were circulated on a single campus. A rather more recent instance is the continent's second largest movement, Peru, which used the same combination of methods for outreach on a national level in 1981. A team of ten travelled some 13,500 kilometres; prayer weeks, fasts and vigils backed up evangelistic talks by Samuel Escobar and Nelson Ayllon, along with the distribution of 1,000 New Testaments and 20,000 tracts. Many students started Bible study courses, and there were numerous conversions.

In the late 1970s and early 1980s a particular openness became evident in the high-schools work. In Brazil, one high-schools staffworker remarked that 'The fruit is so ripe it is just falling off the trees!' In the Dominican Republic, which went for two years in the late seventies without seeing any conversions at university level, high-school students have been forming new groups. The work has expanded 'just as we asked the Lord', they say – necessitating the speedy development of much greater collaboration with local churches. At least thirty new high-school groups began in 1982. (By then the university work had recovered momentum: the National University had eighteen weekly Bible studies, many of them evangelistic.)

The opportunities in Mexico's high schools were what brought forth the IFES Asian movements' first missionary to Latin America. In 1976 no work existed among the half a million high-school students in Mexico City. There was a shortage of Mexican staff. IFES worker Doug Stewart had taken over the general secretaryship after Jorge Chao's departure, and he knew there was no-one to spare for this ministry, so he began to pray for someone from across the border in the USA. 'One day God seemed to ask him why he wanted an American, and from that point on he began to pray for a worker from anywhere in the world.'

Dick Dowsett, an OMF missionary working with IVCF-

Philippines in East Asia, saw the rest of the story. 'The very day he changed his prayer, Leni Sison, a colleague of ours in the Philippines, began to get the message about Mexico. After a week she came to my wife and said, "Rose, do you think I'm crazy? I cannot get Mexico out of my mind. Do you think God could be calling me to go there?" We lent her magazines about Mexico and in time it was wonderfully confirmed that God was calling her there...A man prayed in Mexico City. God answered by speaking to a woman in Manila – just the person for the job.'[13]

Leni was supported in prayer by students in the Philippines, Japan, Trinidad, Barbados, Canada and elsewhere. In some ways Mexican and Filipino cultures proved similar, such as the size of students' families. Yet in other respects, Leni had to face cross-cultural adjustments that a missionary from anywhere else would encounter. 'For example,' she wrote, 'I could not get over the fact that casual Mexican friends (a boy and a girl) could embrace each other warmly as a matter of course to greet each other. Such demonstration of affection would make the ordinary Filipino blush...Neither was it altogether easy for the Mexicans to understand some of my "odd" ways. When I talked about how we eat avocados with milk, sugar and ice in the Philippines, they grimaced: it is eaten here plainly as a vegetable! They almost did not touch my dessert when I served them sweet beans one time....' But Leni survived the adjustments; the students received her warmly and within a year she was able to start ten student groups.

Towards the end of her term of service with IFES, she married a fellow-staffworker in the Mexican movement, Alejandro Juarez. Alejandro had for some years been the sole Christian student in Mexico's Polytechnic University, and was a good example of what could be done by a student with evangelistic vision at tertiary level. He developed a novel evangelistic technique; as Doug Stewart explained, 'He has portable Bible studies. He carries his briefcase with little Gospel portions in it, and sometime, maybe, he gets talking with two or three students... "Let's have a Bible study on it!" and he opens his briefcase, passes out New Testaments and sets up a study!' Eventually, the years of witnessing bore fruit: there were a few conversions, a few other Christians turn up, and at last a group emerged.

Sergio Sanchez, Mexico's general secretary in 1980–81,

[13] Dick Dowsett, *God, That's Not Fair!* (OMF, 1982), pp.137–138.

provided another example of student initiative. Sergio was largely responsible for getting a group started at the militantly Marxist university in Chapingo. 'For two or three years,' says Doug, 'he was faithfully witnessing, inviting speakers, giving out tracts, doing everything, but there was no real response – and suddenly God broke through. Sergio gave out a tract with his name and address on it and one of the first years came to talk with him. He then went back to talk with other first year students, and that began a sustained contact.' A number were converted (including a professor of physical education), and a group of twenty grew up, with an aggressive evangelistic approach. Four meetings would be held a week – one for evangelism, one for training in apologetics, one for prayer and sharing among the leaders, and one for follow-up. A new Christian would always be encouraged to identify his new stance, publicly and immediately. And – since Sergio noticed how Marxist students would go into classrooms between lectures to review and sell attractive Communist literature – he persuaded his fellow-Christians likewise to go from classroom to classroom selling Christian literature.

Mexico provided a third example after Sergio became general secretary. The work in Guadalajara had died out, and in October 1978 the Mexicans made a request in the IFES *Praise and Prayer Bulletin* for prayer for its recommencement. Students and pastors were seeking help, and prayer was needed 'that God will guide and equip those who will be initiating the work'. Evidently that prayer was answered. In June 1980 Sergio wrote in the *Bulletin* praising God for 'the vision and responsibility of the Guadalajara group', who had 'travelled to the city of Tampico to establish a student witness there, by evangelism and discipleship courses'. In October 1981 he wrote more generally of 'a new awakening amongst our local group leaders. For example, the Guadalajara students are carrying out an extensive evangelism programme, including several cities like Chihuahua in the north and north-west of the country. These brothers also have a social project with the refugees from El Salvador and poor people in Guadalajara. A good number of local churches are involved.'

THE GOSPEL FOR LATIN AMERICA TODAY

An army of students with such a vision is urgently needed in a continent where, despite all the efforts that have been poured into evangelism, a massive amount remains to be done. Even the

Brazilian movement contains in its membership only a couple of thousand of the country's million university students; and all the other movements have less than 1,000 members nationally. Less than one tertiary student in every thousand is involved in the groups in Puerto Rico, El Salvador, Bolivia or Ecuador; less than one in 3,000, after all these years, in the two countries where the Latin American work began, Argentina and Mexico. Uruguay and Costa Rica still have no IFES-linked groups at all.

And it cannot be assumed that the pioneering vision will pass on automatically to those who follow. 'We see a generation of student leaders who can *talk* the jargon of discipleship, commitment, lifestyle, etc.,' agonized Samuel Escobar in the *IFES Newsletter* of May 1978. 'But they are not making disciples, they are not disciplined in studying Scripture, they are not practising the basic virtues of veracity, dependability, self-denial, and concern for the non-Christian which have been the secret behind the growth of their movements. "Back to the basics!" is the answer, I know. But it is also: "O God . . . do not drive me from thy presence or take thy Holy Spirit from me" (Ps. 51:11). Do not let our national movements be like King Saul, who began well and ended so tragically. O God we know that there is generational fatigue in every movement, but O God with thy might, overcome sociological fatality . . .'

Still, God is continuing to surprise His people with new things. For several years, IFES staff have been in contact with pastors in Cuba who have been involved in student work. In general it has not been possible for IFES representatives to visit Cuba or for Cubans to attend IFES events. But on one occasion, a pastor named Obed Gorrin was able to attend a training course in Lima, and shared news of the grace of God in raising up evangelical student witness in Havana and Santa Clara. He himself lived on campus in Santa Clara, where his wife Persida lectures in maths. Back in 1971 she had been asked to leave her job because of her Christian commitment. They appealed to different university authorities, but the decision seemed irrevocable. After much prayer they decided to appeal to President Fidel Castro. Within two weeks they received a reply stating that the case would be investigated; and Persida found herself re-instated, with back salaries paid! As a result, the Christian students became bolder in their witness.

Obed was enthusiastic about the opportunity to spend time

with people from evangelical student movements elsewhere. 'We sometimes feel like orphans,' he said. 'It is so wonderful to be welcomed into the family of IFES. Our student work is similar in aim and in evangelical basis to that of the Latin American movements. We even sing the same songs!' Obviously, unusual missionary opportunities are open to Christian students and graduates from Cuba, and this deserves prayer.

There have also been new beginnings in two countries where the work had stopped. In 1980, Dutch IFES staff Henk and Marieke Jochemsen went to Paraguay, where a handful of Christian students had been meeting in a Bible study group begun by Miriam Luster (née Miriam Lemcke, formerly on staff in Mexico). By mid-1982, six or seven Bible study groups had come into existence in different faculties in Asuncion, there were contacts in other cities, and the Grupos Biblicos Universitarios del Paraguay had come into being. A structure based on small group Bible studies – some more or less evangelistic – plus a monthly large-group gathering was meeting the problems posed by irregular lecture time-tables and students' jobs.

In September of that year, the GBU collaborated with the Baptists' student group in a student meeting with Luis Palau, and in the distribution of 12,000 tracts containing material from *Certeza* magazine. The auditorium – which seated 800 – was packed with over 1,000 people: over 100 students expressed a desire to receive Christ as Saviour, including some who had been involved in GBU evangelistic Bible studies. At the GBU's next meeting, nearly half of the fifty-five students present were there for the first time! The Paraguayan group are looking forward to the day when they will be able to minister to high-school students and professionals too.

In Bolivia, also, the work has recommenced. For Felicity Houghton, who had pioneered the Chilean work with such persistence from 1963 onwards, starting all over again nearly twenty years later in La Paz (the highest capital city in the world) was no small act of courage. But the Lord confirmed her call in a remarkable way. In 1981 Felicity was travelling to the Latin American movements' Congress in Armenia, and was anxious to get a seat on a particular flight that stopped over in La Paz. It looked extremely unlikely, but somehow she knew that a seat on that plane would be God's confirmation in what she was planning. Five days before the flight, she was given a seat: and sitting next to her was a Bolivian student, Marcelo Vargas, who had arrived that morning without a reservation to try to get a place.

Marcelo had been studying in Brazil, and had been converted through the student movement there; now he felt a call to serve God back in his own country, and he too was on his way to the Armenia Congress! At that Congress, fellow Latin Americans felt very much that God was answering prayer and opening up the way for student work in Bolivia. Other friends had expressed an interest too. Sven and Berit Kloster, formerly linked with IFES in Ecuador, were now based in Bolivia, a few students were meeting for Bible study and prayer, graduates of the old, now-defunct Bolivian movement were sympathetic, as were local pastors and missionaries. At the time of writing, Felicity, Marcelo and Maggie Anderson (seconded to IFES from EUSA) are hard at work alongside the Christian students; and over twenty students are involved in the group.

Perhaps a poem of Felicity's supplies a fitting way to conclude this account of some of the Lord's dealings with students and staff in Latin America:

JEREMIAH'S ALMOND

Once the tree's woken
there is power
which will not lag
until the bud is flower,
beauty unwrapped,
blossom in sight,
dark wood grown bright,
after cold night
the sunrise hour.

Lord, wake the tree,
wake the tree only,
only wake your tree.

Once the word's spoken
there is One
who will not rest
until the word is done,
promise fulfilled,
purpose achieved,
desire turned into deed,
out of the seed
a harvest sprung.

Lord, speak the word,
speak the word only,
only speak your word.

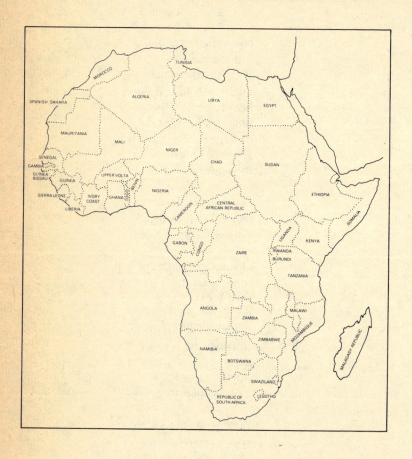

6
Africa

Evangelical student work got off to a much slower start in Africa than in other continents. In recent years, however, the Christian church in Africa has seen massive numerical growth, and this has been reflected in the student work. At the present time it appears that 10% of the tertiary students in five African countries are involved with evangelical student groups, all of them under African leadership; and in a sixth country, Nigeria, the evangelical student movement is the second largest in the entire world. Nevertheless, there is much still to be done in Africa, both in terms of pioneering and also in strengthening and establishing the large groups that God has raised up.

In 1955, there were only about a dozen universities in black Africa, many of them very small; and no evangelical Christian Unions anywhere. An unbiblical theology prevailed; liberal student groups already existed, and many people in the universities were determined to prevent the emergence of separate evangelical groups. As the then IFES general secretary, Stacey Woods, recalls, 'University authorities promised not to permit a second Christian movement... The door seemed shut to the IFES.'[1]

However, 'Unknown or unrealized by us, God had his own strategy'. The means was once again to be something that had begun by prayer. Back in 1938, on the suggestion of IVF-Britain's general secretary Douglas Johnson, a group of eight British graduates, serving in secular posts abroad, had started a prayer fellowship. From this grew the Inter-Varsity Overseas Fellowship, which aimed to give expression to the growing awareness

[1] C. Stacey Woods, *Some Ways of God*, p.54.

of the opportunity such posts gave for Christian service. In the post-war years it had a rapidly growing membership. 'None of us knew where the Lord was leading us,' reflects one of the founders, Tony Wilmot, 'but that's how it is, step by step.'

It was, in particular, the vision of IVF's graduate secretary Freddy Crittenden (a former Oxford student president who had been in Africa as a missionary and during wartime service) both to work with the African students in Britain, and to mobilize British graduates to teach in Africa. These two groups of people, he saw, could play a key part in shaping the future of many African countries. At this time there were more black African students in Europe and America than in Africa, and it is noticeable that several leaders of the student work in later years were involved with IVF-Britain as students (including Gottfried Osei-Mensah, the second African staffworker, and at least two current general secretaries of national movements); besides a number of African academics who have become staunch supporters of the student movements (including three current national chairmen). But that was a long-term development; in the 1950s, non-African graduates were going to play a crucial part.

For it was a critical moment. 'Bewildering change, revolutionary change, everywhere,' was Freddy Crittenden's description of Africa in 1955. 'Beyond the immediate reach of the Church many thousands of Africans are adrift – adrift with a vacuum in the soul. Islam or Communism may quickly fill the void. Time is short… Large numbers of dedicated, qualified Christian men and women are urgently needed for service with missionary societies, colonial governments, industrial and commercial undertakings' – and, of course, 'the African universities and technical colleges from which most of the future leaders of the country will come'.

As openings arose, therefore, prayerful action was taken by IVF to bring them to the notice of their members. Douglas Johnson recalls, 'We put up all our graduates overseas to the idea of getting students together for prayer and Bible study; leaving the initiative in the hands of the students, except for the jobs they hadn't the time to do.' At one stage there were nearly 200 members of the British Graduates' Fellowship active in Nigeria alone, many of them in secondary and tertiary education; and numerous others elsewhere on the continent.

Stacey Woods takes up the story: 'Quite naturally they did what any other Christian lecturer or professor would have done.

On a Sunday afternoon these men invited students, many of whom had had their secondary school education in mission schools and some of whom were Christians, to their homes for a Bible "reading". This was followed by questions, discussion, prayer, tea and biscuits. Some of these students were converted. Spontaneously on their own initiative they banded together, formed Christian Unions and applied for recognition as student societies. There was no propaganda from the outside. The IFES was never mentioned. In the face of such student initiative and responsibility, the authorities had little alternative but to grant the requested recognition.'[2]

In 1955, Tony Wilmot[3] wrote to Douglas Johnson from Accra, asking if someone could be sent out to help this work. 'DJ' was in close consultation with the IFES executive committee on the subject, and wrote back (in true IFES fashion), 'Why don't *you* do it?' Tony visited almost every English-language university in Africa in the last quarter of 1955, using twenty-two aircraft during eight weeks. Although no formal evangelical unions existed, he was struck by the openness to the gospel he encountered and by students' concern for fellowship and united witness. Students also expressed a strong pan-African feeling and a desire to establish effective links with similar students elsewhere, in good measure because they were aware that aggressive witness would provoke opposition.

The evangelicals who had found posts on university staff shared this concern to provide some mechanism for mutual fellowship, in a form that would be wholly African as soon as possible. In 1958, therefore, the Pan-African Fellowship of Evangelical Students came into existence, with a self-liquidating foundation committee working towards its replacement by elected leadership. Meanwhile, organized Christian Unions came into being. Kumasi and Legon in Ghana, and Nairobi in Kenya, were the first groups to affiliate to PAFES, followed by Monrovia

[2] *Ibid.*, pp.54–55.
[3] Tony Wilmot was an Oxford IVF graduate and a member of the student team known as the 'English Seven' who went to Sweden in 1935. After the war he worked in Ghana and Nigeria and acquired a high reputation as an evangelist and Bible teacher. He began annual camps through which a number of African student leaders emerged and caught a vision for starting student groups. Although he was never on IFES staff, he became one of the most widely-used evangelists in the African universities, arranging his work so that he could conduct university missions in both East and West Africa.

(Liberia), Fourah Bay (Sierra Leone), Salisbury (Rhodesia), and Ibadan (Nigeria).

Their numbers were strengthened by healthy Christian work in the high schools, where many graduates were active as teachers. In 1955, Scripture Union sent Nigel Sylvester, who had been converted in an IVF university mission at Cambridge, to Ghana to co-ordinate this work. (He is now SU's International Secretary.) Many young Christians from these groups came up to university with an enthusiasm for Christ and the Bible, and saw the need for a witness that was thoroughly biblical. One Nigerian student, for example, went along to a gathering of the liberal SCM at his university and found it was a dance with an unlimited bar. This was not the Christian fellowship that he wanted, and he helped to form an evangelical group! Student initiative of this kind meshed with the missionary initiative of graduate lecturers and schoolteachers from abroad, and the work grew.

'Attempts were made to prevent the spread of this movement,' recalls Stacey Woods, 'but they failed.' In one instance, an English bishop 'called an evangelical union together and announced to them that he was appointing a chaplain to that university college who would be responsible for their Christian activities. They were too immature and should immediately cease their prayer meetings and Bible studies. An African student quietly stood up and spoke, "Sir, you are an Englishman. We are Africans and we do not propose to be told whether we can meet to pray or to study the Scriptures on our own." The bishop had nothing further to say and hastily left the meeting.'[4]

The role of IFES was now to provide resources for the developing movement. A termly magazine, *Span,* was commenced, and met with immediate – and unexpected – enthusiasm, particularly as the number of African authors increased. (By 1964 it was reckoned that *Span* was read at least in part by nearly half the students in some centres.) In 1960 PAFES acquired its first staff-worker, a black American, Alonzo Fairbanks, who was based in Ibadan but travelled right across Africa. (His travelling expenses were three times as large as his salary!) John Holmes, who had been one of the pioneering university lecturers in Ghana, joined him in 1962, and was based in Nairobi.

Opposition to the establishment of evangelical groups had lessened considerably by now. Al Fairbanks' background as a

[4] C. Stacey Woods, *op. cit.,* p.55.

scientist provided openings into the universities and also a perennial topic; of about a hundred meetings between 1960 and 1963, he spoke on the issue of science and faith at around fifty! 'Everywhere he went he encouraged Christian students to grow,' wrote David Gitari, ' and he gave leaders of Christian groups every possible help.' 1962 saw major university missions conducted by John Stott with the groups in Fourah Bay, Legon, Ibadan, Salisbury and Nairobi. At the last of these there was considerable opposition, but over a third of the 415-strong student body attended the meetings.

1962 also saw the first PAFES conference for West Africa: a similar conference was commenced for the East African countries two years later – with 90% of its cost being met from within the East African region. In 1964 there came the appointment of the first IFES staff for French-speaking Africa. In 1965, when Cape Coast in Ghana and Ife in Nigeria had been added to the list of evangelical Christian Unions, and existing bodies in Khartoum (Sudan) and Addis Ababa (Ethiopia) had begun to show new strength, the first elected committee took over the affairs of PAFES. Daniel Jonah, a lecturer from Sierra Leone, became the first African chairman.

After another year, PAFES appointed its first black African full-time general secretary, David Gitari of Kenya (now an Anglican bishop). Alongside him a Ghanaian was appointed as travelling secretary for Ghana and West Africa, Gottfried Osei-Mensah, who is at the time of writing the world-wide executive secretary of the Lausanne Committee for World Evangelisation. They had a daunting task; David Gitari wrote that he flew to take up the post 'with fear and trembling. Thoughts of the task ahead frightened me greatly: but on landing on African soil my heart gathered courage, and the Lord granted me the power of the Holy Spirit to proclaim Him.'

At a time when very few ministers in the African churches had university degrees, a speaker who was an African and a graduate attracted considerable crowds. When David visited one Ethiopian college, 450 of the 600 students turned out to hear him, and in Khartoum he was invited to speak both at the Cathedral and the city's leading free church. When Gottfried passed through Khartoum he was asked to speak in the Students' Union, something the Christians had never dared to arrange before. Probably half of his audience of a hundred were Muslims, and it caused a stir in the Khartoum press that such a meeting should be held in a Muslim university.

THE FIRST NATIONAL MOVEMENTS

Tertiary institutions were now increasing in number, and 1966 and 1968 saw the emergence of the first national evangelical student movements in black Africa, in Ghana and Nigeria.

Ghana

Ghana Inter University Christian Fellowship – or Ghana Fellowship of Evangelical Students, as it became with the affiliation of diploma-awarding colleges – was formed in December 1966 with three member groups. By 1977 it had grown to eight groups with 700 members, and by 1981 to twelve groups with 1,500 members. T. B. Dankwa became staffworker in 1971 (making regular visits also to Sierra Leone and Liberia). When he started, his support came from Britain; but within three months he was able to raise it locally, and since then the movement has been self-supporting, with most of its income coming from graduates (85% in 1981).[5]

GHAFES is a movement that has been marked by evangelistic vision. Audrey Osei-Mensah wrote in 1971: 'In the past two terms I have been able to get to several of the Saturday evening fellowship meetings at Legon, where the large lecture room is crowded with between 400 and 500 students, and I have found myself wondering what has led to the large increase in the numbers in the fellowship. Certainly one factor is the missions which are held every three years.' As early as 1965 such a mission in Kumasi drew about half the total student body to its main meetings, with an estimated 80% of the students coming to at least one meeting: students were rushing through their supper to get seats, and all other society meetings that week had to be cancelled. About 200 made professions of conversion, including some who came to faith while reading suggested New Testament passages.

The Legon mission the following year was 'not just another university mission...it was a battlefield against the powers of evil', wrote Tony Wilmot. 'These men and women knew God and believed in prayer.' The Kumasi students joined in this prayer warfare, and 'were so conscious of their involvement that 25 of them travelled down by bus after lectures on Friday and spent all of Saturday night in prayer with their brothers and

---

[5] T. B. Dankwa has been IFES regional secretary for English-speaking Africa from 1980 till the time of writing.

sisters at Legon. The power of the Holy Spirit was apparent. God visited and blessed the mission.' Some 150 students made a profession of faith.

However, it became apparent that more work was needed after the missions. 'Many professions have been made,' wrote T. B. Dankwa in 1977. 'The problem has been lack of effective follow-up, and the fruit of these evangelistic efforts has not always been well conserved.' Indeed, Legon's membership was at that time under 300, considerably less than in 1971.

Mission '80 in Kumasi 'came after a long break during which we had not been able to hold major evangelistic activities', wrote staffworker Kofi Owusu, 'so both Christians and non-Christians were excited about it. The Christians spent time praying and fasting.' They also organized training in follow-up. The main missioner, S. M. Atiemo, was a past president of two GHAFES groups. On the first day of the mission over 1,000 of the university's 4,000 students attended. 'It was one of the greatest works of God I have seen,' said Kofi. 'There were over 500 professed conversions, with many and varied testimonies of healing and deliverance. Many brought their charms and protective amulets to be burnt.' A further 200 indicated their desire to accept Christ at Legon's mission the next year. But following up so many people still presented difficulties.[6]

It is worth noting that this evangelistic vision has not been divorced from socio-political concern. During the 1970s GHAFES students were concerned to present a biblical standpoint at times of student unrest, and some were elected to the students' representative councils. When tension arose between students and university authorities on a campus, the Fellowship executive would meet to discuss their approach to the problem. After the 1981 coup all Ghanaian students were sent to work in the rural areas for a period of months; and during this time the Christian students won their fellow-students' respect for their spirit of hard-working service, to such an extent that GHAFES members were elected as president and secretary of the National Union of Students.

[6] A comparable reflection was made after the 1981 mission in Ibadan, Nigeria, where some 160 professions were made, but only about one tenth of these remained in the group in the long run. In another mission two years later, 300 came forward for counselling, but staffworker George Moses again described follow-up as 'our biggest problem area'.

GHAFES's vision continues to be to reach every tertiary institution in the country, and to see a Christian teacher in every secondary school who can help the Scripture Union school groups – those same groups that played a real part in the birth of GHAFES. They are encouraging students to enter the pastoral ministry, with the aim of producing articulate evangelical ministers for the churches. Missionary vision is growing too; GHAFES has appointed an associate travelling secretary to work with the French-speaking African IFES movement, and Kofi Owusu looks forward to GHAFES being able to send 'graduate teams to needy areas both at home and abroad; to do there what the British movement did in our universities!'

Nigeria

Still greater development has occurred in the work in Nigeria. It began more slowly than the Ghanaian work, but by 1966 Tony Wilmot could write that the Ibadan group 'had been endued with a spirit of prayer, and week by week Christian students were experiencing the effective work of the Holy Spirit in leading their fellow-students to Christ. Weekly evangelistic meetings were accompanied by unprecedented blessing and many were being saved.' The following year one British leader described the group as 'probably rather keener and more active than any we have in Britain'. By this time the tradition of a three-yearly evangelistic mission was more or less established, as in Ghana.

Meanwhile, new groups were springing up. The Ibadan Christian Union and the Fellowship of Christian Students at Ahmadu Bello University, Zaria, had in good measure been the result of the involvement of lecturers from overseas. But the groups now emerging were often the result of Nigerian students meeting fellow-believers from established groups and catching the vision to begin work on their own campus, with the aid of the 'quietly helpful' visits of Gottfried Osei-Mensah. Such links naturally gave rise to a desire for a national fellowship and the Nigeria Fellowship of Evangelical Students was inaugurated by representatives of eleven groups meeting at Ilorin in August 1968.

One group not represented at Ilorin was the Nsukka Christian Union. Civil war had broken out in Nigeria, and Nsukka was situated in the heart of secessionist Biafra. During the war the CU members 'found they had the capacity for a quality of Christian life which hitherto they had thought it possible to find only in the New Testament'. Many were won to Christ; CU members were able to get involved in the leadership of local Scripture Union school groups. But conditions worsened; hunger grew, a week's salary would pay for a small cup of salt. 'The unbeliever or the non-committed "Christian" could try to alleviate his/her lot by a little dishonesty,' wrote John Onuera, 'e.g. sell a little government petrol, or if a girl, be the girlfriend of the boss. It took more than nominal Christianity to be clean honest, to refuse the request of a VIP or an army officer for relief food and to be impartial with friends as the rules demanded.

'These problems were discussed at the students' conference. Essentially, a greater willingness to surrender to the will of God was urged. To combat hunger, the system of communal feeding for groups of Christians, small-scale gardening, more giving by those better off were further stressed. All were reminded that suffering trains us to endure and that Christ makes a difference in *all* conditions. Members were again reminded of their responsibility to provide true leadership in their local SU groups. We had to prepare our own Bible study outlines and other aids since outside supplies were cut off by the blockade.'

The war ended in January 1970 – whereupon the group nearly split over 'extreme pentecostalism'! In March the students returned to a campus without tap-water, electricity or beds. Lecture notes were taken standing or sitting on cement blocks; textbooks were luxuries. But the CU 'was marked from beginning to end by more sincere prayer, Bible study, evangelism, and warm love. We prayed with faith and boldness born of experience of the power and love of the living God Who had stood by us in the dark days of the war. We prayed for everything as we were wont to do in the war – for exercise books, for water, for money, for health. We told other students that Christ is the answer to all situations. The war had proved beyond dispute that indeed, as the Bible says, "the heart of man is deceitful above all things and desperately wicked." Christ alone could change lives...

'The group demonstrated love in action. Some gave up one or two of their few clothes, others distributed exercise books and biro pens while still others gave cash. An encouraging number of students were converted and soon the number rose to about 100 consistent members.' Christian students from recently hostile parts of Nigeria showed spontaneous love which 'though natural for normal Christians, is nonetheless a *miracle* worked by the

Spirit of Christ', wrote John. 'Let us thank God that we of the CU/SU have no problem of reconciliation. Indeed, we never quarrelled. During the war Christian friends on both sides prayed for each other by name. We had all along been one in spirit even though physically separated. We praise God!'

By 1971, there were estimated to be possibly 1,500 NIFES members: and no staffworker. The result was the appointment of Kola Ejiwunmi, an untiring labourer, pastoral worker and poet just over five feet tall and with an enormous laugh, 'Uncle Kola' to a whole country and NIFES general secretary to the time of writing. Until March 1972 he had no car; and until 1975 he was the sole staffworker for the whole country.

It was not an easy task. God was blessing the work with rapid numerical growth. By 1973 there were thought to be some 2,500 students involved in groups linked with NIFES. By 1975 Kola was ministering to fifty-two such groups on safaris that might last four to eight weeks.

But there were serious problems. Throughout the early 1970s the Nigerian groups were torn by disagreement over the charismatic issue. As early as 1972 Kola wrote in *Span* of the 'perennial problem' of 'small but vocal and undoubtedly zealous splinter groups...raising the issue of the Person and work of the Holy Spirit to the point of controversy'. Over the next couple of years the crises reached their height.

Two unfortunate results were the alienation from the national body of certain groups that had come to see tongues as the 'one thing needful', and also the distancing of student leaders from senior friends who would have been their advisers. This could manifest itself in disagreement over secondary matters in which no fundamental doctrinal issue was involved – clapping, for example, or repetition of choruses. In some cases senior friends had perhaps not succeeded in 'incarnating' themselves within the prevailing campus culture. One experienced Nigerian leader felt that difficulties arose not because they disagreed with the Christian books popular on campus, but because they had not even read them. The generation gap could be worsened by the occasionally remarkable arrogance of student leaders who were convinced that God had begun a 'new thing' with them, and hence they had nothing to learn! Too often relationships no longer existed where advice and discussion would go deeper than polite conversation.

The consequences of this alienation became apparent when far more bizarre teaching swept the campuses in 1975–76. One popular speaker taught that the Rapture was so close that believers could hope to participate in it right now. Several reputable sources relate how at conferences students could be seen 'jumping up and down, practising the Rapture, trying to fly'. Soon the idea spread that running backwards might bring about translation to heaven, and on at least one notable occasion a whole group spent part of their conference running backwards around a room. Another widely-used speaker taught that, after having received the baptism of the Spirit, the believer should expect the 'baptism of fire', after which he would never physically die and his clothes would never wear out. (Half the leadership of one of NIFES' largest groups went over to one of these teachers, including the president and vice-president.)

By 1977 Kola wrote that 'after two to three years of upheavals in most groups there is a greater determination to "maintain the unity of the Spirit in the bond of peace"' and 'many genuinely spiritually-gifted students have been able to minister freely and effectively'. Even so, 'what may be called the "over-pentecostal" fringe' were 'on the increase' still.

In such a situation the importance of the student leaders and staff of NIFES in maintaining a faithful witness to biblical Christianity cannot be overstated. Kola had to wrestle with being labelled as anti-charismatic and therefore 'unspiritual' at the very time when hyper-charismatic groups elsewhere might be using his name to gain entry to a fellowship – without letting him know. Many groups guarded their independence jealously, informing neither the travelling secretary nor senior friends of their plans for missions or retreats. A second worker, Bayo Famonure, joined the staff in 1975, but money was short (and IFES internationally was facing a mid-year deficit far larger than in any previous year); a third worker was not appointed until 1977. With only two NIFES staff, a group could be visited only twice a year – perhaps for five to seven days in a whole year.

Various measures were taken to improve the situation: the appointment of associate travelling secretaries (*e.g.* lecturers) and the division of the country into zones. Each zone would have its own conference for teaching on such areas as programme planning, Bible study training and personal evangelism, besides practical discussions on current issues. Such events were welcomed by virtually every group. These were very necessary developments, because higher education was expanding rapidly; by 1980 NIFES had about 120 member groups, and by 1982 this had increased to over 260.

Slowly the situation has stabilized, although new movements and 'new things' have continued to rise and fall. In recent years a heavy stress on faith in healing has led some students to consider it unspiritual to go to a doctor or to wear glasses; there were three occasions during 1981–82 when Christian students went to a graveyard to attempt to raise a dead body.[7]

In some places, a 'deeper' Christianity has been taught that majors on externals, prohibiting tea and coffee, commanding the wearing of sandals as 'less worldly' than covered shoes, and discouraging shaking hands with the opposite sex 'in case you lose your sanctification'. Exorcism has occasionally been invoked for anything problematic, whether a malfunctioning film projector, a raincloud, or the 'demon of sleep' in a second consecutive all-night prayer meeting; and prophecies have been made – particularly in the area of political developments – with embarrassing inaccuracy.

And yet many of these problems are the kind of thing that has arisen on the fringes of revival movements throughout history. There can be no doubt that large numbers of students have continued to be brought to the Lord throughout these years. Many of the eccentricities have been the excess of something good, a desire to know more of God that has led to an uncritical acceptance of anyone claiming a 'new anointing'. The task facing student leaders in the coming years is to retain the evangelistic momentum while bringing a greater biblical depth and solidity into the lives of the groups.

Staffworker Joe Omeokwe wrote from southern Nigeria in 1979 that there was 'no other way to account for the current growth in the university CUs than the influence of the Holy Spirit... Almost everywhere this year there has been the same story of larger numbers of first-year Christians than ever before, so that many CUs have doubled their membership in the last three or four years. Evangelism is still very fruitful and many are coming to the faith each term. Quite often the CU has the largest

---

[7] However, a European observer cannot help wondering whether even these misguided attempts to live by faith may not be less displeasing to God than the inability of some Western Christian students to trust God for anything at all!

signed-up membership of any society, and it regularly has the largest meeting attendances in many universities... But it is easy for a group to become preoccupied by numbers and to be more concerned for quantity than quality. Large attendance and a full programme of meetings can sometimes mask inner hollowness .... Many members are young Christians, to whom doctrine at first seems peripheral: their emphasis is on personal subjective experience. Much youth evangelism begins there.... What seems to have declined is the habit of personal Bible study, and here we perhaps reflect conditions in the churches at large. A large part of our ministry must be to encourage and instruct students in how to study the Bible, alone and in groups... All this is hard work.'

But it was an essential task. Otherwise, he added, there develops 'an emphasis on sharing meetings, where personal testimony features more prominently than Bible exposition, a diet of subjective experience rather than objective truth. Group pressures can be very strong in such a situation and dominant personalities assume a disproportionate influence. The end result seems to be the introversion of the group and the emphasis on the "holy huddle", as the spiritual temperature rises. It would be nothing short of tragic if the groups were to be deluded into a wrong preoccupation with their own blessing in a day when the evangelistic opportunities are unparalleled.'

Three years later, Femi Adeleye (himself a former national student chairman of NIFES) expressed a fear that many students from such groups in his region 'are spiritual on the surface, but inside there is confusion, and after graduation they cannot cope. We send out thousands of Christian graduates, but at times we can search and search for them and they are not there. These are people who pray fluently, pray zealously, witness zealously on their own campuses, yet a year later you cannot find them anywhere.'

In the present situation, then, the ministry of NIFES student leaders and staff is one of tremendous strategic importance. The movement is by any standards a remarkable work of God. Somewhere between 20,000 and 30,000 students are involved nationally; NIFES outstripped the British movement in size in the early 1980s and must now be rivalling the IVCF-USA as the world's largest IFES movement. There are probably several thousand more tertiary students involved in the IFES-linked groups of Nigeria than in the rest of Africa, Latin America and the Middle East put together! The NIFES conference has for some time been the largest annual conference of any IFES movement, drawing 4,000 students by the early 1980s. It is where the Lord has been active that the enemy has been active too. Allowance has to be made, of course, for religious nominalism in the country. In 1975 general secretary Kola Ejiwunmi went so far as to estimate the proportion of 'definitely committed Christians' in the groups as 55% to 85%, and five years later he sought to put the movement's continued growth into perspective by suggesting that only 40% to 60% could be counted on as genuinely converted. This, again, has many historical parallels in situations of high numerical growth.

Taking the estimates at their most pessimistic, however, there is still tremendous cause to praise God. Even the large 'nominal fringe' represents a great opportunity for evangelism and discipling. On many campuses the fellowship will be over 300 strong, and virtually any student can direct a visitor to a CU member. In Benin, for example, up to 500 of the 4,000 university students are involved with the group. This strength appears to be directly linked to a widespread commitment to fervent, believing prayer. In Benin, again, over 250 students attend the 90-minute weekly prayer meeting; and throughout the country, days and nights of prayer are frequent occurrences. This commitment is doubtless connected to the fact that many students will have encountered the reality of black magic, and seen in practice the triumphant liberating power of Christ. Such a realistic awareness of the supernatural, free still from the undermining by media humanism which has occurred in the West, may occasionally go several steps further and run into excesses. But it is likely to place a high priority on prayer; and that will bring its own results.

The groups are strong even in the Islamic north of the country. During the Pope's visit to Nigeria in 1982, fanatical Muslim students demonstrated in Zaria with placards threatening to kill him; yet on that same campus the NIFES group draws over 200 to its prayer meeting and has 300-400 members. The ancient walled city of Kano is perhaps the Islamic centre for much of West Africa, and in December 1980 about 10,000 members of a fanatical Muslim sect rioted there for two weeks, causing thousands of deaths. And yet even here there are at least two sizeable NIFES groups. Femi Adeleye, one of three staffworkers ministering to some 5,000 NIFES members in this zone, was a former Kano group president; as president he received three death threats, besides a letter stating a date on which the entire fellowship were to be butchered.

Obviously, the student fellowships in such situations can provide good training-grounds for future missionaries. There remains a great need for training in personal and small group Bible study, and for the raising up of Nigerian Bible expositors in the churches who can provide a robust biblical grounding for the students' faith. In recent years the government has agreed to support some short-term staff as part of the National Youth Service Corps, and at the time of writing NIFES has its largest-ever staff contingent, seven long-term and at least twenty short-term workers. Thus, as the groups emerge from the instabilities that marked the 1970s, there is every reason to hope and pray that God will use them to spread His word throughout Nigeria and beyond.

Back in 1974, says Alastair Kennedy, 'a bold evangelistic effort to preach Christ within the closed Muslim society of the walled city of Zaria nearly ended in tragedy. A group of Christian students had obtained permission to witness in the open air in the town. They were listened to in silence, but when an invitation was given, and some young Muslims responded, the furious population stoned the evangelists. Injured and bleeding, but still praising, they barely made it to safety and to medical help in the nearest hospital. The bitterness of this response to their message did nothing to quench their zeal. Instead, God used this dramatic incident to challenge them to do more for the Muslim peoples of inland Africa.'[8] A Nigerian missionary society, Calvary Productions (CAPRO), was formed to send out evangelistic teams, mostly graduates, into the predominantly Muslim French-speaking lands of West Africa. Bayo Famonure, formerly NIFES staffworker based in Zaria, was in that small group of students and is now CAPRO's director. Perhaps this indicates the spirit of Nigerian student Christianity at its best, and the dynamic potential it has for world mission in the years to come.

EAST AFRICA

Across in the English-speaking countries of East Africa the work has seen similar blessings. In this part of the continent, the

---

[8] Alastair Kennedy in *The Wider Look*, July 1982, p.8.

groups have been linked together in the Fellowship of Christian Unions (FOCUS), which came into being on the initiative of the East African student leaders in December 1972. This was another step in a steady process of regionalization. PAFES was formed, as has been indicated, to enable isolated Christians on campuses right across Africa to give each other mutual support in the difficult struggle for a biblical faith. With the growth of the evangelical student groups, something more suited to the local needs of the East African region was required, and so FOCUS was created. In time the process was to move on logically to a third phase, when individual national movements began to feel strong enough to affiliate to IFES on their own. This stage was reached in the late 1970s and early 1980s.

The only FOCUS staffworker, Ahuma Adodoadji, soon found that with seventeen groups to cover in the region there was simply not 'time to be creative and go into depth with any group'. IFES staffworker Eila Helander was sent out to join him later in 1973. She was a graduate from Finland, and her conversion had to some extent been the result of listening to missionary speakers. ('They told me they went to faraway places to tell about Jesus and I started to think, "Well, what is so fascinating about Jesus that they *travel*?" So I saved my pocket money and bought me a little Bible.') One of Eila's objectives was to train an African to succeed her, and in 1975 her job was taken over by Emmy Matiti, who served with FOCUS as lady staffworker until a year after her marriage to fellow-staffworker John Gichinga in 1978. John himself had become Ahuma Adodoadji's successor in 1974; a far-sighted strategist, he was responsible for the East African work as the national movements came into being in the late 1970s and early 1980s.

Kenya

1974-75 was a period of mixed blessing for the Kenyan work. Large numbers of students attended a training course for the whole of East Africa in June 1974. It was the first course of its kind; it emphasized evangelism and Bible study, plus some discussion of contemporary issues. When the academic year began in July, coffee-house projects were arranged to reach the incoming first-years, and many conversions resulted, particularly in Nairobi. In August, however, both the University of Nairobi and Kenyatta University College were closed down for five months because of campus unrest. The December FOCUS regional conference in Dodoma, Tanzania, drew a good number of Kenyans despite the long travelling distances involved. ('Some of us had to spend days and nights stranded in small towns or on roadsides in the middle of nowhere,' said Gichinga.) When the two institutions reopened in January 1975 many students seemed to have matured in their faith and showed a willingness to put it into practice. Many others, however, seemed to have given up their faith in the intervening months.

Staff shortages presented serious problems in training up mature student leadership. In 1975 FOCUS had three staff for the whole area from Sudan to the borders of South Africa, when, as Professor George Kinoti wrote, 'The minimum number required for effective ministry to students is one for each country' – which would mean twelve staff. IFES, however, was in severe financial crisis at this time, as has been indicated already.

'One result of this shortage of indigenous labourers is that the vacuum is being filled by all kinds of foreign Christian groups who have the personnel and the money,' George Kinoti continued. 'This is a most unhealthy situation, because not only are these foreign groups apparently confirming the popular image of Christianity as the white man's religion, they are also introducing party spirit and unhealthy rivalry. Instead of building upon the foundation that has already been laid, they found new groups in competition with existing ones. One Christian leader has described this simply as an instance of American imperialism.'

Only late in the decade did the goal of at least one FOCUS staff per country begin to be approached, and in the intervening years the situation grew still more complex. By 1980 Gichinga could count thirteen organizations working in Kenyan high schools, colleges and universities. (A few of the additions were indigenous.) Most of these were evangelical, and therefore presumably working on precisely the same basis, and for the same purposes, as FOCUS; unlike the SCM groups which had existed earlier and tended to be theologically liberal. While the increased number of 'harvesters' is a good thing, as Gichinga says, the unnecessary situation of competition has also produced 'suspicions, lack of clear sense of direction, and a little "behind-the-back" talk.' Nevertheless, mutual acceptance has been growing.

Another feature of the 1970s was that 'Kenyan campuses experienced the beauty of the outpouring of God's Spirit in a special way', says Gichinga, 'mainly through the spread of the charismatic movement. Unfortunately, with it also came a lesser zeal to search the Word of God personally. We are so very grateful to God that we are gradually re-learning to combine a serious and systematic study of the Word of God with these experiences.' But still 'The great need is for more workers! Medical training centres have no-one to visit and encourage the groups. We have two polytechnics and other institutes whose groups would be eager to affiliate to FOCUS.' The answer at present seems to be the recruitment of teams of associate volunteers to work in Nairobi, Nakuru and elsewhere, especially in establishing small group Bible studies and writing appropriate materials.

Sudan

There can be no doubt as to the opportunities that could have been seized had FOCUS had more staff. In Khartoum, the capital of Sudan, for example, there has been a large Christian Association including Catholics, evangelicals, and Coptic Orthodox students; they have the rare distinction (for an Islamic country) of having a chapel on campus. But only rarely have FOCUS staff from elsewhere been able to visit them, because of the difficulty in obtaining entry visas. In 1975 the CA's chairman, Pitya Kedini, wrote of 'a lack of shape and strength'; five years later Erisa Owino, a Ugandan student who was one of the leading evangelicals there, wrote that 'Since 1977-78 we've seen God slowly but surely transforming our group. By His grace we now have three small Bible study groups.' But there was a need for prayer that 'We might all, *with the same mind,* strive toward the mark', he said. In 1982 KUCA secretary Mary Zaki shared in the IFES *Praise and Prayer Bulletin* her concern that 'the group isn't well organized and many students do not have a vision for sharing the Good News'.

One of the problems is that northern Sudanese are Arabic in race and language, whereas the southerners are black and English-speaking: so, to begin with, there are difficulties at the level of language. But there is a definite need for at least one staffworker – preferably Sudanese rather than a foreigner! – who can give the impetus for a thoroughly biblically-based work in all of Sudan's four universities and one polytechnic.

Ethiopia

In Somalia no evangelical students' groups are known. But in Ethiopia there have been great opportunities. Here evangelical students from a college and six high schools formed a Students' Christian Fellowship in 1955, and within two years thirteen institutions were involved. A monthly united gathering in Addis Ababa linked the groups together. This movement did not last, however, and a 'loose fellowship of Evangelical Unions' reappeared around 1963 as a result of Christian professors holding meetings in their homes. The Ethiopian University Students Christian Fellowship finally came into existence as a movement in 1967. At least 100 students were involved in Addis Ababa, and seventy at Gondar – a fifth of the student body. Government policies forced the movement to develop a sturdy self-sufficiency, and it was never affiliated to IFES.

Early in the 1970s there was a significant movement of God among Ethiopian young people, and large numbers of students were converted. The Coptic Orthodox church leaders were both perplexed and disturbed, particularly because of the students' all-night prayer meetings; and as a result the government imprisoned most of the student leaders in Addis Ababa and sentenced them to several months of hard labour. (The very gifted Ethiopian staffworker was not arrested because he overslept and was absent from the meeting when the police came.) Because of international pressures, however, the students were released.

IFES general secretary Chua Wee Hian visited Ethiopia in November 1973 and was struck by the students' avid desire for Bible teaching. 400 students packed out the hall where he spoke, some sitting two to a seat, and they were not really satisfied with one sermon only! At the end of 1973, Wee Hian was speaking at the Urbana convention, and met Mildred Young, an American-born Chinese who had been serving with the student movement in Hong Kong. Wee Hian enquired whether Mildred would be willing to go to Ethiopia for two years to do Bible study training: and, despite the unrest in the country, and the fact that she had cancer (and had thought God was calling her to work among the Eskimos), Mildred agreed. She began work in April 1974.

Later that year the Marxist Revolution took place. To begin with, this made life marginally easier for the students; non-Copts had had difficulties under the previous regime. Mildred

Young was able to continue work, and wrote in the *IFES News-letter* of the continued 'famine of the Word...Often as I shared with students from the Word, I noticed how intently their eyes were fixed upon me, absorbing every word like parched ground drinking in every drop of water during drought.'

Pressures began to mount, however. When the Addis Ababa group's 150 members were scattered throughout the country in the government's rural development campaign, some were able to form small fellowship groups; but often this was not tolerated by the non-Christian students. Nonetheless, as Mildred noted, 'they often elect Christian students to positions of trust, such as camp treasurer or purchaser for the food committee. Tolerant or hostile, they know who is to be trusted!' Mildred was responsible for editing a highly-popular newsletter for these students, with excerpts from letters and Bible study questions for use in 'quiet times'. Very close links existed with the high-schools work, including mutual invitations to meetings. A tremendous spirit of unity marked the movement in general. 'No-one can tell whether the students are Lutheran, Baptist, Pentecostal or what – they are just one, as the Scripture says,' commented one leader. They were spending 'much time in prayer and Bible study – that's what helps them stay with the Lord'.

Prayer is needed that God will continue His work in His own way in the years to come. For the time being, the Ethiopian student work, as an organized movement, has ceased to exist.

Uganda

Political pressures were experienced from a different type of government in Uganda. Here there was no evangelical student group in the early 1960s: many students went to university at Makerere and ceased to witness, or even lost their faith altogether. The only groups existing were limited each to its particular residence; these varied greatly in outlook and effectiveness, and there were few conversions. In the mid-1960s, however, a Christian Union was formed, and it grew rapidly until early in the seventies it numbered about 150 in membership. But then came the Amin regime.

'In 1976 the soldiers came to the University,' recalls Beatrice Odonga, a former Makerere CU executive member who is now on IFES staff in Zambia. 'I was in my room with a group of friends when the soldiers were rounding up and beating students.

There was a loud pounding on the door, and a soldier burst in. My friends had hidden under the beds, and the man pointed his machine-gun straight at me. But I knew that God was in control, and that the soldiers could only go as far as He allowed. And I knew too where I would go if I died.

'My friends and I were beaten and marched at gunpoint to where the other female students were being rounded up. Soldiers stood around with their guns pointed at us as we were beaten. Amidst the screams of the students, a Christian friend turned to me and said, "Beatrice, Jesus lives!" and I replied, "Amen, He does!"

'When it was over, a CU executive member sent out letters to Christian students to encourage them and tell them to trust in God. But his letters were misunderstood by the government and he was imprisoned for it. The CU and other friends joined in praying much for him, and he was released, but he had to flee the country.'

Nonetheless, personal evangelism and Bible study groups in the halls of residence continued actively, and evangelistic rallies too; although these had to be held on church premises, otherwise, as David Ssekabira explained, 'It would not take long to be misinterpreted as being linked with subversive elements.' The biggest blow was the expulsion of Scripture Union's high-schools staff; the high-schools groups declined, and when their members came up to university, many had backslidden. 'They had not understood why or whom they believed,' says David, 'so on being exposed to the world they lost their faith. Usually you'd expect about fifty Christians among the new students and God would add 100 or so while they were at university. But during this period the number of committed Christians graduating was about thirty to fifty. Others were dropping all the way – or else when they left they were heard of no more. Those converted at university tended to stand more.'

All this time the Ugandan university and college students had very little staff support. But when the Amin regime fell, David was appointed as staffworker, and was succeeded in 1980 by David Zac Niringiye. One of the first aims was to provide libraries for the Christian groups at each of the eighteen institutions with which they had contact, and Tear Fund generously assisted this with a grant. The groups were scattered distances of up to 120 miles, which made it imperative to get the graduate associates involved in backing the work in their locality, besides evangelizing their colleagues. ('Not just saying, "You have to be saved, you have to be saved",' David Ssekabira added, 'but having open homes and evangelistic Bible studies.')

In this they had some success. Many Christian graduates who could have left the country chose to remain, despite adverse economic circumstances. (David Zac told *His* in 1981 that a shirt would cost 'two-thirds of your monthly salary, and then the rest can buy food or necessities for one week or less...We've learnt to depend on God for soap, for toothpaste, for anything.') As a result, some were able to play a significant part in Ugandan society and the church, besides supporting the student movement. The Entebbe graduates' group committed themselves to assist three local student groups; but they also became heavily involved in the ministry of a local church, and helped it reach out highly effectively to unchurched sections of the population. With their assistance it grew in size from three to 250! Oliver Barclay of UCCF-Britain described this group as the most impressive graduates' fellowship he had seen anywhere in the world.

But even with the effective mobilization of graduates, the student groups still needed visits from the staffworker. And he had no transport! Eventually a German church synod raised the money for a minibus. But the country's economic problems meant that petrol had gone up to $35 a gallon; an average graduate's salary for two months was needed to fill the vehicle with gasoline! So it was not unknown for students to walk ten miles before 9 a.m. to a one-day conference, attend meetings till 5 p.m. and then walk back.

Tanzania

In the early 1980s the Tanzanian groups likewise began to develop a national movement. FOCUS had had an affiliate in the university at Dar-es-Salaam for some years. But in 1975-76 a deep work of the Spirit swept through the high schools. Many students and teachers were converted, and of course within a year or two this affected the tertiary groups too. The Dar-es-Salaam group grew to 100, on a campus of 2,500.

'They have been very bold to speak about their faith,' said one of the Tanzanian leaders, Charles Philemon. 'But with this blessing, the devil brought division, and in some circles much emphasis was put upon experience rather than the Word.' Still, by 1982 'the gap has been narrowed in many areas, and national conferences have been used as platforms to bring unity'.

Zambia

In Tanzania's south-western neighbour, Zambia, the work has developed more rapidly. Here the University of Zambia was founded in 1966; the following year IFES associate staffworker David Bentley-Taylor passed through the country and found Christian groups, of the SCM type but containing a number of evangelicals. After one meeting his audience 'unleashed a flood of questions: "Can a sincere Buddhist be saved?" "What is the sin against the Holy Ghost?" "What use is the Old Testament to Christians nowadays?" "Is heaven to be on the earth or another star?" "What is the purpose of life?" "If God punished men for building the tower of Babel, will He punish them for space research?" "How could Christ, so long ago, have borne my present sins?" After grappling with all this they crowded around me cheerfully at the end, till I simply had to protest that I could no longer think straight!'

By 1969, however, the University Christian Community was under the influence of theologically liberal chaplains and holding two services, a Catholic mass and an ecumenical service tending to deal mainly with social and racial issues. Some Zambian first-year students and a number of British postgraduates met at a local church and found they shared a desire for Bible study and for witness to their fellow-students, many of whom had never been confronted with the Jesus of the Bible. They began to meet for Bible study and prayer in a student's room; then they decided they should come out into the open, and launched the Friday Christian Fellowship, in the home of a maths lecturer from Germany, Rainer Güting.

The start of the new academic year of 1970 saw only four of these pioneers left, facing considerable hostility! But the group slowly grew, in particular through the addition of former members of Scripture Union high-schools groups. Before the end of the academic year Bible study groups had been started in the halls of residence, and the fellowship applied for affiliation to PAFES after a visit from travelling secretary Daniel Kyanda.

The following year numbers increased to forty – and the fellowship's chairman was elected chairman of the university Student Union! But disputes began between the students and the government. Violent demonstrations broke out, the riot police were called in, and the chairman was one of the student leaders expelled from the university. It was a severe blow, which caused much questioning; but slowly the work was resumed.

In 1972 a mission was planned. Three days before the mission, at the start of a prayer meeting, a telegram arrived announcing that the speaker could not come! This provided fuel for prayer, to say the least. 'God surely heard those sincere prayers from people at their wit's end,' says Dorothea Güting. 'The Lord provided a speaker from Zambia, and obviously gave him His power.' There were many conversions, but equally important was the fact that the change of speaker necessitated a change of posters. 'To make sure they were noticed, many Christian students pinned posters on their backs, round their arms and on their briefcases. They were no longer "ashamed of the gospel of Christ". That was a big step forward, and it continued long after.'

In 1974 former IVCF-USA staff Hank and Cathy Pott came to Zambia as IFES workers, with a vision for seeing groups develop throughout Zambia's post-secondary institutions. By agreement with Scripture Union, FOCUS took over some SU groups in the colleges. Area conferences and discreet staff presence helped draw the students together. Within five years a national movement, the Zambia Fellowship of Evangelical Students, was formed, and an African ZAFES staffworker took over, Derek Mutungu. (His conversion, incidentally, had been a result of the British movement's outreach to foreign students in their midst.)

The university group had a unique opportunity in 1980 to lead a service of worship and intercession at State House. President Kaunda and four topmost leaders were present. Student chairman Trevor Mwamba delivered a lucid and incisive message, boldly proclaiming that God demands repentance: unrighteousness in leadership, in the church and the nation would not go unjudged, he said. Such plain speaking made some of the students feel highly uncomfortable! But the Lord was in the midst. In closing the President remarked, 'I confess I was weeping throughout the service, but it was tears of joy.' He quoted the story of Eli and Samuel and commented, 'People in my age group talk about God loosely. But we do not understand His power and love and the meaning of His creation. But God has given to you, the youth of Zambia, to understand and respond to the message of love. I hope you will continue to proclaim it.'

By 1981 ZAFES numbered eleven fellowships, with four more working towards full membership. Nearly 1,000 students were involved, including over 400 of the 3,000 students at the university. Derek had been working hard 'to develop leadership, broaden the programme content of each group, and improve its quality'. But the work had grown far too big for one staffworker. 'We were not successful in our attempt to launch a student magazine,' he lamented in 1981. 'Nor were we consistently able to provide study and training aids. The bottleneck was personnel. On all the campuses there is a need for a personal ministry to students. One sometimes wishes for a 48-hour day and vast reserves of energy. From my experience of the past few months I know that overwork and exhaustion lead to depression and discouragement...ideal recipes for Satan. We need more workers!' The following year Beatrice Odonga, who had studied and served on the UCF executive at Lusaka as well as in Makerere, Uganda, during Amin's time, joined IFES staff and was seconded to ZAFES: and since then a team of associate staff has developed. The associates' ministry is also vital both for tackling the problem of graduate backsliding after university, and for mobilizing graduates to make a real impact on their churches and professions and in society at large.

Meanwhile, Hank and Cathy Pott moved on. In a very important sense they (and other pioneers in Africa too) may be said to have been ideal IFES staff. 'Let's pray Hank in,' Chua Wee Hian said to the Urbana 1973 convention, 'and after two or three years let's pray him out, because we want to see him training Africans to be staffworkers and to lead their own movement.' In Zambia, Hank and Cathy helped raise up a student movement, trained a national as successor and turned the work over to him. Then they moved on to Zimbabwe – or Rhodesia, as it was then – and did precisely the same thing.[9]

Zimbabwe

Zimbabwe was in the middle of a guerrilla war against the white government of Ian Smith, and at the University in Harare (then called Salisbury), the Christian Union was the only effectively multi-racial group on campus, with a presidency sometimes

[9] All of which makes it most interesting that, according to Cathy Pott, the one thing that kept her from full commitment to Christ during high school was the fear that God might send her to Africa!

white, sometimes black. Hank spoke at a camp in Umtali in 1977; Cathy and their son Cholwezi were refused government permission to join him, because the speaker's cabin had been the site of a number of abductions in the previous year.

But Hank was thrilled to work in this country. 'Almost everyone knows of a death in his extended family due to the ongoing hostilities,' he wrote of the university group in the *IFES Newsletter*, 'yet these students are probably the most joyful and confident I have ever had the privilege to know. The campus is aware of their presence. Last spring a new Christian joined the family daily for several weeks in a row: and today in our group at least one in three has become a Christian since arriving at university.'

The final steps were being taken to establish a Zimbabwean national movement too. A little over a year later Hank could write in *In Touch*, 'All but one of Zimbabwe's colleges have affiliated to FOCUS in the past year, or are in the process of doing so. Colleges in Gwelo and Umtali have 100 Christians each. The CU at Salisbury University is a lively one of 75 or more, and added at least 25 to their numbers during one term by joyful personal evangelism!' (The following issue of *In Touch* reported that a further 100 students had responded in a university outreach.) By the end of that year Hank had handed over responsibility to Zimbabwean staffworker Roy Musasiwa, a former chairman of the university group, and his own field of service had shifted again.

Hank enjoyed the lively large-group meetings at the university. 'Admittedly the numerous choruses are not noted for their theological profundity,' he said, 'but the smiles are genuine, the heartfelt involvement is real, and the strong voices, clapping hands, raised arms (and walking bodies, with near chaos, in some choruses!) are a great source of togetherness. Short testimonies, seemingly endless "items", an occasional well-polished skit, and a strong message from a visiting speaker, round out the 2½ hour programme.' (Meetings could sometimes be a little longer than that – the last two meetings of 1979 had ended at 2.30 and 4.15 a.m.!)

But there were weaknesses too, of course. 'There is sometimes less interest in the demands of discipleship than in the magic of many meetings,' wrote Hank in 1980. 'The sure fellowship of song is more attractive than the possible fellowship of suffering.

Even the University's fifteen small groups are occasionally more oriented around sharing experiences rather than serious study of God's Word.'

There was a particular problem in the area of singleness and marriage. 'I vividly remember sharing a room with a Ugandan speaker and asking him his greatest joy and greatest disappointment in five years of close association with students. "Well, Hank, my wife and I lived on Makerere campus all this time," he told me, "and of all the young ladies we have known and counselled, I know no more than a handful who married Christians and are building Christian homes." I was quite surprised, but found a similar situation in Zambia during four years there, and similar pressures among Zimbabwean friends today.' (Similarly, Eila Helander reported in 1975 that students in one Kenyan college felt 80% of backsliding among students and graduates was the result of relationship problems.) This area saw considerable improvement in the following years: in 1983 Hank wrote with enthusiasm of 'the sharply escalating number of godly marriages getting under way in both Zambia and Zimbabwe – one of our greatest sources of hope for Africa's future.' But there remains a great deal of need for teaching, pastoring and prayer.

One significant event in the history of FOCUS Zimbabwe – and, indeed, of the student work in East Africa – has been omitted. In July 1979, at the IFES General Committee in Hurdal Verk, Norway, FOCUS Zimbabwe, Zambia FES, FOCUS Uganda and FOCUS Kenya all affiliated to IFES as independent national member movements. The process of local initiative that had been highlighted by the development of FOCUS East Africa in 1972 had taken another step forward. Proportionally these are some of the largest student movements in the world. There remain serious needs and problems, as has been indicated: but nonetheless, in Kenya, Zambia and Zimbabwe God has brought around 10% of the students into the IFES-affiliated groups.

When we consider that a similar percentage of students are involved in the groups in Ghana, and that Nigeria now has the second biggest IFES movement in the world, it is obvious that, numerically at least, the African student movements are unusually strong. What reasons can be given for this?

One factor, doubtless, is the effectiveness of the high-schools work of Scripture Union, continually supplying the groups with keen Christian students who will be active witnesses. At many places in Zambia and Zimbabwe, for example, said Hank Pott, 'the same pattern held true': groups were usually formed by former leaders of SU groups, with the aid of one or more lecturers. When the SU work suffered, as in Amin's Uganda, the tertiary work suffered too. On the other side of the continent, David Bentley-Taylor wrote in 1967 that the work in Ghana owed its strength to the 'widespread Scripture Union work in schools' and that the 'extraordinarily strong' work in Ibadan University was 'fed by the remarkable Scripture Union work'.[10]

Hank also suggested in 1977 that 'the strongest groups in our part of the world invariably have at least two things in common: they genuinely care for one another, and they are committed to pray with one another'. At Zambia Institute of Technology students were praying together at 6 a.m. and 5 p.m. every day, and at Chancellor College (in Malawi) close to a hundred attended weekly prayer meetings for a year in preparation for a mission. These were two of the largest groups in southern Africa at that time. In Uganda, all-night prayer meetings on Saturdays and Sundays were the students' response to the worsening situation during the Amin regime.

At the University of Zambia, the 400-strong UCF hold 'Operation 0530', a Saturday morning prayer meeting where they pray for the nation: also, they say, 'daily "quiet times" are emphasized, and much of the personal witnessing grows from this'. At the main university in Zimbabwe, the 'official' prayer meeting disappeared around 1977, since daily prayer meetings were taking place in every residence. (By 1980, however, a daily early morning prayer meeting for the whole group had recommenced, under the name of 'Operation 6.05'.) And as we noted earlier in the chapter, the large numerical growth of the groups in Nigeria and Ghana has likewise been accompanied by a massive commitment to prayer.

SOUTHERN AFRICA

Malawi

In southern Africa there are several countries that were not affiliated to IFES at the end of the 1970s. In one of these, Malawi,

[10] The same is undoubtedly true in many other parts of the world. For example, Ian Burnard wrote in *IFES Journal* in 1970 that the size of the Australian university groups was 'very directly related to the successful work of God' through SU at secondary level.

the Universities and Colleges Section of the national Student Christian Organization has applied to join IFES since that time. Here, too, as has been indicated, there is a thorough commitment to prayer. Chua Wee Hian visited Chancellor College and commented on the 'spiritual thirst and hunger' he noticed in a group of seventy students who met each weekday for prayer and Bible study before lectures. (Chancellor College is the most prestigious of Malawi's seven tertiary institutions, and had an enrolment of 850 at this stage.)

SCO started in 1961 as a work of the churches in the secondary schools, and has grown in step with the expansion of the education system – in good measure through the efforts of its first travelling secretary, Franklin Chunga, now Malawi's chief censor. It is currently active in nearly ninety schools. The Universities and Colleges Section is officially just what its name implies, but has developed a vibrant life of its own. Missions led by Africans from neighbouring countries, such as Maurice Ngakane and Phineas Dube, and the encouragement of expatriates such as Martyn Cundy (an IVF-Britain graduate lecturing at Chancellor College) and chaplain Terry McMullan, have contributed significantly to the growth of the university witness. A number of UCS graduates have been encouraged by evangelical student fellowships while doing further studies elsewhere in the world. (Many UCS graduates are now in senior posts, including senior lecturers Boyce Wanda and Kings Phiri, and World Vision's Malawi director Peter Mkolesia.) UCS obviously shares a common vision with the evangelical student movements in the surrounding countries, and its affiliation with IFES merely recognized a deep spiritual affinity that has existed for years.

Botswana, Lesotho and Swaziland

Further south still are the countries of Botswana, Lesotho and Swaziland, in which Hank and Cathy Pott were working in the early 1980s. Botswana has one university, at Gaberone: the FOCUS-affiliated Christian Union had fifty members out of the 800 students on campus in 1980. It was marked by effective student leadership and a healthy daily prayer meeting. Lesotho was a country that until late 1978 had a university campus of 800 students and virtually no Christians with a clear, evangelical witness; but by mid-1979 a lively group of ten to fifteen were meeting several times a week who, as Hank said, 'really ministered to us by their enthusiasm'. A Scripture Union high-schools work is just beginning in Lesotho.

In Swaziland, in contrast, there are many evangelical students. Over 200 of the 1,000 students on the two university campuses attend gatherings of the Student Christian Movement. (This is the name used by evangelical students in Swaziland, and also in Namibia and among South African blacks; unlike groups of the same name in some other continents, these SCMs are firmly evangelical and unconnected with the WSCF.) The groups are student-led and evangelistically effective, and Honor Ward writes, 'The first question might be, Why are numbers so large? "The Spirit bloweth where it listeth"; but it is useful, all the same, to look at the ways growth has come. Good grounding in the faith, from mission schools, Christian homes, evangelical homes and Scripture Union has certainly been helpful. Many students come up fully resolved to identify themselves with the Christians on campus.' Christian lecturers, including a number of graduates from IFES movements elsewhere, and workers from parachurch groups such as Campus Crusade, have had a deep influence. And, as in Malawi, a significant number of Swazi graduates have gone abroad for postgraduate studies and become involved with IFES movements, returning with a vision for the work in their own country. 'This is perhaps the most important development of all,' comments Honor Ward.

The name 'Christian' arouses so little prejudice in Swaziland that any special event such as a retreat or conference may attract non-Christians. Students preach at high schools, prisons and hospitals; the university group has made long trips to rural areas to visit high schools and tell them about Christian work on campus. The SCM choir is famous, and has to limit its acceptance of invitations to sing at wedding and engagement parties!

Span reported a Swazi national conference in 1972 where a decision was taken to form a national movement; little came of this, but a meeting of the committees from the university and college campuses was held for the same purpose in 1977, and an independent Inter-Collegiate Student Christian Movement was formed, with Joshua Mzizi as its first president. Since then it has held conferences and retreats every few months, with a considerable and very positive effect.

In these last three southern African nations – and, indeed, many parts of Africa – evangelical lecturers have played an important role, including Patrick and Cynthia Whittle in Lesotho, John Woollard in Botswana, and Alan and Honor Ward in Swaziland. (The Wards are IVF-Britain graduates who have spent over thirty years lecturing in Africa, and were in at the birth of the groups in Legon, Ghana, and Lusaka, Zambia.) But there is a need for a staffworker for these countries at the present time.

In the two Portuguese-speaking countries of the region, Angola and Mozambique, no national evangelical student movements are known to exist. Periodical visits by African staff have made some contacts, and in one part of Angola a doctor converted in the Zaire groups in acting as adviser to a small group of Christian students.

Namibia

In Namibia, there are no universities, but God has raised up a very strong high-schools work, again known as the Student Christian Movement. Namibia's population is only 883,000, yet the twenty SCM branches in Namibia have over 6,000 members, and there were over 1,000 at their 1981 conference! They have reached this size without any full-time staffworker. SCM in Namibia is determined to be 'the arm of the churches in our schools' rather than something separate, and in 1982 the movement's secretary, A. Kaulinge, reported some of the reactions he was receiving: 'We hear comments such as, "Many of the youth leaders in various congregations are those who have been SCM members"; or, "Our young people have learnt a lot from your students. For most of them it was the first time they had seen their fellow young people testifying freely about salvation in Christ"; or, "We were really surprised to see that there are sincere and devoted Christians among students nowadays!"'

The Namibians have already started a Student Mission Fund which supports a Namibian missionary family outside the country; in 1981 they raised no less than $11,000, which, as IFES staffworker T. B. Dankwa commented, was a 'remarkable achievement... considering that the Movement is mainly among high-school students in a war zone!' In this movement, there is once again a strong commitment to prayer. 'We are accused of praying too much,' pastor Kaulinge told *In Touch*, 'though we firmly believe we should pray to God till the earth shakes! We are accused of moving too much when singing – though we are fully convinced that our whole being should give praise to the Lord!'

As Namibia moves towards independence, there is an obvious place for an evangelical, interracial student movement. At the present time, SCM's work is concentrated among black students in Ovamboland. There is a need for a worker who can build up the ministry, particularly around the capital, Windhoek, so that it is truly national and interracial.

The Republic of South Africa

So in the far south of the continent we come to the Republic of South Africa, where the student movement's history stretches back far beyond the foundation of IFES to the evangelical awakening among the students of the nineteenth century. From its beginning, described in our first chapter, SCA was predominantly Afrikaans (*i.e.* whites of Dutch origin). However, in the 1920s a sturdy English-speaking work developed too, largely due to the efforts of a former member of the CICCU at Cambridge, Oswin Bull. The movement remained evangelical even when many other WSCF movements had changed position.

After the Second World War, a number of tensions within the movement came increasingly to the surface. To begin with, the Afrikaans work faced increasing pressure from the Dutch Reformed Church, which desired a greater control over its young people. Most of the Afrikaans members of SCA belonged to the DRC. In the early 1960s a number of local congregations brought about the disbanding of SCA branches in local Afrikaans schools.

Then there was the multiracial nature of SCA, which did not make it any more popular within the DRC. Work had existed among black students since at least 1919 and among 'coloured' students since 1936. In 1951 the whole movement was reorganized into four sections (Afrikaans, English, black and 'coloured'), by unanimous consent, for administrative purposes; but the intervarsity conference continued to be interracial, which stressed SCA's unified nature. These conferences were criticized by conservative political groups such as the Volkskongres on communism, which labelled SCA as 'communistic and liberalistic'. The movement was criticized from the left for compromising with apartheid and from the right for liberalism. Groups at Rhodes, Fort Hare and Wentworth Medical School disaffiliated for one reason, while the Heidelburg Training College group left for the other reason and other groups threatened to follow.[11]

[11] *Cf.* M. G. Andrew, 'Historical Foundations', *South African Outlook*, July 1967.

Doctrinal tensions existed too. In the 1930s evangelicals in SCA had worked for the adoption of a doctrinal basis. They found opponents on the Afrikaans side, where it was seen as making SCA into a church, and on the English side, where both the concept and the contents of the doctrinal basis met with opposition. Nonetheless, the University of Cape Town adopted the basis, and the Western Province regional committee worked steadily to have it accepted by the entire movement.

In 1962, an independent Evangelical Christian Union was established at Rhodes by students unhappy with the doctrinal position and general outlook of Rhodes SCA; the same year evangelical students at Cape Town drew up a memorandum stating their dissatisfaction with the lack of clear-cut evangelical, biblical testimony in the English-speaking universities. The following year a conference of evangelical students took place in Cape Town to discuss the position of evangelicals within SCA. They recommended to the national movement the acceptance of the IFES doctrinal basis, disaffiliation from WSCF and affiliation to IFES, the appointment of an evangelical staffworker, and positive action towards unity of all believers, regardless of race. (It should be noted here that an evangelical theological position was not being linked to a pro-apartheid outlook.)

The South African Fellowship of Evangelical Students was formed in 1964, with the aim of acting as a parent body to the Rhodes Evangelical Christian Union, encouraging the formation of evangelical groups elsewhere, and affiliating to IFES as soon as three such groups existed. Meanwhile, matters had come to a head in another area highlighted by the Cape Town student conference. The WSCF had called for immediate action to bring pressure on South Africa to abolish apartheid, an action hardly likely to meet with approval among the Afrikaans majority in SCA, which consequently disaffiliated the same year.

In January 1965, SCA's general meeting at Bloemfontein dissolved the association, on the understanding that four separate bodies would be set up – the ACSV among Afrikaans students, the SCM among black students, the CSB (later VCS or ACS) among 'coloured' students, and the SCA among the English-speaking whites. Since the general meeting was democratically organized, the Afrikaans majority was a key factor in this decision; the movement's other three sections were largely opposed to it. In particular, the new SCA's choice of name expressed their desire to change as little as possible, and their protest at what had occurred. From the very beginning, their membership was always open to all Christian students, irrespective of racial identity.

The following year, the new SCA adopted the IFES doctrinal basis by a two-thirds majority. As a result, SAFES dissolved itself, and SCA was welcomed as an affiliate to IFES.[12] Within South Africa itself, however, the newly-defined evangelical position of SCA brought immediate opposition. A liberal student grouping, the University Christian Movement, was launched, with encouragement from the Archbishop of Cape Town and the backing of the Presbyterian, Methodist, Catholic, Congregationalist and Church of the Province (*i.e.* Anglican) denominations. That backing did not guarantee its orthodoxy: David Bentley-Taylor visited one SCA group that had moved over to UCM and found they had 'no fixed programmes but held occasional symposiums, the latest having been on "Does God Exist?" On this they had reached no conclusions, their purpose being to pool opinions and raise questions, not to give answers.' Nonetheless, UCM was said to 'represent the mainstream of Christian thought',[13] and as Bill Houston says, 'SCA was consigned to a corner to fade out quietly.'

But it was not to be. 'The Lord looked down on this weakened, dismembered lot, with no staffworker, no co-ordination between branches in English-speaking universities (let alone other groups),' continues Bill, 'and He gently licked and nudged them into some sort of shape. The movement began, gingerly, to take a few steps....' One of the first was the appointment of IFES staffworker Jim Johnston, a former IVF-Britain travelling secretary, as SCA's staffworker, and later general secretary. SCA's first national student conference, in 1967, drew only forty students, but they were the foundation for future development. A national student committee was appointed, to be responsible for the running of all directly student-related activities; this resulted in innovatory leadership and the emergence of a suc-

[12] Robin Wells (one of the key figures in SCA's adoption of the doctrinal basis, and now UCCF-Britain's general secretary) comments that 'it bears testimony to the singlemindedness of the SAFES Council, who were prepared to sacrifice the movement for whose existence they had been working for three years, acknowledging that the real reason for their action no longer existed'.

[13] UCM went into voluntary liquidation in the early seventies when the black members pulled out to form a separate black consciousness organization.

cession of outstanding student leaders. The independent Graduate Christian Fellowship, which was largely based in Cape Town, dissolved itself to allow SCA to begin a nationwide Graduate Fellowship.

SCA moved into the 1970s on a 'high tide of growth'. The 1968 conference attendance was double that of the original conference; the following year it was up again to 140, and reached 350 by 1973. By that time every campus was holding an evangelistic mission every three years and the movement could find 100 students ready to spend a large proportion of their summer vacation in a mission project in the Transkei.

SCA has not been a 'whites-only' movement. On the advice of Indian students, an Indian Work Committee was set up to be responsible for the development of the ministry in their colleges. This committee was dissolved in 1976, again at its own recommendation, but its work continued, being taken over by SCA's integrated regional committee in Natal. The same year SCA established as a five-year goal the uniting of all evangelical students in South Africa.

This was more easily said than done, however. In particular, a yawning gulf existed between the political assumptions of Afrikaans and black students, and the journey towards unity has proved to be a long one. The Afrikaans movement was still huge. In 1979 its twelve field staff were ministering to 53,800 high-school, university and college students in 5,000 weekly Bible study groups, with the aid of 3,000 teachers and ministers involved on a voluntary basis: besides some thirty-two beach missions each year, and 150 camps attended by over 10,000 students! But it was becoming more and more a part of the Dutch Reformed Church, which increased the problems in the development of organizational links with its sister movements.

Much closer partnership has taken place between the black student movement, SCM, and SCA. SCM is working with up to 100,000 students at high-school level and 3,500 at tertiary level. Their 2,000 high-school and fifty-six tertiary-level groups are ministered to by just four full-time and four part-time staff. Clearly, God has set a wide-open door before these large and prayerful groups. SCM has enjoyed close relationships with IFES – although it is not directly affiliated at the time of writing – and IFES has been able to help with the funding of a mobile bookshop, among other things.

There remains much that students can do in expressing the gospel of reconciliation in South Africa. Andrew Judge wrote in 1976 of the importance of developing contacts at a personal level between the students in the different groupings, pointing out that in meetings between English-speaking and Afrikaans students 'the deep division between the two white communities becomes obvious. There is a history of prejudice and lack of understanding from which Christian students are by no means exempt. It is a long and painful process to build up real friendship and trust, and it is an effort which, until fairly recently, English-speaking students have been reluctant to undertake...'

And although superficial contact with the black students has always been easier, since few English-speaking white students support the government's policies, yet the two groups' living situations are markedly different. 'Most white Christian students have not really questioned their right or attachment to the high standard of living they enjoy,' said Andrew. 'So they are unwittingly highlighting the existing barriers between them and their black brothers, who see them behind a wall of tape recorders, cars, costly holidays and other expensive tastes. Would it not be helpful if, as a visible demonstration of Christian love, a start was made in dismantling at least this particular wall?'

In 1980, the SCA students produced a Declaration to 'make our position clear with regard to some of the issues facing us'. It begins with a lengthy statement of the biblical principles relevant to the South African situation, affirming from Scripture that 'God requires justice and righteousness' and 'will judge those who oppress others', that 'all people are created in the image of God and therefore every person of whatever colour...shares a common dignity', that 'salvation affects...the whole person in all areas of life', and that 'all human institutions are tainted by sin. God is concerned with corporate or structural sin...All Christians must willingly submit to the laws and requirements of those in authority over them. If a particular law conflicts with the law of God as clearly expressed in Scripture then Christians ultimately are to obey God rather than men.'

They apply these and other principles to the church, calling for the visible demonstration of unity, the rooting out of racial discrimination and materialism, and a witness against 'all forms of injustice, unrighteousness, oppression and discrimination', matched by practical involvement with need while working at the 'root causes of poverty and disease'. They affirm that the racial classifications of the apartheid system give 'many opportunities, rights and privileges' to whites that are denied to others: 'This we believe is unjust.' Loving our neighbours, they affirm, includes seeking for them the privileges we enjoy, which in South Africa include freedom to travel, own land, live together as a family, vote, enjoy a just wage, *etc*. Further applications are made in the areas of lifestyle, patriotism, law and order (including a condemnation of such legislation as the pass laws and the prohibition of mixed marriages as 'unjust and indefensible'), military service and submission to authority.[14]

Christian students in South Africa need the prayers of their brothers and sisters outside the country. In so many situations some sort of political stance is inevitable – for example, when a university integrates its residences or sport teams and attracts opposition, or when a mass boycott on a black campus results in many students being expelled, including SCM leaders. Anyone concerned for South Africa should pray for the Afrikaans work. It is plain that the position taken up by the Dutch Reformed Church is of crucial significance in the South African situation; and what happens in student groups such as the ACSV fellowship at Stellenbosch – which numbered a staggering 3,500 in 1978 – is of incalculable importance in the country's future.

We have been concerned in this section with the issue of social involvement, not because that is the dominant element in students' lives, but because it is that which is most frequently of interest to praying friends abroad. Before moving on, however, it should be noted that these movements are, first and foremost, evangelizing and discipling movements. And missionary movements! Trevor Gow noted that 'as a result of the unhappy internal situation here, the tendency to become totally inward-looking is very strong'. He has been involved in leading a joint SCM-SCA missions training programme called SCaMP, which has sent a number of short-term workers abroad during the summer vacation. The apartheid system and the resulting international barriers have not meant that the Great Commission is

---

[14] The entire document appeared in *IFES Review* in 1981. One of the students who drafted the Declaration, Richard Steele, was later one of a number of SCA graduates who were given long terms of detention for conscientious objection to military service with the South African Defence Force.

inapplicable to the church in South Africa, and the two movements are anxious to be biblically obedient in this area too.

FRENCH-SPEAKING AFRICA
First fruits

Work in these countries is both younger and somewhat less well
documented than in the English-speaking countries. Two small
groups existed in **Benin** as early as 1954; but the real birth of the
regional work came in 1964, when Swiss IFES staffworkers Louis
and Denise Perret came to Dakar, **Senegal.** At this stage IFES had
only individual contacts in any French-speaking African country.
The shortage of missionaries from French-speaking Europe had
meant historically that churches in this area tended to be smaller
than in English-speaking Africa; the foundation of high-schools
work that was so crucial in English-speaking Africa was lacking,
since there were few evangelical teachers; and many missionaries worked in the vernacular languages, rather than French,
the language of secondary education.

In Dakar the Perrets found that 'the Protestant students do not
appear anxious to engage in evangelism. The tendency is almost
to discourage such an undertaking, perhaps through fear of
Muslim fanaticism.' To be known as a professional Christian
worker 'is often to have doors closed in one's face'. Still, an open
home proved to be an effective means of evangelism. 'If a student
will walk four or five kilometres to visit me in my home,' said
Louis, 'surely this is an indication of the high value placed upon
personal friendship, interest and affection.'

Over the next twelve months a Groupe Biblique Universitaire
(GBU) took shape. Student organizations were illegal, but the
group continued to pray, and asked a Muslim government
minister if they could be registered. As a result, in a country that
was 95% Muslim, the GBU became the only officially organized
student group! A problem has been that a large proportion of its
members have tended to be from other African countries, with
Chadians in particular playing an important part: and this has
made Christianity appear a foreign import. (In 1982, only one
Senegalese was involved.)

In 1965 the Perrets left Dakar for Abidjan in the **Ivory Coast,**
and their place was taken by Alastair and Helen Kennedy, WEC
missionaries seconded to IFES, who had been working in rural
Senegal since 1953. (From 1971 onwards, Alastair was IFES

regional secretary for French-speaking Africa – which included being sole staffworker until 1967 for the whole area, comprising twenty countries.) In Abidjan the Perrets saw a group of six students formed in 1966, in close fellowship with the Mission Biblique, and with the additional help of Gauthier de Smidt, who was appointed as an IFES associate staffworker in 1967. Abidjan became the GBU base for the entire continent, but the Abidjan group itself had problems to contend with – widespread opposition among the churches to an interdenominational witness, a preponderance of foreigners in the GBU, and some years of defeat due to leadership difficulties and problems with priorities, solved only with the voluntary separation of one section of the group in the mid-1970s.

The French-speaking African work had an international aspect from early in its history. At the region's very first camp, in 1965, four countries were represented by the six participants! The Groupes Bibliques Universitaires d'Afrique Francophone came into existence as an international body along the lines of PAFES, at a congress in Abidjan in 1968. *Lianes* was launched as its journal; Alastair Kennedy was staffworker. In the following years he travelled through Africa, encouraging the pioneering of GBUs in central Africa, and strengthening ties of friendship with the student work in **Chad** and the **Central African Republic,** which formed part of independent evangelical youth movements working under the name Union des Jeunes Chrétiens. (At Bangui, the capital of CAR, the university opened at the end of 1970, and a GBU was immediately formed by seven of the sixty students.)

In **Zaire** the student work had developed in a different way again. Jean-Claude and Thérèse Schwab went to Zaire from Switzerland in 1969 as IFES staffworkers. It was a time when Zairois churches were being united in the Église de Christ au Zaire, and the churches had written to GBUAF suggesting that the Schwabs should not come until their relationship to the new body could receive consideration. Unfortunately the letter never reached Abidjan, and Jean-Claude arrived in Zaire 'in blissful ignorance of its contents', as Alastair Kennedy says. 'Not surprisingly his first contact with the church was less than friendly!' Nonetheless, several church leaders welcomed him warmly, and to Jean-Claude's astonishment he was appointed by the national churches' council as the official protestant chaplain at Kinshasa, the largest central African university. So a group came into being there; others followed in Lubumbashi, Kisangani and Brazzaville (the capital of the neighbouring **Congo Republic**) by the time GBUAF's first Central African Training Course was held in 1971.

That course in Kinshasa was quite an event. It included practical experience in evangelism with the aid of a 'Good Friday Questionnaire' ('What does Good Friday mean to you? Are you surprised that centuries before Christ's death, details of His crucifixion were foretold by David, Isaiah and others? Have you ever tried to explain this? Was Christ's death an accident? If not, what does it mean to you?') Many participants admitted later that they had gone out in doubt and trembling, but were amazed to find that God was with them and that so many students were eager to discuss the meaning of the cross.

For the evening session, the Kinshasa group had booked an amphitheatre seating 300, and advertised with a poster asking 'Is God dead?'. 'Of course not!' said a handwritten reply. 'He lives on in the souls of the feeble and ignorant...' That set the tone for the evening. At the start all seats were taken and there were fifty people standing. A Salvation Army quintet was much appreciated – in fact it was not easy to get the girl soloists away safely at the end – but the rest of the programme was punctuated by whistles and catcalls, and when Zairois evangelist Jean-Perce Makanzu rose to speak, fifty students walked out. But the speaker stayed calm and friendly, and little by little his sense of humour and his message (announced, to great applause, as being on 'God is dead! Long live science!') carried the day. When the meeting ended, he was surrounded by a crowd of students; finally he waved them back to their seats, returned to the platform, and spent the next two hours fielding difficult and hostile questions. Over seventy students were still listening at midnight, and many requested follow-up. Coming at the end of the course, it was a practical proof of the power of God operating in the midst of human fear and weakness. Spiritual warfare continued, however; one participant addressed a thoroughly destructive report to the church leadership.

In the years that followed there continued to be many conversions at the university in Kinshasa; some were delivered from demonic forces and several called into Christian service. In 1974, the Schwabs left Zaire; their successor, Marini Bodho, was thoroughly committed to the work, and progress continued. By the beginning of the 1980s the Kinshasa group had seven groups on the university campus (including two for lecturers), twelve in the town (with between twenty and fifty participants in each), a Bible study group in every higher institute and a developing high-schools work. In Kisangani too fourteen Bible study groups were meeting by 1978, and work had also begun in Bukavu. In all of these cities the student work is a 'parish' of the church.

Madagascar and Cameroun are the two other French-speaking African countries where the work has seen most significant growth. The movement in **Madagascar** came into existence largely through the faith and vision of Gerard Kuntz from France, who taught in Tananarive from 1967 to 1972 (soon after which he became general secretary of the French movement), and Claire Rasiliarivony and others, who had studied in France, been involved with the GBU there and had caught the vision for something similar in their own country.

A university GBU grew rapidly and 'spilled over' into a number of colleges and schools elsewhere. By 1975 the university group numbered fifty, while some 400 members were involved in the eleven high-schools groups. 120 students attended the first national congress in January of that year. The theme – appropriately for these evangelistically-minded students – was 'Go into all the world and preach the gospel to every creature'. The Union des Groupes Bibliques de Madagascar was formed and a medical student, Daniel Rakotojoelinandrasana, took six months off from his studies to serve as staffworker. He was succeeded by Solomon Andriatsimialomananarivo, now the IFES regional secretary for French-speaking Africa. A lady staffworker, Eliette Andrianaly, was added in 1977: she had found Christ at an Easter camp while studying in France, and was living proof of the strategic importance of work among international students! At the time of writing 1,300 students are involved in UGBM's twenty-six groups. But there is an increasing need for literature in the national Malagasy language.

The work in **Cameroun** began after a visit from Alastair Kennedy in 1969, on the initiative of a Chadian student who had been involved in the high-school work in his own country. A cell group started meeting at the university in Yaoundé – with a membership drawn entirely from Chad and Zaire! In 1972 IFES staffworkers Claude and Anne-Marie Décrevel from Switzerland became based in Cameroun. GBUAF's international congress was held in Cameroun that year, and it was hoped that the

Yaoundé group would be present in force.

In fact, although fifteen enrolled, not one member turned up, apart from the enthusiastic Camerounian university chaplain; and as Alastair Kennedy wrote, 'inevitably this strange boycott cast a shadow over the Congress'. It was not even known whether someone had worked to keep the students away, or whether it was merely the result of slackness and poor leadership. At any rate, Alastair was concerned enough to ask *IFES Journal* readers to pray that the Camerounian work would not be seriously damaged.

Fascinatingly, it was such contacts as did result from this very Congress that the Camerounians later saw to have been the crucial stimulus for Camerounian participation and leadership; an apparent disaster helped to change the GBU from a group mainly composed of foreign students to something indigenous. Meanwhile, a number of students coming from Scripture Union high-school groups in the English-speaking part of the country were seeking to develop a similar fellowship at the university, and soon efforts were joined.

However, there were many obstacles in the next two or three years. Only 700 of the university's 7,000 students lived on campus in 1975, and the rest were hard to locate. The zealous followers of the Baha'i sect were making a real impact on campus. Police surveillance could mean that students were hesitant to become involved in a student group that was not officially recognized, but procedures to legalize the GBU were blocked.

Claude himself was meeting misunderstanding from church leaders, although growing friendships developed with pastors of some of the bigger churches towards 1975: besides that, the Swiss authorities were demanding that he come home to teach, a problem finally removed in answer to specific prayer. The GBU had some fifty members and was slowly growing: nonetheless, many members were Sunday Christians with only the vaguest idea of what 'new life' meant.

One problem was the shortage of evangelical work in Cameroun's French-speaking high schools. Very few committed Christian students were coming up to university, and there never seemed to be sufficient time to develop the necessary maturity in the university group. There was only one solution: to start working in the high schools.

Once again, the triennial continental Congress of GBUAF served as the stimulus. Some high-school students were present and caught the vision: Claude and Anne-Marie made circuits of thousands of kilometres, contacting interested students and church leaders. Throughout the French-speaking territory, cell groups sprang up. God was at work.

But in 1977, the Décrevels had to leave Cameroun. (Claude is at the time of writing leading the French-speaking work in Quebec.) And new problems were developing: government recognition and hopes for a national staffworker did not materialize. In September of that year, Ann Bennighof arrived in Cameroun from the USA as a graduate exchange student on a Fulbright scholarship – and also as an IFES Field Partner.[15] She became involved in the GBU, was rapidly accepted by the Camerounians and invited to become their staffworker. At the same time, the movement gained legal status by affiliating with 'New Life For All', a national evangelistic organization.

'We began the 1978-79 school year with another storm to weather,' recalls Ann. 'Doctrinal differences divided the national evangelical community, and it was painfully difficult for our movement to maintain its scriptural and interdenominational identity. Within the university group, mutual confidence grew thin and group witness was almost paralysed. In outlying areas, on the other hand, some school groups were still without a single born-again Christian, and in most groups, even converted leaders did not know how to bring others to Christ! Very few school groups had capable adult advisers.' And many high-school members were living away from home, facing the pressures of widespread corruption and a multitude of occult and heretical sects.

Christmas, however, brought a leadership training camp, addressed by the graduate fellowship's president, Daniel Etya'ale. 'It was the starting-point for the healing process that took place through the year as students learnt to think through Scripture for themselves. Young Christians who arrived anxious and timid went home transformed with a new joy and confidence. A new zeal appeared in the university group; high-school group members transferring into schools without groups started new cells, and some groups even pioneered neighbouring schools.' Even in the Islamic north of the country, the students were persevering – although many of them would be from animist or

---

[15] *I.e.* a self-supporting graduate helping the student work part-time.

Muslim families – and warm co-operation existed with the churches. Ann's visits and the movement's newsletters helped the more struggling groups to feel part of the national body; while leadership training, and the Bible study guides that Ann was preparing, brought Scripture into focus as the heart of group activities.

July 1979 saw the movement's first national Congress, at Libamba, attended by thirty-five university and 100 high-school students. René Daidanso of Chad spoke on 'God's Word and Us', laying down a well-reasoned and heartfelt loyalty to Scripture; while consecutive 'quiet time', small group and expository study of Romans 1–8 deepened delegates' understanding of biblical faith. By the end of 1980, the first English-language high-schools camp had been held, and large numbers of high-schools members were moving on to university and swelling the numbers there.

Ann described one camp in the heart of a 'Muslim-oriented area': 'The daily hair-plaiting session in the girls' dorm; doling out nivaquine, aspirin and prayer every day for malaria, headache, earache; sand between the toes all day; quiet tears and shouts of laughter...Last year, A., from the local junior high, thin, shy, very unsure of himself, attended our training camp. Now on the organizing committee, he leads three boys to Christ in the first three days. B., tall, quiet, partially deaf, suddenly comes alive as he leads a traditional northern song, the kind that begins "THE Lord GOD is THE Cre-A-tor OF the HEAV-ens AND the EARTH, HE'S the O-ONE who GA-ave LIFE to MEN, AL-LE-LU-IA!" and goes through the entire history of redemption in about 25 rhythmic and oft-repeated couplets, finally ending "JE-SUS is COM-ing BACK in POW-ER and MIGHT, We shall ALL BE raised UP to HEAV'N with HIM, AL-LE-LU-IA!"

'The afternoons of December 25 and 26 were set aside for witnessing in the town, if possible to friends and relatives (usually harder than to strangers!). Three teams spoke with classmates who confessed that only fear of being thrown out of the house kept them from coming to Christ. "Please come again to talk to me about Jesus," they requested. "Please lend me more books about God." Another team shared with a group of people gathered to celebrate. To their astonishment, the Holy Spirit came upon some of the women with such conviction that they began to weep spontaneously and openly repent of sin. C. took his team to visit one of the school authorities. She too repented and believed.'

1980 finally brought official recognition – a sign of the churches' growing confidence in the movement, and a tremendous answer to prayer after an alarming period when the government had decided that the university group's legal situation was not yet acceptable, and ordered all activities to be suspended. At the end of 1981, Ann handed over the co-ordination of the work – now involving over sixty-five high-school groups besides the university work – to a Camerounian, Jules Simo, and moved into a new ministry as Bible study secretary for the whole of French-speaking Africa.

The younger groups

The 1975 continental Congress that stimulated the Camerounian high-schools work was important for French-speaking Africa in other ways too. Alastair Kennedy handed over leadership of the work to an African IFES staffworker, Isaac Zokoué, from the Central African Republic. Isaac's involvement in the growing high-school and university work in the CAR had produced much-needed improvement in relations with the evangelical churches in that country; and earlier that year the CAR students' first national training course had been held. Isaac's concern was to see national movements develop within the French-speaking region, and these years saw GBUs pioneered in many new countries.

A group had formed in Niamey, **Niger,** in 1973. Niger is 86% Muslim, with very few evangelicals, and once again the founders were all students from other African countries, particularly Upper Volta. This was a hindrance in obtaining government recognition. Only in 1981 did three Niger nationals come into the membership of the group. In **Upper Volta** itself, ironically, the group began slightly later, in 1974-75, and almost immediately suffered a heavy blow when half its members were transferred to other universities. Nonetheless, it survived and grew in numbers, even establishing high-schools work in close co-operation with Scripture Union. A visit from Solomon Andriatsimialomanan-arivo, who succeeded Isaac Zokoué as GBUAF general secretary, led to the formation of a graduates' group in 1981.

A group began in **Togo** the same academic year, after several attempts that had collapsed through apathy; and, as in Cameroun, a Chadian student was responsible. In Togo – as elsewhere in the region – many students face the reality of black magic. (Alastair Kennedy wrote of a Togolese student's deliverance from demonic oppression during the 1973 Congress: 'His whole life had been ravaged by the effects of the black magic practised years ago by his father: the latter had even mutilated his eight-year-old son to get a finger and some blood for his rites. During the conference we became increasingly aware of his need, and near the end met in a small group to claim his deliverance from all that had darkened his life, even since his conversion. On the return journey, we were struck by the difference in him.') Students from a supernaturalistic context needed a particular approach in evangelism. Many unbelievers might sometimes come to a prayer cell wanting prayer as a 'spiritual insurance' – particularly during exams or sickness. But they might remain very vague about faith as a life-commitment. So the introduction of evangelistic Bible study into the cell groups has been increasingly important, in order to confront such students with the reality of the gospel. Gradually, more Togolese students have become involved.

Further to the north, in **Mali**, the population is again more than 85% Muslim, and for a long time youth work was permitted only through the church. But a vigorous Bible study group for students and civil servants came into being in the mid-1970s and enjoyed friendly links with the GBUAF. At the time of writing it has some fifty members, though only half of these would attend regularly. Similar legal difficulties faced the students in the **Congo Republic** during these years, as the government had prohibited religious activities on campus. In 1974, they affiliated as a student sub-section to the Protestant youth movement; but it remained difficult for them to know how best to evangelize in view of the legal restrictions.

Before the end of 1975 a group had sprung up in the small central African country of **Rwanda**, followed by neighbouring **Burundi** in 1977. In Burundi the old problems reappeared of the majority of group members being foreigners, and the need for government recognition. A beginning was also made in **Réunion** and **Mauritius**, two small islands in the Indian Ocean over 400 miles east of Madagascar and 1,000 miles from continental Africa. The Réunion group was formed in 1974, but the majority of members were not national and were 'only passing through'. In 1976, however, the work recommenced, and by the end of the decade had a team of leaders, 'heads bubbling with ideas...but without a penny!'

They attempted to set up a literature table, and a programme based on audio-visuals. However, as Jean-Marie Langevillier wrote, 'We ran up against financial problems in the first instance, and indifference and finance in the second – and sheer geography when we tried to hire films from organizations overseas! So many times the barriers created by the enemy have seemed insurmountable, and so often we've wanted to give it all up. But praise be to God who, patient, loving, has known how to find words of encouragement in the Bible for each of us.' In that spirit, they have ventured into high-schools work too. In Mauritius, the university enrolment of around 800 includes a number of Chinese. In 1977 Stella Chan, a missionary from Hong Kong, passed through the campus and witnessed to some students who later found the Lord. A GBU came into being; but without staff support it has dwindled, and is down to two part-time students at the time of writing.

The most recent countries to develop student witness have been **Benin**, where a group began in the capital in 1978, followed by others further north during the early eighties; and **Guinea**, where an independent youth movement, the Jeunesse Chrétienne Evangelique de Guinée, emerged in the late 1970s under the wing of the evangelical church. Simeon Zoumanigui wrote in the IFES *Praise and Prayer Bulletin*, 'In the past it has been very difficult to find Christians among the students. But since the organization of a Christian group, a good number have joined us, and it is the students themselves who are bearing witness to their neighbours. We praise God!' In 1982 they held their first-ever national Bible camp, with sixty-one participants.

Plainly, French-speaking Africa is at a time of need and opportunity. In many countries, there is real openness: some groups are flourishing despite most unpropitious circumstances. In **Chad**, where tens of thousands died in the civil war in the late '70s and early '80s, many of the groups stopped meeting, the bank account was cut off, the publications stopped for lack of funds, and the headquarters were pillaged. But honorary travelling secretaries were appointed to keep contact with group members, and to encourage the formation of cell groups so that activities could continue. About twenty cells came into being, including some in areas where the movement was previously

287

unknown; and some 150 took part in leadership training sessions for the cell group leaders. A national assembly was held at Koumra, with 106 participants, and the movement took the step of faith of appointing its first staffworker, Djikoloum Magourna. Each group promised to contribute a certain number of litres of petrol for his ministry. He and the zonal co-ordinators traversed the country unceasingly despite transport problems and physical danger from the continued unrest, and by late 1980 thirty-four groups existed.

But even today there is no work in **Gabon,** or in **Mauritania** (indeed, there are no known national believers in Mauritania). In many countries the work is in need of assistance. GBUAF's basic problem has been its chronic shortage of staff. In the mid-1970s, Alastair Kennedy, Isaac Zokoué, Claude and Anne-Marie Décrevel and IFES Graduate Team worker Stan Le Quire were all actively involved. But around 1978 Isaac was not only responsible for the entire region as GBUAF general secretary, but was also the only staffworker for fourteen countries! He wrote a year later, 'We keep increasing our contacts in the hope of recruiting more travelling secretaries, but the only response is "We're praying for you"... People most likely to join the GBUAF team are those their local church or denomination is most loath to part with...' Going into full-time service for God, even short-term, remains rare among former GBU members. For a graduating student in many of these countries 'the need to support his family (in the African sense of the word) is a priority. This conditions his choice of profession.'

At the time of writing, GBUAF has two workers with regional responsibilities; and at least a dozen countries will not be visited by any other full-time staff. Things are beginning to change, however, and a number of potential African staff are at last emerging. Developing links with the student movements in the English-speaking countries are also alleviating the situation: Togo with Ghana, Benin with Nigeria, Rwanda and Burundi with Uganda, for example.

Two other types of ministry are designed to help in this context. One is the crucial work of Bible study training and producing Bible study guides, so that student leaders can feed themselves on God's Word; Ann Bennighof's current assignment is in this area. The other is the literature ministry. Nancy Felix – again, from Switzerland – went to Abidjan in 1978 as GBUAF's literature secretary. She became involved in conceiving and producing a high quality, four-colour student magazine entitled *Découvertes*, in collaboration with Scripture Union; and also in travelling across the continent leading workshops to develop the awareness and use of literature. This was not an easy ministry in a context which is still, in many respects, an oral-based culture.

'French-speaking Africa', says Solomon Andriatsimialo-mananarivo, 'is at the crossroads of three religions: animism, Islam and Christianity. Islam seems to fit in well with the African culture, but it faces two major problems. Firstly, people see it as synonymous with fanaticism, represented by the Ayatollah. Secondly, it seems that for Islam the only way of getting converts is through oil, that is to say, petro-dollars.' But then 'Christianity has not had any more impact on the students: it is always considered a European import, linked to colonialism. Animism remains the strongest of the three, because of the emphasis on a "return to authenticity". More than 80% of the African population is rural, and they often resist foreign culture, especially foreign religion.' It is a situation in which GBUAF has a crucial role to play. In French-speaking Africa only a fairly small percentage of people receive higher education, and GBUAF can raise up from among them disciples for Christ whose faith is both authentically biblical and authentically African. There is a need for prayer.

And there is no other part of the world from which pleas for prayer come with such fervency. When requests for items for the IFES *Praise and Prayer Bulletin* are sent to some of these small, isolated groups, they frequently respond with delighted gratitude. 'It is a profound joy for us to find that other Christians are thinking of us,' wrote Jean-Marie Langevillier from Réunion; 'we appeal to all Christian university fellowships for mutual support in prayer.' 'We are really thankful that you'll pray for us,' said Alice Wong from Mauritius. Etienne Coulibaly of Mali replied, 'I don't know how to put into words the joy I felt on receiving your letter. I'm very happy to know that the Lord takes care of us, and that He has placed in your heart a desire to pray for us and make our problems yours. Your letter shows me once again that we belong to the same family, and together we form the body of Christ.' Believers in these pioneering situations know the crucial importance of the prayers of fellow-Christians elsewhere.

THE AFRICAN FUTURE

In 1900, Africa had nine million Christians; now there are an estimated 160 million. The African church is a growing church – and a church with a great need for teachers and leaders of calibre. The IFES movements can play a part in meeting that need.

But it is a huge task. There is pioneering work to be done in Somalia, Angola, Mozambique, Gabon, Mauretania and elsewhere. Shortage of funds hinders the existing national movements from employing an adequate number of staff, and providing materials and training for student leaders. Many countries have only one staffworker – or none at all.

The importance of associate staff has already been mentioned: and the movements' graduates in general have a crucial role to play. This was clearly demonstrated by the emergence of two of the most recently-formed national movements, **Sierra Leone** FES and **Liberia** FES. These movements contain two of Africa's oldest university groups. But it was only when graduate fellowships appeared in these countries in 1977–78 that steps were taken to appoint a national staffworker, Mlen-Too Wesley, who could give leadership in the formation of national movements linking the large university groups with seven smaller groups in Liberia and four more in Sierra Leone.

The vision of the African movements is to see trained student leaders running balanced programmes, that make disciples able to think and act biblically at home, in the church and in society. They look forward to mobilizing an army of graduates who will all be active in local churches, with some serving as pastors, and others lecturing in theological faculties. All these developments will, of course, need to be backed by intelligent, biblical literature. John Gichinga wrote sadly in 1982 that 'We neither have money nor facilities to guarantee the publication of even the best manuscripts'. Such a situation should not be permitted to last. There is much to be done in evangelism, in discipling, in financial support and in prayer if the African movements are to fulfil their vast potential.

7
North America and the West Indies

The two national movements of the North American continent, IVCF-Canada and IVCF-USA, are among the oldest and largest IFES movements, with a history stretching back before the Second World War. In the West Indies, however, the IFES ministry commenced after the war, through a combination of student concern and mechanical malfunction!

The West Indies
The University of the West Indies did not come into existence until 1948, so many Jamaican students went to universities in Canada. Some were involved in IVCF groups there – particularly at McGill University in Quebec – and returned home with a vision for student work. In 1944, Stacey Woods was on the way back from an exploratory journey through Central America, and the flying boat in which he was travelling developed problems in take-off. ('The captain ordered, "All passengers sit in the rear of the plane on one another's knees. We'll have another try." I had two people on top of me.') When they reached Jamaica the plane landed for repairs, and Stacey was marooned for five days. 'This unplanned, unscheduled layover was in God's plan and fore-sight,' he says. 'I was able to visit schools, learn of the preparation for the opening of the University, and meet with church leaders and Christians in education. They urged that we help them.'[1]

As a result, IVCF-Canada staffworker Cathie Nicoll – who served with IVCF from 1930 right through until 1982! – was sent by IFES to Jamaica for three months in 1948. She succeeded in

[1] C. Stacey Woods, *Some Ways of God*, p.53.

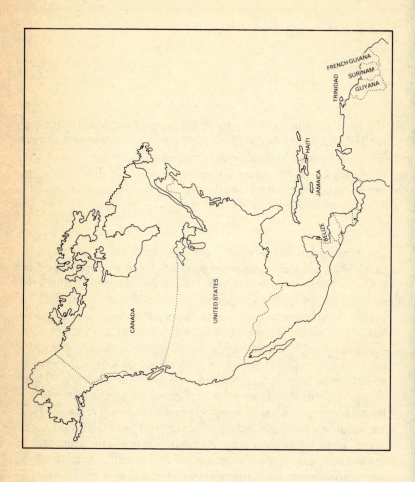

pioneering a high-schools work. In 1952 a university group developed too, through a second visit from Cathie Nicoll; and four years later the first full-time staffworker, Richard Bell, was appointed. He also travelled to other parts of the Caribbean. In 1958 only two Inter School Christian Fellowship groups existed outside Jamaica, but before the end of 1959 there were eight in Guyana, four in Barbados, three in Trinidad and one each in Antigua, Grenada and St Kitts, besides the fourteen in Jamaica.

These developments were made much easier by the presence of graduates from IFES movements elsewhere who now occupied strategic positions, such as Alfred Sangster in Jamaica. Graduates of the Jamaican Inter-Varsity group were playing a significant role – Ruby Thompson in Trinidad, Joy O'Jon and Winston McGowan in Guyana. As university-level education expanded in the Caribbean, tertiary groups appeared too. A few Trinidadian tertiary students began a Bible study in the home of a lecturer, and adopted the name Inter Varsity Christian Fellowship, on the model of Jamaica, after a few of them had attended Trinidad's first ISCF camp in 1961.[2] Similar groups emerged in Barbados and Guyana; and in 1969 a regional IVCF conference was initiated. Up to that time West Indies students had gone to IVCF-Canada leadership conferences for training.

During the 1970s the different countries began to appoint national staff for the burgeoning work. By 1977 some 200 high-school groups existed in twelve Caribbean territories, involving at a modest estimate some 6,000 students. The need for staff support was also felt in the tertiary sector. After a visit from IFES general secretary Chua Wee Hian in 1976, the national movements decided to invite Eila Helander – the Finnish staffworker who had just succeeded in working herself out of a job in East Africa – to come to the West Indies. Eila played an important part in the development of the tertiary work. Subsequently, in 1981, the first IFES regional secretary for the Caribbean was appointed, Frank Goveia from Guyana. Doug and Adele Calhoun, formerly with IVCF-USA, were also appointed to IFES staff, to work alongside the student groups in Trinidad in particular. Their contribution was valuable, and when they returned home two years later their place was taken by a Trinidad national, John Fung.

[2] Eila Helander, *Cultural change and persistence in a religious group in the Caribbean context: a case study of the IVCF in Trinidad*, pp.23–24.

293

At the beginning of the 1980s, God had raised up ISCF groups in 150 schools in Jamaica, 100 in Guyana (although most of these were in the areas around the capital), eighty in Trinidad and forty in Barbados. Barbados has seen striking developments in evangelism; staffworker Terry Frith reported in 1980 that the witness of students in one institution had led to sixty responding positively to the gospel over two years! Evangelistic films have proved particularly effective. In Jamaica, the movement faced severe economic problems as many supporters were emigrating to the USA. Nevertheless, during the early 1980s they were able to increase their staff team to six, and the work has been put on a firmer footing as a result. Of particular note is a strikingly well-presented newspaper named *Manna*, produced by the students for the twenty tertiary groups. Its circulation reached 2,000 by 1982. The Jamaican movement has now merged with Scripture Union and is called Students Christian Fellowship and Scripture Union (SCF/SU).

Students currently comprise more than half of the English-speaking Caribbean population! Yet some of the greatest needs in the region exist in the countries that are not English-speaking. Spanish-speaking countries are closely linked with the IFES work in South America, as was indicated in chapter 5. In Surinam, where Dutch, English and Taki Taki are spoken, university students have pioneered a group. In French-speaking Haiti, with its culture heavily dominated by a mixture of Roman Catholicism and occult voodooism, a group came into existence in the late 1950s through Paul Decorvet, who had been on staff in French-speaking Switzerland. But it still amounts to no more than twenty-five students. A pastor named Esperance Julsaint has been working with them since 1974. One major difficulty is that any gathering of university students tends to result in police surveillance.

At high-school level, a strong work has developed in the rural island of La Gonâve, off Haiti, through the efforts of Hans Spruijt, a Dutch development worker with Tear Fund and the American development agency Compassion. Hans was involved in drilling wells in the area, and in 1979 he invited three students from the university group in the capital to help him start Bible study groups in the schools. (In Haiti, it is not unknown to find a twenty-year-old at primary school!) Since then around a dozen groups have developed, and Hans has found a co-ordinator for them, Yves Joseph. His has not been an easy ministry, since the groups usually meet at night and the only way to visit them is by long journeys on horseback.

Canada

The work of IVCF-Canada has faced inevitable problems as a result of the country's immense size. As late as the 1950s, staffworker Tony Tyndale was working with universities in an area stretching from Windsor, Ontario, to St John's, Newfoundland, a distance of nearly 3,000 miles. Again, when a national staff conference was held in 1979 – for the first time in seven years – travelling expenses took the cost up to about 3% of the movement's budget! During the 1960s, the western regions of Alberta and British Columbia became large entities within the movement, and the movement's structure moved towards decentralization into seven regional divisions. This enabled the work to develop in ways expressing the different regional consciousness of each area.

But the same decade saw what the Canadians have referred to as 'some fuzziness in focus'; there was a lack of clarity as to the movement's purposes. When general director Wilber Sutherland – the movement's leader since 1952 – moved on in 1970, no Canadian successor was in sight. The Canadians took the imaginative step of appointing a non-Western IFES staffworker, Samuel Escobar of Peru, as general director from 1972 to 1975; he was succeeded by a Canadian, Don MacLeod. With the support of several other able leaders, a new direction emerged. One mark of this was the clarification of the movement's doctrinal basis, with the adoption of the IFES statement in place of a wording that had proved to be somewhat ambiguous.

Today, God has given IVCF some 4,000 tertiary members in 155 groups, and 4,800 high-school members in 410 groups. An intriguing aspect of the high-schools work has been its emphasis on student leadership. The Ontario division, for example, have in recent years invested much energy in training camps for high-school students, with planning weekends in September and January and a week-long leadership camp in June. A travelling Student Team exists for non-staffed areas; they have had many opportunities to participate in classroom situations, and to speak on such topics as ecology or family relationships. There is an Ontario ISCF student executive that meets together four weekends a year. This student leadership is backed up by adult advisers, who are likewise encouraged to meet together as often as possible, and by the Canada ISCF manual, developed during the 1970s and focusing on the work's philosophy, besides giving many programme ideas.

The Canadian universities work contains a broad variety of situations. The University of British Columbia group has 250 or more members. The VCF at Edmonton has (among other achievements) probably done more to support IFES financially than any other single student group in the world: their second-hand book exchange has made possible regular donations of up to $7,000 Canadian, which is over 20% of the annual budget of some of the larger African student movements! Many of the stronger groups are on small urban campuses. In contrast, McGill University and the University of Toronto, arguably Canada's two most significant campuses, have of late proved difficult to reach. (Toronto's students have even been proposed as an 'unreached people'!)

IVCF's Pioneer Camp ministry dates right back to the beginning with Howard Guinness. IVCF has eleven campsites, three of them operating all year round; two dozen mobile camps have been added recently. Crafts, canoeing, gymnastics, hockey, music, overnight trips, horse-riding and archery are among the programmes offered. Wilber Sutherland drew parallels with Scripture to explain the camps' evangelistic potency: 'The Lord Jesus Christ did almost all His preaching in the out-of-doors, drawing most of His illustrations from circumstances which lay about Him...When the Lord seeks to restore a defeated servant and then to commission him to a glorious life of service He chooses to make the setting a campfire. After a hard night's toil Peter is called home to breakfast and then to those few simple words which strike home so tellingly.' So, says Wilber, a talk around a campfire 'after a good meal at the end of a hard day's work or a hard night's haul can be very significant indeed'.

It is not just the 'warm camaraderie that binds the hearts of campers', providing 'a God-given opening for heart to heart conversation'; nor is it merely the concentrated time, and isolation from distractions. Rather, he says, it is what the Psalms declare, that 'A true appreciation of the magnificence and wonder of creation can lead a man – or a child – to that sense of awe and humility which is always necessary if a man is really to hear God speaking to him'. This is not 'a nature sentiment which makes emotional enjoyment of the out-of-doors an excuse for evading the broad realism of the Scriptures'. Rather, the glory of nature poses a question to which God's verbal Word provides a response. 'One of the major tragedies of this generation is its preoccupation with the sight of its own handiwork. As long as its vision is filled with its own importance, it is not really interested in what God has to say. But a man – or a teenager – who has lived close to nature has glimpsed a world of more terrifying dimensions than these.'[3]

The camper's perspective was expressed rather movingly in a poem quoted by Marj Long in *Interaction*. It was written by a girl who had come to camp four years in succession, frequently seemed disinterested, and finally, knowing she would be too old to participate the following year, announced, 'It is my last, and I can't be a leader. I'm not a Christian.'

> This is the last mornin'
> that I wake up in this old cabin
> watching the sun
> streaming through the cracks.
> This is the last mornin'
> that I wash in lake water
> since the power in the shower house doesn't work.
> In the next cabin girls are talking;
> I can smell the wood burning
> in the rusty old stoves.
> This is the last mornin'
> that I'm going to hear about God,
> I'm going home.
>
> This is the last mornin'
> that I can breathe the fresh country air
> feel free to be myself
> watch the world turn beautiful.
> This is the last mornin'
> that I line up for breakfast;
> smile and speak to my camp friends

---

[3] The article from which these quotations are taken was reprinted by *IFES Journal* from *The Evangelical Christian*.

who I'll probably never see again.
This is a sweet warm family here,
I guess I'll never forget the times we've had
And I'm so scared to leave,
to be all alone
I'm going home.

This is the last mornin'
that I wear these smelly horse overalls
saddle and bridle those stubborn mules
just for a short ride
and face my loneliness
lying awake at night,
trying to forget my need of Jesus Christ
on the lake the loon is laughing
at my fear of Jesus
as I lay here wondering
where Jesus and I went wrong.

This is my last mornin'
I'm going to have to think about it
I'm going home.

It was three months after her last camp – after spending a weekend with a counsellor – that she wrote to Marj, 'I finally got off the fence – I'm letting Jesus take over.' The Alberta region (where Marj was divisional director for many years) sees many conversions like this; and the camping programme extends to parents too. Family camps have been held, and students can give their parents a trip to an IVCF camp as a birthday present; a number have been converted.

Canada's major pioneering area is traditionally Roman Catholic Quebec. Even as late as 1964, wrote Tony Tyndale, French-speaking Quebec seemed an impregnable stronghold of conservative Catholicism where no IVCF work was possible. In the mid-1960s, however, God placed keen evangelical Christians on each French-speaking campus as students or lecturers: Swiss-German Hanni Feurer and two others at Montreal, another Swiss as lecturer at Sherbrooke, a student called Robert Blanchard – converted through a maths professor who was asked to leave when his religious views became known – at Ottawa, and so on.

Moody films were shown in Montreal, and eventually weekends were held gathering together all the evangelicals in these campuses. Gaston Racine and Frank Horton, who had played important parts in IFES's pioneering work in French-speaking Europe, were helpful speakers at this stage. A small weekly Bible study arose in Montreal; and in 1967 the first staffworker, a former Catholic priest named Joseph Tremblay, was appointed. Tony Tyndale wrote in *IFES Journal* pleading for prayer that would 'break through the strongholds' in the minds of non-Christian students.

The following years saw the grip of institutional Catholicism on the educational system weakening as the anti-establishment mood of the counter-culture led to a questioning of every tradition. In 1972, Ramez Atallah, an Egyptian, took over the work. (He had been converted as an overseas student in Montreal ten years earlier.) It was a time when the French-speaking evangelical churches suddenly began to experience rapid growth. Many of the converts were community college students, and Ramez went from campus to campus encouraging the formation of small Bible study groups. These groups reflected the evangelistic enthusiasm of the converts, who were unashamedly sharing their new-found faith with their classmates. It was not uncommon, year after year, for a third to a half of the participants at a camp to be converts of the previous twelve months. And with the mushrooming of evangelical churches in Quebec, some of these converts were church leaders within a few years!

At one college, St Laurent CEGEP, a single student was praying, 'Lord, help me to meet other believers!' She was joined by another student who had found Christ in the summer vacation. Staffworker Dominique Courbet helped them set up a book-table – but they were asked to move it to an out-of-the-way, dimly-lit room. Apparently depressing – but the anonymity of the location meant that student after student came to share spiritual problems. Six months into the academic year, there were a dozen believers in that college.

Of course, the new situation had its own particular problems. Such a large number of converts created a desperate need for Bible teaching. The cults, and Marxism too, were thriving in the atmosphere of spiritual questioning. The French-speaking high schools remained firmly Catholic, and closed to evangelical work. And, with the rise of Quebecois nationalism, many English-speaking Quebecois Christians began to leave Quebec, so that the long-established work in the English-speaking high schools showed a marked decline. By 1980 Ramez was convinced that English-speaking Quebec had become the most unevangelized part of North America, and was appealing for English-speaking Christians to come to the province. In 1981 there were still only 145 students in the English-speaking IVCF tertiary groups, and 100 in the French-speaking ones. Two years later, however, Ramez's successor in the French-speaking work, former IFES staffworker Claude Décrevel, reported that God had given them another 'new beginning', with at least thirty conversions in the 1982–83 academic year – more than in the previous three years together.

The United States

Inter-Varsity Christian Fellowship of the USA experienced phenomenal growth during the Second World War, despite all the obstacles of the period. When the war ended there were around 200 IVCF groups.[4] Large numbers of independent evangelical student groups were choosing to affiliate with IVCF; the commitment of returned war veterans gave an added impetus. By 1948–49 IVCF was involved officially or unofficially with 500 active student groups, nearly 350 of which were actually affiliated (including Student Foreign Missions Fellowship groups). These were being supported by thirty-seven full-time and three part-time staff.

By 1950 it was reported that some 2,000 conversions had taken place in the previous academic year, and 534 groups had been meeting daily for prayer. In one group, 65% of the students had been converted that year, as had more than half of the 140 students attending one particular weekend conference. IVCF had also merged with the Nurses Christian Fellowship pioneered by Alvera Anderson and others from 1936 onwards. By 1950 one in six of the USA's 1,300 accredited schools of nursing had groups.

IVCF continued to seek new ways of increasing their evangelistic effectiveness. Experiments with the mass distribution of Gospels proved not entirely effective; university missions seemed

[4] Much of the material that follows on the period up to the mid-1960s is based on C. Stacey Woods, *The Growth of a Work of God*. Stacey was IVCF-USA general secretary from its formation until 1960.

more promising. 1950–51 saw an all-out 'Year of Evangelism'. Mission speakers were recruited from throughout the USA and Canada; Leith Samuel, an IVF-Britain staffworker with a particular gift for this kind of evangelism, was invited over for the year. The entire field staff concentrated on training for this undertaking. Some forty missions were held. Often they were not the climax, but rather the start, of an evangelistic thrust. A mission meant that the student group had declared themselves publicly, and there were cases where more students were converted during the continuing outreach afterwards than during the mission itself.

An interesting aspect of this period was IVCF's clear commitment against racial segregation, long before civil rights became an issue nationally. From 1948, in fact, IVCF official policy stated that 'All national conferences shall be on a non-segregational basis...Since coloured people tend to relate segregation and the Christianity which we represent, we must demonstrate that in Christ there is neither black nor white.' In one case, IVCF lost financial support through refusing to use a New York home where blacks were not welcome – something tragically common among whites in that area. In another case, a Victorious Life director threatened to refuse black students admission to his conference centre; whereupon Stacey Woods was 'so moved in spirit and anger' that he promised the man he would 'blast your reputation...as someone who preaches victorious life but has no victory over racial prejudice' if the ban was maintained. (It wasn't.) Most traumatic of all was when the appointment of a black staffworker was opposed by some IVCF board members, including a famous preacher from the South. Finally, the appointment was agreed – but only under the title 'Negro Staff Worker'. Stacey Woods indicated he would resign unless the worker had the same status as the rest of the team, and virtually all the staff followed suit. And the principle was carried.

The later 1950s and early 1960s saw considerable weakening in the movement, however. Many groups which had had memberships in the hundreds were reduced by up to 70%, and some virtually died out. At the end of the 1950s IVCF 'presented a grim picture', says Stacey: 'a dispirited staff and visionless students who had lost their enthusiasm for winning their friends to Christ.' He suggests a number of reasons why this occurred. The universities as a whole were growing more secularized, and in particular the student mood turned against large meetings. Signed group membership largely lapsed; procedures for electing student leaders altered, and anyone who turned up could vote. The absence of signed membership also meant that commitment to the group weakened, and regular involvement in its outreach began to seem optional. Groups tended to disintegrate into semi-autonomous Bible studies, without a weekly united meeting to give teaching and strategy.

Other problems existed at a national level. Stacey's world-wide responsibilities as general secretary of IFES were taking him out of the country for three or four months a year, but repeated attempts to find a new leader for the American movement failed. Meanwhile, tensions grew between senior staff and the board. At staff level, there was a hesitation to refuse anyone who claimed to have a call, with a consequent decline in the calibre of the staff team. The influence of the counselling theories of Rollo May led to a distrust of anything that seemed to involve imposing one's convictions on someone else, with marked results on staffworkers' approach to pastoring. Straight Bible exposition 'largely went out the window'. In one area 'permissive Christian liberty and antinomianism reached a disastrous peak. Regular "quiet time", Bible reading and prayer were discouraged as legalistic. A wide gap opened between Inter-Varsity and many of the local churches which themselves were entombed in an unrealistic, compulsive lifestyle. In that area Inter-Varsity, after unsurpassed blessing, almost collapsed for a time.'

At this very same time IVCF suddenly faced unashamed and sometimes ruthless competition on campus from a number of new evangelical organizations. 'Competition is good for American business, and it's good for Christian work,' a leader of one of these groups told Stacey. 'If you have a first-class staff-worker, I will do my best to compete and get him for my organization.' Exaggerated propaganda, and offers of 'guaranteed results' (one organization advertised offering so many conversions for so many dollars per month), made for an impressive image. IVCF lost the support of hundreds of students and church leaders because they refused to climb on the bandwagon. And meanwhile IVCF itself over-reacted; instead of throwing all its energies into a more biblical evangelism, the movement became introverted and 'like a snail, drew into its shell'.

It is striking that when one talks to IVCF leaders today there seems unanimous agreement that the movement was revitalized, humanly speaking, by the appointment of John W. Alexander as its president in 1964.[5] God can still use just one man to redirect the history of a movement even as big as IVCF-USA, it seems!

John had a reputation for being 'a man of prayer who loves students', and also a man with real management abilities. It was a much-needed combination at that time. Pete Hammond comments that where the movement had been 'a collection of extremely gifted people... with little or no unifying vision', and was 'fraught with internal conflicts', the new president brought 'a combination of vision and integrity. What he said matched up with what he did.' Jim Berney concurs: 'His godliness brought trust to the movement and he was able to delegate responsibilities very cleanly.' 'He had an extraordinary ability to free people to use their gifts,' says Peter Northrup – not an insignificant attribute in a man who was setting about building a unified strategy and organization.

This unification operated on several levels: through a commitment to training, the production of manuals for the movement, an insistence on staff all being able to teach the basics of evangelism, an emphasis on accountability, and a concern for efficiency – a concern expressed in his book *Managing Our Work*, which covers such areas as the practical management of time and the establishment of realistic goals.[6] (It is interesting to find a leader writing about management who has also produced booklets on the 'quiet time' and on Scripture memorization.) It was at this time that Barbara Boyd and others developed IVCF's 'Bible and Life' weekends, a systematic programme of training covering the Lordship of Christ, daily 'quiet times', friendship evangelism, evangelistic Bible study and discipling others, that ensured these basic areas were adequately taught to students throughout the country.

It was imperative that the movement succeeded in putting its

---

[5] John W. Alexander was to retain this post until 1981. He has also served as chairman of IFES from 1979 to the time of writing.

[6] It is arguable that some of John Alexander's contributions were completing a process Stacey Woods describes, whereby IVCF-USA changed (or became contextualized) from a movement with a basically British ethos, stemming from its historical roots, to one with a distinctively American 'face, structure, character and modus operandi' (*op. cit.*, p.30).

house in order, because later in the decade America's campuses exploded. It was not an easy time. IVCF issued a 'riot kit', urging students to keep their cell groups going even when campus violence made large meetings impossible; to build strong bonds of prayer fellowship with local churches; to think biblically about the issues, looking out for comparable scriptural situations (the Minor Prophets were emphasized); and to seize every opportunity to respond Christianly by word (meetings, handbills, posters) and deed (first-aid and deliberate peacemaking). And when it came to the deeper longings of that era, partly epitomized by the Beatles' song, 'All you need is love', the IVCF groups had something to offer. (Across the border in Quebec, a hippie visiting an IVCF-Canada community set up to witness to the 'Expo '67' event commented that it 'beat all love-ins'!)

But of course the counter-culture led to a great disillusionment, and that moment of despair with the ideological and utopian options was the time of the rise of the Jesus Movement. Thousands of students, particularly in high schools and colleges, made commitments to Christ, and when they came on to university one of the groups they sought out was IVCF. 'New life from the Jesus Movement revitalized us and caused hundreds of IVCF groups to grow,' recalls Jim Berney, co-ordinator of the expanding California work during this period (and now general director of IVCF-Canada). 'There was an opportune meeting of a structure led by John Alexander with the impulse of new life in Christ all across the USA.'

Many other factors were being used by God to deepen the life of IVCF, of course; such as the efforts in evangelism of Paul Little, author of *How To Give Away Your Faith*. IVCF's small group Bible studies have been another major emphasis. Their success no doubt owes something to the fact that American students are perhaps more naturally expressive than many of their counterparts elsewhere, but a great deal of work has gone into training small group leaders, and making available Bible study guides and methodology.[7] Paul Byer of California pioneered 'manuscript study' courses, a method of Bible study in quantity that involved giving out (for example) forty type-written pages of Mark's Gospel without verse or chapter divisions, so that students could grapple with discovering thought-

---

[7] See, *e.g.*, *Small Group Leaders' Handbook*, ed. Ron Nicholas (IVP-USA, 1982).

units and themes for themselves, for perhaps six six-hour days. ('I will never again be satisfied with a mediocre "quiet time",' was one typical reaction.) And there was InterVarsity Press, developing into a highly-respected publishing house under the leadership of Jim Nyquist, and providing essential literature for IVCF and indeed other student movements world-wide. (IVP has also given practical assistance in helping other IFES movements set up their own publishing ministries; particularly after Jim's appointment as IFES honorary literature secretary in 1977.) By 1979 IVP were selling a million books and another million pocket-size booklets annually.

And then, of course, there were the famous Urbana Missionary Conventions, organized jointly by the IVCF movements of Canada and the USA. The first such conference took place in Toronto, Canada, in 1946, with 575 students attending, and a team of speakers that included veteran missionary Samuel Zwemer, Indian evangelist Bakht Singh and IVF-China general secretary Calvin Chao. It was calculated that half the conference delegates went abroad as missionaries, including Jim Elliot of Auca fame. (He had been president of an SFMF group at Wheaton College that drew a regular 300–500 of the college's 1,500 students.)[8]

The next convention was held at Urbana, Illinois, as were all that followed. They expanded rapidly, with 1,500 participants by 1951, 5,000 by 1957, 12,000 by 1970, and 17,000 by 1976! By the 1970s a wide variety of speakers from all continents would challenge, report and preach on a broad range of mission topics. Expositors like John Stott, Philip Teng and Eric Alexander would expound large stretches of Scripture, or perhaps the biblical basis of mission, with a depth and solidity to which many students would be unaccustomed.

In 1976, all 7,000 copies of Elizabeth Elliot's book on guidance sold out before it became book of the day. In 1979, participants gave half a million dollars (besides $20,000 raised for hunger agencies in a lunch-time fast), leaving quite a responsibility on the IVCF administrators to use the money in the same spirit of prayer and sacrifice. Bel Magalit of IFES East Asia received one of the conference's few standing ovations for a talk in which he urged his hearers to 'make sharp the difference between

---

[8] David M. Howard, *Student Power in World Missions*, p.113.

American culture and the eternal gospel'. (When Bel saw the first students rise to their feet, he feared they were walking out!)

Many participants would share the reaction of the Philadelphia student who said that 'Christ's Lordship in my life, the effect of His Lordship in the lives of others and the effect of their lives awed me'. Billy Graham has written that 'Virtually every place I go in the world I meet men and women who first received their call to missionary service through Urbana, or who have been influenced by Inter-Varsity in other ways'.

Urbana is only the centrepiece of a massive commitment to missionary vision that has marked IVCF throughout its history. Through the Student Training in Mission programme, for example, and similar ventures such as the Overseas Training Camps, several hundred IVCF students have been given an in-depth, carefully-planned cross-cultural exposure designed to equip them for missionary service. Throughout much of the early history of IFES, IVCF-USA contributed the lion's share of the IFES budget, and still contributes more than any other country.[9] (In recent years its contribution has been roughly equivalent to that of the IFES affiliates in western Europe, who have approximately the same number of tertiary members as IVCF-USA.)

At the same time, the Urbana Conventions highlighted the need to come to terms with the fact that America's student population was not all white. This became acute with the upsurge of black consciousness in the late 1960s, when black Christian students were having to live with the argument that Christianity was just a manipulative tool to isolate and control them. The issues came to a head at Urbana '67, which had consciously shifted away from the discussions of race, nationalism, *etc.* that had marked the two previous conventions, to a more traditional missionary emphasis. This was in response to a feeling that Urbana was growing 'too problem-centred, rather than Christ-centred'.

But for blacks present for the first time, this made the conference 'tremendously difficult to absorb', recalls Elward Ellis, now IVCF's black campus director. 'Because whether it was cultural barriers, bad economic conditions, the need for holistic ministry,

---

[9] IVCF-USA contributed nearly 90% of IFES's income from 1947 to 1963. This dropped to around half in the early 1970s, and to a third by the early '80s. The IFES budget in 1983 was over four times as large as that of 1973.

you name it we had it here in the USA too.' These issues seemed to be related only to overseas contexts. An all-night prayer meeting was held in one of the residences in Florida Avenue, and the black students petitioned the conference director for a chance to present their concerns. 'We were given one small meeting, and we thought, OK, we'll take it and run with it. The place was packed out! – 300 people, blacks, whites, the press. We had prayed for that meeting, and people's hearts were burdened. We were angry that all this hadn't occurred to someone earlier, and we said that too.'

It was noticed, for example, that 'the only blacks in the Urbana promotional film were Africans! Which made a black viewer feel, "This is not about me, it doesn't speak to the issues I'm concerned about."' Elward pointed this out, and as a result found himself being asked to write a filmscript for the first time in his life. But the problem went deeper. 'At IV camps, for example, the whole mode was alien to us. We were well-received, but the environment didn't make us comfortable. There was a need for music and speakers that blacks could partake of.' And the later sixties saw students form two specifically black IV groups. Also, Paul Gibson 'decided God wanted him to take the plunge and go into the organization', becoming IVCF's first black staffworker since 1961.

At Urbana '70 there were 500 blacks. 'We succeeded in getting the mainstream there', says Elward, 'and some were very uneasy with what they heard. Until Tom Skinner, George Verwer and Warren Webster saved the day by tackling the race issue head on.' Two of those three were white. 'Whites had spoken to our concerns too! The evening Tom Skinner spoke, we filled up the front few rows. It was a time when there had been lots of riots, and the convention organizers were going out of their minds and asking, What's going to happen? But it was our night, the Soul Liberation music group were on the programme, our man was up there, we were included. Skinner was up till 3 a.m. discussing with us: Did co-operation with white Christians make any sense? Why were we here?'

Afterwards came something of a lull. Urbana '73 'didn't have the same content', from the blacks' point of view. Not that nothing was happening on the local level; in highly multiracial Brooklyn College, New York, for example, a small group of Christian students and teacher Barbara Benjamin succeeded in

307

pioneering the only integrated group on campus. 'Thanks to the leftist rhetoric,' says Barbara, 'our consciousness about inter-racial relationships had been aroused. We determined to do what they talked about but were never able to realize...In Christ this is possible, though not as easy as we anticipated.' Not easy, because blacks joining an integrated group faced hostility from their own community; and extremists of other ethnic origins also saw the Christians as a threat, stole literature, and even violently disrupted a meeting, besides making various attempts to have the Christian group outlawed. Nonetheless, a fellowship emerged with students of 'Oriental, Irish, Hispanic, Norwegian, Black American, Italian, Jewish, Turkish, German and Caribbean descent' – a mixture with vast differences in culture and attitudes to worship, but whose unity was a powerful witness.[10]

But total integration was not always appropriate. Barbara conceded reluctantly that to reach particular ethnic groups it was sometimes necessary to give them a particular emphasis and a culturally-appropriate setting. 'It is best on campuses to have Blacks evangelize Blacks. I hated to admit it, but we had to... work from there as a starting-point.' Elward Ellis argued that blacks needed a culturally-oriented evangelistic strategy: most 'have a sort of basic ontological awareness of God, so apologetics for us needn't start with the existence of God. To talk about God as an abstraction is a kind of sacrilege to us. Apologetics needs to be closely related to our survival concerns: What did you confront that you could not contend with in your own resources? In what way did God bring you out?'

In the mid-1970s the IVCF national leadership became increasingly concerned to reach black students and recruit black staff. This concern met with some reluctance from potential black workers. 'I didn't want to work for a predominantly white organization,' says Elward. 'I'd suggest what IV should do, but never thought they would bring it in, or that there would be the quality of trust that would permit indigenous leadership...But the things I hadn't dreamed of ended up happening. I was getting nervous!' Within the black community, an IVCF staff-worker faced tensions. 'People would feel I should be in the black clergy: Why are you working with whites? Because of an identity

[10] The whole story is told in Barbara Benjamin, *The Impossible Community* (IVP-USA, 1978).

308

deficiency? Because you're dropping out? But the Lord confronted me with Eph. 2:14, that the dividing walls of hostility were in fact broken down. And yet folk didn't want to be bothered with white people. We were trying to avoid, racially, culturally, the reality of the gospel – just what we accused IV of in 1967.'

The willingness of Elward and (by 1982) seventeen other black staff to 'go into the organization' has been matched by the development of black IVCF groups on thirty-four campuses. Fund-raising remains a real problem, as not all black evangelicals understand what black IVCF staff are doing. But Elward is convinced that 'IV's distinctives – giving a *reason* for the faith that's within us – will be increasingly important as more blacks go to university, and as more get shattered by atheistic or humanistic teaching. We can help them deal with the questions, help them in the discipline of growth through the Word of God.' IVCF-USA is also developing ministries among the Asian, Native American and Hispanic sections of the student population. (In the latter instance, IFES input was of some significance. Hispanic co-ordinator Ruth Lewis attended the 1981 IFES Latin America Congress and thought it was 'just fantastic... If God was doing that down there, then why was it not happening among Hispanics here?')

As time goes on these ministries will be of increasing importance. The student population of New York, for example, contains only a small section who are 'White Anglo-Saxon Protestants'. By 1990, the American student population will be more than 12% black, 5% Hispanic and 4% Asian, besides 10% made up of foreign students. (The USA has the fifth largest Spanish-speaking population in the world!) Considerable sensitivity is necessary as IVCF seeks to develop. This was demonstrated when the movement ventured into a major conference on urban issues, Washington '80, which drew 1,100 participants.[11]

To begin with, scheduling the conference over New Year's Day was a cross-cultural miscalculation that kept the Hispanic

[11] Speakers included Congressman Walter Fauntroy (a Baptist minister and close associate of the late Martin Luther King, Jnr.), Ozzie Edwards (director of Harvard's Center for Urban Studies), and Samuel Escobar (IFES associate general secretary for Latin America), plus many others involved in practical urban ministries.

attendance low. And early on, as Harry Genet noted in *Christianity Today*, there seemed to be a tacit assumption that 'IV basically needed to apply the logistics know-how it has acquired over eleven Urbanas', until two black staff warned Pete Hammond that planning an urban conference without major black input would destroy their credibility: 'You'll kill us, if you go ahead like this.' The convention planners responded; and the result was a series of 'listening conferences' around the country to find what black church leaders had on their agenda.

But once the blacks were basically shaping the programme, the whites and other ethnic groups began to have problems. At the conference 'many exhibited the symptoms of culture shock', observed Genet. 'Many even found it awkward to keep time to the music, conditioned as they were to clap on the (white) downbeat instead of the (black) upbeat.' Asian-American staff Jeanette Yep was struck by the continual comments from the audience – 'Well!', 'Yes!', 'Careful!', 'Tell us about it!', 'Preach it!'. 'At first it was all new and interesting, but by the third or fourth day I began to feel pain and frustration...I was eager to go home.' All the difficulties of building bridges! Still, IVCF had taken the plunge, and started on the journey of discovering together how their movement can give to America's cities.

But there remains a massive amount to be done in terms of IVCF's primary task of making disciples on campus. IVCF believed that in 1981–82 God had given them over 2,600 conversions, the greatest number in the movement's history. It was estimated that one in five IVCF students would have found Christ at university. However, this was a much smaller percentage than in the heyday of the Jesus Movement, as Bob Fryling observed; and there were few states where more than 1% of students were involved with IVCF. One reason was the astounding proliferation (or fragmentation, as a foreigner might call it) of Christian campus organizations. The University of Wisconsin at Madison had forty-four, for example. But putting all these groups together, and adding in the estimated 100,000 students in America's Christian colleges, it was doubtful whether 200,000 of America's 12 million students were active in Christian student groups.

Considerations like these have shaped the growth-oriented approach of John Alexander's successor, James McLeish, who has taken IVCF a great deal further in the direction of management planning and expansion of IVCF's 300-plus staff team.[12] He has sought to stimulate new initiatives in evangelism, particularly in major outreaches, and in penetrating every grouping in the university community.

University missions died out in America in the late 1960s; many of the major outreaches since that time have been based around productions of IVCF's gifted multimedia team, *Twenty-onehundred Productions*. This began in California under the leadership of Eric Miller, with a presentation using slide and movie projectors, lighting effects and folk and rock music. After becoming part of the national ministry in 1972, the team created a wide variety of two-projector slideshows such as *The Effective Ambassador* (evangelistic training), *Waste Paper* (pre-evangelism), and *The Promise and the Blessing* (the biblical basis for world mission). In 1980 they launched a major evangelistic multi-image presentation entitled *Where is the God of Heaven and why is He taking so long?* – 50 minutes long, with an original music score and two dozen automated slide projectors, which meant multiple projectors functioning for each segment of a 50-foot screen. The theme, surprisingly, was the little-known Old Testament book of Habakkuk.

The initial impulse came from a 'manuscript study' session, where it was pointed out that Habakkuk was a very visual book, having many words to do with seeing and hearing. After that the team put in a year's study of the book's three chapters, and a great deal of prayer. The visuals that resulted were designed to tie the prophet's struggle and conclusions into the contemporary context – the search for security through lifestyle, possessions or career, for example – and so provide a basis for students to discuss the issues of the gospel with their friends. 'Sometimes still images race across the screen in animation-like sequence; at other times, the entire screen forms one congruous scene; at still other times,

---

[12] IVCF-USA's full-time staff team is larger than all the IFES movements in East Asia, Africa, Latin America and the Middle East combined. (The combined total of the European movements is around 220.) Part of the development away from the British heritage has included what to a British observer might seem a considerable shift of authority from students to staff, particularly given the absence of an American national student committee and the presence of a multi-level management structure. But IVCF-USA has a reputation for a distinctive emphasis on student leadership, compared with other student movements working in the American cultural context.

one image breaks up into many different images,' wrote David Singer of the production in *Christianity Today*. 'The pace is ever-changing, unpredictable, all-absorbing...The depiction of God actively judging unrighteousness on personal, national and international levels is both convincing and, at moments, frightening.' At the secular International Multi-image Festival in Colorado, the Habakkuk presentation was the only show to win a standing ovation. In its first fourteen months, audiences totalling 38,000 saw it on thirty-eight campuses, and there were many conversions.

But multi-image has not made traditional preaching obsolete; and in the early eighties IVCF began to move back into university missions. One of the first was with Billy Graham at Chapel Hill, North Carolina, an event initiated by IVCF and co-sponsored by United Christian Fellowship (a black group), Campus Crusade and the Fellowship of Christian Athletes. IVCF at UNC was the country's biggest group, with nearly 750 members – although it had nearly disbanded in 1971, when its membership dropped to two. (During its twenty-year existence its membership had never passed forty. But the last two students, Roger Anderson and Jeanne Haibach, felt that 'the Lord had something in mind for UNC', and after prayer they got in contact with every new student at the start of the academic year. By the end of that year the group numbered forty, and it kept on growing, with an emphasis on clear vision, evangelism, reaching out to new students, and small groups with thoroughly-trained leaders.)[13]

The IVCF UNC students had decided to invite Billy Graham after sending two observers to his 1980 mission with the CICCU in Cambridge, England. During his time at Chapel Hill, attendances went up to 7,500 per night, of which about three-quarters were students. Nearly 60% of the 13,000 UNC undergraduates came at least once. Three dozen assistant missioners were involved in discussions in residences each night: 800 students indicated a profession of faith. 400 students had been trained to handle the follow-up. IVCF's dream was that similar missions should take place on other campuses, and thirty IVCF staff were at UNC as observers for this reason. (A similar 'chain reaction' has occurred in Australia, as we noted earlier.)

[13] Much of this paragraph draws from a report by Jim Hummel (with Susan Wheelon) in *His*.

Like everywhere else, America's campuses need evangelizing. The abortion rate in one north-western university is estimated at one in ten female students. More than half the University of Michigan's students admit cheating in exams. In New England campuses, voodoo and witchcraft are resurfacing. It is estimated that half of the college students born in the seventies will have lived in single-parent families, with all the accompanying stresses and needs. IVCF-USA has a huge task.

Nor does its size – IFES's largest tertiary-level affiliate, though with Nigeria following close – guarantee freedom from problems. Many IFES national movements experience a loss of finance as giving drops in the summer months, but to a movement the size of IVCF this can mean a cash shortage of $1 million. In recent times this has more than once caused severe concern. IVCF, too, survives by God's power alone! The worst fate of all would be to forget that simple fact. As James McLeish has commented, 'It's the grace of God that keeps you going, and the worst that can happen to a movement is to keep going when the Spirit has departed.'

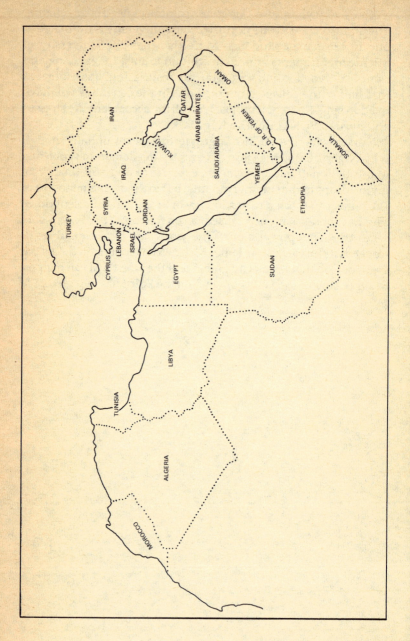

8
North Africa
and the Middle East

We come finally to the most difficult area of the world.

This region is the stronghold of Islam, and it includes at least twenty-two countries. There are the North African lands of Morocco, Algeria, Tunisia, Libya and Egypt[1]; the Near East – Turkey, Syria, Lebanon, Israel, Jordan, Iraq, and (in the Arabian Peninsula) Saudi Arabia, Yemen, South Yemen, Oman, the United Arab Emirates, Qatar, Bahrain and Kuwait; and, further east, Iran, Afghanistan and Pakistan.

Over 300 million people live in these countries. Many of them belong to tightly-knit Muslim communities. For a student from such a background to change his religion is to bring shame on his family – and perhaps severe persecution, even the possibility of assassination, on himself. In some countries, conversion is, theoretically at least, an offence carrying the death penalty.

But the vast majority of Muslims cannot be said to have rejected the gospel. They have never heard the real gospel or seen it lived! Muhammad himself seems to have had contact mostly with 'Christians' holding heretical views on matters such as the Trinity, and this has shaped the history of the region since. Many Muslims today view Christianity through hundreds of years of accumulated prejudice. They know it only as something associated with Western imperialism or economic self-interest or materialistic decadence, or with the minority traditional churches of the area. And these churches in turn are often made up of people who scarcely believe it is possible, or necessary, to win their Muslim neighbours.

[1] Sudan was covered in chapter 6.

SMALL BEGINNINGS

This region of twenty-two countries extends from the Atlantic to the borders of India; and in that vast area, a national, interdenominational evangelical student movement has arisen in just two countries, Pakistan and Lebanon.

Pakistan

David Bentley-Taylor served as IFES regional secretary for the Islamic world from 1968 till 1974, and his numerous and lengthy travels throughout the area established a network of contacts on which the work has continued to be built. A national student movement finally emerged in Pakistan – a country which, unlike most others in the area, had a sizeable evangelical minority – when God brought together a number of such people in a common vision.

Perhaps the first seeds were sown, as David Penman has suggested, 'in the way God moved from 1956 onwards in Lahore', in northern Pakistan. Here Gordon Olsen was working as a missionary, seeking to establish an evangelical student fellowship and to find national co-workers. (He was an IFES staffworker from 1962 onwards.) It was not easy. Nevertheless when he returned home in 1964 he had trained Maqbool Gill to be his replacement in a loosely organized individual ministry in some parts of the Punjab. Maqbool carried on, mainly alone and with many difficulties, until 1969. 'There was no team behind him, no committee, and the IFES seemed a long way away,' as John Ray explains. No permanent groups emerged; yet there were indications that God was preparing a number of people who would later join together in the ministry.

One reason for the lack of supporters was that SCM groups already existed in the five Christian colleges, and they and others were working through local church fellowships. However, the thrust of much youth ministry in Pakistan was largely institutional, or at least highly structured, rather than being a matter of students witnessing to fellow-students. In many instances, concern had shifted from student evangelism to social uplift, and from reliance on the authority of God's Word to dependence on human reason. Nonetheless, the early FES workers had little desire to begin a separate movement, and efforts were made to co-operate with SCM leaders while introducing a biblical, evangelical emphasis. They met with little success. When

Pakistan SCM was forming its organization and writing its constitution in 1956–59, evangelical missionaries proposed amendments (including a doctrinal affirmation) that would have made it an evangelical movement. But neither this nor overtures by FES workers and helpers in 1967–69 met with great response.

By 1968 it became clear that there were many who had agonized over liberalism and superficiality in the student world and prayed for years for an evangelical witness, yet never knew of Maqbool's existence. Visits by IFES staff such as David Adeney and David Bentley-Taylor brought increasing awareness that the time had come for the formation of such a movement, emphasizing God's holiness, man's sinfulness and salvation in Christ. Maqbool was feeling that God was leading him into a different ministry as principal of Lahore Bible Institute. This, says David Penman, 'caused several of us to recognize the need for a team behind whoever else was appointed'.

Representatives of many churches and areas met together at Murree in August 1968. As a result, Michael Nazir Ali was appointed staffworker and a national board was formed. 'The years of sowing and careful nurturing of the country's Christian leadership resulted in the drawing together of a particularly effective, representative and dedicated team of voluntary co-workers,' says David Penman. Within the next three years the work 'developed beyond expectations'.

David was himself a New Zealand CMS missionary who had been converted through Howard Guinness. He became an IFES associate staffworker in 1970, and began to give his whole time to student work. But when Michael Nazir Ali departed for theological training, no national staffworker was left. There was much prayer, with what David calls the 'amazing result' that one of the country's leading evangelists offered to become a staffworker. B. U. Khokhar was an executive with Burmah-Shell, and 'few thought he would be willing to leave such a financially secure position to become an evangelist among students. God planned otherwise.' (He was to be PFES general secretary until 1980, when he handed over to Irfan Jamil.)

Together the two workers strove to strengthen the dozens of cell groups that were coming into being. In late 1971 two lady staff were appointed, Chaeok Chun from Korea in the south, and former OPKO-Finland staffworker Anja Sainio in the Punjab; besides two more national staff, Salamat Masih and Aslam Ziai.

In 1972 they were joined by John Ray, son of the Bishop of Karachi (and at the present time IFES regional secretary for Central Asia). By then there were several dozen cell groups existing in almost all Pakistan's university cities. In Hyderabad, there were many conversions, and twelve cell groups existed. A literature ministry had commenced, as had the Karachi Institute of Theology for graduates, under the leadership of Sam Pittman. And God had 'raised up supporters above what we could have ever thought of a year ago', said John Ray; in that year local giving had more than trebled.

Christian groups could not meet officially on campus, so cell groups were the movement's main focus. This emphasis was also linked to a desire to avoid the 'convention mentality', where the holding of public rallies sometimes served as a substitute for planning and practising personal evangelism. Cell groups were usually started by a graduate, who would slowly disengage as student leadership emerged; a local committee would pastor the groups, with the staffworker playing a crucial role in day-to-day contact with the leaders. Occasional city-wide meetings provided a sense of belonging and an opportunity for training in Bible study, leadership and evangelism.

The continuity provided by B. U. Khokhar's leadership – with the aid of many others, including Tara James and IFES staff-workers Ed and Donna Bradley – helped the movement win the respect it had lacked among church leaders; particularly because of its clear stand on the Word of God and its emphasis on Bible study and evangelism. A Teachers' Christian Fellowship (joint with Scripture Union), a Graduates' Fellowship and a Christian Medical Students' Fellowship have emerged. But there is still a real need for a much more sustained outreach to the largely-untouched Muslim students. (Pakistan is 97% Muslim, and has gone through a period of intensive Islamicization in the early 1980s.) 200 students and graduates attended a PFES conference in Lahore in 1981 on 'The Challenge of the Unfinished Task', which raised the question of their responsibilities beyond the borders of Pakistan. PFES is obviously a movement of great potential for this whole region in the days ahead.

David Penman wrote in 1972 of PFES's hope that 'God is calling us in Pakistan to develop patterns in this rigidly Muslim environment that will be broadly applicable to many of the nations of Muslim West Asia'. He dared to suggest that a Pan

West Asian Evangelical Student Movement was 'a vision that is no longer far beyond our reach'. However, political developments since then – the resurgence of militant Islam, the rise to power of the Ayatollah Khomeini, the Russian invasion of Afghanistan – have changed the picture.

Iran

During the late 1970s some seed was sown among Iranian students and young people, but a promising beginning was brought to a complete halt after two years by the events of the Islamic Revolution. The full-time staffworker wrote in the IFES *Praise and Prayer Bulletin* of a two-day gathering led by the Iranian Christian young people, where they were 'trying to understand the new social order since the Islamic Revolution and the price we will have to be ready to pay for continuing faithfulness to our Lord... I thank God for the growth in many of them. Even if we have to leave, the Holy Spirit will continue His work. Pray for the young converts...' Within a few months his own position finally became untenable, when his name appeared on a death-list produced as a warning by one of the guerrilla groups, and his work ceased.

Lebanon

David Penman had moved on to Lebanon in 1972, along with his wife and family. Lebanon is unusual in the Arab world in that it contains large communities both of Muslims and of nominal Christians. It has complete religious freedom and is a strategic bridgehead for the penetration of the entire area. Bible study groups emerged in Lebanon in the late sixties, with former IFES staff like Al Fairbanks (who had served in Africa) and Bob Young (Latin America) playing a significant role. By 1972 a committee of students and graduates was in charge of organizing the groups, besides arranging international dinners, trips and conferences. During the following two years the Lebanon Inter-Varsity Fellowship came into being, with this committee as its executive. Work was restricted to the English-speaking universities, but a vision was developing for the Arabic- and French-speaking campuses.

David was conscious of the lack of staff and resources – doubly so once he became IFES regional secretary for the entire Islamic world, from 1974. But, he affirmed, 'These are problems which

319

are surmountable, because we have God on our side and we believe that we're in the right place at the right time in history'. He was a man with a great ability to delegate and to share his vision; he was joined in 1973 by Pamela Harris (who came out to Lebanon on a BMMF six-week project and stayed), and soon afterwards by Samuel Abdel Shahid from Jordan and Victor Atallah from Egypt. The number of Bible study groups increased from one a week in 1973 to one a day in 1974; by 1975 there were groups meeting in or near five of Beirut's seven universities besides the graduates' fellowship. Most of these groups contained six or seven nationalities (two out of every three people in Lebanon were non-Lebanese in 1975!). Conferences regularly had fifteen countries represented – a number of them 'closed countries'. Altogether, over seventy-five students and graduates were involved, compared with a core of a dozen two years earlier.

In 1975 David Penman was succeeded as regional secretary by Colin Chapman (also seconded from CMS), who moved to Beirut with his wife Anne and their two children. An IFES Graduate Team arrived in Lebanon to spearhead the next steps. But at that point civil war broke out, and within a short time all foreign workers had to be withdrawn.

Yet right through the darkest days of the civil war one of the student groups kept on meeting. When it became impossible for students to leave their homes, group Bible studies continued by telephone. Members would study the set passage, then call each other to share what they had learnt. After the war ended, work recommenced in three campuses, though without a full-time staffworker until Afaf Musullam, a Palestinian, joined the staff in 1978. (When the civil war broke out, said Afaf, 'I cried to the Lord to take me away from a city gone mad. The Lord proved himself to me by providing a very good job in London. I was satisfied for two years; and then I knew He was calling me back to Beirut against my will and reasoning. I knew there was no running away if I meant business with the Lord.') She was followed by Alison Walley, formerly editor of the IFES magazine *In Touch*, and Eve Lanchantin from Paris.

By the late 1970s some seventy students and graduates were again involved. But the partitioning of Beirut into 'Muslim' and 'Christian' sectors posed problems. Students studying across the boundary from their homes were concerned only to attend lectures and get home before dark. Finding a time for a meeting during the day that fitted all potential members' lecture schedules was not easy. The unrest and carnage have recurred throughout recent years, and it has been difficult to set the work on a firm foundation.

Israel

Israel presents a slightly different picture. At the 1979 IFES General Committee, Israel was highlighted as a country where there were no immediate prospects of student work beginning. The gathering agreed to ask God for at least an observer from Israel at the 1983 General Committee. That prayer was answered. In Easter 1980, John Woodhead, a student leader in the group at Edinburgh University in Scotland, made an exploratory trip to Israel with the enthusiastic backing of the Scottish Christian Unions. He had been brought up in an Arab community in Nazareth, and educated in a Jewish school; consequently he had friends in both communities, and his objective was to see if anyone he had known might be interested in starting a Bible study group. But he was aware that most of the Christian students he had known had left to study abroad.

However, when he got to Israel, he found that the Lord had answered prayer and raised up no less than six Bible study groups already! These ranged in size from six to twenty, and included both Hebrew and Arab students. Some had begun through foreign students and others from abroad, particularly the USA. But three were entirely the initiative of national believers; and the six groups had arisen quite independently of each other. It was indeed a work of God.

John toured the country, visiting the groups and other interested Christians. 'There was real excitement right across the denominational spectrum,' said John. 'Our contacts gave us more contacts and this led to still more contacts. Throughout the country I met students who didn't know about any of the groups and were longing for one.' There were also a number of Christian leaders who were graduates of IFES movements elsewhere and who gave their encouragement. In 1980, about fifteen students met for a national conference. A co-ordinating committee was formed not long afterwards.

After the initial impetus came a stage of patient building. Four groups met regularly in 1981, five in 1982. A graduates' fellowship came into being that year too. There has been a real need for prayer that denominational, cultural and traditional differences among believers will be lost in a deep spiritual unity, so that others are forced to see the reconciling power of the gospel.

Egypt

The Egyptian situation has been different again, in that there is a large Christian minority in the country. There are tens of thousands of students in the Coptic Orthodox church, many of whom have shown an increasing interest in Bible study; and there are up to 3,000 students in the evangelical churches. Many city churches have meetings for university students, and hundreds of students attend summer camps and conferences in or around Alexandria. A number of parachurch ministries are seeking to provide assistance. In the early 1970s IFES worked closely with the Emmanuel Centre in Cairo, and a Graduate Team worker, Hugh Goddard, was actively involved. More recently, God has opened doors for new roles of service to the churches: two key areas at present are Bible study training and the production of appropriate literature. Ramez Atallah is co-ordinating this ministry. He is an Egyptian who left the country at the age of fourteen, met Christ in Canada and became leader of the rapidly-growing work in Quebec, as described in the previous chapter. He and his wife Becky returned to Egypt in 1980. An American couple, John and Nancy Berg, worked alongside them until 1982.

IFES has no desire to import some foreign pattern of work into Egypt. Rather, the objective is to provide as much assistance as possible to the evangelical churches, as they co-ordinate their witness and work out their own pattern. Egypt may well be the most strategic country in the Middle East at present. If God raises up a large number of Egyptian students, fervent in witness, grounded in Scripture and burdened for the world, they could play a tremendous part throughout the surrounding region.

These, then, are the main features of IFES work in the Middle East: national movements in Pakistan and the Lebanon, a developing movement in Israel, no movement but exciting potential of other kinds in Egypt. In other countries, it is likely that the work will take a different form. From two Near Eastern countries reports have come of students meeting regularly for

Bible study during the last decade or so. In Turkey, which has about 100 known believers from the 99% Muslim majority (over 45 million people), there were five to ten known Christians among the 350,000 students in 1981. One of these, the only known Christian in a university of 10,000, was living in a student hostel; and the secret police came to the hostel three times in one year to spread rumours among her friends that she was immoral, or an enemy of her country. Turkey was evangelized by the apostle Paul, but its eighteen universities have no Christian groups today!

And that is just one country. Throughout the region, the catalogue of virtually unreached campuses is huge: Rabat, Algiers, Tunis, Benghazi, Tripoli, Ankara, Baghdad, and many, many more. What is to be done?

POINTS OF STRATEGY

The strategy that has developed in the region has had, as its first step, simply finding the Christian students scattered throughout these campuses! To this end, IFES staff such as Colin Chapman and Vivienne Stacey (seconded by BMMF) have travelled many thousands of miles, developing a steadily-growing network of contacts that build on the friendships established from the time of David Bentley-Taylor onwards. Many of these students will be in countries where the authorities' attitude makes it almost impossible – barring a miracle – that an organized student movement will emerge. The task facing IFES, then, must simply be to provide Christian students with the resources they need to grow in Christ, and to be effective disciples where they are.

Conferences have an important part to play. Apart from overcoming isolation, such events enable Christian students to see in practice that Muslims can discover Christ. Some Christian students find the thought of outreach inconceivable, and God has used the conferences to give new vision, especially in recent years.[2] Regional conferences were held for the whole area from 1976 onwards; but in the early 1980s it became apparent that gatherings for smaller geographical areas might have more use. North African students, for example, may benefit more from

[2] These had to be held in Cyprus, the only country in the region in which all the students could meet without visa problems, *etc*. Nonetheless, some would be questioned on their return home about the people they had met and what they had heard.

participating in conferences of the French movement than from travelling all the way to the eastern end of the Mediterranean.

Another area is literature, a ministry in which Alison Walley has been active. Bible study guides are of particular importance – the experience of participating freely in group Bible studies at regional conferences has been quite a revelation to some students! – and two significant Arabic publications have been a booklet on *How To Lead Group Bible Study*, and a translation of the IVP personal Bible study aid *Search the Scriptures*. 'We believe this book has great potential in our area, where there is such a dearth of books which can help the Christian student dig deeper into the Scriptures,' wrote Alison. The first guide they published to a single Bible book was *Salvation and Suffering* on 1 Peter – a production of particular relevance to Lebanon, where the publishing was done. Books of this kind can be of help to churches and youth groups throughout the Middle East.

A fourth step is to send more labourers. Most of these countries will not accept missionaries; but there are literally thousands of jobs available for doctors, nurses, engineers, accountants, lecturers and teachers, and many opportunities for Christian graduates to study in Middle Eastern universities, some of which (*e.g.* Beirut, Cairo, Tunis) have courses in English. There is a huge need for Christians with experience in student work elsewhere who can find jobs in university cities, and strengthen or begin Bible study groups. Perhaps the openings are greater for Christians from Asian, African or Latin American countries that are not associated in the Muslim mind with the iniquities of the Crusades; but European and American Christians are wanted too.

Such workers need great discretion, the ability to enter sympathetically into the national culture, the willingness to accept loneliness, and the patience that does not expect immediate 'results' and 'successes'. Part of the ministry of IFES staff in this region has been to encourage, pastor and pray for believers in various positions who appear to be quietly pouring out their lives for little or no visible fruit. But only if such people are found – men and women willing perhaps to invest years just to help a couple of students come a little closer to faith in Christ – will the foundation be laid. In a country with less than a dozen known national believers, like Libya, or with no officially-known believers at all, like Saudi Arabia, each contact is of massive significance.

Ruth Stewart, a former IVCF-USA staffworker who joined the North Africa Mission and became an IFES associate staffworker, is a good example. She was active in Algiers from around 1954 until 1977. IFES general secretary Stacey Woods passed through Algiers in 1966, and mentioned the Reading Room operated by the student workers in Rome. Ruth and her co-worker Marge Ballard saw the potential for something similar in Algiers; and this, along with English language teaching, provided excellent opportunities for contacting students. It was a hard situation. But as David Penman reported, 'Daily there are fruitful contacts with dozens of Muslim students who have come to trust and appreciate Ruth's ministry.'

There is a fifth approach, whereby mostly members of the IFES-linked groups in many countries can begin to serve the Middle East. This is through friendship with students from abroad. In 1979 there were more Muslim students in the universities of Europe and North America than in the whole of the Middle East and North Africa! Away from the pressures of their community, these students are facing new experiences and world-views, and are far more open than they would otherwise be to the challenge of Christ. Even so, the issues the gospel poses to them are awesome. 'You are asking me to die!', one Muslim student told IFES staffworker Terrell Smith as they discussed becoming a disciple of Christ. This too is no ministry for anyone seeking rapid results. New disciples will come only through years of untiring friendship. But, again, every contact counts.

Finally, student work in this region is, above all, spiritual warfare. Bob Young, who helped pioneer the IFES work in Latin America and then moved on to the Middle East, summarized the difference between the two by saying simply, 'South America was ready. The Middle East is not.' This raises the question, Ready for what? For even if these lands are not ready for the kind of movement that exists elsewhere, yet there is plenty of scope for some kind of Christian presence and witness. Thus our goal as a world-wide student family is to provide whatever is needed – resources, training, personnel – for the work of God among students in the Middle East; whatever shape that may take. But above all, perhaps our responsibility is to create an overwhelming torrent of collective prayer that will break down spiritual strong-holds (2 Cor. 10:4). For what makes a campus 'ready', and the hearts of students – and governments – 'open'? Is it, first of all, research, funds, gifted workers, personal dynamism, might, power – or the Holy Spirit graciously answering the prayers of God's people?

9
Until He comes

God has done mighty things among students in the period since the Second World War. And by His grace He has given students linked with IFES the opportunity to play a significant part. Nine national movements were involved in the meeting at Oxford in 1946 that led to the formation of IFES. That number of movements doubled by 1959, and doubled again by 1971. Over fifty movements are now affiliated to IFES. If we include pioneering areas, IFES is active in around 100 countries. Some 270,000 students (at a conservative estimate) are involved. And for this we give the glory to God alone. Hallelujah!

And yet today we find ourselves in the middle of an enormous task. There are so many Christian students facing new knowledge, new experiences, new ways of thinking, and needing fellowship and support, to witness and to grow as disciples of Christ. There are so many non-Christian students who are more open to the gospel than they will ever be in later life. China's campuses are still unreached; in parts of Europe, India and Latin America – and even North America – a vast percentage of the student population remains unevangelized; the Islamic world has hardly been penetrated. What kind of movement does the IFES seek to be for the glory of God and the evangelization of the student world in the years that remain?

Perhaps twelve features can be singled out. IFES seeks to be

1. an evangelizing movement
2. a movement that makes genuine disciples of Christ
3. a movement giving itself to prayer
4. a movement unambiguously obedient to Scripture

5. a movement of thorough Bible study
6. a movement producing effective Christian graduates
7. a movement that builds up God's Church
8. a missionary movement
9. a movement active for God's Kingdom in every area of life
10. a movement of creative Christian thought and literature
11. a movement committed to student responsibility
12. a movement committed to national leadership.

1. An evangelizing movement

At this stage of our account that should hardly need saying; yet it does. We praise God that IFES movements have gained a reputation for solid teaching, training and discipling, and for the way God has enabled them to pioneer a wide-ranging expression of the biblical world-view, for example in its social aspects. But as a result it has sometimes been suggested that the IFES movements are not evangelizing movements. Neil Graham of IVCF-Canada has observed that IVCF has sometimes been seen as 'a nurturing movement. Sometimes we have believed this "tagging" and thus may have lost our sense of being on the cutting edge of evangelism.'[1]

Undoubtedly there have been times when our evangelism has been sporadic. There have been many groups where, as one staffworker wrote, a tendency exists 'to remain safe and warm in the Christian group and never move outside of it'; where group members have no non-Christian friends, and evangelism goes no further than 'shoving a tract under a door or inviting someone to a meeting'. Often we fail to seize the opportunity that university life offers to 'let our light shine before men', demonstrating the fruits of the gospel in our long-term, prayerful friendships.

But every IFES member movement believes that without Christ men and women are genuinely lost, and should be active both in friendship evangelism and in unashamed proclamation of the gospel; by evangelistic Bible studies, university missions, booktables, music, drama, street preaching, or whatever other means are possible and appropriate. This is our primary and consuming purpose. IFES is an evangelizing movement, and if it lost that, it would lose its reason for existence. When a student group fails to

[1] Neil Graham, '"Roots": Reflections on a Self-Renewing Vision', *IFES Review* 1978, 1.

keep witness at the top of its agenda, the result is often introversion, loss of direction, and the production of very few well-
taught graduates.

There is no 'IFES evangelistic formula'[2]; the aim of student
groups world-wide is simply to be active in evangelism that is
biblical (presenting the whole counsel of God), intelligent (giving
honest answers to honest questions), and effective (producing
conversions that genuinely last).[3]

2. A movement that makes genuine disciples of Christ

Our goal must be to make disciples who will love and serve Jesus
Christ throughout the world – rather than merely harvesting
decisions that survive less than a month! In one Asian country,
sixty-five students at a camp of 150 made 'decisions' to follow
Christ, but the speaker immediately warned that he expected
only 10% to last. In most countries, particularly where there are
many new converts or where local churches are weak and liberal,
much effort has to be spent by student groups in helping each
new generation to grasp the basics of the Christian life: for
example, how to have a 'quiet time' ('a meeting with God that
impregnates the whole day', as Hans Bürki describes it), how to
pray and study the Bible, how to witness effectively, how to be a
useful member of a local church, *etc*. And, above all, creating a
hunger and thirst for God, an absolute and costly self-dedication.
It is all too easy to be evangelical and yet motivated by ordinary,
human self-interest, rather than a consuming passion for Christ
Himself. This is true even at leadership level.

The practical ethical implications of the gospel have to be
taught too. In one country, an IFES staffworker was alarmed to
find that entering into marriage as a virgin was almost unheard
of, even among Christian students; and indeed he reported that
many Christians 'found it difficult to understand that the gospel
has something to say in this area'. There has to be training in
practical holiness and in developing an attitude of servanthood
like the Christ who came 'not to be served but to serve'. Student

[2] Although at least two IFES staffworkers, Bel Magalit and Branse Burbridge,
have produced gospel outlines to assist students in becoming familiar with the
basics of the gospel; *IFES Review*, 1977, 1 and 1982, 2.

[3] Books on evangelism by staffworkers of IFES movements include Bel Magalit,
How To Share Jesus; Paul Little, *How To Give Away Your Faith;* Rebecca Manley
Pippert, *Out of the Saltshaker.*

leaders and graduates must model an attitude towards their qualifications that sees them as tools for God's service rather than status symbols. René Padilla insists on the importance of the area of simple lifestyle: 'If you fail to learn not to be wasteful as a student, it is unlikely that you will learn it once you graduate.'

Conferences are of crucial importance in this respect. In particular, the IFES International Student Conference held at Schloss Mittersill, Austria, has meant much in the lives of many students year after year: particularly those from pioneering countries in Europe and the Middle East. Reactions have included 'I have learnt to converse with God', 'The idea that academic studies must be done to God's glory was new to me', 'I had thought of leadership as "dictatorship" but I learnt that Christian leadership is service' (a reaction of a student from a totalitarian country), 'Greece, my country, used to be my neat little world. Most other countries existed only on the map for me. But I found myself at Mittersill, and my world was never the same again'. And from Britain, 'I believe I learnt more than in the previous two years of my Christian life!' The Spanish movement is one of many that has singled out the Mittersill conference as having been of vital importance in their history: 'IFES helped us but never robbed us of the initiative.'

Similar conferences and training courses are organized by student movements in every continent. In Asia and Latin America in particular, camps and courses of three weeks or more take place. In the Philippines' month-long leadership training camps, says Willie Girao, 'Each day starts with one full hour of "quiet time". Mornings are devoted to lectures followed by questions. Most of these lectures focus on doctrines. Workshops on leading small group Bible studies or actual small group Bible studies occupy the latter part of the morning. In the afternoons, campers discuss prayer, personal Bible study, understanding God's will, social action, love, courtship and marriage...They also discuss principles affecting relationships with the national movement, the IFES, the local churches...Devotional messages are in the evening. At the end of the day, small groups share what they have learnt in their log cabins, and they close the day in united prayer ...At one point in the camp, campers go to the nearby city of Bacolod for two days. There they practise what they have learnt about person-to-person evangelism with strangers – otherwise known as "commando evangelism". The campers enter a local

university campus and seek to evangelize individuals. Later...
they evaluate their evangelistic efforts...' Outdoor life, sports and
physical work assignments are also included in the programme.

The considerable sums of money spent on such events, locally,
nationally and internationally, are well invested. Inevitably,
when so much is at stake, spiritual warfare may be as evident in
conferences as in evangelism. Doug Stewart wrote in *In Touch* of
crises taking place at a Mexican training weekend as student
leaders grappled with crucial issues of discipleship: 'Satan will
oppose the operation of God's power in our lives. As long as the
kingdom for us consists only in talk he has nothing to fear.'

There is the slight sense of frustration in having to cover the
same topics year after year – 'building sandcastles on a conveyor-
belt', as one staffworker described it. But that is balanced by the
thrill of knowing that every year hundreds of graduates go out
into all the world and into the whole of society, adequately
equipped to be God's servants wherever they find themselves. It
is a strategic and unending task. Maintaining a group's health in
these fundamental areas requires continual effort and enthusiasm
from student leaders and staff. Stacey Woods warned in 1966 that
an evangelical group born in struggle can grow lukewarm through
acceptance and academic respectability, with a resulting drift in
its members' discipleship. 'Like Joseph and Mary of old who
supposed Christ to have been in the company with them as they
journeyed from Jerusalem, we can imagine all is well...Do our
unions all have a daily prayer meeting? In reality, are students
being converted? How many of our graduates actually are entering Christian service? Is there missionary vision and commitment
to world evangelism?'

3. A movement giving itself to prayer

One of the things that has been most striking to the writer in the
preparation of this history has been to see the commitment to
prayer that marked the early student groups, particularly before
the Second World War. The records seem full of this emphasis, in
a manner that would perhaps be rather more typical of Africa
than Europe or North America today. (Noticeably, the African
IFES groups have in many cases outgrown their European
counterparts. It is worth asking what factors in European culture
have militated against the continued practice of a heavy
expenditure of time in intercessory prayer.)

In 1936, a questionnaire was mailed to the existing student movements asking them what was their most important activity. Almost unanimously, the reply singled out the daily prayer meeting.[4] Ole Hallesby, the father-figure of the Norwegian movement, stressed that 'God Himself in the beginning of our work taught us to work on our knees'. In 1951 he wrote in *IFES Journal* urging students, 'Pray every day for your non-Christian friends. Surround them with your prayer. Each time you pray you plunge a holy explosive into their soul, and one day it will scatter the ice from around their hearts.' David Adeney emphasized in *His* in 1942 that a prayer meeting characterized by definite and unselfish prayers is 'a powerhouse for all the other activities'.

This commitment has been fundamental to IFES's working philosophy. In 1958, Yale University Divinity School called for an examination of the essential difference between the North American IVCFs and SCMs. Stacey Woods expected them to focus on the authority of Scripture. 'Not so. The conclusion was that Inter-Varsity consciously depended upon the Holy Spirit, upon his leading and enablement. We believed in supernaturalism, in contrast to the Student Christian Movement which was judged to be much more naturalistic and humanistic.'[5] 'Since then I have often prayed that this dependence on God might not be lost', says Stacey.

IFES came into being, not because of the brilliance of a few evangelical supermen, but because God raised up student leaders in country after country, and then provided more people (virtually all of them from among these leaders) to back up the work and ensure its continuity. It resulted from 'separate initiatives of people who had the same idea because they read the Bible', says Oliver Barclay, 'rather than being some one person's brilliant scheme... Enormous numbers of people were involved who set about the task locally and more or less independently, and then rejoiced when they found one another and joined hands to spread it still further.'[6] Time and again, an IFES worker has arrived in a country to find that God had raised up campus

---

[4] C. Stacey Woods, *Some Ways of God*, p.99.

[5] C. Stacey Woods, *The Growth of a Work of God*, p.145.

[6] *Cf.* Hans Höeg in the welcome address at the 1937 International Conference in Budapest: 'It is something quite unique the way the Lord God at the very same time in very different countries put the very same thoughts into our hearts... If God will use us as His tools, we wish to give our lives as living sacrifices!'

witness through student initiative just a little earlier. Israel, the South Pacific, and Spain – and, in the 1930s, New Zealand and the USA – are good examples. Such things occur through the unpredictable and glorious work of the Spirit, not as the fruit of a transcontinental master-plan on the part of IFES!

IFES movements have always believed a foundation of prayer to be indispensable for all other activities. The problem has been giving that faith practical expression! From early on, it was a rule in both the Filipino and Taiwanese movements that no staff-worker should begin a day's work before spending an hour with God in Bible study and prayer.[7] Howard Guinness began to win people of his own age group to Christ only after making a resolution in his third year as a student that 'From today the central thing in my life shall be prayer' – and reorganizing his activities accordingly. Roger Mitchell writes from his experience of evangelistic university missions that 'the place of intercession is crucial in the front line... An important strategy is to discover the people who are open and make them targets for specific prayer. I never cease to be amazed how these prayers are answered, how the day-to-day incidents during a mission are overruled. I don't know why in the world we don't take this sort of specific prayer more seriously in ordinary church life!' Dave Bryant of IVCF-USA's missionary department wrote in *His* that 'there is a dynamic behind missions mobilization that goes beyond exposure to missions, such as Urbana, or training in missions... Spiritual mobilization has to be anchored and sustained by prayer.' His reaction has been to call for large-scale 'concerts of prayer... united, sustained, intentional, targeted on revival and world evangelization'.[8]

As a movement committed to Scripture, we must believe what Scripture says that 'you do not have, because you do not ask God' (James 4:2).

4. A movement unambiguously obedient to Scripture

Since the very beginning, IFES groups have seen their submission to the final authority of Scripture as part of their obedience to Christ. As Gottfried Osei-Mensah of Ghana affirmed at the 1979

---

[7] Chua Wee Hian, *Out of Asia*, p.88.
[8] *Cf.* David Bryant, 'Concerts of Prayer: Waking Up For A New Missions Thrust', in Cindy Smith and Joe Cumming, *Rebuilding the Mission Movement*, pp.164–191.

IFES General Committee, 'The Lord Jesus did not only cherish a high view of Scripture; He submitted to it Himself as the ultimate authority in His life and ministry, with certain conviction that, "what Scripture says, God says"....When therefore we affirm the divine inspiration, truthfulness and authority of both the Old and New Testament Scriptures...we do so on Jesus Christ's authority.'[9]

In that affirmation Gottfried spoke for the IFES movements throughout their history. As we have noted, when the Cambridge students made their lonely but crucial stand before the First World War, they emphasized that it was 'sufficiently reasonable' to hold the view of the Bible 'which Christ Himself held'. It was Christ, the Messiah Himself, who unflinchingly responded to Pharisaic traditionalism or Sadducee anti-supernaturalism with 'Haven't you read...?'[10], setting God's Word authoritatively against human tradition, even that of the chosen people[11]; it was He who challenged the rebellious Jewish theologians, 'Are you not in error because you do not know the Scriptures?'[12] His teaching frequently alluded to the very Old Testament passages that made later, theologically liberal, academics squirm with embarrassment;[13] and He treated biblical prophecy as the entirely trustworthy Word of God, the fulfilment of which governed the future, with no capacity for error.[14] Clearly, His attitude to Scripture was not a minor accommodation to His surroundings; rather, His use of the Old Testament prophecies showed it to be fundamental to His self-understanding.

It was for this reason, therefore, that the early evangelical student groups made the crucial refusal to correct Scripture by contemporary opinion, preferring rather to allow the temporary conclusions of their decade to be corrected by the eternal Word. It was on Christ's authority that they took the Bible as a final criterion supreme even to the teaching of the church, and were

---

[9] Gottfried Osei-Mensah, 'The Authoritative Word', *IFES Review* 1979, 1. For fuller statements of the evangelical position, see John Stott, *Christ the Controversialist* (IVP, 1970) and *The Bible: Book for Today* (IVP, 1982) and J. I. Packer, *'Fundamentalism' and the Word of God* (IVP, 1958) and *God Has Spoken* (Hodder, 1965).

[10] Matthew 12:3, 5; 19:4; 21:16, 42; Mark 12:26.

[11] Mark 7:6–13. [12] Mark 12:24.

[13] Matthew 11:23–24; 12:41; 23:35; 24:37.

[14] Matthew 26:24, 54; Mark 12:10; Luke 4:18–21; 18:31–34; 22:37; 24:25–27, 44ff.

willing to 'contend for the faith'[15], just as Paul was willing to stand up to Peter at Antioch when the nature of the *gospel* was at stake.[16]

For the issue was not a matter of the trustworthiness of the Bible as a mere philosophical abstraction. The pioneering students' concern was rather that refusal to submit to the final authority of Scripture led in time to a different approach to Christian life and discipleship. And, in particular, they were concerned for effective outreach, for a collective witness that was proclaiming the biblical gospel rather than offering salvation by works or sacraments – or, worse still, mere religious discussion with no real passion for conversion and the new birth. 'Evangelical' means 'people committed to the *evangelion*, the gospel'; and the issue of salvation by faith in the atoning death of Christ was what was at stake in Cambridge in 1909, in Norway in 1921, in Singapore and India in 1950.

When Paul reminded the Corinthians of what is 'of first importance', he stressed that the gospel he was preaching was 'according to the Scriptures'.[17] And it was to ensure that the gospel they preached matched the realities of God's dealings with men, 'according to the Scriptures', that the International Conference of Evangelical Students, and later the IFES with all its member movements, became firmly committed to a doctrinal basis. 'God has given us the message', said Ole Hallesby at the first International Conference in 1934. 'We have neither found out, discovered it, nor have we thought it out, but the message is from God... This gives us a firm position in this world of chaos today.'[18]

The doctrinal basis of IFES is, as Chua Wee Hian says, 'an anchor rather than a flag'.[19] It is not itself our message for the campus; rather, it is a summary of the crucial facts undergirding that message, anchoring it to the New Testament. And that is a matter of no small importance. The apostle Paul declared, 'If anybody is preaching to you a gospel other than what you accepted, let him be eternally condemned!'[20]

Obviously, the IFES statement does not claim to be a complete summary of Christian belief. The doctrinal basis of the IFES is 'the fundamental truths of Christianity, including:

a. The unity of the Father, Son and Holy Spirit in the Godhead.

[15] Jude 3.   [16] Galatians 2:11ff.   [17] 1 Corinthians 15:1–4.
[18] Quoted in Douglas Johnson, *A Brief History of the IFES*, p.180.
[19] Chua, *op. cit.*, p.36.   [20] Galatians 1:9.

b. The sovereignty of God in creation, revelation, redemption and final judgment.

c. The divine inspiration and entire trustworthiness of Holy Scripture, as originally given, and its supreme authority in all matters of faith and conduct.

d. The universal sinfulness and guilt of all men since the fall, rendering them subject to God's wrath and condemnation.

e. Redemption from the guilt, penalty, dominion and pollution of sin, solely through the sacrificial death (as our Representative and Substitute) of the Lord Jesus Christ, the incarnate Son of God.

f. The bodily resurrection of the Lord Jesus Christ from the dead and His ascension to the right hand of God the Father.

g. The presence and power of the Holy Spirit in the work of regeneration.

h. The justification of the sinner by the grace of God through faith alone.

i. The indwelling and work of the Holy Spirit in the believer.

j. The one Holy Universal Church which is the Body of Christ and to which all true believers belong.

k. The expectation of the personal return of the Lord Jesus Christ.'[21]

The founders of IFES saw that summary as one that would unite all Christians who based their witness and life on the authority of the Bible. And – along with the very similar doctrinal basis of the British movement – it has indeed been something of a rallying-point for evangelicals. The influential evangelical magazine *Today*, for example, described the UCCF version as 'the standard statement of biblical faith'.[22] These basic tenets, and the lifestyle that must accompany them, have, says Samuel Escobar of Latin America, 'been liberating truths, dynamic elements within movements of renewal that God has used to keep His Church alive in terms of crisis or advance. This is how we in the IFES understand them.'[23]

The doctrinal basis is not, therefore, merely a negative exclusive device. It has also served as a positive foundation for unity, by defining a platform upon which all students committed to the

[21] For an exposition of the basis see Hans Bürki, *Essentials* (IFES, 1975).
[22] Derek Williams and John Capon, 'Advance and Divide', *Today*, July 1982, p.40.
[23] Samuel Escobar, 'Our Evangelical Heritage', *IFES Review* 1983, 1.

biblical gospel can unite and work together. And this is perhaps one of the most exciting things about the student movements. Precisely because the groups' objectives do not necessitate taking up positions on issues that divide equally biblically-minded evangelicals, students from different denominations can labour in partnership and enrich one another. There can be few members of IFES-linked groups who have not gained by this exposure to the different perspectives of other biblically-minded believers. In turn, the links created in the student scene serve to build essential bridges within the evangelical community in the following years. (René Padilla has described this as 'one of the main contributions of the student movement' in Argentina.) Like everything else, however, this interdenominational unity is preserved only by 'constant vigilance...to resist the inroads and the peculiar emphases which are not representative of the church as a whole. Such emphases, while having an appeal to a few, will result in division and a "holier-than-thou" attitude, and this will divert from the primary task of evangelical witness in the universities.'[24] It is a question of keeping our objectives clear, of 'keeping the fundamentals fundamental'!

Effective student group life, and in particular a thorough exposure to the Bible, should 'make disciples' who do indeed 'speak the *truth* in *love*', maintaining both a faithfulness to the New Testament gospel and a unity with everyone else who is building on that foundation. Adequate teaching must relate these concerns to the new situations that develop. In 1980, for example, the IFES executive produced a 'Call to Renewed Evangelical Awareness' responding to the changing situation within the Roman Catholic church and IFES movements' increasing contacts with Catholic students. This statement thanked God for the 'considerable number of students of Roman Catholic background who come to our activities, join our Bible studies, and, where they have a personal faith, enjoy fellowship in our groups...We welcome such students and want to offer them genuine friendship.' It emphasized the 'new avenues' that had opened up for evangelism. At the same time, it stressed that students from non-evangelical backgrounds would be 'helped best' by a clear proclamation of the nature of the gospel, 'as well as by displaying a warm-hearted and loving biblical faith and life'. It proceeded to

[24] C. Stacey Woods, *The Growth of a Work of God*, p.52.

set forth the crucial points at which a biblically-based gospel differs significantly from the official Catholic position; and it stressed the need for all leaders to be people clearly committed to the evangelical faith. The aim, said Chua Wee Hian, was to help student leaders 'to handle this subject with biblical firmness where it relates to crucial theological issues and with love as they relate to their Roman Catholic friends'.[25]

Doctrinal clarity will continue to bring the besetting danger of doctrinaire lovelessness (and lifelessness); and it will continue to have its price. 'These are truths for which many people have gladly died', Carl Wislöff reminded the 1979 General Committee. As another early Norwegian leader observed, 'All schism within Christian circles must be regretted; but when our most precious possession, the free gospel, is at stake, we dare not compromise on a single point.' It is at times of numerical strength that complacency and a weakening emphasis on Scripture's authority and reliability can appear. If God Himself has indeed spoken through the Bible, it would be foolish to expect the Enemy ever to stop asking the age-old question '*Has* God said?' (Genesis 3:1).

5. *A movement of thorough Bible study*

An orthodox doctrinal commitment is not enough in itself; it is only of use as a prelude to a lifestyle that is marked by biblically-based thinking and action. Our aim must be that all group members should, as Colin Chapman says, 'apply their minds to the study of the Bible with the same thoroughness and intellectual integrity with which they study their own academic subjects'. Where this thorough commitment to the study of Scripture is present, even inexperienced leaders will be preserved from over-emphases and mistaken trends.

When asked what had kept the large British movement healthy for over fifty years, its former general secretary Oliver Barclay singled out the 'solid diet' of Bible study in personal 'quiet times', small groups, and Bible expositions in larger meetings. 'Where God has given a heart to love, study, obey and meditate on His Word, He has made us strong. Where we have substituted other kinds of spirituality or human wisdom, we have become weak.' René Padilla noted such weakness operating in some

---

[25] *Cf.* 'A New Consciousness?', *In Touch* 1981, 2 and 'A Call to Evangelical Awareness', *IFES Review* 1980, 2.

Latin American students who divorced experience from teaching: 'I was astonished to find that at one training course students spent several hours of the day singing and praying, but received very little instruction on Bible study and gave no importance to the reading of Christian literature. As a result most of them are not prepared to face the ideological bombardment to which they are subjected at the university, and tend to retreat into the circle of Christian friends' – with calamitous results for evangelism.

Group Bible study has come to be a key part of the life of most IFES movements;[26] not only for building up Christian students, but also as an *evangelistic* method that can function in any context (and under any regime). At first, however, it 'seemed quite daring to go to a passage of the Bible and believe that what it said would be opened up by the Holy Spirit as a group of people tried prayerfully to understand its meaning and application. The aim was to find a way of studying the Bible that did not depend on an "expert" but could be profitably pursued by an ordinary group of students'[27] – people not dissimilar to the recent converts who were the original recipients of much of the New Testament.

The 'innocent-looking' leaflet *How to lead a group Bible study* was developed by two staff of the British and American movements at an IFES conference soon after the war, and was a forerunner of many Bible study guides and training sessions since. Well-prepared Bible study guides have also been of importance, as Ann Bennighof emphasizes, in preventing cell-groups becoming either monologues dominated by one person, 'topical' studies ranging all over the Bible and grappling with nothing in depth, or sessions that use the text as a pretext for 'sharing personal experiences and airing personal opinions'. Users of well-prepared Bible study guides will gradually begin to pick up intuitively good habits of Bible study and interpretation.[28] Part of Ada Lum's ministry as IFES Bible study secretary has been training national staff to write Bible study guides appropriate to their country's cultural context.

[26] Significant IFES materials on group Bible study include three books by IFES Bible study secretary Ada Lum, *How to Begin an Evangelistic Bible Study*, *Learning and Leading*, and (with Ruth Siemens) *Creative Bible Studies*. A useful selection of evangelistic Bible study outlines is *Jesus – One of Us*.

[27] *For the Faith of the Gospel*, p.15.

[28] Ann Bennighof, 'Written for our Instruction – the Old Testament: Its Values and Use in African Student Fellowships', *IFES Review* 1982, 2.

It is worth noting in passing that the two methods of Bible study common to most IFES groups, the small-group inductive study and the large-group Bible exposition, have given student fellowships the combination of 'cell' and 'congregation' units emphasized by Peter Wagner and his fellow church growth missiologists.[29] Where the small group level has been weak, personal application and fellowship have tended to be lacking; where the large group is weak, in-depth teaching and awareness of and commitment to the fellowship's overall strategy have sometimes been lacking. The two levels in balance have made for effective group life.

6. A movement producing effective Christian graduates

Neither biblical orthodoxy nor Bible study are sufficient unless they lead to long-term biblical obedience. And graduation brings its own pressures. Camilo Torres, the Latin American guerrilla priest, complained that 'At the end of a university career the nonconformity disappears...The rebel students...convert into bourgeois professionals who, to buy the status symbols of the middle class, have to sell their consciences in exchange for a higher salary.'[30] The sudden acquisition of a high salary can easily produce 'conformity to the world', and such apparently obvious basics as continual personal evangelism, regular 'quiet times', the moment-by-moment practice of the presence of God and the insatiable desire for more of His fullness can seem like student idealism.

Sometimes it has even been argued that few graduates retain their faith after university. There may, indeed, be situations where group life has come to lack depth and solidity, and graduating students have not been trained in a robust, biblically-grounded discipleship that will survive testing. Staffworker Femi Adeleye was quoted above expressing this fear regarding some

[29] Peter Wagner, *Your Church Can Grow* (Regal, 1976), ch. 7. Wagner postulates a third level, the large 'celebration' unit; and it may well be that, in IFES, national and regional conferences fulfil this role. Few better descriptions could be envisaged than this account of an early British conference: 'Until I went to the conference I often felt that I was almost alone, struggling with a feeble few to carry the banner of Christ in our place. When, on the first night... the hymn was given out and everyone burst into song (as if to lift the roof) I almost cried for joy! I was no longer alone, for here were people from every place, filled with enthusiasm for the Lord' (quoted by Douglas Johnson, *Contending for the Faith*, p.337).
[30] Quoted Jack Voelkel, *Student Evangelism in a World of Revolution*, p.42.

Nigerian groups. However, such research as has been done suggests that the majority of group members continue as 'live and effective Christians'.[31]

Nonetheless, many graduates do undergo real difficulties. The answers to these problems have much to do with personal discipleship, and deliberate involvement in a healthy, biblically-based church, of course. But the establishment of strong Graduate Christian Fellowships focusing on the particular needs and concerns of graduates and professionals is also of importance. In our sections on Singapore and Uganda we have given some indication of the massive potential these groups can possess.

Undoubtedly the health of the student movements has often depended on graduates with a continued vision for student evangelism. Although many students give sacrificially to the work, a high proportion of the income of national movements – and of IFES world-wide – comes from graduates. (Perhaps it is not surprising that people who have benefited from the student work will be keen to ensure that it continues!) Graduates are involved at many levels: as sponsors of high-school groups, as speakers, counsellors, even evangelists. In the late 1970s the Norwegian movement sought to establish a graduate prayer group behind each student group. In a number of countries, particularly in Africa, graduates serve as associate staffworkers to complement an overstretched staff team. The movement in Papua-New Guinea, that has grown to a membership of 3,500 without a staffworker, has done so in good measure because of graduate support.

Graduates who have been called by God into the academic world have a particularly significant part to play. Stacey Woods commented in 1972 that 'relevant apologetics' seemed to be 'an increasing lack in our member movements'. Graduates of IFES groups are often in a position to meet their successors' need for

---

[31] UCCF-Britain's *For the Faith of the Gospel*, pp.24–25, quotes two 1960 surveys of group members of 1950. One gives 100% continuing as active Christians, the other states that over half of sixty members were now in full-time work while only four had disappeared from the Christian scene. The 1979 UCCF annual report, p.6, quotes two more recent surveys indicating that at least 85% of CU members continue as active Christians. An encouraging picture emerges also from Singapore; *cf.* the surveys in Chua Choon Lan, 'The Graduate and the Church', *Impetus*, November 1979, pp.1–3. In both of these countries graduates have access to a considerable number of strong evangelical churches, of course.

such tools – albeit at the possible expense of academic respectability. Carl Henry wrote in 1977: 'I venture one prediction. In the next decade the credibility of evangelical Christianity among university students...will turn upon the polemical and the scholarly attacks that are unleashed against their positions by non-evangelical scholars who cannot agree on an alternative but will concentrate their fire on our positions. The reply will have to come from Christian faculties gifted with intellectual and writing skills. If it does not come from them, Intervarsity...will be under the same pressures as was the Student Christian Movement.'[32]

7. A movement that builds up God's Church

This, obviously, is the central contribution of the graduates produced by IFES groups, and has always been an integral part of the IFES vision. Ole Hallesby warned the first International Conference in Oslo in 1934 against an 'academic, individualistic' faith: 'Our message is a message of the communion of saints.' Bobby Sng likewise insists that 'to be a Christian is not only to be personally converted. It is also to belong to a body of believers of which the local church is an expression.' IFES has worked on the principle that student groups, with their limited objectives and membership made up of one age-group, are not local churches. Students, therefore, need to be thoroughly committed to – and cared for by – a local church fellowship as well as their campus group.[33] Colin Chapman says firmly of the Middle East ministry, 'We believe that our ministry will be successful only to the extent that it builds up existing churches and enables them to grow.' And Ada Lum recalls being very impressed on arrival in Asia by the way her colleagues in the Asian movements were asking, 'What is our responsibility to the national church?'

There are many ways in which the campus groups can collectively serve the local churches. In Ghana, the 'Students in Church Evangelism' programme arranges for students to join with a village church, helping with farming during the day and evangelism and teaching during the evenings, including Bible studies

---

[32] *Evangelicals Face the Future,* ed. Donald E. Hoke (Pasadena, 1978), p. 166.
[33] Bobby Sng, 'Student Work and the Church', *IFES Review* 1982, 2. Bobby adds that 'New converts should also be encouraged to be baptized. It is disappointing to see how few student groups take the latter seriously enough.' The whole paper deserves careful study. *Cf.* also Michael Griffiths, *Cinderella with Amnesia* (IVP, 1975), ch. 7 (published in the USA as *God's Forgetful Pilgrims*).

and open-air evangelism. These outreaches are commenced by three days of prayer, fasting, study and planning, and are followed by a day for review and reports. Student church campaigns in Wales involve afternoons and evenings spent in evangelism, and mornings in reporting back and study; for example, an hour of Bible teaching, an hour of prayer, and an hour of training in apologetics, covering a topic that would then be preached in the evening. Such campaigns build up strong links between the movement and the local churches. Graduate groups sometimes exercise similar ministries: in Taiwan, for example, they have set up gospel teams especially to work with small local churches.

Many other forms of involvement exist. At a national Baptist congress in one Latin American country, representatives of the student movement were responsible for training the Bible study group leaders. In Vietnam, the leadership training which the students had received resulted in many of them becoming leaders in youth groups and Sunday schools. These are just two examples of the ways in which students – just like any other members of the church – can bring the benefit of the particular experiences and training that God has given them to the enrichment of the Body of Christ locally.

This should be a normal pattern after graduation. As Bobby Sng points out, various aspects of the experience gained by student leaders – the basics of personal evangelism, running small Bible study groups, planning a balanced programme – should in the long term prove useful in church situations. The discipline of reading widely and setting things down in writing is a training worth putting at the disposal of local church magazines. 'Young people especially will appreciate the encouragement and practical aid that graduates can offer.'

It would be foolish to be over-idealistic, however. Sometimes graduates have real problems in adapting from a lifestyle where many of their needs were met by a student group made up of members with similar outlooks; they become restless and unable to 'incarnate' themselves in the more diverse fellowship of a local church. Also, as Bobby warns, behind their attempts at involvement 'there must be the spirit of humility...Sometimes graduates in their impatience and enthusiasm have forced the issues and unfortunate confrontations have resulted' – to the eventual impoverishment of all concerned. And sometimes, obviously, there have been problems resulting from the attitudes of church leaders. Mobilizing the full potential of graduate involvement in local congregations requires (like most other things) prayer, love, persistence and enthusiasm.

Countless members of IFES groups have gone on to become church leaders and pastors, of course. A survey of thirty-nine student leaders from the 1971-77 period in VCF-Singapore showed that ten were in full-time ministry or in theological training, two were church elders, six church deacons, and a further thirteen serving on church committees. 35% of men entering the Anglican ministry in England in 1963 were IVF graduates. There were 200 KGK-Japan graduates serving as pastors by 1974. In 1975 it was estimated that over half of the pastors in the Church of Norway were NKSS graduates. In the episcopally-organized churches, numerous graduates of IFES movements have become bishops, and several – Donald Coggan, Howard Mowll, Hugh Gough and Donald Robinson – archbishops.

Similarly, large numbers of parachurch organizations are staffed by former student leaders and staff of IFES movements. The burgeoning Neighbourhood Bible Study movement, for example, was begun by two former IVCF-USA staff taking their Bible study techniques from the campuses into the wider world. And more generally, there can be no doubt that in their defence of the biblical gospel the IFES movements have been able to serve as a mouthpiece of the evangelical community in general. Juhani Lindgren of Finland has singled this out as a feature of the rise of the student movement there; the publications of IVP in Britain and the USA have undoubtedly played a similar role.

On the international level, it is noticeable that when the World Evangelical Fellowship was formed in 1951 and set up four working commissions, two of the chairmen were René Pache (at that time IFES vice-chairman) and Hugh Gough (IVF-Britain's first full-time travelling secretary). IFES leaders have likewise played an important part in the activities of the Lausanne Committee for World Evangelization. Gottfried Osei-Mensah, formerly on staff in Africa, is the executive secretary of LCWE world-wide; IVCF-USA loaned two of its staff – Paul Little and David Howard (now WEF general secretary) – to help organize the congresses at Lausanne in 1974 and Pattaya in 1980 respectively. At both of these, Chua Wee Hian was responsible for a plenary session; the contributions of Samuel Escobar and René Padilla were undoubtedly two of the most widely-quoted papers at Lausanne, and indeed 'the Escobars and Padillas' became a recognized shorthand for the emerging third-world evangelical voice. René edited the post-Lausanne anthology *The New Face of Evangelicalism*.

IFES is concerned to act as an integral part of the Body of Christ world-wide; to be, in Brazilian Dieter Brepohl's phrase, 'the arm of the church in the faculty', or in that of UCCF-Britain, 'the missionary arm of the church in the university' – or college or high school. It is a sign that this is taking place when a leader in the Evangelical Alliance such as Morgan Derham can refer to the rise and growth of the student movement as 'the most significant phenomenon in British evangelical life in the past half-century.... Today, if one has to set down any signs of hope in the Christian situation in Britain, at the top of the list (or very near) one has to put the size and vigour of Christian Unions in all the institutions of tertiary education.'[34] It is likewise striking when a *New York Times* writer singles out 'evangelical groups such as IVCF' on the USA's campuses as attracting 'by far the most students to religion; in providing models for church growth, they are showing similar initiative, and in the foreign mission field they are notably showing the way'.[35]

Recognition and respectability of this kind undoubtedly have their own dangers. It is through the 'foolish...weak in the world ...low and despised in the world' that God has chosen to accomplish His purposes, according to 1 Corinthians 1. These things must be a stimulus for thanksgiving – and then a challenge to ensure that the original vision has not been lost, and that student groups really are producing graduates who are *visibly* of use to the churches; not just mavericks and malcontents, but people using their abilities to be radically biblical in every part of life, who have retained the enthusiasm for making disciples that they learnt as students.

It is our prayer that more churches will follow the example of congregations in Sao Paulo, Brazil, who consciously 'set apart' their students as the church's missionaries to the university

---

[34] A. Morgan Derham, 'Student Ministry', *Third Way*, December 1979, p.31.
[35] Kenneth A. Briggs, 'U.S. Mainstream Evangelicals Gain in Protestant Influence', *New York Times*, 14 March 1982.

through the student movement. East Asia missionary secretary Ellie Lau spoke for IFES as a whole when she expressed her desire to work 'so that the churches consider the student movement as part of their outreach', and in turn to ensure the return of 'the graduating students back into the churches to serve'.

8. A missionary movement

'If the time should come when we do not live and work for foreign missions, the Christian student work will die', said Ole Hallesby at the first International Conference. By the following year, IVF-Britain had already sent out over 300 missionaries. In 1975 it was reported that one Norwegian missionary estimated three-quarters of Norway's missionaries to be NKSS graduates. Stacey Woods quotes two American missionary agencies as saying that half their recruits were IVCF graduates. As we have seen, the maturing of a national student movement – India, Brazil, Taiwan, the Philippines – has time and again been marked by developing missionary concern. Graduates of the student movements in Asia, Africa and Latin America will undoubtedly play a major part in the new missionary task force that will arise from these continents in the next few years.

Missionary vision is frequently a good indicator of group health. It was the sturdy missionary-oriented Student Volunteer Movement that gave rise to the first world-wide student movement. Forty years later, when IVF-Britain emerged, they immediately became involved in responding to God's call to the campuses of Canada; within a few years of IVCF-Canada's birth, they were used to reach out to the USA; and the birth of IVCF-USA was almost immediately followed by the pioneering of Mexico.

David Howard tells the story of missionary pioneers like Samuel Mills, C. T. Studd, Robert Wilder, Jim Elliot and others, and shows how 'students have played a decisive role in many of the greatest forward movements of the church in world evangelism'.[36] Many current leaders of missionary societies are graduates of IFES-linked groups. Joe Church, who was commissioned in 1927 as CICCU's own missionary, maintains that the Cambridge students' emphasis on revival was what sparked off,

[36] David M. Howard, *Student Power in World Missions*, p.62.

under God, the East African revivals.[37]

And in a day when many countries have closed their doors to missionaries, students are graduating with the professional qualifications that continue to provide openings. The question of stewardship of time and money arises here. Jimmy Kuswadi, who pioneered the Indonesian student movement, argues that every Christian should consider giving at least a tithe – 10% – of his lifetime to serving God overseas. Such service is not easy. One graduate took a lecturing post in another country and reported afterwards, 'I consider it a broadening experience, having been cheated, misled, lied to and abused in a greater and more unashamed way than ever before!' Another wrote, 'In the university it is patent that, unlike all others, we "fear no man". Lectures are prepared and given to the best of our ability, exam papers are marked impartially, time is given to any student who has a difficulty or a question, all (sadly) in contrast to the established pattern here. It earns respect from some quarters, but definite opposition from others. We had never known what it was to have real enemies before.'

In a time when nearly half the world – 16,500 people groups – still have not heard of Christ, it is imperative that IFES groups remain dominated by a passionate missionary vision; like Joshua, directing their attention to the land that 'remains to be possessed'. The people of Israel lost that vision, and it was a mark of their decline in the book of Judges. Fellowships that cease to be motivated by a vision to advance into the unevangelized areas around them, and, beyond that, 'all the world', begin to be marked by purposelessness, discontents, overemphasis on secondary matters. Deliberate efforts have to be made to ensure the inclusion of world vision in all group activities – prayer and teaching programmes, for example. The Enemy will do his best to see that such vision does not come automatically.

9. A movement active for God's Kingdom in every area of life

Christ included in the scope of the Great Commission the entire human world, and challenged his disciples not merely to a superficial proclamation but to teach '*all* that I have commanded you'. The challenge before Christian students and graduates,

---

[37] Quoted in Derek Williams, 'These are the Days', *Christian Graduate*, June 1978, p.5.

then, along with every other disciple of Christ, is to 'out-think, out-live and out-die the worldlings of all types' (the phrase is that of former India general secretary P. T. Chandapilla). A robust evangelicalism is neither a static conservatism nor an unanchored radicalism. Rather, as John Stott – himself a CICCU graduate and an IFES vice-president – has stated, the Christian is called to be a 'radical conservative'. He is to be unshakeably committed to 'the truth which has been handed down to him from Christ and the apostles' in Scripture, but in everything else – social and church structures, lifestyle, mission, and much else besides – 'he is obliged to be as radical as Scripture commands and is free to be as radical as Scripture allows'.[38]

The Great Commission, the command to 'love our neighbour as ourselves', and the mandates of the opening chapters of Genesis together present a programme as universal in its scope as anything set forth by any humanist or Marxist. Within it, there is a place for every aspect of the life of Christian students and graduates. This includes mounting a prayerful and prophetic challenge to all injustice and to all godless ideologies and lifestyles wherever they appear. 'Believing students need to distance themselves from the spirit of their age', wrote Indian graduate Prabhu Guptara in *In Touch* in 1982. 'We need to recognize that the Bible speaks in judgment against the imaginations of man's mind, whether it presents itself as "humanism", secularism, "liberalism", existentialism or any other "ism". The challenge before us is to see what the Bible teaches about philosophy, economics, politics, sociology, psychology, business, industry, and so on – and not merely be misled and brainwashed by the secular consensus that comes at us from every side – from radio and television, from our friends and neighbours, from our teachers and textbooks.' And on that basis, affirms former IVCF-Philippines staffworker Melba Maggay, we may aim at 'capturing once again the imagination and conscience of entire nations... this calls for artists, journalists, economists and political scientists, as well as practical, nuts-and-bolts gifts of service. We need ideologues as well as technocrats, ideas-men as well as organization-men who shall bring fire and freshness of vision.'

The rediscovery of such a vision by evangelicals is generally seen as a phenomenon of the 1960s and 1970s. But an expression

[38] John Stott, *Christ the Controversialist* (IVP, 1970), p.37.

of new life in Christ in terms of practical service has been a mark of evangelical student groups since the very beginning. The Christian student groups of the 1830s and 1840s were deeply concerned about issues such as temperance and slavery[39]; and, as we noted in our opening chapter, the first forerunner of the CICCU in Cambridge was a group of students active in evangelism and literacy work in the Jesus Lane Sunday School. Nor was that the end of CICCU's evangelical social commitment. In 1906 the Cambridge Medical Mission was launched in Bermondsey, at that time a very poor London area, in partnership with a local church. It included a boys' club and public dispensary, and was based on the conviction that the 'only remedy' for the many evils of the district – gambling, violence, prostitution – 'was the power of Jesus Christ'. CICCU undergraduates were involved in the vacations, but the main work was done by graduates. It was 18 months before the first conversion was seen, but slowly the work developed. 'The ideal and ambition...has been to prove that spiritual regeneration is the threshold of social regeneration', declared the organizers.[40]

As early as 1944, *His* explicitly attacked the polarization of evangelism and social concern, in an article written by Kenneth Taylor, later translator of the Living Bible. 'Uncompromising in truth, (Christ) was also uncompromising in love', it asserted. Paul likewise 'held the truth *in love*. Pleading against the heresy of salvation by works, he did not hesitate to organize and plead with Christians to send relief to the church at Jerusalem when the brethren there faced starvation. Nor did he stop, in his urging of practical kindness, with those who were Christians. He strictly admonished to ''do good unto all men, especially those that are of the household of God'' (Galatians 6:10).' Accordingly, evangelicals 'ought to be foremost in our practice of the social aspects of the gospel along with the proclamation of the Saviour'. This was expressed practically in IVCF-USA's strong stand against racial segregation.

We have already mentioned the contributions of IFES staff Samuel Escobar and René Padilla at the 1974 Lausanne Congress,

---

[39] Clarence Shedd, *Two Centuries of Student Christian Movements*, p.xix.

[40] John Pollock, *A Cambridge Movement*, pp.154–155. It should be added that a more negative attitude to social action marked some CICCU publications in the 1930s; *cf.* the quotation in Oliver Barclay, *Whatever Happened to the Jesus Lane Lot?*, p.119.

were widely recognized as instrumental in the re-
ening of evangelical social action, and we have described
e of the practical social projects that have been undertaken
the Latin American student movements.[41] These could be
matched from many other parts of the world. Chua Wee Hian
wrote in 1969 of Asian students active in contexts of social
need: Singaporean and Malaysian students giving free tuition
to children in slum or poverty-stricken areas, Korean medical
students combining medical service with evangelism in the rural
districts. IVF-Vietnam students were active in distributing food,
clothing and medicines to refugees and flood-stricken areas in
1970-71. At the height of student unrest in the Philippines, IVCF
issued a list of practical suggestions for Christian social
involvement which included supporting slum families, giving
medical aid to tribes people, serving in camps for destitute boys,
helping in literacy campaigns, and being active in the elections,
including volunteering as 'poll watchers' to discourage vote-
buying and terrorism. In more recent years *In Touch* has carried
similar accounts of small-scale, practical projects in New Zealand,
Nigeria, South Africa and Hong Kong.

The Nigerian students' rural work camp in the animistic village
of Aguleri-Otu ('200 gods big and small for the estimated population of 1,500') was a good example of biblical social action. It
was no holiday; indeed, the student team was only recruited
after much prayer. ('Nobody was prepared to be caged in such a
forsaken land for two whole months.') For accommodation,
reported Charles Amuzie, 'We had a five-room house abandoned
some six years before by the Forestry authorities, situated at a
place originally used as a burial ground for twins and for people
who died of horrible diseases, quite isolated and standing alone
in the forest...On arrival I met the horrifying sight of animal
carcasses and droppings that had accumulated over the years to a
height of three to six inches. There were also some live scorpions
here and there. This information was cautiously concealed from
the brethren while I earnestly prayed that God would shield His
children from every danger!' Ikodiya Uka recorded one day in
the group's journal, 'Lunch: we don't have any drinking water
again. Choice: colourless water with taste or tasteless water with
colour. Someone swallowed a live pupa.'

[41] See also Samuel Escobar, 'Our Evangelical Heritage', *IFES Review* 1983, 1.

The village was marked by very poor sanitation, rampant tuberculosis, poor health care and a high mortality rate. The student team sought to assist with adult literacy, agricultural help, building latrines, and thatching houses for widows and the poor; besides education in health, hygiene and feeding habits, making use of songs to the tune of 'Read your Bible, pray every day'. 'We taught them (in the local language) "Drink good water that is boiled", "Eat beans and crayfish weekly", and "Use vegetables in your soup, your yam and beans".' There was much personal evangelism, preaching before classes and at the local church services, and evangelistic filmshows and drama, where 'the response to the altar call was such that we had to ask those who were not sure to return to their seats'! Much prayer was taking place. 'It was glaringly clear that the arm of flesh would fail us and that we had to depend on God completely...A daily "quiet time" of 45 minutes was incorporated into the programme, starting at 5 a.m., followed by another 45 minutes of corporate prayer. At night, we had 90 minutes prayer time. All this helped to keep us spiritually lively.'

Such projects bear the stamp of an authentically biblical faith. In the essay quoted above, Samuel Escobar reaffirmed the need to combine evangelical social action with the pietistic heritage. 'It is unfortunate that the term "pietistic" has become derogatory', he says. 'In light of history and human need, we have to recover this dimension and realize that intense personal piety in no way needs to be divorced from serious theological reflection, or from committed social and missionary action...When this dimension has been abandoned, the whole life of a student movement has been weakened.' Christlikeness includes both a passion for God and service to men, and involves both being '*in* the world' and '*not of* the world'. Our goal must be a fully-rounded discipleship.

Probably the most important contribution that student groups can make in this area is the winning and building up of large numbers of Christian graduates; people who have been trained to think biblically about whatever they are doing, and who will be determined to live out a radical discipleship in the service of Christ and their neighbour wherever they go. Sometimes this has resulted in the establishment of task-oriented groups arising out of, but organizationally unconnected with, the student movement. Oliver Barclay notes that the student movement may provide the impulse to start such groups but not be in a position to be directly associated with a group's adoption of controversial policies – *e.g.* in medicine, education, social work or law. Once again, it is a question of knowing a movement's objectives and creating a different structure for another group with equally biblical but different objectives. 'Therefore, there may come a time when developed professional groups should be hived off from the student body which initially set them up.'[42]

The Shaftesbury Project, a pioneering social action group in Britain, grew originally from the student movement in this way. Likewise, in the Philippines, the Institute for Studies in Asian Church and Culture arose through the vision of a group mostly made up of IVCF-Philippines graduates. It is strongly oriented towards social and political action against injustice, and includes fellowships of Christian theologians, psychologists, social activists, writers, artists and social scientists. One of its leaders, Melba Maggay, pointed to the unique strength of an evangelical social action group in the context of the need for perseverance (a need that concerned the Latin Americans too, as we noted in an earlier chapter): 'It's Christians who had kept the vibrancy in their faith that you could use, people with a very deep spiritual life. When you have to pay the price, it's your spirituality that counts.'

10. *A movement of creative Christian thought and literature*

It is difficult now to realize just how little evangelical literature existed fifty years ago that was suitable for students. Most scholarly literature was non-evangelical; most evangelical literature was aimed at a different audience. Consequently, literature work has become an important part of the student ministry.

The initial phase was the development of publishing houses in some of the older movements; and their books were soon exported and translated. This process has continued up to the present time: a total of 657 translations of IVP-Britain titles have been published or contracted, for example. (Their most translated book is John Stott's *Basic Christianity*, based on a series of university mission addresses, and now in thirty-three languages. This is followed – significantly – by *Becoming a Christian, The Quiet Time, The Evidence for the Resurrection, Search the Scriptures* and Francis Schaeffer's *Escape from Reason*). Translations were mostly

---

[42] Oliver Barclay, 'Student Work and the World', *IFES Review* 1982, 1.

out of English, but some books from other languages were welcomed too, a notable example being Ole Hallesby's *Prayer*. Programmes based on translations went ahead in such countries as Argentina (Ediciones Certeza), Brazil, Spain, Italy and Korea, besides books in Chinese and Arabic. IFES began to provide revolving loan funds to provide the initial capital for such work, besides financing magazines like *Certeza* in Latin America, *Span* in Africa and *The Way* in East Asia.

But, some years later, there still remains a massive need for literature in many languages. In 1982 a group of student leaders in one European country finished a camp, shrugged off their weariness and went away together to translate an urgently-needed book into their own language. But translations can only partially meet the need. It is essential that large numbers of writers be found who can produce books appropriate to the needs of each country, rather than literature filled with practical examples from the alien cultures of Britain or America! Hans Bürki of Switzerland, who served as IFES literature secretary from 1963 to 1971, contributed much in this respect, as a result of his deep concern to stimulate Christians to write well.

In the late 1960s Ada Lum went to the Philippines to help the movement there launch their literature programme. Their first production was a songbook for the groups. It combined hymns, choruses, gospel folk songs, fun songs and even the national anthem, topically divided with attractive Filipino illustrations and appropriate Scriptural introductions. 'To our delight, churches and other Christian organizations, as well as the student groups, kept making big orders, so that since then it has gone through several reprints...It was needed, and it was different.' This bestseller helped to launch other books; the next was an adaptation of IVP-USA's Bible study guide *Grow Your Christian Life*, amended for the Asian context. Ten selected Bible studies were shared out among a team of ten staff; they researched and wrote individually, coming together for mutual editing. Final editing was done by the general secretary, Bel Magalit. The result, *Start Right*, has been used as a basic follow-up guide throughout the Philippines and in a number of other countries too.[43]

IVCF-Philippines' literature ministry has continued to grow

[43] Ada Lum, 'Developing and Using Literature', *IFES Review* 1980, 2.

since then. Many similar operations – Ediciones Certeza in Latin America, the *Jyoti* publications of the Indian movement, the publishing houses of Taiwan and Brazil, and many others – started small but have become increasingly significant.

During the 1970s steps were taken by the French-speaking IFES movements, and Scripture Union, to produce effective literature for their movements. Maurice Gardiol of Switzerland was appointed to head up the Presses Bibliques Universitaires, based in Lausanne. PBU's first titles were a symposium on suffering, a translation of John Stott's commentary on Romans 5–8, and a collection of essays by IFES staff René Padilla, Hans Bürki and Samuel Escobar entitled *Evangile, Culture et Idéologies*. These sold 2,000-3,000 copies – good sales for evangelical literature in French. But it was plain that, if PBU published what was needed, it would probably not be a commercial success: the number of potential customers was too small. (No doubt this is a major reason why 100 Christian books exist in English for every one in French!)

Literature ministry is also a way in which the student movements can be of use to the church as a whole. Church historian Ian Rennie, speaking at the 1974 Lausanne Congress for World Evangelization, described IVP-Britain's publications as a key factor in the 'renaissance of evangelical theology' in recent years.[44] Their commentaries – a vital area – have won particular praise: David C. K. Watson described the *Tyndale* series as 'invaluable', while J. I. Packer remarked that 'No commentary series is more consistently satisfying'. The publications of IVP-USA have had a comparable impact. Once again, this kind of recognition represents both a cause for thanksgiving to God, and a cause for prayer. Daniel Bresch of Presses Bibliques Universitaires told the 1979 IFES General Committee that 'Publishing literature is for many publishers a spiritual battle. So don't just remember titles or money, remember the spiritual battle.'

11. *A movement committed to student responsibility*
IFES and its movements are above all a *fellowship of evangelical students joined together in witness to other students;* rather than a missionary organization of professional outsiders sent in to witness to students. This is basic both to IFES-linked groups'

---

[44] *Let the Earth Hear His Voice*, ed. J. D. Douglas (World Wide Publications, 1975), p.1319.

evangelistic attractiveness, and to their ability to produce future leaders. As René Padilla observes, 'There is no better evangelist among students than those who are students themselves.'

Obviously, that does not mean that the campus fellowship exists as a self-sufficient unit. It is usual for IFES-linked groups to enlist the aid of local church leaders and graduates for major evangelistic presentations or Bible exposition. But the principle of student leadership means that a pioneering staff seeks to raise up Christian students who – like Christians in any other place – will take responsibility for active witness where they are, rather than relying on an outsider to do it for them. It means, too, that the gifts that God has given to every believer amongst them – as to every believer anywhere (Ephesians 4:7–16) – should be given the fullest opportunities for development, rather than concentrating the planning, organization and implementation of all activity in the hands of an indispensable specialist.

This is, of course, one aspect of the fundamental Reformation principle of the 'priesthood of all believers'. It is visible in Acts 11 where Barnabas visits the young believers of Antioch, and instead of seeking to bring them under the strict control of a centralized organization, he commits them to the Lord and encourages them to get on with the work. It could be said that Barnabas was exercising a ministry similar to that of a travelling IFES staff-worker today!

In IFES groups, then, leadership is usually taken by students. Orders are not sent down from the administrative office in Harrow or anywhere else! And it is undoubtedly because of this development of the leadership gifts of group members that so many go on to become pastors and Christian leaders. Senator Mark Hatfield has commented that in IVCF-USA the 'basis in Scripture combined with student leadership produces top quality people to be leaders in our society'. Even radically liberal theologian Harvey Cox, who considers IVCF's biblically-based theology 'indefensible', nevertheless wrote in *The Secular City* that he would not attribute the movement's 'strength and tenacity' to 'its appeal to the stupid and closed-minded'(!), but to its student-led nature. 'On the campus where I was an undergraduate...IVCF sponsored scores of student-led Bible studies, where the discussions were often hotter and more valuable than those carefully supervised by clergymen...IVCF was a lay-led, highly visible, and extremely mobile organization which did not have enough money to erect separate facilities so was forced to live in the same world with everybody else.'[45] In short, it was genuinely *indigenous*.

This does not always work instantly, as we have noted in our section on Latin America; sometimes the student leadership takes a long time to emerge. Noor van Haaften has speculated that the tradition of Catholic cultures, for example, discourages lay participation in religious matters, and creates a mind-set that expects everything to be done by specialists. The underlying socio-cultural factors have not really been adequately researched as yet; what is clear is that in such situations a great deal of input may be needed from a staffworker if effective student leaders are to be raised up. (This is particularly so where there is a lack of strong evangelical churches and high-school groups giving good Bible teaching and mobilizing their members in active, participating discipleship.) That in turn has implications for the extent to which such staff can be itinerant. As Ross Douglas of Brazil indicated, a 'necessary minimum' of staffworkers (and graduates) must be available.

And of course the emergence of student leadership does not mean that the staffworker's role is purely passive. There will always be a need for student leaders to be backed up by staff who model discipleship and also can serve as a fund of resources, ideas and relevant biblical principles. Many staff are actively involved in programmes on a regional or national level where the decision-making may be done in partnership with a representative student committee, but the implementation requires full-time personnel. As John Bowen of Canada has remarked, 'We believe in student initiative, and we believe in staff initiative too.'

It might seem that the actitivity of staff compromises the principle of indigenous student leadership, since by definition staff are not students! But the distinctive thing about the IFES working philosophy, compared with other organizations active on campus, is that it has chosen to live with this tension. Instead of accepting the drift of decision-making into the hands of professionals, it has sought always to keep responsibility in the hands of students whenever possible. This is something that requires a more deliberate effort as movements grow. Its original ethos has been maintained because it has had many leaders – people like Stacey Woods, Chua Wee Hian, Douglas Johnson,

[45] Harvey Cox, *The Secular City* (SCM Press, 1965), p.224.

Oliver Barclay, Samuel Escobar – who have been marked by a determination to lead in a way that safeguards this principle. The heavy emphasis on Bible study at every level, combined with constitutional safeguards obliging leaders to be committed to the doctrinal basis, has tended to produce an environment where student leaders will not drift away from the original vision, but instead become permeated by Scripture and hear the voice of God speaking into their decision-making.

The whole subject was summarized in an interview with Oliver Barclay in the Singapore magazine *Impetus*. Asked if doctrinal weaknesses necessitated more staff supervision, he replied, 'I don't think it is usually necessary. It's partly a question of how we train our leaders. A question to ask is, have we enough stable people with good Bible knowledge amongst the leaders?...So long as we can ensure that they are studying the Bible, then even if they come up with strange ideas, they'll eventually grow...I want to say to students, "Before God you're responsible for what happens here on your campus." I believe it's a very important training-ground. I want to take the sort of risks Paul took.[46] He ordained elders in every place he went, even though they were young churches...I still find his leadership very real. He says, "I urge you, I encourage you." He was persuading even as he laid down the law of the Word of God. But if you don't give students responsibilities you don't develop people who can carry responsibilities later on.'

12. *A movement committed to national leadership*

This too is an application of the indigenous principle. All IFES national movements govern their own affairs. IFES is not like one of the old colonial empires ruled from a capital in the West. Rather, it aims to be a somewhat more brotherly(!) equivalent in the Christian student world of the United Nations, an association of autonomous national bodies who are equal partners. The aim is

---

[46] *Cf.* also Dr. Barclay's observations on the argument that the cost of student leadership is having a certain proportion of groups in difficulties at any given time: in New Testament times too, he says, the appointment of indigenous leaders who were recent converts led to 'some disasters, as the Epistles bear witness, but there was also widespread evangelism... – far wider than there could have been otherwise... Whatever we may think about its practical consequences, this is the New Testament model' ('Notes on Student Leadership and Responsibility', *IFES Review* 1980, 2).

that the work in each country should develop a genuinely national character rather than being a foreign import. This was clear from the very beginning, when it was obvious that the student movements of (for example) Britain, Holland, Norway and the USA were all equally evangelical but nonetheless had very different approaches, because of the different cultural and ecclesiastical contexts in which they had arisen.

The need for such a policy was highlighted by Chua Wee Hian in 1969 when he described an Asian coming to a Christian meeting in his own country: 'On the walls, he sees pictures of an Italian Christ and he concludes that Christ must have been a European. He sings choruses or hymns with Western overtones, he hears a Western missionary speak and he observes that his fellow-countryman also speaks with a Texan drawl. Surely, such impressions would support his hypothesis that Christianity must be a Western faith...We have to communicate the unchanging gospel in the thought pattern and culture of our nation and refuse to parrot Western orientated programmes or slavishly adopt Western methodologies.' In the more nationalistic student world, a failure in this respect would be catastrophic. Hence the importance of indigenous leadership. 'Local people themselves usually know better than an outsider how to adapt basic truth to their culture', says Ada Lum.

That should be obvious; and certainly IFES has worked on this principle. The 1956 General Committee re-affirmed the necessity of 'movements being indigenous and representative of their own organizational and cultural pattern...In no way should Western patterns be imposed upon movements.' Yet it is no easy task to distinguish between a pattern or assumption that is based on biblical principle, and one that pretends to be biblically-based but stems in reality from our own cultural background. Hence the importance of having movements led by nationals rather than foreigners; even if there is room for foreigners working under the nationals, once the latter are firmly in the saddle.

Three events in IFES's history bear particular witness to this process. The first was the move of the IFES office from the USA to Switzerland in 1962. This was a time of increasing tension between the Western and Communist blocs, and letters were coming in from some of the younger student movements, particularly in Africa, making clear that it was difficult or even impossible to join the IFES while its office was in the USA.

Certain governments mistakenly equated an American office with a loyalty to American foreign policy. The move to a neutral country was of considerable importance. And it led to a great improvement in spreading the load of the financial burden of IFES, which had been left mostly to the North Americans up to that time.

A second significant event was the General Committee of 1967, when business sessions started off dominated by a few Western delegates familiar with the operation of parliamentary procedure. It was evident that delegates from some other regions were bewildered by what was taking place. After a while, John W. Alexander of the USA (later IFES chairman) rose and expressed his astonishment 'that so much talking is being done by so few delegates who speak on so many topics. We need to hear more from other brethren...I suggest that in the spirit of fellowship we provide a freer and looser atmosphere in which our "silent brethren" will feel free to...give us the message that is on their hearts'. His assessment had considerable impact, and was later strongly endorsed in a statement from the Asian movements: 'The business sessions tend to be dominated by some delegates whose insistence upon the minutiae of organization have deflected us from discussing the really important issues. We feel the need for spending much more time in prayer...'

A third major milestone was the appointment of Chua Wee Hian of Singapore as the IFES general secretary in 1971. This was possibly the first appointment of a non-Western Christian to the leadership of a major evangelical international organization. There can be no doubt of the effect this has had in demonstrating that IFES was not Western-dominated. Wee Hian's Asian nationality is an obvious advantage in his ministry of working alongside the general secretaries of the younger national movements, most of whom are, of course, not Westerners.

IFES has moved into an ever-deepening partnership between the different cultures, for which the Urbana 1967 theme 'God's men – from all nations to all nations' may serve as a watchword. The West still has much to offer. For example, Inter-Varsity Press of the USA and Britain have given tremendous assistance to younger movements seeking to develop their own literature ministries. Many staffworkers from the younger movements have gained from a brief period visiting the work of one of the founding countries. But the West is not the only training-ground.

When Vinoth Ramachandra went to Sri Lanka in 1980, for example, his training consisted of time spent with the movements in the Philippines and Singapore.

And now the West is beginning to receive from other parts of the world. The rediscovery of evangelistic Bible study in the European movements, for example, owes much to impulses from Asia. The 'contact group' system of Singapore has proved of use to a number of other countries. In 1972, the Canadian movement invited Samuel Escobar of Peru to become its general director, a post he held with distinction until 1975.

And finally, it must be said that many Western students have been challenged to a new seriousness in discipleship, prayer and liberation from materialism by exposure to Christians from other parts of the world. In particular, the sheer scale of the growth of the church – and the student movements – in countries like Singapore, Nigeria and Brazil is a continually effective challenge to European Christians to throw off their defeatism and claim equally great things from God.

The structure of the IFES reflects these principles of national, culturally indigenous leadership and grass-roots initiative. IFES is not a missionary society, but a fellowship of students witnessing to students. Hence its 'vital centre' is not a head office; rather, the 'vital centre' of the Fellowship is its cutting edge in the local student group. The national movements exist to develop and strengthen the witness and discipleship of Christian students in the groups where God has placed them; these national movements are themselves autonomous, free to appoint their own leaders and develop their own working pattern. The collective voice of their representatives, the four-yearly IFES General Committee, is the ultimate decision-making body of the Fellowship. As will have been apparent, this gathering of delegates from all the movements is a forum for sharing vision and making policy; 'GC' is also the level at which new member movements are accepted, the IFES general secretary is appointed, and staff appointments are ratified. Any constitutional amendments are made at 'GC'. And it elects the 15-member IFES executive committee, which meets for four days each year and gives more specific direction to the world-wide work.

The staff team, appointed by 'GC' and the executive committee, has its own structure. Working under the leadership of the general secretary are the associate general secretaries, currently from Peru and Japan, and regional secretaries, currently from Guyana, Wales, Madagascar, Ghana and Pakistan – a thoroughly cross-cultural combination!

So the Fellowship's overall structure is grass-roots-oriented rather than hierarchical. The national movements express the collective fellowship of the local groups; their representatives at 'GC' and on the executive committee make policy and appoint the staff team; the staff in turn complete the circle by using their abilities to mobilize and strengthen the witness and initiative of students in the local groups.

CO-LABOURERS FOR A MOVEMENT OF STUDENTS

Besides senior staff, and workers attached to a particular country,[47] IFES's team of workers includes a number of specialist staff. Branse Burbridge, for example, is the IFES high-schools consultant; he has been active in this area since 1946, when he became the first staffworker of the Scripture Union-linked Inter-School Christian Fellowship in Britain. (In those days he and one other staffworker were responsible for all the high schools in England and Wales!) Other IFES specialist staff with a world-wide brief include Jim Nyquist, honorary literature secretary; Ada Lum, Bible study secretary; and Jim Stamoolis, who serves as theological students' secretary, a post previously held by Harold O. J. Brown and Bruce Demarest.

The importance of this last ministry cannot be overstated. Evangelical theological students inevitably find themselves in a position of critical distance from some of what they are taught, wondering, as Douglas Johnson puts it, whether the 'web of increasing hypotheses' of some liberal higher criticism is really scholarly. IFES theological students' secretaries have the task of encouraging evangelicals in this field to produce something that is both more biblical and more scholarly, and also at the same time to persevere in the difficult task of maintaining their evangelistic zeal and warmth of personal fellowship with God in such an environment.

Bruce Demarest tells of a visit to one prestigious theological

[47] Apart from senior and specialist staff, the majority of IFES field staff are in pioneering situations. Once a national movement develops in a country, workers in that country will be responsible to that movement rather than to IFES. However, national movements also request IFES workers to be seconded to them.

college in India where 'students relate that every possible ideology – liberal Protestant, Hindu, Marxist – is given a fair hearing, *except* the historic Christian point of view. The small group of students who hold to an evangelical faith are often chided by professors as intellectually simplistic, while those who engage in prayer and other devotional exercises are ridiculed by fellow-students'. One keen Nigerian couple who came there to prepare for a biblical ministry found their commitment to the historic gospel had largely vanished after six months. But they were challenged by a lecture given by Bruce, and encouraged through small group Bible studies and personal counselling, with the result that they made a fresh commitment to the gospel of the grace of God. Obviously, giving assistance in such situations to the students who will be future pastors and teachers is of massive importance.[48]

Full-time staff work with IFES – in any capacity – has its price. Staff stay with IFES for only a few years, as a rule, after which there is the challenge of finding a new ministry or discovering a way back into their secular profession. For many, accepting God's call to full-time service is very much a repetition of the abandonment of all human security to which God called Abraham in Genesis 12. One staffworker turned down highly attractive research posts to come and pioneer with IFES, and has since played a crucial role in the development of a national evangelical student movement in his home country. But he met with some astonishment from friends at home that he had opted out of the 'brain drain' to the West.

In the early days field staff also had to do without much training. Some staff recall that 'The general secretary gave me three addresses and said, "See what you can do about starting a Christian witness in the universities of this country"'; or, 'They just said to enrol at the university and make new friends'; or, 'I was told to get my passport, a mosquito net and see Pastor X when I arrived'! This undoubtedly helped to make men and women of prayer and faith – qualities that can sometimes exist in inverse proportion to the amount of resources in manpower, finance and intellectual support that is available. Still, these

---

[48] IFES's other contribution in this field is the theological magazine *Themelios*, produced in partnership with the British Theological Students' Fellowship, and aiming to provide practical, down-to-earth articles and book reviews directly related to the needs of evangelical theological students.

resources are gifts of God, gifts that we have to learn how to use, and, indeed, to make available. In recent years a significant part of the IFES budget has been spent on training staff.[49] And, since 1977, theological training scholarships have made possible brief spells of theological training for over thirty national leaders with senior responsibility in their national movement.

The least glamorous part of the staff team is that section involved in administration and central support. Financial support for pioneering staff is always easier to find than for the typists who produce the resources they need! A crucial ministry within this section – particularly during the recent years of recession – has been that of the finance secretary (currently Jacques Beney of Switzerland[50]) who is responsible for administering the IFES budget, in partnership with the honorary treasurer (currently Sir Fred Catherwood of Britain) and the finance committee. IFES has always sought to maintain a very modest and frugal central office; as late as 1972 the central office team consisted merely of four people, and even at the present time there are only eleven. The Fellowship has not wanted its decision-making to become divorced from the realities of the student culture and fall instead into the hands of a group of highly-qualified professionals remote from the practicalities of student evangelism. In the last resort, the field, that is, the campus, is where the action is.

THE UNFINISHED TASK

There remains a tremendous amount to be done in the student world today. It is a task for which no team of people could be adequate. Rather, God is reaching the campuses through a vast number of Christian students that He has raised up; backed up by the support of graduates, church leaders and staff.

This work needs the prayers of every reader of this book. It is true that God has done great things. But it is a fragile work. It can fall into excesses; it can drift towards liberalism; it can freeze into ineffectiveness. When we consider the 10% of the student enrolment involved in some of the African countries, it is a cause for rejoicing; but what human power could possibly be adequate to ensure that such vast movements are kept from the Enemy,

---

[49] The *IFES Review*, which commenced in 1976, is a periodical designed for people in student ministry and is concerned with the principles and practice of such work.

[50] Jacques Beney was IFES treasurer from 1963 to 1980.

channelled to maximum effectiveness, kept from complacency and close to the Lord? And when we consider the pioneering countries, it is plain that in many cases the task has scarcely even begun. Many are lands requiring a real breakthrough at the level of spiritual warfare. It is for this reason that IFES produces prayer materials such as the *Praise and Prayer Bulletin,* and *In Touch*[51] (the successor to *IFES News* and *IFES Journal*); the student work world-wide needs the involvement of people who will deliberately set aside time regularly to labour in prayer.

Massive opportunities exist in many countries for outreach to international students. The importance of this work has been demonstrated time and again in the history of IFES. The current general secretary of the Zambian movement, Derek Mutungu, became a Christian while studying in England. 'No sooner had I unpacked than Christian students descended on me', he wrote later. 'Initially they just wanted to make me feel at home. But Easter found me at their colleges conference' – and there he found Christ. Ramez Atallah, now active in Egypt, became a Christian when he went to Montreal, Canada, to study. Eliette Andrianaly, Madagascar's first lady staffworker, was converted while studying in France, through a student camp – and other students who had had contact with the French movement played an important part in the development of the work in Madagascar. At least three early leaders of the Japanese movement were converted while studying in the USA. In one pioneering Asian country, a small group of national pastors are giving vital support to the work, despite opposition from other sections of the church; and this is largely because they were all converted or built up in their faith through the IFES-linked groups they met while studying in the Philippines, India or Singapore.

Karl Marx was a 'foreign student' once; so were Mahatma Gandhi, Chou En Lai, Fidel Castro. Future leaders from many countries are studying on campuses with strong IFES-linked groups at the present time. Many are from 'closed countries' – China, Iran, Iraq, Saudi Arabia, for example. Many foreign students are extremely lonely – some will have left their families for three years or more – and are seeking genuine friendship. This is a need that the love of Christ should enable us to meet.

Some IFES groups organize an 'international welcome week' at

[51] Obtainable from the IFES office at 10 College Road, Harrow, Middlesex HA1 1BE, England.

the beginning of the academic year, where they meet incoming foreign students and help them with the many initial problems of settling in. This can be followed up by social evenings, weekend houseparties, camps and outings, particularly at times like Christmas and Easter. (One Egyptian student told how he spent Christmas walking round a cold Welsh city, and described it as 'the worst day of his life'.) Graduates can play an equally important role, inviting foreign students to meals or longer visits and introducing them to a Christian home. Colin Chapman points out that for Muslim students in particular the value of special meetings 'is limited unless they introduce foreign students to our *homes*....It is hard to overemphasize the importance of hospitality'. Long-term, unselfish friendships can break down misconceptions about Christianity and lead into evangelistic Bible studies. Muslim students generally have heard of the New Testament (from the Qur'an) as the 'Injil', and are often curious to know what it contains. Thus, over a period of years perhaps, they may come to an encounter with the living Christ. At the present time IFES has an Arabic staffworker who was converted as a result of picking up a Bible at a Christian student bookstall in Paris.

Many IFES movements are active in this kind of ministry, for example in North America, Australasia, and Asia (strong outreach to foreign students exists in such countries as Japan, the Philippines and Taiwan). In Europe, IFES staff have contributed to the development of such work recently in France, Germany, Holland and Italy, and hope to be able to play some part in other nations within the next few years.

But the international student phenomenon has other potential besides. In country after country, students from abroad have played a significant part in the development of campus witness, as we have noted – Norwegians in Austria, Latin Americans in Spain, Americans in Israel. From France, Gerard Kuntz has thanked the British movement 'for regularly sending us "assistants"' (students spending a year abroad) 'who are often the driving force in the group. African, Malagasy and Asian students have more and more of a place...' Asian and Nigerian students have pioneered campus groups in Britain; one UCCF group is 80% Malaysian Chinese at the time of writing. The IVCF group at University of Nevada-Reno, USA, was started by a Kenyan student. Throughout French-speaking Africa, as has been indicated, the groups have been begun by students from

365

other parts of the continent, and in fact there has been a recurrent problem of bringing nationals into membership and leadership so that the fellowship ceases to appear a foreign import. Stories have occasionally reached us of African students – both French- and English-speaking – going to Russia, or other parts of eastern Europe, and starting evangelistic Bible studies – even in Moscow. They can be God's missionaries to many other foreign students grappling with the same problems of settling in; and some of these will come from 'closed countries' such as Afghanistan.

We need to pray for the right people to take such opportunities. Former Australian staffworker Jill Stewart took a course in a university in Delhi, India, and noted that 'Being a fellow-student put me on the same level. I was "foreign", but I was one of them. I didn't have a status or a role which gave me a position and authority. I was just there, attending lectures, working on assignments, meeting deadlines, relaxing, socializing – conspicuous because of the colour of my skin, but part of the scene.' Many government scholarships are available for study in countries with little or no student work.[52]

Other workers are needed too. IFES full-time staff are usually people who have already 'learnt their trade' as active and effective members of a student group and then as staffworkers with their national movement. Other workers are seconded to student work by missionary societies such as BMMF or OMF, or denominational mission boards. IFES 'Graduate Team' and 'Student Team' members are active in certain areas, particularly cities like Paris with large numbers of international students.

IFES 'Field Partners' are 'tentmakers', professionals in secular posts – sometimes the only way to penetrate 'closed' countries. Such people can make contact with students and begin or strengthen Bible study groups, although in the toughest countries developing relationships between expatriates and nationals is not easy. But it is sometimes the only way. Lecturers and teachers in particular are strategically placed, of course; we have noted in this history a few of the countries where such people have played a crucial role. The massive numbers of textbooks in the English language means that openings exist for teachers of English throughout the world.

The task continues. And underlying and motivating all these,

---

[52] See UNESCO's handbook *Study Abroad*.

we need a fervent, worshipping vision of God and His work. Vision is not maintained automatically – as most Christian graduates notice. We all – individually and collectively – need to assess our faithfulness to our 'first love'. Chua Wee Hian reminded the delegates at a recent General Committee of the need to 'arm ourselves against complacency, respectability and the temptation to compromise biblical authority. The words of Moses still address us today, "Take heed lest ye forget the Lord your God by not keeping His ordinances, His commandments and His statutes...lest when ye have eaten and are full...then your heart be lifted up and ye forget the Lord your God. Beware lest you say in your heart 'My power and the might of my hand have gotten me this wealth'. You shall remember the Lord your God, for it is He who gives you power."'

The words of Howard Guinness, whom God used to pioneer the student movements in Canada, Australia and New Zealand, are an appropriate challenge: 'Where are the young men and women of this generation who will hold their lives cheap, and be faithful even unto death...who will lose their lives for Christ's sake – flinging them away for love of Him? Where are those who will live dangerously, and be reckless in His service?...Where are the men of prayer? Where are the men who...count God's Word of more importance to them than their daily food? Where are the men who, like Moses of old, commune with God face to face as a man speaks with his friend?...*Where are God's men in this day of God's power?*'

Member Movements of IFES

DATE OF AFFILIATION

1946 Australia — Inter-Varsity Fellowship (later Australian Fellowship of Evangelical Students)

Canada — Inter-Varsity Christian Fellowship

France — Union des Groupes Bibliques Universitaires de France

Great Britain — Inter-Varsity Fellowship (later Universities and Colleges Christian Fellowship)

Netherlands — Calvinistische Studenten Beweging (later linked with other groups in the Commissie Nederland IFES)

New Zealand — Inter-Varsity Fellowship (later Tertiary Students' Christian Fellowship)

Norway — Norges Kristelige Student-og Gymnasiastlag (later Norges Kristelige Student-og Skoleungdomslag)

Switzerland — Groupes Bibliques des Ecoles et Universités (later the German-speaking Swiss groups became separate as the Vereinigte Bibelgruppen in Schule Universität Beruf)

United States — Inter-Varsity Christian Fellowship

1947 China — Inter-Varsity Fellowship (no longer in existence)

1950 Finland — Suomen Kristilinen Ylioppilasliitto (later disaffiliated)

Sweden — Sveriges Evangeliska Student-och Gymnasiströrelse

1953 Germany — Studentenmission in Deutschland

Mexico — El Compañerismo Estudiantil

1956	Japan	– Kirisutosha Gakusei Kai
	West Indies	– Inter-School and Inter-Varsity Christian Fellowship

1959	India	– Union of Evangelical Students of India
	Italy	– Gruppi Biblici Universitari
	Korea	– Korea Inter-Varsity Christian Fellowship
	Malaya and Singapore	– Fellowship of Evangelical Students
	Philippines	– Inter-Varsity Christian Fellowship

1963	Brazil	– Aliança Biblica Universitaria do Brasil
	Costa Rica	– Agrupacion de Universitarios Cristianos de Costa Rica (no longer in existence)
	English-speaking Africa	– Pan-African Fellowship of Evangelical Students
	Hong Kong	– Fellowship of Evangelical Students
	Peru	– Asociación de Grupos Evangélicos Universitarios de Peru
	Puerto Rico	– Asociación Biblica Universitaria de Puerto Rico
	Vietnam	– Tong Doan Sinh-Vien Hoc-Sinh Tin-Lanh (no longer in existence)

1967	Argentina	– Asociación Biblica Universitaria Argentina
	Denmark	– Kristeligt Forbund for Studerende og Skoleungdom
	Finland	– Opiskelija- ja Koululaislähetys
	Malaysia	– Fellowship of Evangelical Students
	Paraguay	– Agrupación de Universitarios Cristianos Evangélicos del Paraguay (no longer in existence)
	South Africa	– Students' Christian Association of Southern Africa
	Venezuela	– Movimiento Universitario Evangélico Venezolano

1971	Dominican Republic	– Asociación Dominicana de Estudiantes Evangélicos
	French-speaking Africa	– Groupes Bibliques Universitaires d'Afrique Francophone
	Ghana	– Ghana Fellowship of Evangelical Students
	Nigeria	– Nigeria Fellowship of Evangelical Students
	Portugal	– Movimento de Estudantes Evangélicos de Portugal (no longer in existence)

1975	Chile	– Grupos Bíblicos Universitarios de Chile
	COMCEDE	– Comunidad Centroamericana de Estudiantes Evangélicos

	Iceland	– Kristilega Skólahreyfingin
	Lebanon	– Lebanon Inter-Varsity Fellowship
	Pakistan	– Pakistan Fellowship of Evangelical Students
	Spain	– Federación de Grupos Bíblicos Universitarios de España
1979	Colombia	– Unidad Cristiana Universitaria
	Kenya	– Fellowship of Christian Unions
	Papua New Guinea	– Tertiary Students' Christian Fellowship
	Portugal	– Grupo Bíblico Universitário de Portugal
	South Pacific	– Pacific Students for Christ
	Thailand	– Thai Christian Students
	Uganda	– Fellowship of Christian Unions
	Zambia	– Zambia Fellowship of Evangelical Students
	Zimbabwe	– Fellowship of Christian Unions
1983	Jamaica	– Student Christian Fellowship and Scripture Union
	Liberia	– Liberia Fellowship of Evangelical Students
	Malawi	– Universities and Colleges Section of the Student Christian Organization
	Sierra Leone	– Sierra Leone Fellowship of Evangelical Students

Bibliography

Adeney, David, *China: Christian Students face the Revolution* (IVP, 1973).

Barclay, Oliver, *Whatever Happened to the Jesus Lane Lot?* (IVP-Britain, 1977).

Beahm, William H., *Factors in the Development of the Student Volunteer Movement for Foreign Missions* (unpublished dissertation, University of Chicago, 1941).

Benjamin, Barbara, *The Impossible Community* (IVP-USA, 1978).

Braisted, Ruth Wilder, *In This Generation: The Story of R. P. Wilder* (Friendship Press, 1941).

Chua Wee Hian, *Out of Asia* (unpublished dissertation, Fuller Theological Seminary, 1972).

Coggan, F. D., *Christ and the Colleges* (IVF-Britain, 1934).

Cumming, Joe, *The Student Volunteer Movement for Foreign Missions*, in Cindy Smith and Joe Cumming, *Rebuilding the Mission Movement* (National Student Missions Coalition, 1982).

Escobar, Samuel, *La Chispa y la Llama* (Ediciones Certeza, 1978).

For the Faith of the Gospel (UCCF-Britain, 1978).

Guinness, Howard, *Journey Among Students* (Anglican Information Office, Sydney, 1978).

Helander, Eila, *Cultural Change and Persistence in a Religious Group in the Caribbean Context: a case study of the IVCF in Trinidad* (unpublished dissertation, University of Helsinki, 1982).

Howard, David M., *Student Power in World Missions* (IVP-USA, 1979).

Johnsen, G., *Evangelist i Sentrum* (Credo Forlag, Oslo, 1949).

Johnson, Douglas, *A Brief History of the IFES* (IFES, 1964).

Johnson, Douglas, *Contending for the Faith* (IVP-Britain, 1979).

Laget 50 Ar:1924-1974 (NKSS-Norway, 1974).

Lagsbevegelsen gjennom 40 Ar (NKSS-Norway, 1964).

Miller, William McElwee, Jr., *Evangelism among University Students Overseas in the non-Communist and non-Roman Catholic World 1960-1962* (unpublished dissertation, Princeton Theological Seminary, 1964).

Orr, J. Edwin, *Campus Aflame* (Regal, 1971).

Pollock, John, *A Cambridge Movement* (John Murray, 1953).

Porta 25 (SMD-Germany, 1978).

Rohrbach, Hans, *Studenten Begegnen der Wahrheit* (SMD-Germany, 1957).

Rouse, Ruth, *The World's Student Christian Federation* (SCM Press, 1948).

Shedd, Clarence P., *Two Centuries of Student Christian Movements* (Association Press, 1934).

Tatlow, Tissington, *The Story of the Student Christian Movement* (SCM Press, 1933).

Voelkel, Jack, *Student Evangelism in a World of Revolution* (Zondervan, 1974).

Woods, C. Stacey, *The Growth of a Work of God* (IVP-USA, 1978).

Woods, C. Stacey, *Some Ways of God* (IVP-USA, 1975).

Glossary

CF or CU – 'Christian Fellowship' or 'Christian Union'; the term used for a local student group in a number of countries.

GBU – 'Groupe Biblique Universitaire'; the term used for a local student group in French-speaking countries.

High schools – The educational systems of different countries vary very considerably. In this book we have used 'high schools' to describe pre-university education. This may begin as early as the age of 11 or as late as 15; it may finish as early as 16 or as late as 20.

Mission – A major outreach to a university or college, usually including several major preaching events.

Quiet time – The basic discipline of meeting with God daily for a period of Bible study and prayer that has been fundamental to the health of most evangelical student movements.

SCM – Student Christian Movement; a local group, or else national movement, deriving from the great student movements of the late nineteenth century; most of which began by being evangelical, but broadened out to include all theological positions, and usually ended up very liberal. These were linked together in the World's Student Christian Federation or WSCF. The exceptions to this definition are the student movements calling themselves SCM in Swaziland, South Africa and Namibia, which are all evangelical and unconnected with the WSCF.

Tertiary education – The post-secondary educational sector; universities and colleges.

Acknowledgments

Much of the material in this book has been quoted from elsewhere. Lengthy quotations have been made from other histories, as indicated in the footnotes. No acknowledgment has been made of material quoted directly from *IFES News*, *IFES Journal*, the *IFES Praise and Prayer Bulletin* or *In Touch*; nor *His* magazine, in the case of material from the 1940s relating to events in Central America, Japan and the pioneering areas of Europe. Considerable use has also been made of numerous memoranda and reports in the archives of our Harrow office, and of manuscript histories sent us from various countries, such as Australia, Austria, Colombia, Pakistan, South Africa, Spain and Zimbabwe.

Special thanks are due to C. Stacey Woods and to Alison Walley, who compiled extended drafts of historical material on the IFES; and of course to Douglas Johnson, whose *Brief History of the IFES* appeared in 1964, and who has helped with much other information. We are grateful for permission to quote extensively from *For the Faith of the Gospel* (UCCF-Britain), *Rebuilding the Mission Movement* by Cindy Smith and Joe Cumming (National Student Missions Coalition, 1605 Elizabeth Street, Pasadena CA 91104, California), *A Cambridge Movement* by John Pollock (John Murray), *Whatever Happened to the Jesus Lane Lot?* by Oliver Barclay (IVP-Britain), *Contending for the Faith* by Douglas Johnson (IVP-Britain), *Student Evangelism in a World of Revolution* by Jack Voelkel (Zondervan), *The Growth of a Work of God* and *Some Ways of God*, both by C. Stacey Woods (IVP-USA), and *No Ordinary Union* by Peter Lineham (SU-New Zealand).

Thanks are also due to the thirty or more leaders of IFES movements who responded to a questionnaire in 1977, and provided much material that has been used in this more recent compilation; and the eighty-five or more leaders around the world who have kindly commented on sections of the history. In particular, Chua Wee Hian, Jacques Beney and Oliver Barclay have given much time to reading large sections. Needless to say, none of these many readers would have written the account in quite this way; for the biases, cultural blindspots and inaccuracies that still remain the author takes full responsibility. It is impossible for any reader to assess the accuracy of every detail! Finally, many thanks to the members of the IFES office team in Harrow – and friends outside it – for their support, prayers and assistance; in particular to the IFES editorial assistant, Judy Hanson, for her efforts in map-making, research, deciphering, transcribing, and much else. May the result be worthy of the intercessions that have enabled it to be completed!

outline of paper

Issue: Assessing "fruit in ministry"
in task (USA) vs person
oriented culture (Asia + pacific)

components:

- AFR form
- Asia + Pacific paper
- Task vs person def's (winzenpelter
- Δspirituality paper (Houston)